LESSONS AND LEGACIES

LESSONS AND LEGACIES

The Meaning of the Holocaust
in a Changing World

Edited by Peter Hayes

NORTHWESTERN   UNIVERSITY PRESS   EVANSTON,   ILLINOIS

Northwestern University Press
Evanston, Illinois 60208-4210

Copyright © 1991 by Northwestern University Press. All rights reserved.

Printed in the United States of America

First published 1991
Second paperback printing 1995
Third paperback printing 1996

ISBN 0-8101-0956-5

Library of Congress Cataloging-in-Publication Data

Lessons and legacies : the meaning of the holocaust in a changing
    world / edited by Peter Hayes.
        p.   cm.
    Includes bibliographical references.
    ISBN 0-8101-0955-7.—ISBN 0-8101-0956-5 (pbk.)
    1. Holocaust, Jewish (1939–1945)—Congresses. 2. Holocaust,
Jewish (1939–1945)—Historiography—Congresses. 3. Holocaust,
Jewish (1939–1945)—Influence—Congresses. I. Hayes, Peter, 1946– .
D810.J4L4 1991
940.53'18—dc20   91-14707
                                                              CIP

The paper used in this publication meets the minimum requirements of the
American National Standard for Information Sciences—Permanence of Paper for
Printed Library Materials, ANSI Z39.48-1984.

In Memory of
Samuel and Gizella Weisz
and their children, Meir and Sarah,
who died in Auschwitz and Buchenwald

Contents

II. Deeds

III. Encounters

Theodore Zev Weiss
President, Holocaust Educational Foundation

Foreword

THE HOLOCAUST EDUCATIONAL FOUNDATION WAS ESTABLISHED IN 1980, dedicated to preserving awareness of the reality of the Holocaust. The foundation's chosen means to this end are (1) to videotape the testimony of survivors and (2) to encourage the study of the Holocaust at colleges and universities. Through these projects, we seek to give students an understanding of the place of the Holocaust in history and of the current and universal implications of the event. Making our young people conscious of the enormity of this tragedy will, we hope, contribute in some measure to preventing another human calamity of this magnitude.

In 1987, Northwestern University became the first of now more than twenty institutions of higher learning to work with us in establishing a course on the history of the Holocaust. The overwhelming student response to that initial course, taught by Professor Peter Hayes, led directly to the Lessons and Legacies Conference. Without Professor Hayes's dedication and diligence, neither the conference nor this book would have materialized.

We wish to express our thanks to Northwestern University for its support in arranging the conference, especially to President Arnold Weber, Provost Robert Duncan, Dean Lawrence Dumas of the College of Arts and Sciences, and Dean Donald Jacobs and Associate Dean Stuart Greenbaum of the Kellogg Graduate School of Management, who made the beautiful and efficient Allen Center available as the site for the conference.

We are also deeply grateful to Earl Abramson, Judd Malkin, Mort Minkus, Robert Stempel, and Howard Stone. Their constant interest, encouragement, and help turned the idea of this conference into a reality.

It is difficult to find words to express my appreciation to the committee whose members worked so hard to make the conference and this book possible: Earl Abramson, Sharon Abramson, Dr. Leonard Berlin, Lenore Blum, Gitta Fajerstein, Leland Fisher, Larry Gerber, Ira Glick, Joel Greenberg, Elizabeth Jacobs, Sondra Kraff Fineberg, Esther Lauter, Mort Minkus, Sabra Minkus, Barry Pitler, Beverly Reinglass, Heidi Rosenberg, Louis Rosenblum, Lya Dym Rosenblum, Chaya Roth, Elsa Roth, Professor Kenneth Seeskin, Dr. Allen Siegel, Robert Stempel, Rachel Stempel, Howard Stone, Fern Stone, and Professor David Vital.

I want also to say thanks to my wife, Alice, my son, Danny, and my daughter, Deborah, for their patience and understanding during my many absences.

Finally, to my co-chairman, Professor Peter Hayes: your keen insight and tireless effort brought this conference together, and we all thank you.

Peter Hayes

Introduction

BEFORE, WHILE, AND AFTER IT HAPPENED, THE NAZI ONSLAUGHT against the Jews of Europe literally defied human comprehension. Indeed, the sheer incredibility of the Holocaust did much to make it possible, drive it forward, and provoke both the denial and fascination that it continues to arouse. Certainly, had murder of such a degree and kind been imaginable to contemporaries, fewer Germans in the 1930s would have dismissed Hitler's antisemitism as mere rabble-rousing, fewer Jews in the early 1940s would have clung to false hopes, and fewer citizens and officials of the allied nations in both decades would have discounted reports of Nazi barbarism. Had clear precedents for the savagery existed, fewer perpetrators could have derived such pride from the enormity of what they had undertaken or tortured the victims with the claim that no one spared the camps would ever believe accounts of them. Had later generations possessed a convincing explanatory framework in which to fit the slaughter, fewer scholars would have struggled to establish the what, why, and how of its occurrence; fewer readers would have turned to the books and fewer students to the courses that reflect these efforts; and probably a smaller handful of putative "revisionists" would have won less attention by twisting the shocking proofs of purposeful massacre into the familiar shape of a by-product of war. Precisely because incomprehension seems both a cause and a result of the Holocaust, the subject draws and disturbs so many people still.

But, is the Holocaust incomprehens*ible,* as some authorities maintain? Are we and our descendants doomed to fail to grasp what occurred, more or less as contemporaries did, because the cruelty seems beyond our ken or because the number of victims confounds our minds or because the priority the Nazis assigned to annihilation appears so irrational? If so, will the assault on the Jews appear steadily less instructive to our and succeeding generations, despite the proliferation of research and writing on the subject? How can and should serious thinkers try to affect the answers to these questions? As the number of surviving eyewitnesses dwindles and the Holocaust becomes a matter of recorded rather than living memory, these concerns grow more pressing.

These issues not only occasioned the conference at Northwestern University to which earlier versions of the chapters in this volume were presented in November 1989, but also gave rise to vigorous and searching discussion during the proceedings. Whether or how one can formulate the "lessons," "legacies," and "meaning" of the Holocaust obviously depends on whether or how one can explain persuasively what the Nazis caused to happen and why they wanted and were able to act as they did. Thus, from the opening and keynote addresses of Raul Hilberg and Saul Friedländer to the closing remarks of Geoffrey Hartman, the twin themes of comprehensibility and memory predominated. Of course, the participants did not provide conclusive answers to the questions "How much can we know?" and "How can we best preserve, extend, and apply what we have learned?" But, in keeping with the conference logo incorporating the Hebrew letter *chai*, symbolic of hope, the contributors did suggest important ways of increasing and refining our comprehension, avoiding pitfalls that surround this effort, and acting on our knowledge.

To professors Hilberg and Friedländer, who raised the issue of comprehensibility, the problem has essentially the same source, though each thinker describes it differently. The apparent inexplicability of the Holocaust results, in Hilberg's view, from the fact that it marked so radical and disturbing a departure from the perceived direction of history that people then and since have been unable to fit what occurred into a view of human development with which they can live calmly. Friedländer's doubts about the "relevance" of the catastrophe to future generations make a somewhat similar point, to which he adds another: the force of repression bars us from access to the psychology of the perpetrators.

Beneath the differences of phrasing and argument lies a common perception: the Holocaust is but incompletely comprehensible because it is so fundamentally deviant. Our notions of our selves and societies cannot make use of or bear full confrontation with what happened. So we recoil.

In elegant form, Hilberg and Friedländer bring us to the heart of the practice of invoking the incomprehensibility of the Holocaust: it is an intellectual and moral reflex, all the more powerful for being propelled by hope and decency. The strength of these impulses helps explain why references to the unfathomability of Nazi evil have become virtually expected of any civilized commentator on the subject. Although such statements about another subject might be taken as disappointing confessions of (sometimes lengthy) explanatory failure, we crave them in this context as part of a reassuring pact between asserter and audience. The former, in effect, avows that "*I* cannot understand, since *I* could not have done or permitted such things," and the latter, eager to say the same, nods in agreement. Some thinkers, including my colleague Kenneth Seeskin, see great value in this ritual. "If we could understand . . . then the Holocaust would no longer be alien," he argues. "Thought would have a purchase on it. From a moral perspective, this is an impossibility. We *ought* to be overwhelmed by evil on this scale. If so, the old categories do exactly what we want them to: . . . prevent us from thinking we understand what is too horrible to contemplate."[1]

But I wonder if the chief appeal of this reasoning—the way in which it distances us from the Holocaust—does not also have a dangerous aspect. Does it not shield us from the impact of Hans Mommsen's observation that "the Holocaust is a horrifying example of the seductability of otherwise normal individuals"?[2] After all, as Istvan Deak has recently noted, even the most sadistic of the individual perpetrators—like perhaps the German nation as a whole between 1933 and 1945—frequently "grew into" a brutality that expanded with the opportunities for its exercise. Meanwhile, too many bystanders demonstrated what Zygmunt Bauman has called "the facility with which most people, put into a situation that does not contain a good choice . . . argue themselves away from the issue of moral duty."[3] And, on occasion, some among the victims behaved ignobly under the enormous strain. That we should want to turn away from similar possibilities in ourselves or our own world is understandable. But it is also escapist; people can only learn less about their own place and time, as well as the past, when they give in to this temptation.

Nor is this the only ground for debating the wisdom of calling the Holocaust incomprehensible. Michael Marrus alluded to a second line of objection during the conference by noting that, when it comes to identifying the "meaning" of the catastrophe, specialists cannot avoid contending with an intellectual version of Gresham's law, the economic dictum that "bad money drives out good." Proclaiming our inability to understand does not look like a promising weapon in this struggle. Perhaps I can make the point best by shifting the analogy: incomprehension strikes me as an artificial intellectual condition, rather like a vacuum in the physical world. Sooner or later, something rushes into its place, and researchers had best try to control what does so. To concede, however, that a sphere of human agency and interest is beyond comprehension is, in effect, to discredit rational tests of the explanations that inexorably intrude. It virtually invites mystification and manipulation, then abandons the field to them. This is especially so when the subject, as with the Holocaust, excites elemental human fears about the nature of one's fellow beings and the controllability of life. Still a third analogy may best suggest the consequent perils. As a sage observer of politics in early twentieth-century Europe once remarked, "When people cease to believe in God, the danger is not that they will believe nothing, but that they will believe anything." Under these circumstances, a sense of intellectual responsibility would appear to call for acknowledging and reducing the blank spaces in our understanding, rather than affirming the impossibility of it.

Both in his chapter and during the conference sessions, Professor Yehuda Bauer articulated a third line of dissent from the idea that the Holocaust is incomprehensible. Strictly speaking, he insisted, incomprehensibility is a commonplace concerning things that happen to others; it is as true and false for the French Revolution as for the Holocaust, for the particular physical or emotional responses of even a relative as for those of a person far away. Sometimes similarity of experience narrows the gap; sometimes unflinching introspection helps. The more remote from us the situation, however, the more we must rely on our imagination, and on the knowledge that extends and informs it. Almost never do we insist on precise duplication of another's feelings to establish a claim to understanding. If we did, we would have to despair of the possibilities of mutual engagement, of empathy, and of writing meaningfully about the past at all. Instead, we struggle to overcome the limits of time, place, and self. To be sure, conceiving of the mental and physical worlds of the ghettos, the hiding places, the transports, the camps, the SS barracks and *Einsatzgruppen* bivouacs, and even the planning conferences and the occupied cities and countrysides—all of this poses formidable mental challenges to people living in gentler circumstances years later. But success in the effort is no less attainable in principle with regard to the Holocaust than any other human experience. Though Professor Bauer did not say so, one might add that contending otherwise amounts to elevating an important purpose of studying the subject (and much of history)—namely, memorialization—into the only purpose.

There is still a fourth basis for challenging the incomprehensibility of the Holocaust, namely the element of inconsistency often embedded in the notion. Like many other writers who sense enduring impediments to our understanding, professors Hilberg and Friedländer also suggest significant ways in which these have been or might be reduced or removed. In Hilberg's deft outline of the "discovery" of the Holocaust, one can recognize the considerable progress of historical explanation to date, valuable lines of future inquiry, and the importance of a "search for moral certainty" in propelling continuing student and professional interest in the subject. While meditating brilliantly on the "opaqueness . . . at the core of historical understanding and interpretation," Friedländer also provides two searchlights with which to penetrate the motives of those who acted unspeakably: the "exaltation" and the "bond to the Führer" that many of them experienced through repeatedly carrying out his desires. A starker, much less fruitful, case in point is Arno Mayer's recent and widely discussed book *Why Did the Heavens Not Darken?* In the preface, the author states that "at bottom the Judeocide remains as incomprehensible to me today as . . . when I set out to study and rethink it." Yet his work argues vigorously that "the disaster visited upon the Jews" emerged from

(1) a "historical context...of general crisis" which made the slaughter possible and (2) a particular set of "short-term events" which made it happen.[4] More specifically, Mayer highlights the responsibility of German elites in facilitating Hitler's power and purposes, the role of anti-Bolshevism in inspiring the murder of Jews, and the importance of German military reverses on the Eastern Front in setting off the carnage. That most specialists have judged his treatment of these points as inaccurate and overstated is not the issue here.[5] What matters is that Mayer simultaneously advances a way of explaining the Holocaust and reveals that, still and all, he finds it inscrutable. Which claim is the reader to be guided by, the one made emphatically and extensively over 450 pages of text or the one contained in a single paragraph? The allocation of space implies an answer.

If the foregoing arguments have merit and dubbing the Holocaust incomprehensible appears imprudent and illogical, one may well ask why it is so common. The answer suggested above is that it seems more comfortable than the alternatives. Having recourse to incomprehensibility can be a form of emotional resistance, a way of underlining our moral revulsion at the horrors of the subject, of refusing to assemble the available data in ways that arouse self-doubt, and, as perhaps in Arno Mayer's case, of excusing the presentation of strained explanations. But these are not the only emotional defenses at work. Equally powerful is the apparent awe most researchers feel in the face of the Holocaust. Confronted by the extent and viciousness of the massacre, scholars have trouble finding words adequate to describing what happened, let alone analyses equal to accounting for it. The usual, scientific and Cartesian, solution to complexity—to divide the problem into parts, unravel them individually, and connect the results—strikes many people as yielding findings incommensurate with the consequences. The piecemeal explanations that emerge seem too small or too chancily related to have brought forth such a catastrophe. Though it is generally understood—by analogy with mutations in biology or some reactions in chemistry and physics—that individually minor but simultaneous variations in specific historical conditions can aggregate to produce major departures from previous patterns, a felt need for proportionality between cause and effect seems to inhibit explanation of the Holocaust and foster a sense of its incomprehensibility. Again, one is bound to sympathize with an honorable reaction, but also to ask whether it is salutary or sound.

Agreeing that the Holocaust should be treated as a comprehensible event in history does not resolve the issue of precisely *how* we can most intelligently conceive of it. This is the question the chapters in Part I of this book powerfully address. For professors Bauer and Katz, the first step is to define the distinguishing features of what happened and why. Each man offers a learned and detailed analysis of what set the Holocaust apart from other brutal persecutions of human beings both before and during the Nazi years and made it exceptionally lethal. Though the case studies examined in the two chapters differ, the authors identify strikingly similar prerequisites to an attempt at complete annihilation: the mutually reinforcing absence of ideological constraints on mass murder and willingness of social and political elites to participate. Professor Lang's chapter also stressses the historical contingency of the Holocaust and its distinctness from earlier assaults on humanity. But he uses the skills of a philosopher to add another attribute to that distinctness, seeing in the Nazis' deeds, rationales, and desire to conceal their crimes a terrible new feature in the history of human evil. In his view, Himmler and his minions transgressed against received standards of decency, not in order to serve some supposedly "higher" purpose, like other antinomians before or since, or out of lust for destruction, like some ancient tyrants, or in self-defense, as antisemitic ideology taught, but "deliberately, i.e., with the consciousness of it as a wrong," and in so doing established genocide as a more constant potentiality in the human future than ever before.

The final chapters in Part I by professors Marrus and Vital offer provocatively parallel and divergent discussions of the postwar public reception of the Holocaust. On the one hand, both experts trace and warn against distortions that stem from inclinations to sanctify the tragedy or to satisfy popular preconceptions. On the other hand, whereas Marrus worries that many Jews have been too gripped by an "irrational fear" for their future and a desire to offset internal political and religious differences in reacting to the Holocaust, Vital is troubled by the lasting impact of decimation on the Jewish people and the disunity of their responses to it. Both graceful and pointed, these two chapters provide not only valuable correctives to hasty or superficial readings of the historical record, but also stimulating models of how serious thinkers' views of the past and present can intersect in the conceptualization of the Holocaust.

Central to any explanation of the Holocaust are answers to the two questions taken up by the contributions to Part II of this volume: How could people do or permit these things? Why did so few brave souls try to intercede? Hans Mommsen ascribes the spiral toward annihilation not to widespread and fervent antisemitism in Germany, but to the conjunction of intraparty politics and popular passivity. On his showing, the Nazi regime tended to compensate the minority of hard-core radical racists within the Party for their exclusion from other spheres of policy-making by allowing them relatively free play in attacking the Jews. In this context, deference to authority, segregation from Jews, fear of the Gestapo, and the compartmentalized and semi-concealed nature of the persecution process did the rest, spreading apathy and stifling potential resistance. Similarly, Claudia Koonz is concerned with the way in which activists' murderous notions came to control the behavior of wider segments of the German population. She locates the "genesis of genocide" in the Reich's propaganda campaign against "life unworthy of life" during the 1930s, arguing that this drive succeeded in getting key groups and millions of average citizens to dissociate themselves from the targeted categories and to accept their elimination as scientifically justified, thus predisposing Germans to acquiesce or participate in the "Final Solution."

Whereas professors Mommsen and Koonz demonstrate how national developments structured societal behavior and values in the Third Reich, the remaining three chapters in Part II focus on individual conduct. Robert Gellately directs our attention to a daily manifestation of popular involvement in the persecution of the German Jews, the practice of tipping off the Gestapo to infractions against antisemitic legislation. His close examination of case files in Würzburg establishes not only the dependence of the understaffed police on widespread readiness to assist them and the intimidating effects on other Germans but also the predominance of petty and personal motives, rather than ideological conviction, in animating denouncers. Even more prosaic bases for still more heinous deeds take center stage in Christopher Browning's chilling report on the German reserve policemen who shot to death, one by one, 1,500 Jewish women, children, and elderly residents of a Polish village in July 1942. Neither political fervor nor fear of punishment seems to have prompted their willingness to kill. Most acted out of a nearly automatic impulse to conform—to appear strong in the eyes of their comrades—strengthened in a few cases by an interest in advancing their careers. Conversely, if antisemitism is virtually absent as an active impetus to persecution in these accounts, Nechama Tec's study of occupied Poland suggests that opposition to antisemitism seldom figured prominently in decisions to save Jews from the Nazis. Instead, she finds that persons who opted to defy the enormous perils associated with rescue generally had long records of aiding the needy and acting on the basis of individual conviction. Such people chose to render assistance at great personal risk just as unreflectively in most cases as the German reservists chose to carry out their assigned task. Taken together, these three chapters attest to the decisiveness of personal character in moments of historical extremity. In doing so, they help demystify the littleness and the largeness of which individuals proved capable.

Part III of this book comprises chapters devoted to the subject of memory—its content, its plasticity, its application, and its collection. Lawrence Langer's extraordinarily sensitive piece seeks to reveal what oral testimonies tell us about the impact of the Holocaust on survivors and to throw light on the issue of comprehensibility. He discerns in the recollections of the persecuted our only possible inkling of the "knowledge as disaster" that has stamped their lives, leaving them with an enduring but barely recognizable "violated self" that haunts the person each subsequently became. Alvin Rosenfeld takes the iconography of Anne Frank as an illuminating example of the transformation, even banalization, of memory, showing how the contents of her diary have been sentimentalized and bowdlerized, according to local taste, in the process of translation onto the stage or screen or into other languages. The result is a chronicle, not of fear, suffering, and death, but of uplift, inspiration, hope, and triumph, one made to offer reassurance and forgiveness at the price of historical accuracy. James Young's analysis of Holocaust memorials in Israel details another process of integrating memory with interpretive preferences, in this instance with "national myths and ideals." His examination of commemorative sites in the Israeli countryside discloses a recurring emphasis on the Holocaust as a display of Jewish helplessness and heroism, the former as proof of the need for a Jewish state and the latter as demonstration of how it can survive. Franklin Littell draws similarly explicit connections between understanding of the past and action in the present and future, but his vantage point is international and ecumenical. Without neglecting the specific theological and historical roots of the assault on the Jews, he recognizes in the rise of the Nazis and the Holocaust guidelines for identifying potentially criminal political movements and an injunction to prevent them from taking control of states in an age when the popular ability to dislodge dictatorships has declined and the world has grown increasingly interdependent.

The final chapter in Part III and Professor Geoffrey Hartman's closing remarks provide fitting conclusions to a scholarly volume on the Holocaust by raising directly the issue of education and the role of survivors in it. Each chapter narrates the procedures and dilemmas of gathering testimony from those best equipped to tell us the "feel" of what happened and in the videotaped form suited to conveying exactly that sort of understanding. Both essays alert students and researchers to the availability of an extensive and significant new means, as Lawrence Langer writes, to "narrow the space that separates us from the event" and thus to reduce incomprehension.

Although the foregoing summaries can hardly capture the richness of the contributions to this book, they suggest, I hope, the resourcefulness with which the scholars who came to Evanston met the challenge of identifying the lessons, legacies, and meaning of the Holocaust. That they, nonetheless, did not exhaust the currently plausible responses to that challenge, let alone the ones that future experience will suggest, should go without saying. One lesson, legacy, and meaning is, however—at least to my mind— firmly documented here: comprehension of the Holocaust is not only possible, but essential. For, to quote my colleague Kenneth Seeskin once again, "How can reason oppose something it cannot understand?"[6] So long as that is the question, I submit, there can be no effective answer.

Raul Hilberg

Opening Remarks: The Discovery of the Holocaust

THE HOLOCAUST IS A FUNDAMENTAL EVENT IN HISTORY—NOT ONLY because one-third of the Jewish people in the world died in the space of four years, not only because of the manner in which they were killed, but because, in the last analysis, it is inexplicable. All our assumptions about the world and its progress prior to the years when this event burst forth have been upset. The certainties of the late nineteenth and early twentieth century vanished in its face. What we once understood, we no longer comprehend.

It happened unexpectedly, in the middle of our century in the middle of civilized Europe.

Least of all did the victims, already marked with yellow stars and concentrated in their ghettos, fathom what was about to happen to them. Regardless of what they heard, notwithstanding insistent rumors, few of them could grasp that the evidence pointed to the abyss. There were at least three ghettos in Poland—Lodz, Bilgoraj, and Bialystok—to which the Germans shipped the clothing of gassed Jews for cleaning and for sorting—clothing still filled with identity cards, passports, and religious objects that no religious Jew tosses away. Despite these bureaucratic errors, it was hard for the ghetto dwellers to grasp the reality, stranger and more fierce than anything ever imagined, that had descended upon them.

The disbelief extended to the Jewish organizations that watched the process from the outside. With a budget of less than $1,000 a month, the World Jewish Congress maintained an office in Geneva for the purpose of acquiring information about the happenings in Europe. All that this very small staff could do was to pass on the most important published data and some of the reports and rumors that filtered across the Swiss frontier, always with the caution that there was not enough money to put everything into telegrams.

There were at least, so we are told by the research of Laqueur and Breitman and others, three German emissaries who crossed into Switzerland in the summer of 1942—Ernst Lemmer, Arthur Sommer, and Eduard Schulte. The third of them, by roundabout ways, got the message across. It had to come from Germany! It had to come from a German to be believed. And even then, it was subject to endless checking, for it was, in the words of an American consul in Switzerland, "Fantastic!"

Again and again, the information was confirmed but not fully comprehended. We now know and can fairly accurately calculate that by the end of 1942, the most lethal year in Jewish history, four million Jews were killed. The Jewish organizations in Washington, meeting with President Roosevelt in December 1942 and still at that moment reluctant to believe the full truth, presented the number two million. About a year later, a report came from the Polish underground in Auschwitz, delivered at considerable risk by a Polish courier to London, detailing the events at the camp itself, complete with names and numbers. It was disseminated to our Intelligence in the War Department, where it was filed away, to the War Crimes Commission, where it was filed away, to the Office of Strategic Services, where the great historian who was in charge of its intelligence and research branch, William Langer, also filed it away. Thereafter came that famous aerial photography that David Wyman wrote about, when first a South African aircraft and then repeated reconnaissance missions of Allied Mediterranean Command took pictures, in clear skies from the height of 29,000 feet, of Auschwitz itself. No one looked for the gas chambers in the left-hand corner of those photographs.

Not until 1945 was the reality visualized. It took the ground forces of the allied armies that liberated the camps to see the Holocaust, to smell it: American troops who captured Dachau, Mauthausen, Buchenwald; British troops who found the emaciated bodies of Bergen-Belsen; and two divisions of the Red Army, the 100th and the 101st Ukrainian divisions, that captured Auschwitz in January 1945. Vassily Petrenko was a lieutenant colonel, a commander of one of the battalions in the 100th division. He tells us that Soviet commanders had been warned to expect concentration camps on the path of their advance, but: "Nothing prepared them for gas chambers. Nothing."

Immediately after the war, this reality had to be incorporated into policy, into memory. But what happened? In the Nürnberg trials, where the indictments were drawn up and the offenses defined, killing *allied citizens* was a war crime—people of Norwegian nationality, of French nationality, Belgian, Dutch or Polish nationality. Some of them just happened to have been Jews. Those of German or Hungarian nationality were counted as victims only if they were killed on the soil of an allied country. The controlling criterion was nationality or the place of the crime. And so, even at Nürnberg only the perpetrator was identified, but the identity of the victims was half forgotten.

It was not only Nürnberg, it was not only the law, that buried memory. We had no language with which to describe the unprecedented event that had taken place. Look over the early literature, the early correspondence, and the early newspaper accounts and see the descriptions with words like antisemitism, excesses, atrocities. The inadequate terminology appropriate for what happened in the nineteenth century was used for this event. Was there any incorporation into our teaching? Hardly. If there was mention at all of anti-Jewish activities in our textbooks, the epitome was represented as *Kristallnacht,* that is, as the rocks that were thrown into shops in the cities of Germany on November 10, 1938, as if not much happened thereafter.

I well recall a small but telling incident when the *Encyclopedia Americana* prepared its 1968 edition. They wanted a new article on concentration camps, and I said, "Fine, I'll write it for you." And, naturally having looked at the *Britannica,* I had to do better. Apparently I did. They were so pleased as to ask for two small articles also about special topics: Buchenwald was one, Dachau the other. Then I waited, but no request came for Auschwitz. No request came for Treblinka. They didn't exist yet in encyclopedias.

Even when special efforts were made in the world of art to portray what had happened, the Jews were generally left out. For example, in that famous film, "Night and Fog," Jews are not mentioned, though Auschwitz is shown; Jews are never referred to, even though the camera dwells on a gas chamber to the accompaniment of the love and death music from *Tristan and Isolde*. Or consider the well-known play by Peter Weiss, *Die Ermittlung* (The Investigation): the Auschwitz trial itself put into the form of a drama, yet no mention of the word Jew. Clearly, this was more than forgetting; it was repression.

Note what happened to the works of survivors. You will hear at this conference a very illuminating account of that most famous of all works by a victim who happened not to have survived but who lives in our hearts, Anne Frank. How many copies were printed in the first edition? Or look, if you will, at a book published in the Yiddish language in Argentina, *Und die Welt hot geschwigen* (And the world was silent)—an angry book. Who read it? It was in any case addressed to fellow survivors. A starkly realistic and insightful story, the author pared it down, made it into a poem and called it *Night*. It is Elie Wiesel's cut-down version that you have all read. Later, the Italian publisher Einaudi printed 2,500 copies of Primo Levi's *If This Be a Man;* six hundred were on the remainder list and drowned in the Florentine Flood, as he informs us in a book appropriately called *The Drowned and the Saved*. Even the survivor was told: "Forget it, get on with your life."

Under these conditions, how did we discover the Holocaust? At first, the question obviously raised at Nürnberg was the simple one: "Who were these people who did this?" And the answer was just as simple. For inevitably, that missing person, Adolf Hitler, seemed to be the all-encompassing answer—if need be with the help of the SS, that "Negative Elite," as it was called by Eugen Kogon, a former inmate of Buchenwald. It is to the credit of American prosecutors that they—lawyers that they were, but also historians, like Telford Taylor—dug beneath that superficial analytical framework and sought out for trial physicians, generals, and, yes, members of industry—of Krupp, I. G. Farben, the Dresdner Bank, and Flick—but not, to cite but two examples of men who were in the very midst of the destructive arena, officials of the ordinary street police (the *Ordnungspolizei)* and the railways. It was just not fathomable to assume that men untouched by ideology, who'd never read *Der Stürmer* or *Mein Kampf*, could do such things. But then, as one of Himmler's cousins once told me, *he* couldn't understand how Himmler did, as he put it, "such things." We went from the top down. We started, not at the bottom, but with Hitler.

Years later, we discovered the victims in precisely the same way. The occasion was the Eichmann trial, when a correspondent, borrowed from the discipline of philosophy, was sent by a popular magazine to cover that proceeding and hurriedly wrote a report about it. She found herself in a morass of data and quickly concluded that the Jewish Councils were the undoing, the cause of death, of so many people. Had it not been for the *Judenräte*, for the Jewish Councils, for those people who sat collaborating, or cooperating at least, with their persecutors, well, maybe a million, maybe two million Jews would have died, but certainly not five or six. As late as the 1970s, when Isaiah Trunk's path-breaking book, a heavy, 700-page history of the ghettos of Eastern Europe, was published by Macmillan, it did not receive the title "The Ghettos" but was called instead *Judenrat* (Jewish council). I can appreciate the change of plans because the editor had originally asked me to write that book. Mine was to have been a book about ghettos. Trunk's *is* a book about ghettos. But the publisher could not encompass the thought that here was a description of a ghetto society in all of its complexity.

Have we to this day explored the victims? Look at the analytical literature. There were men and there were women, but were their experiences the same? There were children. How often do we hear about the fate of the Jewish children? How important is precisely the fate of these children, for that is what makes the Holocaust a holocaust! I must confess to you, I did not ask that question of myself until at my university the Pediatrics Department requested from me a lecture about the fate of Jewish children. And I said, "My God, these are doctors. No doubt they want numbers and facts, and they want these on handouts." Quickly I raced to what little material I had. I stared at a report of the Lodz ghetto, a document I'd had for years but which I really had not analyzed with great care. Then I saw something that made me call up the chief of Vital Statistics of the State of Vermont, for I had to ask myself whether something was wrong with me or with the report. I said, "Please tell me, what exactly is an infant mortality rate? How do you define that?" She explained, and I looked at my data again, realizing that in the Lodz ghetto it *was* more than 1,000 per 1,000. Think about that. It is possible. It is the mathematics of a holocaust.

Or take another subject. We do not talk about it. We do not explore it, although we mention it more and more frequently and it is in the memoirs. Did money help in a moment of crisis? Did the poor die first? Isaiah Trunk speaks of a food pyramid in the ghettos. Have we explored this subject? Have we counted calories? What of mixed marriages and their offspring? Who talks about converts to Christianity? Who in the eyes of the Germans were Jews? Who in the eyes of the Jews were gentiles?

After the focus had been placed on perpetrators and victims, we became aware of the third personality—the bystander. Once again, we started at the top—after all, the playwright Hochhuth informed us that the name of the chief bystander is Pope Pius XII! Who else? Thank goodness the Vatican published some eleven volumes of documents showing what some historians may have known all along—that even the Catholic Church is not monolithic. When Cardinal Secretary of State Maglione discovered in 1943 the existence of Treblinka, the very way in which he words his memorandum reveals the same surprise, the same astonishment, almost the same disbelief that the victims and the American government had exhibited earlier. Those of you who saw the film *Shoah* by Claude Lanzmann probably saw for the first time local bystanders being interviewed. How late we discovered these peasants. Everywhere, we looked, not from the bottom up, but from the top down.

What meaning in this Holocaust? Different meanings, to be sure, for the perpetrators, for the victims, and for the rest of the population of the world. For Germans, I have always felt there is an insurmountable obstacle. After all, the one question one does not ask of a person of a certain age in Germany whose father was an adult in World War II, the one question that is totally taboo, is "What did your father do?" Essentially, the division between the generations, it strikes me, is far greater in Germany than the division now disappearing between West and East Germany, far greater than the superficial ideological division of a cold war, far greater than any other bifurcation. Yes, Germans would love to forget. They do not have psychological independence, as we learned during the Bitburg crisis, when Chancellor Kohl thought that with one stroke he could end the forty years in the desert by having an American president visit a cemetery. And what happened? "The past returns!" cried the German newspapers, "The past is still here!" So they struggle with that past without letup.

There are those who say this Germany of 1933, 1938, and 1945 was ruled by a government of usurpers. "We can show you the statistics; we have investigated the elections of 1932. We have counted the votes." Political scientists, represented by Bracher and his school, make this argument. "Nazism was an aberration!" Well, listen to the paper of Christopher Browning about one ordinary battalion of police in one town on one day and ask yourself the question again, "Who did these things?" Another German argument says, "All right, something was drastically wrong, something happened to us; we don't know what. But clearly a break occurred in history. Maybe it happened to all of us. But you cannot compare the Germany of the Nazi years with that prior to 1933 or after 1945." "Oh, no," says another school, "there is continuity. It is the same Germany." Continuity theory was already espoused by Thomas Mann in a lecture in the Library of Congress in April 1945. He spoke with pain, for he was a passionate romantic, but he had to admit that, whereas classicism was healthy, German romanticism was enduringly sick. Finally, there are those political scientists around Nolte who say, "All right now, you want continuity, you want to talk about us Germans as a self-perpetuating culture, but let us look at other nations. Who invented the concentration camp? The British in South Africa, the Spaniards in Cuba—not we. Who has the patent on the bullet into the back of the neck? The Soviet NKVD—not we. Who, for that matter, designed gas chambers first? Why, you Americans—not we." And they go on and on. This is called relativization. If all things are relative, one need not worry so much. But whom do they fool? Not even themselves.

For the Jews, the impact is incalculable. In Professor Vital's chapter, you will notice that the author speaks of the literal amputation of one-third of the Jewish people. Can such a people, any people, stay the same after such an event? Can it define itself the way it did before? Will not a thousand years pass before somehow this experience becomes "history" for the Jews? Only three years almost to the day after the end of the Holocaust, Israel was established as an independent state. What a connection. Look at the topography of Jerusalem and the three hills that were pointed out to me. On one are buried those who were killed, mostly in 1948, without whom the state would not have been possible. On another is the transplanted grave of Herzl, without whom the state would not have been conceivable. And, on the adjacent third hill, stands the remembrance authority of Yad Vashem commemorating the Holocaust, without which the state would not have been necessary. One cannot remove this event from the Jewish psyche in a thousand years.

But the Holocaust came to the bystanders, too. Here in the United States, something happened. We now can almost pinpoint when. It was roughly 1978. Naturally such developments don't really have a precise date on which they begin. And yet, here was a television play that the author, Gerald Green, could not have sold to any network five or ten years earlier. Here was a nationalization of the Holocaust by an Executive Order establishing a President's Commission on the Holocaust. Here, at that late date, was the establishment of the Office of Special Investigations, to look for perpetrators on our soil. Here, we see the multiplication of books about the Holocaust, of courses about the Holocaust, of curricula about the Holocaust, and, yes, of conferences about the Holocaust.

How well aware I am of this transformation. I have taught at my university for thirty-four years, and I kept my research a private endeavor long after its first publication. Not until a colleague of mine in the Department of English, of all places, came to my office one day and said, "Let us teach a course on the Holocaust together," did I decide to do it. But I said, "Let us make it one of those topics courses and not give it a permanent number. We'll teach it once, we'll teach it twice, then we'll see." After two years and after three, we realized this is a topic that will not go away. After his retirement, I thought "maybe now the enrollment will drop." But it has not. Nor is this phenomenon confined to the University of Vermont. Moravian College offers a Holocaust course; Moorhead, Minnesota, had a conference on the Holocaust; the University of Hawaii has a regular seminar on the subject. The subject has spread throughout the land. Twenty-year-old men and women come into my office to inquire about the course, and they say, "I've been interested in the Holocaust for a long time." We have some affluent students, and it turns out that when they graduated from high school, their parents gave them a trip to Europe. These are not, by the way, Jewish students in the majority at all. And where did they go on this sightseeing trip? Why, to Dachau and to Mauthausen.

Something in our youth demands knowledge of what happened. We have not created that interest. We have not agitated at all to make it happen. History created this interest—this search for moral certainty, this quest for a definition of evil, this preoccupation with the ultimate truths of the behavior of men toward other men. That is what they want to know.

The Holocaust is the same; it cannot change. But the world in which we live, whether we welcome or do not welcome the development that is before us, changes the meaning of the Holocaust as time passes before our eyes.

I. T·H·E·M·E·S

Saul Friedländer

The "Final Solution":
On the Unease in Historical Interpretation

"THE PAST CARRIES WITH IT A TEMPORAL INDEX BY WHICH IT IS RE-
ferred to redemption," writes Walter Benjamin in the second of
his "Theses on the Philosophy of History." "There is a secret agreement between past generations and the present one. . . . Like every
generation that preceded us, we have been endowed with a *weak*
messianic power, a power to which the past has a claim. That claim
cannot be settled cheaply . . . "[1]

Walter Benjamin wrote these lines before the onset of the catastrophe of which he himself was to become a victim. For him,
historical materialism was to be the redeeming approach toward
the past. After the extermination of the Jews of Europe, Benjamin's messianic gaze might possibly have posed the question on
an entirely new level. He might have discovered that historical
materialism had little to contribute as a convincing interpretation
of these events; he would have wondered, possibly, whether any
historical approach could suffice to redeem, that is convincingly to
interpret that past.[2]

There lies the dilemma of the historian. On the one hand,
historians cannot but study the "Final Solution" as any other past
phenomenon. The reconstruction of the most detailed sequences
of events related to the extermination of the Jews is progressing
apace. On the other hand, for some historians at least, an opaqueness remains at the very core of the historical understanding and
interpretation of what happened.

Such a sense of difficulty was quite obvious during the immediate postwar years, but it was not dispelled by the passage of time, and recently, intimations of this unease have appeared again in the work of several historians. The aim of this chapter is to come closer to the nature of this difficulty. It should be clearly stated, however, that for many historians who deal either directly or indirectly with the "Final Solution," a full historicization seems by now possible and even in large part achieved.

This unease in historical interpretation is, as the French philosopher Vladimir Jankelevitch would have said, a "je ne sais quoi," a "hint of something." For instance, in his recent *Why Did the Heavens Not Darken? The Final Solution in History*, Arno Mayer made a massive effort to contextualize the "Final Solution" within what he called the "Thirty Years War of the Twentieth Century," only to end his preface with the acknowledgment that after more than five years of study, he did not understand the "judeocide" better than when he started.[3] What this lack of understanding was, more precisely, he did not say. When Charles Maier in *The Unmasterable Past* wrote that "Auschwitz was incomprehensible," he probably meant the same thing.[4] Finally, when Raul Hilberg, possibly the historian most thoroughly acquainted with the documents of destruction and the day-to-day aspects of the "Final Solution," spoke recently, of "this event which appears in history and yet (is) apart from it, disturbing so many historians . . . ,"[5] he, again, may have meant this rather diffuse but unmistakable impression persisting after decades of inquiry.

This feeling of incomprehension is probably more often expressed by Jewish interpreters of the "Final Solution" than by others. One could easily argue that the notion is thus highly subjective and derives directly from the emotionally charged vision of the group to which the victims belong. As we shall see, this is far from being exclusively the case, but the element of subjectivity cannot be denied. However, such subjectively accords, in my opinion, with the existentially determined aspect of *all* approaches to Nazism and the "Final Solution."[6]

I shall try to identify the difficulty dealt with here on two different levels: first, that of a specific issue—the psychology of the perpetrators—further, that of the insertion of the "Final Solution" into a global historical interpretation.

Most interpreters try to avoid the problem posed by the psychology of total extermination by concentrating exclusively on specific ideological motives (i.e., racial antisemitism, racial thinking in general, etc.) or on institutional dynamics. There is no way of denying both the importance of the radical antisemitic theme and of competitive internal politics, as well as the dynamics of bureaucracy, in giving general interpretation of the "Final Solution." But an independent psychological residue seems to defy the historian. The psychological dimension, whenever recognized, is usually reduced to a vague reference to the "banality of evil." My hypothesis, in this first part, is that for some historians this particular dimension remains a kind of riddle which is subsumed under other explanatory categories, but accompanies any discussion about the "why" and not the "how" of the "Final Solution." Here I shall try to distinguish between various elements of this psychological dimension in order better to circumscribe what could well be its irreducible core.

Let me intentionally choose one of the most notorious documents of the "Final Solution" in order to direct our questions to a text familiar to anybody dealing with this subject: the Himmler speech given in Poznan on October 4, 1943, before an assembly of high-ranking SS officers.

"Most of you know," Himmler declared, "what it means when 100 corpses are lying side by side, when 500 lie there or 1,000. Having borne that and nevertheless—some exceptional human weakness aside—having remained decent *(anständig geblieben zu sein)* has hardened us. . . . All in all, we may say that we have accomplished the most difficult task out of love for our people. And we have not sustained any damage to our inner self, our soul and our character *(Und wir haben keinen Schaden in unserem Inneren, in unserer Seele, in unserem Character daran genommen)."*

The horror and uncanniness (understood here in the sense of the German word *Unheimlichkeit)* of these lines lies at first glance in what, for the reader, may appear as a fundamental dissonance. It is between, on the one hand, the explicit commitment to breaking the most fundamental of human taboos, that is, wiping from the face of the earth each and every member of a specific human group (eleven million people, according to Heydrich's calculation at the Wannsee Conference) and, on the other hand, the declaration that this difficult task was being accomplished satisfactorily, without any moral damage. This sense of inversion of all values is reinforced by the mention, later in the speech, of those rare weaknesses that have to be ruthlessly extirpated, such as the stealing of cigarettes, watches, and money from the victims.

However, the source of the strangeness *(Unheimlichkeit)* is not limited to this dissonance only. It is augmented by a further key sentence in that part of the speech: The extermination of the Jews of Europe, Himmler maintains, "is the most glorious page in our history, one not written and which shall never be written." Himmler thereby conveyed that he and the whole assembly were, in this case, well aware of some total transgression that future generations will not understand, even as a necessary means toward a "justifiable" end.

In a later speech, Himmler came back to the extermination of women and children. He stated that this extermination is imperative in order to prevent the rise of future avengers. In this context, he restated the necessity of carrying the secret of this extermination to the grave. One could object that the vow of secrecy belonged precisely to the forging and existence of a fanatical elite and was, almost by itself, the distinctive sign of such an elite. This may indeed have been so, except for the fact that for religious movements, as well as for modern political religions, the mass killing of enemies of the faith or the party generally is part of the well-publicized campaigns of such entities (e.g., the extermination crusade against the Cathars, the witch-hunts and the general practices of the Inquisition, the "Terreur," the Bolshevik killings and those perpetrated by the "Khmer Rouge," etc.). Such killings are always linked to the most explicit aims, propagandized with pride by such institutions or movements, and presented as almost self-understood in terms of ideological necessity.

Himmler's vow of secrecy for all time seems to indicate that he saw no higher comprehensible argument that could "justify" such an annihilation in the eyes of posterity. This may well indicate that Himmler himself had doubts about the ideological foundations of these actions and that his arguments about "love of the Fatherland" and "destroying the people that wanted to destroy us" have to be considered, in part at least, as rhetorical.

There can be little doubt about the centrality of the anti-Jewish obsession in Hitler's worldview, as well as about elements of anti-semitic motivation at various levels of the Party and the popula-tion, but the overwhelming centrality of this factor is not apparent in the case of Himmler and his Poznan audience. The core moti-vation may well be more decisively attributed to a series of elements that I shall mention further on, among which are the *Führer-Bindung* ("the bond to the Führer") and the concept aptly pointed to by Hilberg: *Rausch* ("irrepressible exaltation").

There, among other things, lies one aspect of the differences between the Nazi "project" and the Stalinist one. Whatever the magnitude of the crimes committed by Stalin, they were commit-ted, at least on the face of it, in the name of a universal ideal, or, more precisely, the universal ideal was maintained as explanation, most probably in the eyes of the perpetrators themselves. The Nazi extermination of the Jews, if we take seriously Himmler's vow of future secrecy, appears as an aim that cannot be explained by "higher, commonly understandable" ends. Thus, the singularity of the Nazi project seems to lie not only in the act, but, inciden-tally of course, in the language and the self-perception of the perpetrators. If one continues considering the events from this viewpoint, then, in fact, the extermination perpetrated by the Nazis is not an "inversion of all values" (as would be the case if human beings were worked to death or killed for a very specific political aim) but instead represents an amorality beyond all cate-gories of evil. Human beings are no longer reduced to mere instru-ments; they have lost their humanity entirely.

Before probing further, we should ask whether, incidentally, the contemporaries who were not involved as perpetrators in the extermination process seemed to have understood its nature, on the basis of their knowledge of the events. Various recent studies dealing with the "terrible secret" stress in diverse ways the simul-taneity of considerable knowledge of the facts and of a no less massive inability or refusal to transform these facts into integrated understanding.[7] Clearly, each group had its own reasons for not internalizing what, in great part, could be known or was known. One cannot compare the reasons of the victims with those of sur-rounding German society, but one common denominator appears nonetheless: the "Final Solution" was in a way, "unthinkable."

A comparison with Stalinist Russia will, again, put this type of contemporary incomprehension into clearer perspective. It seems that the victims of Stalinism who were not commited Bolsheviks faced no impossibility in comprehending the all-pervasive terror that descended on their country. They grasped the significance of the Lubyanka, of the Siberian camps, of the starvation and the shootings; they may have considered all of it in terms of Bolshevik terror in general, but none of the more detailed accounts of these events, such as Robert Conquest's studies for instance, raises the issue of some kind of paralysis of comprehension.[8]

This type of argument should not be misunderstood as an exoneration of the "bystanders," whoever they were. The widespread knowledge of monstrous crimes perpetrated against the Jews and the almost general indifference that accompanied them is a sufficient indictment; an understanding of the full scope of the "Final Solution" is not a necessary precondition for all the questions later raised about European society, about the behavior of the Allies, the Neutrals, and the Churches, about that of German society in particular.

In terms of the incomprehension of contemporaries, that of the victims stands out in its incommensurably tragic dimension. It is impossible to reelaborate here on the oft-described mechanisms of "denial" in the face of a reality that, at some stage, was only too obvious. But, as is known, "denial" was not the only element involved. What misled the immense majority of European Jews was the compelling belief, as far as Nazi behavior was concerned, in some element of "instrumental rationality" (some rational link between utilitarian aims, such as producing clothing or shoes for the *Wehrmacht* in the ghetto workshops, for instance, and appropriate means, such as keeping the able-bodied Jewish working force alive). The fate of the Jews was sealed in any case; the reason for their extermination they could in no way comprehend.

The main question about interpretation, however, must be addressed to those who acquired full knowledge of the events, after the end of the war. The life span of many of the present-day readers of Himmler's speech still overlaps in part with his. On the basis of the assumption of sharing a common humanity and even a common historical experience, and thus basically common perceptions of human existence in society, we try to overcome the feelings of strangeness and horror and to find the point of psychological identity. We try to identify our own thinking with that of Himmler's world by an understanding stemming from the postulates of these psychological common denominators. By doing so, we assume the validity of the notion of the "banality of evil," as it supposedly allows us to grasp the mind-set we are probing: the "banality of evil" suggests that we all share common propensities eventually leading to ultimate criminality. I will not even attempt to analyze the conceptual fuzziness of the "banality of evil."[9] On a more concrete level, by accepting this notion, we disregard several major elements that I will presently try to circumscribe.

A close analysis of Himmler's speech can lead us to a more precise delimitation of the areas of incomprehension. One could argue that the extirpation of blemishes such as the stealing of the victims' cigarettes, et cetera, belongs to a well-known category: military or monastic discipline as far as minute details of behavior are concerned, such as is found in elite units and religious orders of various kinds. One could argue, moreover, that the elimination of potential avengers by exterminating the women and children can be reduced to the logic of "instrumental rationality." Clearly, however, these aspects are corollaries of the initial motivation; they do not explain the motivation as such. Thus, if we accept the thesis that Himmler and his generals were not driven by an overriding anti-Jewish ideological obsession (in contradistinction with Hitler), we are faced with the *Führer-Bindung* as part of the explanation and some imponderables that indeed seem to escape us, included in the overall notion of *Rausch*.

In the previous pages, I have used the word "strangeness" or "uncanniness" as the equivalent of the German *Unheimlichkeit*. It manifestly brings to mind Freud's famous essay "On the Uncanny." Freud quotes a 1906 article by Jentsch that relates the feeling of the uncanny to the impossibility of distinguishing the animate from the inanimate; in his essay Freud denies, on several occasions, that Jentsch's indications are in any way plausible.[10] I will allude further to Freud's interpretation, but at first glance, Jentsch's intuition appears relevant. Let me repeat Jentsch's position as summarized by Freud himself: "The author [Jentsch, S.F.] believes that a particularly favorable condition for awakening uncanny sensations is created when there is intellectual uncertainty whether an object is alive or not and when an inanimate object becomes too much like an animate one."[11]

When we consider again the text of Himmler's speech, or in more general terms, the mass extermination actions of the various perpetrators and particularly of the higher bureaucracy of death, we cannot but admit, on the one hand, the human ordinariness of the perpetrators and notice, on the other hand, the "mechanical," non-human aspect of their actions. In a sense, we are confronted with some kind of uncertainty as defined by Jentsch, except that we are not dealing with automata approaching the semblance of life, but with human beings of the most ordinary kind approaching the state of automata by eliminating any feelings of humanness and of moral sense in relation to groups other than their own. Our sense of *Unheimlichkeit* is indeed triggered by this deep uncertainty as to the "true nature" of the perpetrators, except, as I mentioned, as far as their own group is concerned. This is the point of inception of *Rausch*.

Could one of the components of *Rausch* itself, as far as killing and extermination of others are concerned, not be the effect of a growing elation stemming from *repetition*, from the ever-larger numbers of the killed others? "Most of you know what it means when 100 corpses are lying side by side, when 500 lie there or 1,000." This repetition (and here indeed we are back, in part, to *Freud's* interpretation) adds to the sense of *Unheimlichkeit*, at least for the outside observer; there, the perpetrators do not appear anymore as bureaucratic automata, but rather as beings seized by a compelling lust for killing on an immense scale, driven by some kind of extraordinary elation in repeating the killing of ever-huger masses of people (notwithstanding Himmler's words about the difficulty of this duty). Suffice it to remember the *pride of numbers* sensed in the *Einsatzgruppen* reports, the pride of numbers in Rudolf Hoess's autobiography; suffice it to remember Eichmann's interview with Eassen: he would jump with glee into his grave knowing that over five million Jews had been exterminated; elation created by the staggering dimension of the killing, by the endless rows of victims.[12] The elation created by the staggering number of victims ties in with the mystical Führer-Bond: the greater the numbers of the Jews exterminated, the better the Führer's will has been fulfilled. *However, precisely at this point—the elation created by the dimensions of the killing—our understanding remains blocked on the level of self-awareness, and this after the events and because of these events.* As the British philosopher Alan Montefiore aptly put it: "The unimaginable belongs to that part of my darkest imagination—or, at least, that imagination which, whether it be mine or not, I may have to recognize within me—to which my whole conscious, 'normally' sensitive being refuses the very right of existence."[13]

Consequently, the greater the moral sensitivity, the stricter the repression will be of a subject deemed too threatening to both the individual and society. *The historian can analyze the phenomenon from the "outside," but, in this case, his unease stems from the noncongruence between intellectual probing and the blocking of intuitive comprehension of events that happened more or less during his or her lifetime, within his or her own society.*

The second possible source of the historian's unease lies, in my opinion, on an entirely differently level, that of the insertion of the "Final Solution" into global historical interpretation. "The National Socialist murder of the Jews," writes Eberhard Jaeckel, "was unequalled because never before has a state, with the authority of its responsible leaders, decided upon and announced the total killing of a certain group of people, including the old, the women, the children, the infants, and turned this decision into fact, with the use of all the possible instruments of power available to the state."[14]

This kind of definition is usually at the center of the debates concerning the comparability or noncomparability of the "Final Solution" with mass murder perpetrated by various other political systems. It is the backdrop to which more subjective interpretations of this exceptionality ultimately refer. Granted this, let us turn again to another level of obstacles encountered by the historian in his subjective apprehension of the events, this time within their wider interpretive context.

The "Final Solution," like any other historical phenomenon, has to be interpreted *in its historical unfolding* and *within the relevant historical framework.* A priori, therefore, we should be dealing with this epoch and these events as with any other epoch and events, considering them from all possible angles, suggesting all possible hypotheses and linkages. But, as we know, this is not the case and, implicitly, for most, this cannot be the case. No one of sound mind would wish to interpret the events from Hitler's viewpoint. Actually, even the "interpreters" belonging to the neo-Nazi lunatic fringe do not try to justify the "Final Solution"; they deny its very existence. Even in regard to much less extreme positions, there is *a sense of self-restraint about the available interpretive repertoire.*

This situation does not stem and could not stem from any ideological "orthodoxy" imposed by any group. What could have been argued during the years immediately following the war—the existence of an overall consensus imposed by victors and victims alike—certainly cannot be argued today. In consequence, the historian feels that, in this case, there are some undefined but clearly felt *limits to interpretation.* This very perception of limits—about the nature of which one can have any number of arguments, but the sense of which is compelling—may indicate that we are possibly facing an exceptional situation that calls for a fusion of moral and cognitive categories in the course of the historical analysis as such.

The questions raised by such limitations on interpretive strategies, by such apparent ethical restraint of historical analysis, can be better defined by some examples. First, does an event such as the "Final Solution" allow for *any kind* of narrative, or does it foreclose certain narrative modalities? Does it perhaps escape the grasp of a plausible narrative altogether? Second, any discussion of the "Final Solution" cannot avoid the moral issue. Hence, a problem arises with the application of certain new interpretative strategies. Is it possible to embrace such strategies and yet avoid moral relativism? To take a concrete illustration: can one write the history of the science produced by experiments made on human beings in Nazi camps or can one use the results of such experiments as elements in ongoing, normal scientific discourse?[15]

In more general terms, the limitations of the approaches to the interpretation of the "Final Solution" put the historian in an essentially insoluable situation. The set of difficulties is compounded by the variety of general theories that take this apparently exceptional situation into account and aim nonetheless at inserting it into a convincing explanatory framework. It is beyond the scope of this presentation to consider these various attempts and show their limitations. At the level of political ideological interpretations, as far as the historical contextualization of the "Final Solution" is concerned, the simplest argument is the following: the point is not that such concepts as "totalitarianism" or "fascism" seem inadequate for the contextualization of the "Final Solution," but, obversely, that these concepts fit much better the particular phenomena they deal with, once the "Final Solution" is *not* included.

The only global historical interpretation that seems to "fit" is the most traditional one: the incremental effect of an ever-more radical antisemitic factor. But even those historians who still remain close to this view have to admit that due to the very nature of Nazi antisemitism and the "Final Solution," "the question of continuity becomes problematic."[16]

The overall gist of these difficulties has recently been expressed in a remarkably clear way by one of West Germany's leading historians, Reinhart Koselleck:

> I consider that the history [of the "Final Solution," S.F.] is confronted by demands that are moral, as well as political and religious, and which altogether do not suffice to convey what happened. The moral judgment is unavoidable, but it does not gain in strength through repetition. The political and social interpretation is also necessary, but it is too limited to explain what happened. The escape into a religious interpretation requires forms of observance which do not belong either to the historical, the moral, or the political domain. In my thoughts on this issue up to the present day, I did not manage to get beyond this aporetic situation. In any case, these considerations point to a uniqueness which, in order to be determined, creates both the necessity of making comparisons as well as the need to leave these comparisons behind.[17]

Finally—and this may be the decisive issue—the historian does not find a convincing element of *relevance* when he or she tries to consider this specific past from the point of view of the present. In an as yet unpublished essay, Bielefeld historian Joern Ruesen writes that "history is the mirror of the past into which present time looks, in order to learn something about its future. . . . We have to understand historical consciousness as an operation of the human mind by which present-day life is understood and its future perspectives are designed . . . "[18]

This general definition of history and historical consciousness seems to fit any major past phenomenon that we can think of, certainly any one that still has hold on our emotions or our interest, any one that seems to be existentially relevant: the two world wars, the Bolshevik Revolution, the French Revolution, and for that matter, industrialization or the modernization process in general, fascism in its most global aspects, et cetera. Contemporary life, one could suggest, may be better understood in the light of these phenomena, and, possibly, we still consider each of them as relevant for our future. Not so, in my opinion, with the "Final Solution." Within the general interpretation of historical consciousness, this past teaches us nothing commensurable with the very enormity of the event; apparently, it does not help us to understand the present-day world or the future of the human condition, except that we know, since "then," that such an event took place within modern, industrial society. It does not seem to teach us anything about modern industrial society as such, notwithstanding some linkages established between modernity and the attempt at total extermination. A priori, the "Final Solution" sets many questions concerning modernity, but either the linkages are kept at such a level of generality that they are irrelevant or the contradictions become insuperable.[19]

The issue of relevance could be set in an even more complex way if, following Ruesen, we accept the appearance over the last three centuries of successive categories of historical consciousness: the traditional, the exemplary category implies the existence of "timeless rules of social life, a timeless validity of values"; the critical category aims at "breaking temporal wholes" and at "establishing value criticism and ideology critique as important strategies of moral discourses." The last category, the genetical one, views the *changes as such,* the open-endedness of possible developments as the very condition for the ongoing relevance of historical consciousness.[20] According to this typology, one could argue that the way I previously posed the problem of nonrelevance of the "Final Solution" carries an implicit reference to some sort of "exemplary" category, whereas the critical and genetical categories are the only significant ones for present-day historical understanding. It is precisely from this perspective that the "Final Solution" seems exceptional in its opaqueness. What critical revision of values could take place in this case? What could be the ideological revision? What could be the relevance of change as such for the understanding of this past?[21]

The most elementary question remains open: how will all this be affected by the passage of time? Will distance from the events allow for the construction of meaningful patterns of interpretation? Some historians have answered in the negative: "I doubt," wrote Isaac Deutscher in the mid-sixties, "that in a thousand years from now, people will better understand Hitler, Auschwitz, Majdanek and Treblinka than we do today." To Deutscher, the biographer of Stalin and Trotsky and the staunch critic of Stalinism, the comparability of the totalitarian modes of terror and destruction did not even occur. For him, the passing decades and centuries did not indicate progressive enlightenment. On the contrary, he added, "posterity may well understand all this even less than we do today."[22]

Paradoxically, the "Final Solution," as a result of its apparent historical exceptionality, could well be inaccessible to all attempts at a significant representation and interpretation. Thus, notwithstanding all efforts at the creation of meaning, it could remain fundamentally irrelevant for the history of humanity and the understanding of the "human condition." In Walter Benjamin's terms, we may possibly be facing an unredeemable past.

Yehuda Bauer

Holocaust and Genocide: Some Comparisons

WAS THE HOLOCAUST UNIQUE? IF SO, IN WHAT SENSE? IS IT COMPARABLE to other genocidal mass murders in the twentieth century? This series of questions has been discussed *ad infinitum et ad nauseam* by historians, philosophers, and theologians. Why go over a scarred battleground once again? The reason is, probably, that the answers we are giving to these questions are somehow incomplete or unsatisfactory. Permit me then to restate my position on this complex of questions, and then try to go a little bit further.

Two preliminary questions have to be addressed: one, whether the Holocaust is an explicable event; second, even if it is explicable, is it an extraordinary aberration, or can it be placed within the continuum of modern history?

The Holocaust, that is, the planned total annihilation of the Jewish people and the actual murder of close to six million of them, is a historical event; it was perpetrated by humans for human reasons, and is therefore as explicable as any other series of violent acts in recorded history.[1]

Clearly, every event undergoes transformations in the memory of humans. First comes the event itself; it cannot be repeated, hence it can never be totally reexperienced, fully remembered, or explained. Reality will, by definition, always loom larger than the fullest recounting and explanation. Second, the interpretations, whether through selective memory—all memory is selective—or by historical analysis, will be influenced by forgetfulness, misinterpretation, hindsight, and post factum considerations unknown at the time the event happened. Each subsequent generation will reinterpret the same event differently, in line with its own predilections. It is the historian's task to try to come as close as possible back to the event itself, and attempt to differentiate between the influences on him or her of contemporary events and his or her analysis of the event from the standpoint of the time it happened.

When we deal with mass murder, there are psychological barriers to understanding. But there is no reason to assume that the Holocaust is different from any other event in history—there were factors, reasons, frameworks of society, socio-psychological developments that made it possible, and all these can be satisfactorily explained, though to do so is extremely difficult and we are only part of the way toward satisfactory explanations. I disagree with writers, philosophers, and theologians who try to remove the Holocaust into some abstract sphere of mystification, and tell us "we shall never know." If they mean knowledge equal to the actual experience, obviously not—but then neither can they experience the pinprick of their little child's finger. There is no barrier in principle to approaching ever nearer to the understanding of the event.

The Holocaust brought to the world's attention extremes in human behavior—torture, sadism, murder. There was nothing new in these. The worst massacres perpetrated by the Nazis have exact precedents, given the level of technical development, from ancient times to modernity. The Mongols at Isfahan, the Catholics at Béziers (1209) in the Middle Ages, the Romans in Carthage, the Danes in post-Roman England, and the Jews toward Midianites and others according to the Bible—the list is endless. The mass murder of children, the annihilation of whole populations in the most brutal way—all this is part of recorded history. In this area, what the Nazis did was to apply modern technical means to older precedents. We try to hide this from ourselves by calling the Nazis "beasts" and their action inhuman. This is a basic error. The actions of the Nazis were very human, unfortunately, and to call them beasts is an insult to the animal kingdom, because animals, by and large, do not act like that.

The problem is that what the Holocaust has shown is that humans, in the technological age, and despite the teachings of the great political and moral philosophers of the past three centuries, are capable of extending the limits of normal human behavior to near-absolute evil. I wish to emphasize the word *normal*, because the murderers were, by and large, absolutely normal people by most clinical standards. An analysis of Himmler's famous Poznan speech of October 4, 1943, shows this. "To have stood fast through this," he said, referring to the mass murder of the Jews, "and to have stayed decent, is what has made us hard. . . . We had the moral right, we had the duty towards our people, to destroy this people that wanted to destroy us. . . . But we do not have the right to enrich ourselves by so much as a fur, as a watch, by one mark or a cigarette or anything else. . . . And we have suffered no harm to our inner being, our soul, our character."[2]

We have, in this extreme and by now famous example, a clear enunciation of a petit-bourgeois morality, combined with an equally clear standing of the accepted morality of the Western world on its head. Mark you, not a deviation from it, but its turning upside-down, its hypostasis, to use a philosophical term in a slightly different way. The Jewish commandment accepted by Christianity of "thou shalt not kill," stood on its head, says "thou shalt kill," but there is no deviation. Theft, cheating, adultery, and so on are forbidden, though of course they continue to occur just as they have always done, but that too is within the framework of accepted morality, and in this the Nazis are no different from us: they lived in the same moral framework, except that with them it was flipped upside-down. The horror of the Holocaust is not that in it humans deviated from human behavior; the horror is that they didn't.

Permit me to look at the same complex of questions from an interpretation of the works of Erich Fromm. What Fromm tells us is that humans have not only a basic life-affirming instinct, Freud's libido, but also a destructive instinct, which was termed "Thanatos" by one of Freud's pupils. It is only the existence of such a basic drive that would explain our tendency to Manicheanism, or our culture, which appears to be a sublimation of its opposite. Fromm hinted, I think, that given certain societal conditions, this destructive instinct might turn into uncontrolled aggression, possibly self-destructive and possibly directed toward others. As, however, society continues to provide the framework, some sort of framework, to the exercise of aggression, it also imposes limits to the aggressive explosion, and may well put it into the framework of the previous, so-called accepted, morality.

These general considerations are important, I think, because they seem to explain why mass murder, genocide, and Holocaust are not one-time disasters but are within the possibility of our society, and are of course comparable. Hence, Holocaust and genocide and mass murder appear, all of them, to be based on similar foundations and cannot ultimately be dealt with separately from each other. And yet, of course, each such explosion is specific, and different from all the others.

The mistake made by so many observers lies in denying the specificity of each such cataclysm. The question they ask is why we should differentiate between death and death, between the killing of an Armenian by the Turks in Anatolia, the death of a French soldier at Verdun, or the gassing of Jews at Auschwitz. The simple answer is that while cholera and cancer are both deadly diseases, you don't treat them with the same medicine, because you know that the causes are different. The purpose of our study of these events is, I hope, to learn something from them. Though the chance of humans learning from their mistakes may not be high, the moral obligation to try is there. In our modern era there is a continuum from mass murder through genocide to Holocaust. The definitions some of us are struggling with are not really the crucial issue. All definitions are abstractions from reality. When new insights into reality occur, the definitions have to change, not the historical analyses.

Genocide, then, is the elimination of a nationality or an ethnic unit. The definition provided in the Genocide Convention of 1948 cannot be our guide, because it was the result of horse-trading between different power-interests. There is no logic to include in it, for instance, religious massacres, not only because religions are not stable groups of culture, language, and ethnic traditions, but because by definition individuals will be able, on the whole, to avoid being caught up in massacres of this kind if they adopt the beliefs of the persecuting religious group. Political persecution should not be included either, for a similar reason—people who will abjure their previous politics may well thereby save their skins. But Czechs who were defined as such by the Nazis, even if they wanted to become Germans, had great difficulties. The Czech people as a people was to have disappeared. Its intellectual leadership murdered, part of it was to have been permanently enslaved, part of it Germanized, its culture and its educational institutions destroyed. The same was to have happened to the Poles and the Serbs, but not the Slovaks or the Croats, for instance; there was no clear Nazi genocidal plan for all Slavs. There never existed any plan to murder all Poles or Czechs. That is the difference between the fate of these peoples and that of the Jews. Although many Poles, knowing what had happened to the Jews, explicitly expressed their fears that they would be dealt with in the same way by the Nazis, that was their perception, not that of the Nazi leaders.

Total physical annihilation I prefer to call Holocaust, and that of course means that whereas that is what happened to Jews—and the fact that a percentage of Jews survived in Europe was due not to any lack of desire on the part of the Nazis to kill them, but to their failure to catch all of them—it could, mutatis mutandis, happen to others as well. The term Holocaust should therefore be used in this double sense, of the specific fate that befell the Jews, and of the fate of other peoples if their experience should happen to parallel that of the Jews.

Are there, then, other peoples whose experiences may parallel those of the Jews? The two cases with which we usually compare the fate of the Jews are those of the Armenians and the Gypsies. However, when we discuss World War II, we sometimes get caught up in futile discussions about other groups. A good example of this is the story that the homosexuals shared the fate of the Jews. A reasonably detailed examination of the evidence appears to show that the number of homosexuals actually interned by the Nazis was in the neighborhood of 20,000. This, of course, is 20,000 too many, but when one reads estimates, quite reasonable ones, that there were in 1933 around 1.5 million homosexuals in Germany, the matter changes from the tragedy of the interned homosexuals to the farce of claims by gay activists. Among the Nazis, as is well known, there were large numbers of practicing homosexuals. When they turned against them, this was in most cases as a result of denunciations, or when the individuals concerned were disliked for some other reason. There was never any drive by Nazi authorities to ferret out homosexuals in German society, and the lesbians were not even discussed. Moreover, only Germans were ever interned for being homosexuals. As far as the other nations were concerned, the Nazis favored anything that reduced their birth rate, especially of the main Slavonic nations, hence their total indifference to homosexuality among the enslaved peoples.

Another example is that of the Jehovah's Witnesses, known in Germany as the *Ernste Bibelforscher.* They were arrested and tortured in concentration camps, not because of their theology in the abstract, but because of its practical implications: they refused to serve in the Army and would not recognize the right of the Führer to determine what they should or should not do. However, any of the few thousand arrested German *Bibelforscher*—the Nazis could not have cared less about Jehovah's Witnesses of other nations— who abjured their beliefs in order to get out of the camps, and there were some of those, too, got out. Most of those arrested survived; they were not targeted for murder.

One can follow the discussions in Nazi leadership circles about the Russians, the Poles and Balts, but not the Gypsies. There is the correspondence around the so-called *Generalplan Ost,* which actually dealt with the future settlement of ethnic Germans and other Nordics in the conquered areas in the East, and then posed the problem of what to do with the indigenous peoples there. We find no such development of policy, however, in the material that is extant about the Gypsies. We know of a number of contradictory directives issued by Himmler from 1938 on. On the one hand, they deal with German and Austrian Gypsies as a population stricken with a racially, genetically conditioned asocial criminality, as a blight (*Zigeunerplage*) that has to be removed by police measures. On the other hand, Himmler, who saw himself as a racial theoretician, averred that each race has its right to exist, and one could not very well deny the Gypsies their Aryan characteristics. After all, if there were any *real* Aryans in Germany, they were the Gypsies. To solve the problem, a Racial-Hygienic Institute was established by the Nazis, which then proceeded to examine racially 20,000 out of the 28,000 Gypsies in Germany. They found that over 90 percent were so-called mixed-bloods. In a fairly logical way, if one accepted the racial nonsense, it was then argued that Nazism had no objection to "pure" Gypsies, who would have to be separated from the mixed-bloods, who were the problem. In October

1942, a Himmler decree separated the "pure" Gypsies from the rest, and in January 1943, they were to receive nine leaders who would supervise the relative freedom of movement that they were to be granted.

However, parallel to this line of development was another one that dropped all pretense at differentiations. In September 1939, Heydrich declared that 30,000 Gypsies were to be deported to Poland together with the Jews of the Warthegau. As the total of the Gypsy population of Germany and Austria was 39,000, this meant in effect the deportation of almost all Gypsies. It was not, however, carried out. When in the autumn of 1941, 15,000 Lalleri Gypsies were deported from Austria to the Lodz ghetto and, later, to the gassing installation at Chelmno, there was no selection. What happened to the decree establishing the "pure" Gypsies as a recognized group with some privileges is not clear. In the end, about 20,000 Gypsies, mostly from Germany, were killed at Auschwitz, over 6,430 of them by gassing. But probably close to 14,000 survived.

One has to notice that most of the literature dealing with the Gypsies to date has dealt with German and Austrian Gypsies, who formed an insignificant proportion of the European Gypsy population. What happened to Gypsies in Poland, the Soviet Union, France, Czechoslovakia, and other countries is by no means clear. Estimates of both the initial populations and the losses vary wildly. Subject to further research, which is essential, one can only suppose that the Nazis simply did not have a policy regarding the Gypsies. Certainly, they did not see in them the kind of supernatural threat that the Jews allegedly posed. In the Ukraine, the *Einsatzgruppe* of Otto Ohlendorf murdered 90,000 Gypsies, probably most or all it met. In the North, however, we find that some Gypsies were murdered but the vast majority were left alone. Wandering Gypsies in Poland were often murdered on the spot, others pushed into Jewish ghettos. But the many Gypsy villages or settlements in towns were not touched. In Croatia, the local fascist Ustasha movement systematically murdered Gypsies along with Serbs and Jews, but there seems to have been no explicit German instigation to do this.

Overall, Gypsies were viewed as a superfluous and bothersome group whose disappearance would be actively advanced if the opportunity offered itself. But there seems to have been no plan, no clear policy, no intention to seek them out and destroy them by concerted action. Insofar as ideology was involved, it was the mixed-bloods who were sentenced to death, rather than what the Nazis considered to be the "pure" Gypsies. However, these are tentative findings at best. Should documentation come to light indicating a Nazi plan for destruction, we might well call the "*paraimos*," as the Rom people call the disaster that befell them in World War II, a Holocaust.[3]

I have tried to address the question of the Armenian massacres during World War I elsewhere; here all I wish to do is to summarize the problem briefly. The concept of a continuum, avoiding definitions that are applied in too hard and fast a way, enables us, I think, to view the Armenian genocide as a Holocaust-related event, somewhere between genocide and Holocaust. The principal characteristic of a Holocaust is the aim of the perpetrators to annihilate the targeted group completely. It is perfectly clear that the Young Turkish regime wanted to annihilate the Armenians in Turkey completely, and the reasons why some of them escaped that fate parallel the reasons why some Jews survived the Nazi onslaught. The parallels extend to a state-organized murder, the use of collaborators from subject peoples, the technique of the death marches; and the attempt to hide the murders, even the denial by the Turkish regime to this day of the mass murder committed forms a kind of parallel with the Holocaust. However, it is not clear at all that the Young Turks intended to ferret out Armenians all over the world in order to kill them or sought international agreements to achieve that end. The main difference lies of course in the fact that with the Nazis there was a pseudo-religious motivation that brought Jew-hatred into the center of Nazi ideology, whereas for the Young Turks the murder of the Armenians was a means to a chauvinistically conceived end, namely the establishment of a Pan-Turkic Empire.

Since the end of World War II, other mass murders have occurred, which some people have tried to compare with the Holocaust. The comparison does not stand up to a detailed critique. The murder of a part of the Cambodian population by another part of the Cambodian people, the regime of Pol Pot, was an auto-genocide. By definition, a Holocaust can be committed only by someone else on a given people, because the aim will be total destruction. The atomic disasters in Japan were designed to end the war, not to kill off all the Japanese. When we come to small ethnic groups, Holocaust-related events are more likely, as with the Hutu in Burundi, whose destruction was aimed at by the ruling Tutsi people, but not achieved.

As historians, we have to check the more distant past in order to see whether there are not precedents in Israel for what happened. Some valiant spirits have been trying to do this, and have come up with problematic results. Starting from the biblical stories, in which the Amalekites and the seven nations of Canaan were destined to be completely annihilated, one finds the idea of total mass murder cropping up again and again both in literary traditions and in the practice of governmental structures. The societal, religious, and social differences between these and our own experience make it extremely difficult, however, to reach clear conclusions. The very definition of a national or ethnic group belongs to modernity and has seemingly little bearing on our subject. And yet, tribal societies and language and cultural groups were sometimes targeted for total destruction, and more research is needed before we decide that genocide and Holocaust are phenomena of our own times only.

Where does all this lead us? A deeper understanding of the Holocaust obligates us to make comparisons. It then becomes clear that the Holocaust had certain characteristics that are unique, on the one hand, but can be repeated in another form, perhaps, on the other hand. Thus bureaucratic involvement is centrally important. But there is one aspect of the phenomenon that has aroused constant and agonized questioning and that one must address when making these comparisons. We hear the question in every undergraduate course: how could a cultured nation such as the Germans succumb to a criminal leadership, and how could it become a partner to the most terrible crime in history?

The beginnings of an acceptable answer have been given by Ian Kershaw, Peter Merkl, and others, who are examining the way the murder machine operated on the level of consensus and of propaganda. The starting point lies in the discovery that in most cases the people who actually killed the Jews had not undergone any special schooling in antisemitism and did not have any past history of Jew-hatred. The conclusion is that most Jews were killed by Nazis who were not really ideological antisemites. Research on German antisemitism has shown that, although this was a very widespread sentiment, it has to be defined in traditional terms, not as the radical murderous type of antisemitism that the Nazi leadership propagated. Also, significant parts of the German electorate in the early thirties voted until the very end for parties that opposed antisemitism. In the years preceding 1933, whereas anti-Jewish propaganda was certainly part and parcel of every Nazi effort, it was not *the* central plank of the Nazi platform. In other words, the Nazis never thought that anti-Jewish propaganda would be the main reason for voting for them. Indeed, it wasn't. People voted Nazi because of the economic crisis, because of the promise of a new Germany devoid of deep social crises, and because they were promised a strong Germany of which they could be proud.

Even though antisemitism was never the chief attraction for the voters, it was most certainly a central issue for the core of the Nazi leadership. The leadership elite, and one has to use that term despite its jarring note, quite consciously withheld from the masses their true convictions. The masses, however, became totally identified with the leader and the Party. Had there been free elections in Germany in 1937–38, there can hardly be a doubt that Hitler's Party would have won hands down. This identification was made easy because there was an intermediate social stratum that served as a transmission belt, namely the intelligentsia, significant portions of which were among the first to join the Party. The intelligentsia—not only the Dr. Mengeles and Dr. Claubergs, but also the university-educated bureaucrats, engineers, professors, and officers—identified with the father figure of the Führer as the representative of a regime which they would not just follow, but within which they could use their considerable initiative and energies to find better and better solutions to problems posed. When at last the elite came to the point of murder, there was no question but that via the intelligentsia the message to the simple souls who did the killing would be a consensus that everything was fine and that this was the way one should serve the Fatherland. The intelligentsia of course also murdered: three of the four heads of the *Einsatzgruppen,* quite a sizable proportion of the lower officers in them, and some of the commanders of concentration and death camps were university educated. They, too, did not have schooling in antisemitism; however, they identified with a regime whose leadership saw the elimination of the Jews as a central issue. And all this could be done because the traditional, deep antisemitism of the masses prevented any significant opposition, such as arose in response to the Euthanasia program, which was challenged not only by the churches, but even by many Party members.

What are the conclusions from this? The most serious one surely is that whenever a genocidal elite gains power and there is no traditional opposition to eliminating a targeted minority, the psychological capture of the intelligentsia can pave the way to mass murder. The comparisons have to be made between a society in crisis, such as Germany in the early thirties where this happened, and other societies in which roughly similar processes might lead to roughly similar results. Whether such outcomes can be avoided is something we should think about very seriously.

Steven T. Katz

Ideology, State Power, and Mass Murder / Genocide

RECENT HISTORICAL RESEARCH HAS INCREASINGLY EMPHASIZED NON-ideological elements in the unfolding, in the actuality, of historical events. This new approach is especially evident and intensive in the dispute between so-called intentionalists and functionalists over the nature of the *Sho'ah,* though it now has its counterpart on a less developed level in the revisionist historiography being written by Sovietologists such as Sheila Fitzpatrick and J. Arch Getty, as well as by scholars in fields as diverse as the history of colonialism and the history of the American Indian. This revision-ist-functionalist work adds important elements to our total grasp of the *realia* under study; it calls attention to pluralistic factors and empirical circumstances that older historical construals ignore, often at their own peril. Yet, in this chapter, I want to reaffirm the centrality of ideology in historical phenomena, in particular in relation to governmental action during occasions of mass death. To anticipate my larger conclusion, let me say that ideology is both consequential as a cause of mass death and genocide and, very importantly, sets the conditions, more often than not the *limits,* of this execrable behavior. Or put another way, occasions of mass death differ—very few are, for example, genocidal—because ideo-logical constraints operate upon the crucial mechanisms of state power to delimit and control the bloodshed that does occur.

Were there space, I believe I could show this to be true in every major case of mass murder / genocide that we might consider. Here, however, I have chosen to focus on three events as paradigms of the type of argument that is apposite in the larger historiographical conversation of which this volume is a part. My three "test cases" are: (1) medieval antisemitism, which I choose because of its salience to any comparative deciphering of the *Sho'ah;* (2) the witch craze of the fifteenth to eighteenth centuries, because it is a striking example, as is medieval antisemitism, though now from an inner-Christian dimension, of the constraints operative in traditional Christian society; and (3) the Gulag—a compelling case of persecution by ideological design and one in which there is clear state control of the mechanisms of oppression. In each instance I will lay bare the structure of the socio-political and ideological forces at work, and also try to compare these events to the *Sho'ah,* that is, to explain why they were *not* genocidal whereas the Nazi "war against the Jews" was.[1]

PATRISTIC AND MEDIEVAL ANTISEMITISM

By the patristic era, following upon the basis already set in the New Testament, in particular in the Gospel of John, the encounter between Jew and Christian, between Synagogue and Church, was perceived as the embodiment of Satan's clash with Jesus, of Evil's rebellion against the Good, of the assault of the Sons of Darkness against the Sons of Light, of the Powers of Hell arrayed in deadly opposition to the Powers of Heaven. "The Jews" had become, and were to remain, perfidious and meta-human, opponents of God Himself. They "fight against the commands of God and dance with the Devil" (Chrysostom). How else to explain the monstrous act of deicide? How else to decipher their national demise and exile? How else to account for their abiding unfaithfulness, rebelliousness, unresponsiveness? Their continued rejection of God's love, of His grace revealed in and through the crucifixion, of His presence in the Gospels and in the Church? The Old Israel "has been darkened in the eyes of its soul with a darkness utter and everlasting" (Hippolytus).

What is all-important about these theological caricatures is that, building upon canonical roots, they consigned the conflict between Synagogue and Church to the realm of myth and metaphysics. Though the patristic writers did not invent this interpretive form of decipherment—the authors of the New Testament already spoke in the revaluing idioms of this rhetorical construction—they gave it extensive room for growth, nurtured its most unsavory elements, and assured that it would become the fixed pattern for all subsequent readings of the Jewish-Christian encounter. After the combined hermeneutical assault of the New Testament and the patristic writings, the Jew is never again to be "a man like other men." He has become a *mythic* creature. Seen in its broadest, maximal, terms, the generative Christian myth demands that Jewry provide both God and his Luciferian adversary. The Jew, as Jesus, thus becomes an enfleshment of cosmic powers. But whereas the latter is the embodiment of good, the overflowing symbol of bountiful grace, the former is the incarnation of evil, the symbol of passionate anti-godly defiance. That full-blown diabolization of the Jew that comes to full and concrete expression in the popular culture of the post-Crusader era has its roots here. *Ex nihilo nihil fit.*

Though the patristic authors may not have envisioned, or intended, the translation of these falsifying images into sociological realities, into popular and deadly transgressions, they had sown the seeds, at least conceptually, *theo*-logically, that is, in the name of God, for massive, continuous evil. Thus the Jew was removed, even to our own day, from more ordinary canons of judgment, appraised by other than human values, and transposed unwillingly to dangerous theological and mythographic realms. Jews, a Jew, can be God incarnate, they can be the devil incarnate (or his lieutenants); but they can never again be *merely* human beings. I do not exaggerate here. The whole of Jewish history, understood in its collectivity, in its totality, as played out in Christian time and space is intelligible only on the basis of this deformed idealization. Other seminal factors contribute their perverse share to the saga of anti-semitism (e.g., economics, politics, social realities, and other "ordinary" causes of prejudice), but this determinate metaphysicalizing of Jewish being provides the foundational substratum for all of them. What remains constant, even in large segments of the modern consciousness, certainly in the convoluted Nazi myth, is this transcendentalizing of "the Jews."

The potential liberation of "the Jews," that is, their becoming merely Jews, if not men and women, as a result of the deconstructive revolution of the Enlightenment, ultimately proved impossible in the face of the continuing, subterranean, and visceral presence of this older pattern of stigmatization. Thus new forms of explanation—volkisch, Romantic, nationalist, and, ultimately, racial—would be coined to explain this enduring alterity of "the Jews." With all the vulgar cunning that could be mustered, the empirical actuality of Jewish existence was again, or rather still, capriciously transfigured into an antipodal transhistorical essence. Jewish individuality, the actuality of Jewish life, was subsumed by new "theologies" that, though substituted for the old, continued to insist on the unredeemed *ideal* otherness of the Israel of the flesh. To this degree the canonical Christian portrayal of Judaism retained its overpowering presence even after the quintessential christological proclamation began to lose its force from the eighteenth century on. Thus, and most significantly, though the Nazis would explain this "terrifying otherness" on different grounds from those utilized in classical Christian polemics, *the fact of their choice of the Jew to play this role of cosmic antithesis, of racial meta-racial alien, would be rooted in the pattern established by patristic theology.* The Jew is structurally the defining inversion of the Aryan, as he had been of the Christian. In both metaphysical systems, in both cosmic mythologies, he is the phenomenal representation of absolute, transcendental contrariety, of that determinative spiritual opposition whose luminous perversity is an expression of its essence. Judaism—if not the Jew—for the Church and the Jew *qua* Jew for the Nazis stand in immutable opposition. This transformation of worldly, human conflict over matters of eternal salvation into more than human *topoi* creates the depth and continuity of anti-Jewish sentiment and its polymorphous variations.

This patristic myth, like all myths, is neither open to refutation nor subject to falsification. Anything that refutes the holy tale is itself a "Devil's trick." Any evidence to the contrary is but a misleading manifestation of diabolical cunning. As a consequence, once "the Jew" became a central, if perverse, feature of Christianity's central myth—the crucifixion—he or she is trapped. Only conversion, which is the salvific action sanctioned by the now-sacralized mythic script, can ameliorate the tragic conflict, can undo the damage engendered by the telling of the tale. Despite the variety of readings this constantly reinterpreted narrative received, one element remained fixed: the surpassing depravity of "the Jews."

"The Jews" are not only the enemy of man, but also of God. And thus to hate them, to be their adversary, is, simultaneously, to be God's friend. Paradoxically, this particular hatred thus becomes a cardinal virtue: the more one hates, the more pious one is. Hate is a sacramental activity. To hate Jews is for the church fathers a Christian *mitzvah*. Make no mistake—every major church father is a great hater of Judaism and the Jewish people.

However, this dark depiction of the Jew and Judaism does not lead the Church to preach a crusade of physical genocide. According to Augustine's paradigmatic formulation, Israel's apostasy and subsequent punishment, as well as its continued proclamation of the Torah, even while blind to its supreme meaning, Christ Jesus, reveal important lessons for Christian society. As Cain's treachery verified and exalted Abel's faithfulness, so the skepticism of "the Jews"—and their consequent fall from favor, the destruction of their Temple, and their exile—all reinforce, in an overwhelmingly visible and experiential way, the truth of Christianity. Accordingly, like Cain, "the Jews"—real Jews—are not to be harmed by the Church, by Christians. Jews are certainly not to be killed. Rather, above all else, they are to wander the earth as proof of their rejected status. And in God's good time, as part of the apocalypse, in conjunction with the return of Christ in glory, even this exilic status would end, in the ultimate sign of Christ's power and graciousness. Jewish survival thus becomes, paradoxically, a Christian theological imperative. Both Jewry's present exile and its final redemption play central, and inescapable, roles in this influential version of Christian belief—the former as a mark of God's power, the latter as a sign of His love. Thus to violate this divinely ordained Jewish status—that is, Jewry's wandering until the eschaton—was itself to become, in an ironic reversal, apostate. Moreover, Christian transgression of this covenant of unbelief could only hinder the millenarian consummation, and thus was undesirable from a Christian perspective. To this day (as can best be seen among fundamentalists such as Billy Graham and Pat Robertson, though it is no less part of the dogmatics of mainline Protestants and the Catholic and Orthodox churches), this connection of Jewish wandering, Jewish survival, and Christian eschatological hope remains alive. Thus the triumphalism of Christian supersessionism could not altogether dispense with the root out of which it emerged. Christianity could neither ignore nor destroy—as a consequence of its own profoundest christological imperatives—"the Jews."

This Augustinian elucidation—combined with the earlier New Testament and patristic tradition, over against and in dialectical tension with the rhetorically unconstrained legacy of Chrysostom, which culminated in the tradition of diabolization and Crusader violence—created the ambiguities, conceptual and practical, that defined Jewish existence for the entire medieval era. That is to say, although the tradition of Chrysostom continued to encourage and to cause unbridled vituperation for Jews and Judaism, climaxing in the violence of 1096 and beyond, the modulating Augustinian position became, more or less, the basis of the "official" policy of the papacy and the Church hierarchy from the late fifth century on. This discriminating outlook, which set limits to the diabolization of the Jew and attempted, often with success, to limit anti-Jewish violence, eventuated in the mediating papal and council program that proved so important in creating at least marginal status and some living space for Jews within the orbit of Christian civilization. The existence of this severe yet restrained tradition goes a long way in explaining why Jews and Judaism were able to survive, in however reduced circumstances, centuries of Christian abuse and domination. Despite the continuing human distortions and ethical abuses legitimated by the Augustinian position, its constraining two-sidedness, its limiting, controlling, and even ethical intent must be recognized.

Here it is also essential to note that from the christianization of the Roman Empire under Constantine (325 C.E.) onward, the monumental intrusion of the state into what had heretofore been a largely meta-political struggle between two essentially powerless minorities transformed the nature of the confrontation completely. That is, the extant apolitical symmetries were shattered, to be replaced by a wholly asymmetrical relationship. Henceforth, until the late eighteenth century in the West and still later in Eastern Europe, governmental coercion became the instrument through which the Church made real its scornful commentary on Judaism. Here is the decisive turn in the history of Christian anti-Judaism, a turn whose ultimate disfiguring consequence was enacted in the *political* antisemitism of Adolf Hitler. That is, anti-Jewish prejudice becomes deadly only when supported by the police apparatus of the state. And this unfortunate tradition, this employment of the state machinery to enact and supervise anti-Jewish legislation, begins in the christianizing politics of the fourth century and does not cease until the modern era.

Yet, having indicated, and indicted, the transformative implications of the politicization of anti-Judaism, I must in fairness make a dialectical counterobservation. To wit: all Christian political regimes recognized the existence of real theological, moral, and utilitarian limits under which they operated. Thus state power, for all its intrusiveness and ethical obtuseness, was counterpoised by a governing recognition that the civil authority was not totally free to do as it liked, especially as regards the taking of human life. The Christian polity, that is, recognizes that human life per se is ontologically purposeful, the end product of a divine initiative. Except in specific "legitimate" cases where capital punishment is justifiable (e.g., heresy), the state must preserve and protect *all* human life. Still more, Christian political philosophy acknowledges certain privileged areas beyond the power of the state, including specifically and necessarily the right of Jews, the only tolerated religious minority in most of medieval Christendom, to remain Jews. Salvation, even though desirable, cannot be coerced, at least not in the case of Jews, by the body politic. Moreover, this latter understanding is inseparably united with the peculiar role that eventual Jewish conversion would play in the era of the eschaton. Thus Christians must beware of violating Jewish religious autonomy for fear of injuring, and delaying, their own eschatological hopes. Moreover the Christian state, though elected by God, is always aware, in theory, of its being subordinate to the will of God as revealed in natural and positive revelation. The ordinance against murder, and the obligation that Christians manifest love and charity, even for Jews, are essential ingredients in such revelation. Thus the Christian theological and papal traditions regularly use the terms love and charity to describe the proper Christian attitude toward even Jews—as long as Jews know their servile place. Finally, and perhaps most importantly, the Christian state recognized the need to defer the resolution of a small set of theological issues to the future, to leave certain matters to the Almighty. Included in this set was the final resolution of the Jewish-Christian

conflict. Thus, the civil power acknowledges heteronomous parameters, even as it may continually transgress them. Even kings
must take cognizance of the inhibiting power of transcendental,
universal, ethical valences.

Recognizing the authority of these principles meant that the
abridgment of pre-Christian Jewish juridical and civic entitlements
and their replacement by highly problematic post-Constantinian
political compulsions still did not result in a situation of absolute
moral lawlessness. Even the post-Christian nation-state, for all its
claims to autonomy and its reversal of the church-state hierarchy,
almost always recognized certain "inalienable rights," a revised
recognition of natural law claims, as well as particular constitutional limitations, even as it regularly extended its claims to authority. In contradistinction, the Third Reich recognized no law
outside itself, and more particularly no law outside the will of the
Führer, who was now seen as the supreme intermediary between
the objective cosmic law and the Aryan people. Nothing stood
against the Führer's will and demanded "Thou shalt not." No
natural or positive law was admitted; only the subjective decisions
of Hitler, as Führer, proclaimed as the expression of the gods, were
acknowledged. Thus the way was opened for tearing the long,
earlier, tradition of the politicization of theological confrontation
free of its circumscribing heteronomous ethical and theological
moorings and thereby creating the possibility of transforming it
from a policy of debasement and ostracism into a policy of genocide. As a result, both antisemitism and politics became something
they had not been, something pre-Nazi antisemites and pre-Nazi
politicians did not want to become. And having become what they
became, they were no longer what they were.

As concrete evidence for this argument, consider the behavior
of the Church hierarchy and the monarchs of Europe during the
bloodiest period of medieval Jewish history, that of the Crusades.
There can be no doubt that the Church elite and the royal houses
sought, at times with success, to protect the Jews. In Speyer during
the First Crusade, for example, a large segment of the Jewish community survived because of the direct intervention of Bishop Jean,
who shielded the vulnerable community from the infamous Emi-
cho von Leinigen. Elsewhere the pattern was the same. "It is important to note," as Leon Poliakov writes, "that almost everywhere,

counts and bishops (Adalbert in Worms, Archbishop Ruthard in Mainz, Archbishop Herman III in Cologne, the Count of Mors, etc.) attempted, sometimes even at the peril of their own lives, to protect the Jews, yielding to the Crusaders only under constraint and the show of force." What was true of the clerical establishment was true also of the secular authorities, who sought to contain the popular frenzy. As a rule the Imperial and aristocratic authorities opposed the anarchic devastation wrought by the Crusader bands, which represented a threat to their authority as well as a mortal danger to Jewish communities. Where such secular power was exercised in a disciplined and manifest way, anti-Jewish behavior was limited. Indeed, there was a direct correlation between the degree of real political control that secular authorities were able to exercise and the degree of anti-Jewish violence. Thus the catastrophic tumult in the Rhineland was directly proportional to the weakness of the centralized German Imperial bureaucracy; conversely, the far lower level of anti-Jewish terror in France is attributable to the ability of the French court and the barons to maintain tight control over such hostilities. A contemporary source reports that when the Emperor (Henry IV) was told of the anti-Jewish disturbances:

> The anger of the Emperor was aroused and he sent letters throughout all the provinces of his empire, to the princes and the bishops, to the nobles and to Duke Godfrey—messages of peace and [orders] with regard to the Jews that they protect them so that no one harm them physically and that they provide aid and refuge to them.

Such royal declarations proved insufficient in the face of the fury of the Crusader armies, but this weakness, due in large measure to the underdevelopment of the mechanisms of centralized bureaucratic political control, so essential by contrast in the *Sho'ah,* is not indicative of any genocidal intent on the part of either the Church or the Imperial power. Thus, for example, in his General Peace of 1103 the Emperor (again Henry IV) specifically singled out the Jews for royal protection.

Likewise in France the bishops, with the support of the king, intervened vigorously in 1096 to protect the Jews living in their domains and generally succeeded, with the notable exception of Rouen, in restraining anti-Jewish behavior. In England, too, we hear little of anti-Jewish passion during the First Crusade; the protective behavior of the English Crown is indicated by the refuge that England appears to have given to continental Jews fleeing persecution in their native lands. Thus it is evident, given the behavior of the German, French, and English authorities, secular and religious, and the record of the papacy, that the contemporary Church and state leadership recognized in the outrages of the masses a fundamental distortion of the Crusader ideal. Nowhere did the papal call to free Jerusalem entail a corresponding call for the eradicaton of Jewry. The papal rebuke of the Archbishop of Narbonne, censured in 1063 for aiding in atrocities against the Jewish communities in southwestern France in concert with Catholic efforts to reconquer Muslim Spain, is symptomatic of inherited and future papal attitudes.

Those contemporaries who read the call to the Crusades as legitimating the extirpation of European Jewry were engaged in a deadly *mis*reading that the Church never endorsed and indeed, insofar as it was able, sought to mitigate, even if neither with all the vigor and power at its disposal nor completely out of pure motives. In judging the Church's response, we must not underestimate the rather sizable, militarily formidable nature of the Crusading bands; neither should we forget that the papacy and the regional bishops had no comparable military force at their disposal.

Moreover, it is evident from contemporary Christian accounts that Church authorities, aware of the categorical dictates of canon law, opposed even the antinomian efforts of the Crusader bands to convert the Jews by force. Thus Albert of Aachen unambiguously pronounces: "God is a just judge and orders that no one be brought unwillingly or by force under the yoke of the Catholic faith." Likewise, Cosmas of Prague records that the Bishop of Prague "seeing that [the forcible baptisms] were against canon law and led by zeal for justice, tried vainly, because unaided, to forbid them lest the Jews be baptized against their wills." "Most of the bishops," Riley-Smith argues, "made some effort to protect the Jews [from forced baptism], although with varying degrees of success." Generally, the Church was true to itself in its response to forced conversions. This conclusion is supported, insofar as the available evidence is reliable, by the absence of any overall policy of forced conversion among the Crusader armies in the Near East, where the Jewish community, in most areas, excluding Jerusalem, was not liquidated either by conversion or physical extermination. Although the Crusaders had little compunction about murdering Jews in the midst of the anarchy of 1096, particularly those who saw such vengeance as legitimate reparation for the Jewish role in the crucifixion, a theme several times repeated in the Hebrew Chronicles, the majority of Crusaders and their leaders still clung to traditional Christian eschatological and soteriological notions and preferred, as Robert Chazan has written, "a victory of the spirit (conversion) . . . to a victory of the flesh (murder of the Jews or Jewish martyrdom)."

The saving actions of Bernard of Clairvaux against the anti-Jewish monk Ralph during the Second Crusade are also highly instructive. Bernard, in a classical homily, tells the Christian faithful:

> "God," says the Church, "will show me victory over my foes. Do not kill them, lest my people be unmindful." They [the Jews] are for us living words, for they remind us always of the passion. . . . If the Jews are wiped out what will become of the hope for their promised salvation, their eventual conversion?

As David Berger has commented, "Bernard did not like Jews, but protecting them was the obligation imposed by the Christian *halachah* [religious law], and Bernard as a good churchman obeyed the *halachah*." And it is this requirement of the Christian *halachah* that is so instructive. "Jewish experience was more than a right," Robert Chazan writes in explanation of this Christian imperative, "it was a pre-requisite for the onset of the Christian drama of redemption. . . . this is simply established Church doctrine. What is striking is the readiness of the Church leadership to invoke this traditional argument and its firm resolution to exert control over the vast crusading enterprise." Bernard's actions show that the highest levels of the Church were galvanized during the Second Crusade to assure that the despoliation that resulted from the First Crusade did not repeat itself. Likewise during the Third Crusade. Thus a half-century after the climactic intervention of Bernard, Innocent III declares: "Although the Jewish perfidy is in every way worthy of condemnation, nevertheless, because through them the fruit of our own faith is proved, they are not to be severely oppressed." Indeed during this troubled period the traditional papal *Constitutio pro Judeis* that explicitly ruled against direct anti-Jewish violence was endorsed and reissued on ten separate occasion by successive popes between 1120 and 1250. Of course the repeated issuance of such admonitions is indicative of the widespread and continual abuse to which Jewry was being subjected. Yet these genuine expressions of human concern, of the need for Christian restraint, reflective as they are of the unresolved problematic inherent in the Jewish-Christian encounter, did exercise beneficent and meliorating influences on the circumstances of Jewish life.

This same relatively positive estimation applies to the various imperial policies of Christian monarchs from Constantine the Great, through the Carolingian kings, to the German emperors Otto I (936–73), Henry IV (1056–1106), Frederick Barbarossa (1152–90) and Frederick II (1215–50), and their successors, the kings of England before 1290, the majority of the kings of medieval France and Spain, most of the kings of Poland, and even, if less unambiguously, to the Russian czars down to Czar Nicholas I. Out of respect for law and tradition, in the interest of their own imperial authority, given the royal relationship to and competition with the papacy, economic necessities, and historical precedent ranging back to Roman times, kings and emperors in both Eastern and Western Europe were, as a rule, in practice, Israel's staunchest, most significant, defenders. When in 1171 the Jews of Blois, and all of northern France, were threatened by a "blood libel," Louis VII condemned the false accusation, though it was championed by his brother-in-law, Count Theobold, and gave the Jewish community renewed assurances of his protection. Similarly, when the Jews of Mainz were threatened following news of the Crusader defeat in the Holy Land at the hand of Saladin, the emperor, Frederick Barbarossa, made his position pellucid: "Anyone," he declared, "who harms a Jew and causes an injury, his hand shall be cut off. Anyone who kills a Jew shall be killed." Again in 1189, following his coronation, and an outburst of antisemitic violence in London, Richard I issued royal proclamations warning against the repetition of such episodes. Unfortunately his warnings proved ineffective when he left again for France, as we see from the series of anti-Jewish incidents in England, no doubt spurred by the call to the

Third Crusade, culminating in the communal murder of York Jewry on Sabbath, March 16 and 17, 1190. Yet even here the Jews of York took it as a given that they would find safety in the castle of the Royal Constable of York, the scene of their final annihilation when the York mobs could not be dissuaded from their bloody ritual. There can be no doubt that the absence from England of the king, the archbishop of Canterbury, Hugh de Puiset (the most important churchman of northern England), and Nigel de Mowbray (the most influential nobleman of the area) contributed to the freedom felt by those who would, *contra* official policy, destroy the Jews.

This pattern of royal protection was repeated elsewhere in the Crusader epoch. During the Second Crusade King Stephen protected the Jews of England, primarily following the spread of the Norwich "blood libel." In Germany Count Otto of Burgundy sieged and destroyed parts of Speyer and its environs in retaliation for anti-Jewish acts, and his brother, the emperor, "came and captured the murderers, until they paid him great sums of money." And this money he turned over to the Jews, "approximately five hundred talents and rebuilt their homes and synagogues as before." Again, just as Stephen and Richard I sought to protect English Jewry during the Second and Third Crusades, Louis IX, no friend of the Jews, sought to assure the safety of the French Jewish community following the outburst of anti-Jewish violence connected with his crusading zeal in the early 1250s. In a series of royal ordinances he sought to uproot Jewish usury and reduce the Jewish "presence" in his realm (for example, through proscribing the Talmud and limiting the construction of new synagogues); at the same time, however, he delimited the physical and juridical harm that could be done to these same French Jewish communities. Likewise, Henry IV and William II, in disregard of Church opposition and tradition, allowed Jews who had been made to convert during the First Crusade to return to the Jewish community without penalty. Similarly in Christian Spain the Spanish monarchs (e.g., Juan I during the crisis of 1391, Juan II in the 1430s, Enrique IV during the troubles in 1467) had a remarkable record of protecting the Jewish community, until their own final and decisive act of 1492, and Charles IV, like his Spanish contemporary Peter IV of Aragon, defended the Jews, if only for reasons of economic self-interest, in the aftermath of the Black Death. This list of royal interventions on behalf of various Jewish communities could be extended to include nearly all the royal houses and individual monarchs of European history, if to varying degrees. It was almost always in the interest of the Crown, however antisemitic the monarch's personal sentiments, to defend the Jews. The maintenance of royal authority, if also the health of the exchequer, required it. Thus, as a rule, where there was a strong king, and he was in residence, the Jewish people were spared the more extreme indignities of the epoch.

Anti-Jewish violence, on balance, welled up from the lower and middle echelons of the socio-political order and was expressive of social discontent, economic exploitation (by the king and the nobility often, at least in part, through Jewish mediation), and excessive, often heterodox, theological zeal. The peculiar, and undesirable, role of the Jew in the feudal order, defined by his unbelief, his necessary alliance with the King, and his odious economic activity, linked him to the oppressive socioeconomic forces, as well as the cosmic goblins, that the sporadic popular political eruptions were intended, in part, to dislodge. At the same time, the lower and middle classes of medieval society never possessed sufficient power to do more than create a series of pogroms. They lacked the organized political mechanisms necessary to perpetuate genocide, assuming, questionably, that such was their ambition. Conversely, *between 1096 and 1391 there is only one, very local, and very marginal instance of a state-sponsored, that is, "official," pogrom,* despite the indisputable power of the state to organize such carnivals of death; the absence of such incitement being consistent with Catholic doctrine. Aquinas, the authoritative medieval theological voice, counseled the rulers of Europe: "It would be licit according to custom to hold Jews, because of their crime, in perpetual servitude. . . . however . . . [the Christian Prince must] not deprive Jews of things necessary for life." The continual irony of Jewish history here again manifests itself in the fact that it was also the Crown that eventually, for reasons of its own, forced the Jews from the respective European states beginning with the expulsion of the Jews from England in 1290 and culminating in the Iberian expulsions of 1492 and 1496. Thus we come to understand that, comparable to the dynamics of the medieval oppression of heretics and witches, maximal persecution, and in the Jewish case the eventuality of expulsion, could become manifest only when organized and effected from the top down.

To summarize: The Church's anti-Jewish views were of such a character that when translated into political actualities they led to Jewish oppression and degradation but, quite consciously and purposefully, ensured Jewish survival. The Christian state is *not* genocidal because its reigning ideology forbids its becoming so.

WITCHES, WOMEN, AND THE CHRISTIAN SOCIO-POLITICAL ORDER

The quantum leap in the witch mania of the sixteenth and seventeenth centuries that followed upon the publication of the *Malleus Maleficarum* in 1485–86, to which the Papal Bull *Summis desiderantes* of Innocent VIII was appended as a Preface, was a response to the unfolding theological, political, and socioeconomic conditions of the historic moment, especially Luther's Reformation. But it was a response that occurred within "predictable" parameters, based on the vivid application of inherited metaphysical dualities. The chaotic theo-political matrix of the sixteenth century was taken as confirming the formal traditional cosmological structure that had evolved, to wit, that reality is the plaything of alternate ontological forces. The radical transmutation that Catholic society was undergoing is decisive evidence that the forces of dissolution and corruption are no fictive construals. Both Catholics and Protestants agreed on the Devil's immediate reality in their daily environment. The perennial struggle for the perfection of self and society represents a continual collision between man's inherent desire for sanctity and the luciferian ambition to make all such efforts come to naught. This ramified diabolism was not a new belief, but in a sixteenth-century context it took on a new urgency. In the successive wars of religion Satan was always on the other side. This theological certitude, this theological reading of social transformations, is primarily responsible for the multiplying continental witch-hunts between 1485 and 1750.

The Devil, though omnipresent, is not omnipotent; he must be opposed, engaged, defeated. The witch-hunts are the primal exemplification of this metaphysical struggle. In the new climate of spiritual activism and personal religious commitment created by the Reformation and the Counter-Reformation when, perhaps for the first time, Europe's peasantry was fully christianized, individuals began to see that their personal salvation, as well as nothing less than the fate of Christendom, was at risk. Thus, what the Passion Plays had been for medieval society, a cathartic acting out of its deepest beliefs and profoundest fears, the witch-hunt now became for the newly fractured Protestant and Catholic societies of the sixteenth and seventeenth centuries. The events were no less staged, no less acted according to a pre-extant script, the learned demonologies supplied by Sprenger, Kramer, Remy, Bodin, and others. Society's obsessions now focused upon the Witch. She was to blame for all manner of evil, particularly the collapse of Catholic hegemony in Europe, and she was to atone. Where, amid the new fissures in the Christian polity, the mythography of satanic chaos was not only present but very actively exploited by ruler and cleric alike to "explain" the metamorphic crises through which this era was passing, as occurred especially in Northern Europe, there the craze escalated. By contrast where, as in England, the mythic proportions were controlled, the deadly consequences were likewise controlled. It is true that the absence of torture as a judicial tool in English common law in cases of witchcraft (canon and Roman law prevailed on the continent and Roman law in Scotland) helps to account for this difference. However, that this procedural rule was never changed is due in large measure to the prior absence of any widespread, officially encouraged paranoia regarding witches. The significance of this dialectical interchange between the overarching premises operative in a society and its jurisprudence is made particularly clear when one compares the unchanging legal circumstance in England with the procedural novelties introduced into Massachusetts law when the Puritan collective conscience was taken over by the witch mania.

The most significant manifestation of the work of the Devil and of his agent the witch was now visible in the intense, desperate clash of Protestants and Catholics. That it was felt to be particularly evident in post-1570 Germany, the culture most deeply lacerated by Luther's reforms and the struggles of the Counter-Reformation, the country most affected by the politicization of religion, was almost predictable. It was primarily because of the religious strife

created by the Reformation that the anti-witch phenomenon became institutionalized within the legal-political divisions of Europe and came to acquire a legitimacy and potency that caused the
deaths of tens of thousands. The Devil would have his due.

This is not to deny the constant significance of those major
social and economic changes that Europe was undergoing in this
period, and the local and regional variations thereof that encouraged or deflected certain pressures (e.g., the seemingly anomalous
developmental pattern of England), but it is to insist that what was
determinative for the witch craze was the privileged interpretive
theological frame of reference that emphasized the opposition between God and the Devil now incarnated in the newly divided
political structures of Europe. For both Catholics and Protestants,
reading contemporary history through the prism of classical theological disjunctions, the adversary was always more than a human
other.

However, to properly comprehend the nature of the witch mania, we must connect it concretely to the primary group targeted
as witches: women. Witchcraft received much of its thrust from
the dialectical metaphysics of misogynism. To elucidate the full
meaning of witchcraft as both mendacious doctrine and lamenta-
ble reality one has to investigate the acute existential predicament
of the crucial "outsider" group in this context, women. Moreover,
insofar as one wishes to compare medieval antisemitism to witchcraft, and both these medieval realities to the *Sho'ah,* one can do
so satisfactorily only after full weight has been given to the fact
that the persecution of witches meant primarily, essentially, the
persecution of women.

The medieval conception of women shares much with the corresponding medieval conception of Jews. In both cases a perennial
attribution of secret, bountiful, malicious "power" is made.
Women, that is, are anathematized and cast as witches because of
enduring, grotesque fears of their putative abilities to control men
and thereby coerce, for their own ends, male-dominated Christian
society. Whatever the social and psychological determinants of this
abiding obsession, there can be no denying its consequential reality in medieval Christendom. Linked to theological traditions of
Eve and Lilith, women are perceived as embodiments of inexhaust-
ible negativity. Though not quite quasi-literal incarnations of the

devil as were Jews, women are, rather, their ontological "first cousins," having emerged from the "left" or sinister side of being.

Historically, the most salient manifestation of the unreserved belief in female power and female evil is the recurrent, nearly instinctive association of women and witchcraft. Though there were male witches, when the witch craze accelerated and became a mass phenomenon after 1500 its main victims were female witches. Indeed one strongly suspects that the development of witch-hunting into a mass hysteria became possible only when directed primarily at women. Jean Bodin, one of the sixteenth century's leading intellectuals and witch-hunters, wrote: "it is clear from the books of all who have written on witches that for every male witch there are fifty female witches. . . . [this is due to their] bestial cupidity." The prevalent view, drawing on older New Testament and patristic traditions, was that women were more likely, because intellectually feebler, vainer, and more lustful, to become the instruments of Satan. As Augustine had already pronounced, women were *non posse non peccare*—incapable of not sinning. Just as Eve, at the beginning of time, was the subtle, insidious tool of Satan in the garden, so every generation knows the unsanctified alliance of its womenfolk with the Devil. Playing upon congenital feminine weaknesses, Lucifer involves them in unholy ritual intercourse with himself, violates them, and draws them into his cabal against Christendom. Initially called to defensive action by the regular, often pronounced, role of woman in the many heretical movements of the day, the medieval Church increasingly saw woman, in Tertullian's descriptive phrase, as "the devil's gateway" and reacted accordingly.

The high (low) point of this intertwining of theological antifeminism with witchcraft was the publication of the *Malleus Maleficarum* in 1486, the very title of which is cast in the feminine form, and its horrific reverberations, encouraged by the invention of the printing press, throughout the sixteenth and seventeenth centuries. Expanding on traditional authorities, the two Inquisitorial authors of this text expostulate on the link between women and the Devil: "Why is it," they ask, "that women are chiefly addicted to evil superstition?" Their answer, though many-layered, is essentially that women are inherently impure, their nature, of necessity, corrupt. "All wickedness," they affirm, "is but little to the wickedness of a woman. . . . What else is woman but a foe to friendship, an unescapable punishment, a necessary evil, a natural temptation, a desirable calamity, a domestic danger, a delectable detriment, an evil nature, painted with fair colors." Women are "naturally" satanic.

Above all else it is the power of female sexuality that is the primary cause of the *Malleus'* fear. Through it women ensnare and corrupt, dominate reason, undermine Heaven's rightful order, and facilitate the pollution of Christ's kingdom. "All witchcraft comes from carnal lust, which is in women insatiable . . . a . . . thing which says not, it is enough: that is, the mouth of the womb." It is this insistent concupiscence that causes the witch's heretical and erotic improprieties, the most disgusting of which are her magical castrations of ordinary males and her carnal betrayal with the Devil and his legions. "The Devil uses them so," writes Henri Boguet in his popular *Discours des Sorciers* (ca. 1590) because "he knows that women love carnal pleasures and he means to bend them to his allegiance by such agreeable provocations." Female sensuality knows no limits.

Misogyny is therefore a transcendental imperative, an elemental Christian virtue that situates the hatred of women metaphysically. "More bitter than death (is woman)," declares the *Malleus,* "because that is natural and destroys only the body; but the sin which arose from woman destroys the soul by depriving it of grace, and delivers the body up to the punishment for sin." Accordingly, Inquisitorial activity makes contact with the deepest levels of personal being, braiding together man's most fundamental existential categories, the sexual and the spiritual. Significantly, it was this transhistorical conceptualization, this confident, sexually perverse diagnosis, which gave witch-hunting such longevity by making it immune to empirical counterevidence and, thus, to falsification. Only when the older *weltanschauung* was thoroughly purged by the "new science" did the belief in diabolical feminine potencies become not disproven but rather "unbelievable."

It is also instructive to compare the myriad channels through which the witch was said to perform her perfidious charge and those, often overlapping avenues of satanic activity attributed to the Jew. Both allegedly possessed a diabolical gnosis manifest in the practice of medicine and midwifery, sorcery, the making of potent images, the misuse of human blood, and child seduction and murder. The latter accusations are near-universal archetypes attributed to enemies—real or imagined. One finds them attributed to adversaries in mythological descriptions of the "other" in cultures as diverse as the Roman, the Hindu, and the Polynesian.

Now this angry, menacing description of women, of women *qua* women, is accurate—to a point, but it ignores altogether the dialectical ideology governing the real position of women in medieval society. The whole truth comes into focus only when one recognizes that the adversarial conception of woman as witch was juxtaposed and mediated by countervailing understandings and their institutionalization whose purpose was to integrate women fully and "non-terrifyingly" into the larger social fabric. Women, in effect, were perceived to lose their sybaritic indecency, their ontic negativity, by being absorbed within various anodyne structures whose very existence, as understood by the Church, was tied to their ability to assure just such a transmutational result. From wild, sensual, free, castrating and devouring creatures of natural and supernatural power, women become domesticated—that is, sexually controlled and subordinated—by entering into societal arrangements meant to ensure just this austere transformation. So the institution of the family, that is, of wife and mother and economic partner in nearly every trade and task, and the institution of the nunnery, with its idealized sublimation of female sexuality for non-married women, particularly of the upper and middle classes, come into being and have their sacred function. These culturally defined roles act to neutralize women's inherently anarchic libido, to subdue the undesirable qualities of feminine nature, and hence to curtail the feminine threat to the Divine Order.

But within the ideological parameters created to control women, they were to be protected and loved. Marriage, even if viewed as an exchange of women by men, was, in society's consciousness, a divine blessing, having the status of a sacrament. (See Paul's comments in Ephesians 5:20ff.) Later, for Luther and the reformers, though no longer a sacrament per se—Protestantism having eliminated such sacraments—marriage remained a great good, "the commonest, noblest state." Sexuality when expressed within matrimony was a sacred action blessed by God with children and the cycle of responsibility and care that such procreatic activities engendered. Medieval philosophers and mystics alike described motherhood through such affirmative attributes as generation and sacrifice, love and tenderness, nurturing and selflessness. Moreover, orthodox Catholic doctrine insisted that though women were intellectually and spiritually weaker than men, they were equal in capacity for salvation. And whatever the scholastic theorizing of learned clerics, the many required economic and utilitarian roles played by the woman-wife in the daily routine created mutual dependencies and genuine affection.

The natural affection attendant on the roles of mother, wife, and daughter, and the ideological legitimations offered by such roles as that of nun produced two far-reaching consequences: (a) the understanding of women in medieval society was pluralistic, that is, women were not reduced solely to the status of "alien," "outsider," witch; and (b) most women, having been benignly incorporated into the community through the family or nunnery, were not charged, persecuted, or executed as witches or sorcerers. That is to say, the elemental structural arrangement of Christian society was intended to establish the functional basis for an overtly nonaggressive, male-dominant *modus vivendi* between the sexes, and this, for the most part, it did successfully. This is so *even at the height of the witch craze* between the 1480s and the 1650s, during which the vast majority of women, over 99 percent, protected by their communal role(s), were not directly touched by the mania.

To summarize: the family unit was intended to serve as the medium through which female nature, female sexuality, was controlled and transformed. It appears largely to have succeeded in this ambition. The roles of mother and wife had the desired prophylactic impact and assured both the proper control of women by men and the creation of bonds of mutual affection that served to protect women in moments of social crisis. Insofar as nearly all women entered into and performed these pre-established, socially defined roles, they were, with few exceptions, so protected. The system worked.

Complementing the integrative function of the family was the socio-doctrinal role of the nunnery. On the basis of the dominant negative Christian view of sexuality, coupled with the transcendental meaning of the virginity of Mary, "the mother of God," and the celibacy of Jesus, the Church early came to propound a doctrine that extolled self-willed virginity for both men—what Ernest Jones characterized as "symbolic castration"—and women as superior to active sexuality, even within marriage. As Paul taught: "He who marries his betrothed does well, and he who refrains from marriage will do better" (I Cor. 7:28).

Given this normative hierarchy, the nunnery, and ancillary female associations such as Beguinages, Samenungen, and Gotteshäuser, came into being as an organized, indeed central, feature of Christian communal life parallel to the monastery. As an institution consciously constituted, the nunnery had two cardinal functions. The first was the suppression of female sexuality. This sexual motif, in the sublimative role of "brides of Christ," was the main ideological justification for the nunnery. The second function was the absorption of "surplus" females, who represented a real and pressing danger to community decorum as a whole. Thus the nunnery provided security and a valued social role for women who were not part of normal, "natural" family patterns (as well as protection for the families of which they were not a part). It complemented the family by providing alternative, elective possibilities for women, preventing a serious rupture in the overall pattern of communal life, and controlling potentially disastrous female sexuality. The nunnery thus affirmed the Catholic universe of meaning and order and provided women a second valued form of social incorporation.

Our deconstruction of the mediated societal view of women is yet incomplete. We must add to the familial and monastic ideals the evocative, complex mythography associated with the cult of the Virgin that expresses itself narrowly in theological doctrine and more widely in the emerging ideal of chivalry. "The cult of the Virgin," one of its most distinguished students informs us, "is the most characteristic flower of medieval religion and nothing is more striking than the rapidity with which it spread and the dimensions which it assumed." Here was female-kind at its most exalted, the antithesis of Eve, the evidence par excellence that not all women were satanic creatures, necessary adversaries of God and man.

Of course this romantic idealization, the creation of men's fantasies and pieties no less than the image of the female as feeble bait for the Devil, was not without its profoundly problematic aspects. The most significant of these is the fundamental paradox that Mary though female is *not* like other women. Indeed her theological significance resides precisely in this contrast. Her relationship to sexuality, to sinfulness, to lust, to intercourse, to pregnancy, to child bearing (cf. the long-standing Catholic theological debate over Mary's *in partu* virginity despite the birth of Jesus), and to death is wholly *untypical* of her sex. "Far from being the glory of her sex," Ian MacLean says of the image of the Virgin in the sixteenth century, "[Mary] is not of her sex in its malediction, tribulation, and imperfection. She incarnates certain moral values which are consistent with the social and religious role of women . . . but she does not ever become a model of behavior, so remote is she from others of her sex." Thus, even the panegyric elevation of the feminine in the glorification of the Virgin is not unambiguous concerning the status of ordinary women. In fact, in certain instances, it may even reinforce the radical traditional misogynistic critique of other, real women, who, unlike Mary, are sexually polluting, not paradigms of perfect love and solicitude. Such a disjunctive misogynistic reading appears to have been favored among those androcentric elites in whose circles the cult of the Virgin was especially intense. Yet, even acknowledging this diminishment of real women through the extolling of the Virgin, the larger fact of Mary's female status, however anomalous in form, remains. And in its many variegated resonances it could not but influence the totality of the understanding of women, countering the perverse stereotype over against which it was in dialectical competition. For even in her uniqueness the attributes for which she was admired were "feminine" ones, especially the control of her natural, female, sexuality (i.e., her virginity), complemented by her tenderness and care as *the* mother par excellence, her modesty, kindliness, submissiveness, humility, and obedience. The Virgin may have been an unusual woman, the most unusual woman, but she was still, and completely, a woman.

Let us now bring this discussion to bear directly upon the comparative issues of gynocide, genocide, and the *Sho'ah*. Whereas the witch was, *per definitionem*, an outsider in the Christian commonwealth, women per se were not. To extrapolate from the circumstances of the former to those of the latter as if the two were synonymous is a gross non sequitur. When one correlates the limited demographic role and restricted cultural-historic status of witches with the wider and polyvalent role of women in medieval society, then the marked difference between the status of women and that of witches begins to become clear. The same occurs when one compares the situation of women to that of Jews in the post-Christian matrix, for Jews were *always,* again by definition, *contra* women, outsiders to something approaching the maximal degree. (Only in the twentieth century would the Jew reach the ultimate condition as outsider. It would require, paradoxically, the modern era of emancipation and political citizenship to produce this circumstance.) This disjunction between women and Jews arises directly from the fact that whereas pre- and post-Crusader Christianity worked hard and earnestly to create mechanisms through which to integrate women into the social collective, defined patriarchically, and to encourage love, however hierarchically arranged and objectified, between Christian men and women in authorized institutions, most notably the family, leaving only a small minority of women as outsiders, in the case of the Jew it did just the opposite. Increasingly after 1200, as Christianity gained ever tighter and more monopolistic control of society, it took new steps, or reinforced older ones, to discourage and displace normal human relationships between Jews and Christians. No mediating social avenues or institutions existed to domesticate, to culturally ingest, the Jew other than the traumatic one of conversion. Thus women could be idealized, typologized, and actualized as wife, "helpmeet," partner, caretaker, mother, daughter, heir, nun, lady, and Virgin, but the Jew in late medieval Christendom was always and only a Jew. Papal policy, though consistently molded to protect Jews, also intended to enforce Jewish "servitude," to make existentially manifest the consequences of Jewish "stubbornness" and "rebelliousness."

What these differences in cultural and state policy mean, both in the medieval context and still more pointedly in relation to the *Sho'ah,* can be gauged by considering the demographics of the witch craze. Extreme caution is required in making these calculations, for the estimates of the number of witches executed between 1400 and 1750 vary by a magnitude of at least 300; that is, estimates range from 30,000 up to 9,000,000. Most scholarly estimates of the number of witches put to death during the entire craze cluster between the figures of 30,000 and 200,000, with the higher number, "conservatively estimated," finding many proponents. However, both these figures are open to serious question, one for underestimation, the other for overestimation. It is closer to the complex historical record to put the figure of witches killed over the three centuries of the mania at approximately 100,000, though even this may be too high. Given this demographic total it is clear that those who all too commonly liken the fate of those *accused* of witchcraft to that experienced by Jews under Nazism with its inescapable racial necessities are simply mistaken. Given the huge, and illusory, estimates of witches that were common in the sixteenth and seventeenth centuries, ranging up to nearly two million on the account of the demonologist Henry Boguet in 1602, it is evident that the states of Europe did not—even in Germany, the center of the storm—pursue the witch as ardently as they might have, despite the fact that the various states made witchcraft a secular crime and passed laws against it, the Holy Roman Empire in 1532, England in 1542, 1563, and 1604, Scotland in 1563, and France, Sweden, and Russia in the late sixteenth and early seventeenth centuries. Though this state intervention broadened the hunt and resulted in higher rates of conviction and more severe punishment (e.g., in Scotland, Transylvania, and Poland), thus anticipating in a very preliminary way the politicization of modern antisemitism, one must generalize here with great caution. Without the intervention of the secular courts and legislatures the witch craze would never have reached the dire proportions it did, yet these same state institutions never brought anything like their full weight to bear, either directly via secular power, or more obliquely through Church apparatus, upon the "problem." Had the formal secular and religious structures of Europe acted with full vigor and in concert, given the hallucinatory immensities projected by those concerned to make such projections, the toll would have been far higher.

This judgment is confirmed repeatedly, in differing ways. Thus, it is confirmed in Germany in an inverse manner, by the disproportionately high level of executions carried out there as a result of the *absence* of actualized authority that allowed, even encouraged, local clerics and magistrates to hunt witches as they desired without regard to Imperial or Church constraints. The presence of Imperial and Church authority, of state power, limited the excesses rather than encouraged them. Likewise events in Scotland, with its local courts, followed the German pattern: "the execution rate in Scotland was dramatically higher when unsupervised local authorities heard witchcraft cases than when judges from the central courts did so. . . . the execution rate . . . was 91 percent in local trials . . . 55 percent in the Justiciary court [in Edinburgh], and a very low 6 percent in the circuit courts." Conversely, in Spain, with its centralized Inquisition and developed national bureaucracy, very few witches were murdered. Similarly in France, another strong state with developed controls, 36 percent of all cases of witchcraft appealed to the Parlement of Paris were dismissed and only 24 percent of such cases were confirmed. In England the witch craze was stringently controlled, except for rare instances, because the monarchy wanted it controlled and had the means to implement its will.

In sum, although the machinery of the state was essential in the evolution of the witch craze from a minor phenomenon to an international crusade eventually claiming the lives of tens of thousands of innocent women, the fact remains that it never became more than a highly *marginal* assault. This conclusion is validated by the statistical evidence that over 99.9 percent of all women were not harmed directly by the police arm of either the state or Church, though both had the power to do so, had the elites that controlled them so desired. Thus, although witch accusations did function as an escape valve through which to eliminate social pressure, did work to control "surplus population," did serve as the occasion(s) for collective rituals of purification and societal reconstruction, and did involve the intervention of civic authorities, they did all of these things only spasmodically, and to a very limited extent. And this difference in degree is, ultimately, a difference in kind; the difference between genderized mass murder, albeit of a very small percentage of the target population, and genocide. European society, the European State, partly because of its bifocal vision of women, and the accompanying Christian morality thereof—and partly for institutional reasons—never translated its prejudicial image of women into an active, monolithic, murderous misogynism, *even during the two and one-half centuries of the witch craze.* There simply never was, *contra* Hitler's indubitable program of genocide, a policy of gynocide anywhere in Europe or the New World.

THE GULAG

The Gulag drew upon two imperfect precedents, penal detention and slavery, that mixed together in a particularly bitter way to create the Stalinist camps. Penal institutions, including the use of special incarceration centers for political "dissidents," are an all-too-common historical phenomenon. For example, the Nazi use of internment camps from 1933 (e.g., Dachau) for political enemies such as Communists and liberals belongs to this general history and need not detain us. The same may be said of the evolution of Czarist prison institutions into Bolshevik ones. *The House of the Dead* leaves us no innocent illusions on this subject. The relation of Stalin's Gulag to the normative structures of slavery, however, requires a closer, adequately nuanced look. The basic, compelling comparability of the two oppressive configurations lies in their purposeful, aggressive exploitation of human labor; that is to say, both are rooted in and maintained by specific economic and social needs that are held to be best met by unfree labor. Stalin's policy of the forced acceleration of industrialization was "aided" by reducing a significant percentage of Russia's population into, effectively, "slaves." Through this coercive labor policy, rooted in the Czarist past, the inmates of the camps were made to provide crucial cheap labor for all forms of Soviet industrialization ranging from the mining of raw materials to the building of transportation networks. Representing, at its peak, on some accounts, more than one-sixth of the male adult population, this "enslaved" group composed the largest single industrial working class in Russia. Moreover, it could be set tasks that (a) were necessary to the economy as a whole yet situated where labor on the free market would have been very costly to procure; and (b) could be accomplished by the calculated substitution of a large work force for expensive machines that could be obtained only with foreign currency that the Soviet Union lacked.

This slave labor system was not created as the result of the devastation wrought by the First World War, nor as the consequence of special short-term problems in the life of the Stalinist regime, though the numbers of such workers did vary from period to period. Rather it was inherent, as Solzhenitsyn has so dramatically emphasized, in the very fabric of Stalinism per se. The constitutive excess that was a dominant feature of Stalinism emerged within an already grotesque, authoritarian order. Not only in the Gulag empire but throughout the Soviet economy, coercion was the norm after 1929. The brutalities of agricultural collectivization form an essential ingredient in our schematic deconstruction, and to them must be added the extensive reorganization of (regular) industrial labor in 1930 that led, for example, in December 1938, to the system of industrial passports and in October 1940 to the introduction of severe penalties for lateness and absenteeism and curtailment of the workers' freedom in job selection. Even more significant, analogous in intent to slave labor, is the system of State Labor Reserves established by Stalin in October 1940 that, in effect, created large-scale pools of young *unfree* industrial workers. According to this scheme, as many as one million male teenagers, the majority off the farms, were "drafted" into technical industrial apprenticeships deemed necessary by the State economic planners. After a training period lasting between six months and two years depending on the job for which he was being prepared, the young man would be assigned a task to which he was legally bound for four years. In this way a novel method of industrial serfdom was instituted. The Fourth Five-Year Plan called for 4,500,000 such recruits, a major percentage of all industrial employees. And, as in the Gulag, such unfree labor was expected to provide, in particular, 70 to 80 percent of the new workers in the heavy industries (e.g., coal-mining, the mining of ferrous metals, and machine building). The Gulag, then, can be identified as the end point of a spectrum of Soviet labor exploitation rather than as a discontinuous and radical alternative to the "normal" Stalinist social order.

Hitler, or perhaps more precisely Himmler and Speer, created, during the war, a somewhat comparable slave empire comprising captured prisoners of war, over-run Slavic peoples, and even citizens of conquered countries in Western Europe, not to mention the industrial complexes utilizing Jewish labor at Auschwitz and elsewhere. However, Hitler's use of slave labor, whatever its overall qualitative comparability to Stalin's, differed with respect to the expropriation of Jewish labor. Jews were not utilized as slave labor either in the classical or Stalinist sense, but rather as, in Ferencz's telling phrase, "less than slaves." The German intent was not to foster economic efficiency or substantive production gains but to establish a disutilitarian equation that combined labor utilization with guarantees that Jewish workers would be worked to death in a very specific, highly inelastic period of time.

Stalin's system, in contrast—theoretically at least, and more often than not in practice—was predicated on a fixed period of forced labor. The dominant concern of the regime was the realization of the labor quotas, and it was callously, cynically *indifferent* to the survivability of its prisoner labor force. Whether Kolyma workers lived or died was a matter of little moral or practical import, aside from its bearing on productivity, to Stalin or the camp bureaucracy. If inmates could survive under the prevailing execrable conditions, well and good, but their individual fate—*either that they survive or that they die*—was not primary. In the main, during most of the Stalinist era, the Gulag was uncaring, its state-dictated attitude toward its wards expressed in a skeptical, perverse disinterest in their particularity. Without doubt there was in the organization of the Gulag much malice, sadism, murder. Brutality was normal, the norm brutal. What was absent, however, was a specific, unambiguous, national policy of mass murder. Despite the high death toll in the Gulag, aside from during 1938, the major causes of death in this environment were corollaries of the dolorific natural conditions and the official attitude of unconcern, which had the impact of ramifying the negative consequences of the ecological habitat. No less a critic of Stalin's camps than Robert Conquest has summarized these circumstances in the following terms:

> Previous years [pre-1938] had seen, on occasion, massive casualties. But these had been due to inefficiencies in supply, attempts to carry out assignments in impossible conditions, and in fact—if in exaggerated form—the normal incompetence and brutality of Soviet life. When the difficulties could be overcome, conditions, as we have seen, were tolerable. But above all, prisoners were not subjected to lethal conditions on purpose.

Even in that cruelest of years, 1938, when Stalin and his new chief henchman for the Kolyma region, Major Garanin, ordered an unprecedented wave of shootings, increased every manner of abuse, and saw to it that conditions went from bad to unbearable, even then, for the entire year, the whole Kolyma district witnessed "only" 40,000 shootings, that is, intentional, official murders. And even in 1938, executions were still coupled to work quotas—and generally unconnected to any other ideological or normative category (e.g., kulaks, old Bolsheviks, or Jews).

This is not to argue that Stalin's new ferocity toward the Gulag's population did not take its considerable, if more oblique, toll during this year. Estimates ranging from 200,000 to 400,000 deaths caused by cold, starvation, and overwork are commonly accepted. For this one year, under these exceptional conditions, the Gulag approached Auschwitz *asymptotically*—asymptotically because even in this worst of years, the Gulag did not operate under the same equation of life and death as did Auschwitz. The priorities of labor versus death, of productivity versus dehumanization, did shift toward a heretofore-unprecedented near-equality; yet, even at its nadir, the demands of life, even if translated and reduced to economic units, still had at least equal weight. In this matrix exploitation and annihilation certainly became too casually contraposed, and the original dominant economic drive saw itself paralleled by a corrupt desire to debase, even destroy, many of the camp inmates.

However, even amidst this rueful reevaluation of purposes, at no time was the equation so wholly inverted that death was the supreme unchallenged good. Moreover, and elemental to the Nazi versus Gulag comparison, the Gulag killed people distributively, taking its toll on all groups and singling none out for "special treatment." Then again, the powerful streak of harsh realism in Stalin's perception of reality caused him to recognize the need for "compromise" between actual economic requirements and the primitive desire to "punish" real or imagined enemies, while his Marxist-Leninist ideology allowed for such mediation.

Alternatively, Hitler's severe biocentric "idealism" encouraged no comparable compromise on the Jewish question, while his immolating racial metaphysics permitted none. As a consequence, Himmler's SS empire manifested no such mediating dispositions; nor did it represent similar, primarily utilitarian, priorities, at least not where the *Judenfrage* was concerned. In this arena it was primordially committed not only to Jewish submissiveness, to the exploitation of frightfully controlled Jewish labor, but also, and more rudimentarily, to the unenigmatic biological extinction of each and every Jew trapped within its parameters. Hitler and his Aryan elite were neither skeptical about nor uninterested in, *contra* the controlling rationality of the Gulag, the fate of "their" Jews— they were, rather, passionate advocates of the universal imperative that all Jews *must* die. Under no conditions, no matter how economically advantageous their efforts and no matter how politically cooperative Jewry proved itself to be, could it be left to survive. *Mere* Jewish survival was the active enemy. Compared to 40,000 shootings in the Kolyma in all of 1938, 10,000 Jews a day died at Auschwitz in 1944, Treblinka consumed 1.5–2 million Jews in eighteen months, and the *Einsatzgruppen* efficiently murdered 1.5 million Jews in about the same period of time.

According to the craven operative Nazi calculus, Jews at Buna were already assumed "dead." They had been irretrievably sentenced, only their execution and burial had been delayed for a short, inconsequential duration. Consider as evidence of these alternative logics, the Gulag's and the Nazis', the differing food allocation systems. In the Nazi labor camps, even productive laborers were, as a rule, fed on a subsistence level calculated to exhaust their strength within three months. The commandant of the men's camp at Buna once asked a prisoner how long he had been there. "Seven months," answered the prisoner. "Then," replied the commandant, "you must have been cheating us, because you could not live on camp food [rations] for more than three months." Thus, even economically useful workers were, by design, turned into corpses by the system within a short period, for their own cadavers were the most "valuable" thing they could produce. By comparison, food in Russian camps was regulated so as to provide higher allotments to efficient workers. Those who could not work, or work as per quota, were given, in effect, starvation rations. In this way a tight equation was constructed between labor efficiency and survival. Not so in the Nazi landscape, where food rationing was a key subplot in the larger, near-total, Nazi unconcern with economic rationality as far as Jewish labor was concerned.

Still more broadly, the five-year economic plans promulgated in Moscow by Stalin provided the economic causation of much of the labor camp activity, as they did of the mass movement of nine million peasants off the land and into the cities. Adam Ulam reminds us that these programs became the blueprints for regulating "the economic life of every Soviet citizen. Every Soviet producer, whether in agriculture or industry, would become a soldier in the war to attain the goals prescribed from above." Accordingly: "Fulfillment or nonfulfillment of quotas would become equivalent to soldierly behavior and desertion under fire." The key implication of this policy was not only the dread and intimidation it produced, but the axiological rule that it established. Stalin's "subjects were judged not only according to their degree of submission, but also according to their ability to produce what and as much as the despot commanded. One's daily work would become a test of one's loyalty." This strong linkage of economic development, Communist ideology, and political loyalty to State and Leader reveals the economic motivation functioning at the heart of the Great Terror. Forced and directed labor, however inefficiently managed in practice, became the basic exchange relationship between ruler and ruled, state and citizen. It is relevant to recognize that in this labor situation there were mediating circumstances that softened the impact of the governing imperatives. For example, factory managers needed workers to meet their quotas—and save their own lives—and so bent the harsh centralized rules theoretically directing factory employment; or various managers and middle-level bureaucrats offered material incentives, including job security, to workers to meet obligatory quotas. And it is apposite to compare these mediating situations and structures, as those of slave systems, to the wholly unmediated forms of Jewish labor under Nazism.

Structurally, there is a direct connection between the war against the nation, the increase in slave labor, and the need to meet preordained industrial quotas. The consequences of this coalition can be seen in the fact that it was during the First Five-Year Plan, in 1930, that the Gulag (a Russian acronym for Chief Administration of Camps) was established as a separate agency of the GPU. Only during this period were slave labor and the overall economic plan of the nation synchronized into one, with dramatic effects. The contribution of "convict" labor to the overall economy increased 120 percent in 1931, 235 percent in 1932, and was projected to over a 450 percent increase for 1933; the value of slave labor went up over fivefold between 1930 and 1932. Slave labor was responsible for constructing many, if not the majority, of the large industrial and public works projects of the 1930s and 1940s, beginning with the Belomor Canal, begun in 1931 and completed in 1933. In addition, it extracted much, if not most, of Russia's mineral (gold) and forestry resources, especially in the Kolyma region, in this period. Precisely these two valuable natural resources provided the majority of the foreign currency required to finance the importation of necessary technology and machine-goods from the West. Thus slave labor was essential to all plans to transform Russia into the modern state Stalin and his allies called for. In reverse, had slave labor been reduced or had it evaporated, the whole planning of the Soviet elite would have collapsed in a domino effect. Allied as such modernizing public policy was to Stalin's own intense political paranoia, this now elemental, terrifying, and terrorizing feature of Soviet life continued to expand ever apace.

The Second World War, which caused acute shortages and profound dislocations, exacerbated the abysmal material conditions in the camps while it shifted the labor assignments toward war production goals. The primacy of the principle of economic exploitation became even more necessary for reasons of national defense, especially in light of the fact that Russia was the only combatant that had to finance dramatically increased military expenditures on the basis of a precipitously reduced economic infrastructure. Thus the State Plan for the Development of the National Economy for 1941 allocated 6,180 million rubles out of a total of 37,655 million rubles for investment to the NKVD. This considerable percentage of the national wealth was invested in the exploitation of up to 3.5 million camp exiles in 1941 and the years immediately thereafter. Moreover, under existing wartime conditions, the rhetoric of national survival was relied on to justify every manner of ruthlessness. Mass deportations of many national groups, involving millions of individuals, for example, were carried out, their autonomous republics disbanded in the name of state security, thus helping to restock and expand the required slave-labor population. The Gulag was further reinforced by captured prisoners of war, who again numbered in the millions, as well as by the Soviets' own repatriated prisoners of war, who were treated, bizarrely, as "enemies of the state" and exiled.

The composition of this vast slave population, however, is a complex matter that sheds further light both on state policy and on the differences between Soviet and Nazi state ideology. That is, the precise relationship between group membership, bracketing the nationality question momentarily, and exile was neither uniform nor self-evident. Belonging to a now-disfavored segment of society did appreciably heighten chances for deportation. Thus, for example, being a wealthy peasant or civil servant meant a high probability of being charged with some "crime" against the State. Yet, *unlike* Nazi anti-Jewish legislation, according to Soviet procedures *not* all members of a given group were *by definition* to be deported. Even in the most numerically substantial, as well as outrageously polemical instance, the persecution of the kulaks, only approximately one-third of the kulaks were deported. In all other cases the figures involved need to be qualified by the adjective "some." Only some religious leaders and lay followers were deported, some Jews, some soliders, some party members, some artists, some state experts, some judges, some Chinese, some foreign workers (many), some police, some NKVD operatives, some anti-revolutionary remnants, some intellectuals, some technicians, some professionals, some Komsomol members, some individuals with foreign connections. The exceptions to this general rule were certain national minorities, moved east in the period 1941–44 almost *en bloc*. (And even in these cases, as in the national cases already cited, exile should *not* be equated with genocide for reasons most luminously manifest in the 1957 repatriation of the majority of the deported nationality groups.) Thus, the "criminal" pool cut across all segments of Russian society, isolating none in a particularly invidious manner, as did, by comparison, the Nuremberg Laws. Though the material impact of the Soviet campaign was distributed asymmetrically among different groups, *none* was singled out for physical genocide, and abuse was fairly democratically distributed with the exception of a small class of "politicals," who came in for especially harsh treatment. In all, the tally of victims from these manifold, widely distributed purges and deportations looks like this. Ten percent of the total Soviet population fell into disfavor during the purges of the 1930s. It is estimated that between 1936 and 1939 four to five million people were actually uprooted, and of these approximately 10 percent, 400,000–500,000 souls, were killed.

This was not Auschwitz. Why it was not lies in the differences between the reigning ideologies, let us better call them mythologies, held by the two regimes in question. Nazism was a novel, peculiarly deadly amalgam of racial, Social Darwinian, and Manichean elements that reified the Jew not only as a biological inferior and the enemy of all positive values, but still more importantly as the paradigmatic temporal manifestation of nothing less than the principle of cosmic negativity per se. Conversely, Hitler was the supreme contemporary positive incarnation of the Spirit, its principal medium in the world, the prophetic leader of the struggle for that racial purity that translated itself into the advance of civilization, an advance that simultaneously assured certain victory over the metaphysical forces of universal darkness. It is here that the *Führerprinzip* becomes so consequential, with its meta-legal, meta-ethical legitimacy and authority. All positive restraints, either moral or jurisprudential, must—by definition—give way before the incontrovertible will of the Führer. He, and he alone, discerns the opaque but compelling signs of destiny and leads the *Herrenvolk* accordingly.

Marxist-Leninist-Stalinist ideology parallels this mythic political dogma to a considerable extent, in particular through its heightened self-consciousness of itself as the avant-garde of the uncompromisable historical struggle for existential emancipation from class tyranny. Marx and his many, diverse heirs were convinced that they had discerned, in the materialist dialectic, the root principle of historical change, and accordingly were, in history's primordial struggle for human liberation, on the side of the angels. "The Marxist doctrine," Lenin pronounced, "is omnipotent because it is true."

More technically described, Marxism-Leninism-Stalinism can be said to share, allowing for its own particular ideologically reconstructed analysis of key categories and concepts, two of the three principal metaphysical dogmas of Nazism: (a) a variant form of Manicheanism; and (b) its own special totalitarian rendition of Social Darwinism. Its Manicheanism manifests itself in its definition of the class struggle as an unbounded, yet determinate, war between the inherently "progressive" forces of history and those that are "reactionary," that is, those that oppose the emancipation and autonomy of the proletariat. Marx's revolutionary conceptual breakthrough was his "discovery" of the universal motivating principle of this conflict, the economic dialectic of material productive forces, which allowed him, armed with this "gnosis," to unlock the inner, heretofore secret, code of history's unfolding. Through such knowledge the Marxist can learn how to assist the virtuous, proletarian masses in overcoming their execrable, tyrannical antitheses, thereby ushering in the socialist equivalent of the "Kingdom of God." Such inspired goals demand a war, for all its terror, "making no concessions whatever to the accursed heritage of serf-ownership, asiatic barbarism and human degradation" and "creating conditions in which it will be impossible for the bourgeoisie to exist, or for a new bourgeoisie to arise" (Lenin). This avowed ruthlessness is legitimate because it is directed against a robber class, which manifests far more despotic behavior, and because it brings into being a pristine order, which produces nothing less than a new form of man as well as an unprecedented mode of egalitarian society. Predicated on a changed distribution of power, the concern of this revolutionary transformation is nothing less than a wholly reconstructed socioeconomic order. Socialist Manicheanism, hence, requires a concrete political struggle for control of the state apparatus that creates, modulates, and distributes influence between classes.

In this challenging context, the revolutionary elite—the Party—leads the remorseless assault against all, including liberal-democratic, anti-proletarian forces. It absorbs all power, brooks no opposition in either theory or practice, and thereby gathers the necessary strength to liquidate the malevolent structures of the class enemy as well as to foment the revolutionary struggle from above. The Party is wholly justified by its revolutionary ethic, which aligns with historical necessity to demand that it transform the masses even while they seem unprepared for this apotheosis. It is in this criss-crossed way that the dialectic of organizational structure and ideology become realized: the Party—the bureaucratic vehicle—compellingly implements and rigorously supports the revolutionary Marxist-Leninist synthesis while the encompassing ideology reinforces the enacted Party-organizational structure and its legal superstructure as reflected in juridical formulations such as the notorious Article 58 (on treason to the Fatherland) of the 1926 RSFSR Criminal Code. It is also through this complex interweaving of form and doctrine that the Party legitimates its terror ideologically, as morally required for capturing the future. "Morality," Lenin would assert at the Third Komsomol Congress, "is that which serves the destruction of the old exploiting society." This strident redefinition also authorizes the monopoly of power exercised by the revolutionary elite—the Party and its leadership. Through their peculiar "awareness" of the *Truth,* as well as of the mechanisms by which it works itself out in space-time, they possess the higher ethical right to total power. "People who were really convinced of the fact that they had advanced knowledge," Lenin asserted, "would be demanding not freedom for the new views alongside the old views, but the replacement of the latter by the former." The Party has now been justified, in the context of this class conflict, as the ruthless agent, if and as required, for carrying through this revolutionary purge of bourgeois elements, indeed of all oppositional groups whether of the right or left, whether of the aristocratic or the middle class.

To this degree then there is a formal as well as structural parallelism between Nazism and Bolshevism, with both asserting their claims and coming to power on the basis of a party machinery outside of, and putatively superior to, the state apparatus. In each case the Party justified itself as the spear-carrier of historical laws, as the embodiment of the Spirit. Moreover, each attributed to its leadership special powers. "The revolutionary leadership," argued Lenin, "[is] rule that is unrestricted by any laws." Hitler would agree. As a result, a war against ideological enemies, in the case of Nazism against its racial protagonists, in the case of Bolshevism its class opponents, was not only defended but recommended as a moral imperative. Yet for all the conceptual, mythic, logical, and bureaucratic similarities between these two immensely powerful world crusades, the defining difference between them must also be recognized.

The defining difference between Nazism and Stalinism resides in the seminal fact that each system understands its Manichean manifesto, its energizing first principles, in radically disparate ways. Given the economic basis of Marxist-Leninism, the imperative is to annihilate an oppressive class regime; the real opponent is a "false" exploitative labor-economic system. The class enemy is an enemy by virtue of the place he occupies in the deformed socioeconomic arrangement. "Our policy is a class policy," Stalin reminded the Central Committee. "He who thinks that one can conduct in the countryside a policy that will please everybody, the rich as well as the poor, is not a Marxist but an idiot. . . . " Accordingly, the visionary ambition is to alter the reigning organizational arrangements of society, thereby eliminating the regressive, enervating economic superstructure, and hence the structural immorality of existing political models. Such far-reaching social renovations entail one further, cardinal transposition as well: to eliminate the offending *status* of one's class enemy, that is, to dissolve the very notion of class and hence, necessarily, that of enemy *qua* enemy. Such fundamental repositioning, of course, might require terror on a grand scale, as evidenced, for example, in the protracted and painful war against the kulaks, for the bourgeoisie will not give up its privilege easily or willingly. The intent of such official violence, ideally, however, is not to attack the kulak *qua* being but to transform the power structure that corrupts both the bourgeoisie and the proletariat alike. (This is why at least 65 to 70 percent of the kulaks survived!) Ideologically, even for Stalin, *reeducation, not* physical extermination, is the consummate goal. Bolshevism declares an uncompromising war against the class enemy *qua* class enemy, that is to say, against his class status; it does not declare an unlimited, annihilatory war against his person *qua* person. In this, Bolshevism manifests a conversionary doctrine and militant zeal analogous to that of the classic Catholic approach to the conversion of Jewry (or perhaps still closer to that of Islam toward Pagans). Reeducated, the former bourgeoisie can take its rightful place in the "workers' paradise," just as a converted Jew can become a fully equal member of Christian society, even a "Prince of the Church."

By comparison, Nazism does not merely apply its vengeful Manichean passion against an alternative economic class or sociocultural status, but against an opposing, assertedly biological givenness—that is, Semite versus Aryan. Given the fixed strategic construction of this binary opposition, it cannot take on the character of a war of status versus status—that is, a collision that does not necessarily deny the essential humanity of the other—for, unlike class conflict, racial conflict does not allow for the conceptual or juridical separation of person and status. A Jew by status, defined biologically, is also necessarily a Jew in person. This, and precisely this, is the intended sting of racial claims—no reeducation, no conversion, no alteration in either status or person is possible. Hence, whereas Stalinism sought "confessions" of wrongdoing, of ideological heresy, of "wrecking," as a required if not always successful prologomenon to social or political rehabilitation, Nazism sought no "confessions," no repentence, from Jews—for it allowed no possibility of their social (i.e., racial) rehabilitation. In this elemental sense, Nazism pushes the primordial struggle fundamental to cosmic-historical progress to a deeper level than Marxism—that is, to biological rather than economic-cultural determinants. As such, Marxism-Leninism-Stalinism has programmatic alternatives open to it that Nazism does not possess. Race, as the primary, immutable determinant of the Manichean cosmology, demands a total war different *in kind* from the revolutionary clash entailed by Marxist-Leninist metaphysics. This intrinsic dichotomy defines the qualitative incongruity between Stalin's Gulag and Hitler's Auschwitz.

The instructive case against which to test these deconstructive meta-ideological observations on ideology is, of course, that provided by the treatment of the kulaks. On the one hand, their tragedy makes clear that all theoretical considerations of individual versus corporate categories, as well as all related questions of mediating moral restraints, were settled by Stalin in a most immoral "corporatist" fashion. For Stalin they were an identifiable segment within the overall population for whom belonging to a collective "category" was to be all-consequential. Yet the actual nature of their appalling dismemberment as a "class," which meant such vast human suffering for millions of peasants, provides evidence that Stalin's onslaught against them was different in kind from Hitler's campaign against Jewry. Consider that: (a) Stalin explicitly chose to murder only a minority of the kulaks, though he could have murdered them all; and (b) the main assault, for all its severity, was against a "contingent," "socially alien" identity, the nature of which was, by definition, subject to change. Whatever neurotic fears energized and accompanied this convulsive anti-peasant policy, there can be no reason to doubt that what was elemental in this unstinting war was the kulaks' economic—that is, class—loyalties, loyalties that had to be broken down for the general good to prevail according to the dominant socialist consensus. (Stalin was *not* alone in holding this view, which was *the* view of almost the entire Bolshevik elite, including Trotsky, differences existing only as to how best to accomplish this policy.) The desired alteration in the kulaks' collective class consciousness, and correspondingly the kulak's status as a "class enemy," was to come about through forced collectivization. I estimate that 88 percent of the Russian peasantry, at a minimum, survived Stalin's class war against them in the 1930s. This loss rate of 12 percent or less indicates massive suffering but not a state-dictated, state-actualized, policy of physical genocide based on criteria of socioeconomic "class."

The vastly destructive famine in the Ukraine in 1930–33 has also to be accounted for in light of the present argument, that is, *contra* genocide. Though the sheer size of the Ukrainian tragedy is overwhelming, to understand it properly one must put it into its correct historical and conceptual context. To do so is not to diminish the vastness of its human proportions, but rather to make it available, in an accurate form, to academic study and debate. To begin, the nationalist dimensions of the event need to be highlighted. Both the indigenous Ukrainian population and the alien Soviet ruling class understood that the Ukraine had historically been independent with its own separate cultural traditions. Accordingly the frame of the confrontation of the twenties and thirties was between competing claims to sovereignty—one nationalist, the other putatively internationalist—though the latter, increasingly, was merely a cover for an ever more visible Russian national chauvinism. For Stalin, the ultimate objective was the full integration of the Ukraine into the larger, ideally homogenized Soviet state. Anything less was dangerous, both practically and potentially. Thus in a massively expensive campaign of internal colonialism, Stalin decided to eradicate this recurring challenge to his leadership and to Soviet socialist hegemony. Beginning with the purge of Ukrainian academics and political and cultural leaders in April 1929 and continuing into 1930, Stalin set in motion a movement that would eventually consume literally millions of Ukrainians.

The object of the entire campaign was the complete annihilation of Ukrainian nationalism, much like Hitler's strategy in, for example, Poland (and elsewhere in Eastern Europe). In both cases the purpose of violence was the maintenance of political control, of ensuring either new or continued domination of one group over another. In both situations terror in its myriad forms was employed, but in neither did it intend genocide, for this would have been counterproductive from the perspective of the oppressor seeking to exploit the victim people. Killing off the *whole* of the intended "helot" population makes no more sense than killing off one's slave. Destroying its controlling elite was a necessary condition for achieving the lasting subordination of the conquered nation or group, but destroying the subjugated masses themselves would have been absurd—except in the wholly nonutilitarian case of Hitler's war against the Jews.

Given the Ukraine's specific socioeconomic circumstance (i.e., the importance of the independent, economically autonomous peasantry), Stalin's plan for the extermination of national identity called for, in addition to the removal of the national intelligentsia, a crusade against the "proto-capitalist" peasant. As S. O. Pidharny has described it, Stalin had to move against "Ukrainian nationalism's social base—the individual landholdings." "Stalin seemed to have realized," Robert Conquest has recently written, "that only a mass terror throughout the body of the nation—that is, the peasantry—could reduce the nation to submission." As long as the Ukrainian kulak, a euphemism now for all free peasants, existed, nationalist sentiment would remain; to crush the latter, one had to crush the former. The method to this end was forced collectivization of the agricultural sector and an overly demanding quota for grain exports from the region, which translated into a man-made famine in the Ukraine in 1931 and especially 1932.

Increased pressure was applied against the kulak class enemy, against local party officials who, failing to produce the required quota, had to be in league with the peasant enemy, against all channels of Ukrainian self-sufficiency, economic vitality, and food supply and distribution. And the result was predictable, though I believe its magnitude caught even Stalin and his inner circle off guard: mass starvation throughout the region reaching its climax after March 1933. Of a peasant population of upwards of 25 million, it is estimated that 4 to 5 million, 16.5 to 25 percent, died in this period from lack of food and related medical disabilities. In some areas the death rate was as low as 10 percent, in others nearly 100 percent, depending upon local agricultural and ecological conditions, especially the ability to find other sources of nutrition such as fish or wildlife to replace the lost grain harvest.

Overall, though the human carnage was immense, approaching the number of Jewish victims during the Second World War, the percentage of the Ukrainian peasant population lost was somewhere in the region of 20 percent, plus or minus 5 percent, and the losses for the Ukrainian population as a whole were in the area of 15 percent. These statistical results resemble, if being slightly higher, the figures for population loss in those Eastern European countries overrun by the Nazis, and in both cases, the Stalinist and the Hitlerian, the figures do not indicate that either conquering despot intended, or pursued, a policy of total population eradication, of physical genocide. Had they done so, the number and percentage of dead would have been far higher.

Stalinist ideology created both the Gulag in general and the specific assault against the kulaks. Yet, conversely, this same ideology constrained the behavior of Stalin and his bureaucracy. It created a state that was guilty of mass murder but not a state that sought, or implemented, a policy of physical genocide. And I assert this conclusion with the terrible fate of the kulaks, the Ukrainians, and that of the deported minority peoples very much in mind.

CONCLUSION

What the leaders of nations believe affects what nations do. Because mass murder and genocide have required state intervention, it is essential to understand the direct, causal links between ideas and reality in the historical circumstances that eventuated in slaughter. Conversely, to comprehend why in other specific historical instances these extreme phenomena did *not* occur it is equally imperative to understand those controlling ideological doctrines that operated against the creation of Auschwitz-like solutions. The unmediated character of Nazi ideology is historically unique; of all the destructive belief systems its Judaeophobia alone demanded unlimited physical genocide. It is this fact that makes the "Final Solution" an unprecedented and unparalleled event.

Berel Lang

The History of Evil and the Future of the Holocaust

True lastingness is constantly in the future.—
—*Rosenzweig*

1

SINCE EFFORTS ARE STILL NEEDED TO DESCRIBE FOR THE PRESENT THE events of the Nazi genocide against the Jews, it may seem premature and even offensive to ask about the future of those events—as if they might later be seen or assessed quite differently (perhaps more benignly) than they are now. But I believe it is important also for the present to consider the speculative question of "the future of the Holocaust." One reason for holding this bears on the Nazi genocide considered in its own terms—that is, for the detailed reconstruction of those events and of the contemporary responses to them. This task is most immediately historical in character; it falls not only on the social, political, and economic historians who will be central to carrying it on, but on the social scientist and the literary and cultural critics, all of whose efforts are required for describing the events of the genocide as they occurred and the roles assumed by or imposed on its agents, victims, and bystanders.

This form of historical address is taken up by many contributors to the present volume, and I do not myself adopt it here except to suggest the importance of a projection into the future, even for such accounts which focus designedly on the past. I mean more by this suggestion than only the reflective principle that applies generally in historiography and asserts that, together with the assembling of data, also required for historical discourse is an act of the imagination into the *historian's* future; this projection is required wherever evidence is interpreted—that is, wherever it is found to disclose (or to resist disclosing) a pattern in the causal structure. I mean to emphasize rather that for any present consideration of the Nazi genocide, certain versions of its future are already clear—and that anticipation of these alternatives *as future* bears also on the present analysis of the genocide, which in another, all-too obvious sense is past or concluded.

To be sure, new information about the Nazi genocide will undoubtedly continue to be gathered. But future accounts are unlikely to be affected in a *radical* way by such additions—in part because the factor least likely to be changed by new findings is also the weightiest one—that is, the "disappearance" of between five and six million European Jews; in part because the pattern of future alternatives is a matter of logical as well as historical distinctions that are already visible. The pattern available to historiography in this convergence of historical and logical alternatives is clear: in the view from the future, the occurrence of the Nazi genocide will be affirmed, or it will be denied, or—between those possibilities—it will be reconceived in a way that defines a middle ground between the two.

There is, to be sure, nothing startling in this statement of alternatives (although this, too, attests to our familiarity with the alternatives as actual): affirmation, in institutions ranging from historical scholarship and artistic expression to the openly rhetorical forms of social incorporation in monuments and museums; denial, in the extreme form of exclusion, but also, more noncommittally, by those people who remain or who will be unknowing of its occurrence (the reference to "Holocaust" in E. D. Hirsch's itemization of knowledge required for "cultural literacy"—it appears there between "Sherlock Holmes" and "The Holy Grail"—vividly displays this precariousness); and then the reconceptualization, in the revisionist forms that press in from each of the two sides—from the side of denial, as the genocide is represented as a (perhaps) regrettable but in any event justifiable act of self-defense; from the side of affirmation in the view, for example, that the Jews were somehow the causal agents as well as victims in the genocide—that to a greater or lesser degree they brought their fate on themselves.[1]

What difference does it make to see these alternatives, already active in the present, as projected into the future? In one sense, this recommendation amounts to a variation on Kant's categorical imperative directed now at the historian: write the historical account of the Nazi genocide—this maxim goes—as though you were legislating every future view of its subject. Even this near-truism, however, might have consequences that are less than obvious. It has passed unnoted or at least undisputed, for example, that the reliance in contemporary forms of discourse (including history) on the experimental method of science, with the latter's *expectation* of future revisions, has substantive and not only rhetorical implications for the way what is written is formulated. Even the most dogmatic or ideologically motivated writings have come to reflect this expectation; the results are evident in all the disciplines that have taken scientific discourse as their model—that is, in all the disciplines.

There is also, however, a subtler implication of the projection into the future that bears on representations of the Nazi genocide—and this is as a reminder that the events thus represented were indeed, fundamentally, historical. To envisage them in the present from the point of view of the future makes it more difficult to conceive those events *in their own time* as not having posed a question to the future. It underscores, in other words, their status as contingent rather than necessary, involving factors that may be too extensive to enumerate but not too extensive to conceive and that thus include the element of human agency with its accompanying implication of individual and/or corporate responsibility. It is not that this historical factor would otherwise be indiscernible—but that to view the events from the perspective of the future underscores the role of contingency, which, because of the pressure of "hard" facts, is often elided, if not simply denied, in historical writing—in writing about the Nazi genocide hardly less than elsewhere.

To be sure, anomalous events may occur historically as they do biologically; furthermore, many historians of the Nazi genocide already avoid claims of its "uniqueness" or the related assertion of its "incomprehensibility"—claims that have the effect, whether intended or not, of distancing the occurrence of the genocide from history altogether. But the importance of addressing the events of the Nazi genocide as historical, with the justification for this not only in its material causes but also in its superstructure—in the language it created and employed, in its moral and ideological conceptualization—warrants continued emphasis because of the danger of the alternative. In this sense, such emphasis outweighs even the danger that with historicization, the Nazi genocide may come to seem so normalized, so thinly dispersed in the *alltäglich* world, that any attempt to distinguish it then as having *unusual* historical importance becomes open to question as a matter of principle as well as of fact.

What this proposal comes to in practice is this: that from the point of view of the future—on a modal conception of history that includes possibility and contingency as categories—the work of the historian in detailing the events of the Nazi genocide is itself contingent, with the historian, through his or her writing, present now as agent. The historian is in this sense responsible for his historical representation—a claim that would convey only a verbal platitude and indifferent moral weight if not for the fact that it links the writer of history to the ascription of responsibility *within* the events that he writes about. Insofar as the events of the genocide are now known largely through accounts of the historians, with the factor of contingency evident both in those representations and in the events represented, the historian shares in the responsibility found (or denied) there. From the standpoint of the historian, this becomes a condition of his own future, now joined to the future of the events that are his subject.

2

A second, more specific reason for considering the future of the Nazi genocide as a means of facing it in the present is that the turn in this direction poses unavoidably the question of *which* history (or histories) the Nazi genocide is to be viewed as part of. Formulated in this way, the question suggests an intrinsic perspectivalism for the writing of history ("*which* history?"); and at the level of practice, this conception of historiography as characteristically pluralistic seems unexceptionable. Without judging whether history can ever claim more than this (for example, as intending history "in itself"), and even admitting the approximate boundaries of "particular" histories, it is evident that distinctions among such particular histories are commonly assumed. The place of the Nazi genocide in the context of Jewish history will differ in its proportions (not necessarily as incompatible, but as different) from its representation in a history of Germany or in a history of Russia, and still more, and more obviously, from that in a history of Madagascar. The literary categories of implied author or authorial point of view make a scholarly difference in these instances; this difference is further accentuated in historical accounts of the Nazi genocide which embed it, not in national or ethnic frameworks, but in contexts defined topically or conceptually, for example, in the histories of rhetoric or of socialism or of demography—in all of which the Nazi genocide has a place.

The means for identifying such particular histories are not a priori or fixed, but the conventions they depend on are substantial enough to indicate that they are not arbitrary. I propose here to relate the events of the Nazi genocide to another of these histories, which is in certain respects more problematic than the ones mentioned, but whose subject has arguably been more constant and consequential a presence than anything the other histories have been histories "of". This is the history of moral judgment and conduct—more restrictively, the side of that history that I would represent as the history of evil. It is in relation to the latter history, I shall be suggesting, that a view of the future of the Holocaust becomes more portentous for its—and our—present.

This formulation may seem to have jumped ahead of the argument by several steps, and these need to be mentioned, at least to the extent that they presuppose a concept of evil itself. Without claiming this definition as adequate, I shall be supposing here a conception of evil in which harm is done to a person or group deliberately and without putative justification—that is, with the consciousness of it as a wrong. Without ascribing specific measures of responsibility, furthermore, it will be assumed that this general conception of evil applies to the corporate "act" and to individual agents of the Nazi genocide. Notwithstanding disagreements about the status of the intentions or of the deliberation involved in that genocide, *some* acknowledgment of their relevance is admitted in all but the extreme accounts that deny its occurrence altogether. And for purposes of the discussion here, even a minimal acknowledgment of this relevance provides a basis for relating the two phrases joined in this chapter's title.

To link the question "What is the future of the Holocaust?" to the history of evil encounters a significant obstacle in the second phrase of that proposal as well as in the first. For it is by no means obvious that there *is* a history of evil—and some evidence argues strongly to the contrary. One item of prima facie evidence is especially notable here: that, in point of fact, no histories of the phenomenon or occurrence of evil have been written—not of evil as historical idea or as practice, not in terms of its evolution or development, not even in the simplest form of chronicle. In contrast to specific institutions such as slavery, warfare, and means of punishment, and in contrast to such related (inverse) ideals as natural rights, freedom, or even love, all of which have been recognized as "having" histories or as being part of other histories, evil has not been viewed as a historical phenomenon at all.

This denial, again, is no more than prima facie evidence: the fact that no history of evil has been written does not prove that there is no history there to be written. But the explanation of this lacuna defines the requirements that must be met for something to "have" a history—and also the way in which evil (allegedly) fails to meet them. There are, it seems to me, two principal reasons why evil has not been conceived historically—why philosophers, theologians, and imaginative writers (and then the historians "proper") have regarded it as one of the small class of phenomena for which any representation as historical is so improbable as to deter even the attempt. These reasons are at once conceptual and moral; they correspond, in fact, to the two principal theories of moral evaluation in the history of ethics—moral judgment as determined by the intentions of the agent, and moral judgment as determined by the consequences of an act.

In the conception of history implied by intentionalist theories, the conditions for evil-doing are fully—and finally—realized in its first occurrence. From the standpoint of intentions, *how* an act turns out does not matter morally; it is the will to do wrong that counts, and in this sense—since the will is of one "kind"—all evil-doing is identical and thus complete. If the intention is present, the sometimes very large differences in consequence among particular acts do not enter in. To be sure, varied accounts are given of exactly what that common intention is; these range from the claim of an innate human impulse to one of a deliberate (but still common) project of the imagination. Overriding such differences in content, however, is the view of evil-doing in each occurrence as the exemplification of an original form. And in these terms, there is no reason to ascribe a history to evil, since evil is fully present *whenever* it appears, early or late, small or large.

The reference to an "original" form is an obvious echo of the most radical version of this view—that of "original sin," as it prefigures all other wrongdoing. Even a less dramatic reading of the "Fall"—such as the account of the events in Eden given by the Jewish tradition—argues to this same effect. For on the latter reading, too, knowledge of good and evil comes to Adam and Eve at a moment; neither they nor their descendants have more to learn about *that*—the knowledge itself appearing as both complete and irrevocable. Whatever else constitutes the moral knowledge thus acquired, two of its features are unmistakable: there is nothing to add to it, and there is no forgetting or escaping it.

It is not difficult to infer the motivation for this account in which history begins and ends in a single moment. Dominant in it are the issue of theodicy for the monotheistic traditions of religion and the analogous conflict between reason and wrongdoing for the rationalist tradition in philosophy: how to account for evil, given the existence (in the former) of a beneficent God, in the latter, of a reality that is essentially rational. In the end, no resolution may be possible in either of these accounts, and the rationalist tradition is forthright in conceding this when (as in Plato, for example) it flatly denies the reality of evil. Even when, in the biblical narrative, the existence of evil is acknowledged, moreover, it is located at a single historical point—presumably on the grounds that the difficulty in explaining one moment would only be compounded if there were other ones to explain as well. This practical reason joins a second, more substantive assumption—that a single and common ground is decisive in all evil-doing, namely, the intention or will to do it. Insofar as the latter serves as the necessary and sufficient condition for evil-doing, the explanation it provides for any particular instance of evil applies in principle to *all* its occurrences. In these terms a narrative that details a number of instances of wrongdoing would, nonetheless, be irrelevant as history, since those instances would be only variations on a single theme.

The disposition of the second—utilitarian or consequentialist—argument against ascribing a history to evil is related to the first. To measure evil-doing by its consequences requires an inclusive moral calculus into which any possible consequence can be translated. The difficulty of formulating a calculus that is both general and specific enough to cover the multiplicity of human actions has, however, proved formidable. One source of the difficulty, again, is itself a moral judgment. There is an obvious difference between an act that causes the destruction of one life and another that causes two deaths, a difference that becomes larger as the numbers increase. But it might nonetheless be objected that to measure degrees of evil by such numerical differences denies the value ascribed to any single life and challenges the basis of value itself: is *quantity* the decisive feature in judging the "quality" of evil? Few utilitarians other than Bentham have been willing to accept the implications of this claim; and the reluctance to do so has had the effect of flattening the dimensions necessary for a history of evil. Here, too, that potential history is undermined at its source.

3

These plausible reasons for denying the history of evil do not, however, outweigh other grounds for asserting such history as real. It is these other grounds and a conceptual framework based on them that connect the "future of the Holocaust" to an understanding of the Holocaust in the present. This connection becomes apparent on both "external" and "internal" readings (and writings) of history.[2] In external history, the subject, judged from the outside to have a fixed identity or "self", appears in different historical settings which disclose that identity more fully. It is in this sense that evolutionary histories are written of biological organisms; accounts such as the histories of language or of medicine are also conceived in these terms.

The last of these examples provides a useful analogue to the history of evil. The goal or "final cause" of medicine—the maintenance or recovery of health—is the center around which its history turns; the written history of medicine is then an external—metaphorically, a technological—rendering of the means devised over time to reach the end assumed in them all. In the case of medicine, this history is often regarded as progressive (based, for example, on life expectancy); in other external histories—for example, in the history of art—the pertinence of a progressive ("whiggish") interpretation is itself a theoretical issue. Whether a particular external history is judged to be cumulative or not, however, the identity of the historical subject is presupposed, with the written account then detailing variations over time in its appearance and their connections to other histories.

Does evil have a history in this "external" sense? Admittedly, it is more difficult to identify here than for other histories individual events that serve as chronological markers (and thus as evidence that there *is* a history). But for evil, too, individual factors are distinguishable within the concept of violation or transgression—in motivation, in the role of intention or premeditation, in the conceptualization of the victim; it is also possible to identify differences among these factors as they occur *historically*. Consider, for example, the following statement made about the Nazi genocide against the Jews by Himmler in a secret speech to the SS at Poznan in October 1943:

> The hard decision had to be made that this people should be caused to disappear from the earth. . . . I myself believe that it is better for us—us together—to have borne this for our people, that we have taken the responsibility for it on ourselves (the responsibility for an act, not just an idea), and that we should now take this secret with us into the grave.[3]

On the face of it, this complex statement is dispassionate, reflective. According to it, the "Final Solution" was indeed intended as genocide—the "disappearance" of "this people." It was, moreover, intended selflessly, not for personal gain but as a matter of principle. The principle itself remains unstated in the immediate context, and Himmler acknowledges that in "act and idea," it may be so difficult for others to comprehend (even German compatriots) that it ought to remain a secret permanently—further evidence of the selflessness required. The totality of the "Final Solution," in other words, is meant to encompass the fact of the event itself.

Comparisons are always to some extent tendentious. But it is not tendentiousness that distinguishes Himmler's words from (for example) the statements that Suetonius attributes to Caligula or to Nero, who stand out among the Twelve Caesars and in history since for their regimes of terror and brutality. Himmler's statement is a moral world apart from the latter, distinguished even in its own terms by its "principled" basis. It differs from the professions of Caligula or of Nero by as much as does selflessness from egoism, as totality from partiality, as genocide from murder—even murder on a large scale.

I do not mean to suggest that the historical distance between these examples is impassible, that there are no later echoes of the chronologically earlier one or earlier anticipations of the later one; obviously there are cases even in antiquity, as in Cato's call for the destruction of Carthage, that come close to the ethos expressed by Himmler. But for that, too, as more clearly in the other example, there is a significant difference in the imagination of evil that is asserting itself. It is probably too extreme to claim that Himmler's statement *could* not have been uttered at the time of the Roman caesars or of Cato; but a good measure of the difference between Himmler's intention and that of the others is indeed historical—a function both of changes in the material context and also, more fundamentally, in the conceptualization of evil itself. That the difference is indeed historical is further substantiated by the fact that the changes which thus appear are not only differences in the external sense of variations on a theme—but also *internal*, as they reflect an intensification or fuller realization of their subject, that is, of evil. The debate continues on whether the Nazi genocide is indeed the first historical instance of genocide; but it cannot be reasonably doubted that the "Final Solution" was indeed an instance of genocide. Nor can it be doubted—and this is more important for the claim of a history of evil—that as a phenomenon genocide is a more dominant presence for social existence in the twentieth century than it ever was before. And in connection with this, Himmler's statement, although distinctive even in its own context, epitomizes a more general, and also distinctive, change.

A similar claim, although only indirectly related to Himmler's statement, applies to the phenomenon of torture, as that, too, stands as a representation of evil. Even allowing for the increase in populations, and the means of historical reporting, the evidence suggests that the occurrence of torture in the twentieth century exceeds that in any previous historical period. There is probably no way of fully establishing this comparison, but the implications of its claim gain in force when joined to the fact that what served earlier as a utilitarian "justification" for torture (i.e., the perceived need to obtain information) has been increasingly displaced in the twentieth century by the availability of new technology.

Given such chronological differences, not only does evil appear then to "have" an external history—varying in its proportions over time—but a history that is arguably a progressivist one as well, in which the twentieth century has "advanced" over previous ones. And in that "advance," marked in its most recent stage by the phenomena of genocide and the gratuitousness of torture, the "Final Solution" is a significant datum.

A second sense in which a subject might have a history is "internal"—where the subject has no fixed identity or essence, where its character changes and yet remains recognizable, and where the *process* of this development then defines the subject historically. The development involved here is much like that of a consciousness seen to deliberate on the future in light of its past— as in the historical genres of biography or autobiography. There is something problematic, to be sure, about citing a "consciousness" that impels historical events where the agent is not a person. But in these broader contexts as well, the metaphorical reference to an internal identity is often useful. To write English parliamentary history or the history of the American Civil War requires taking account of decisions by individuals, and there is no need to posit a *literal* corporate consciousness in order to represent the sum of those decisions metaphorically. (There is an obvious danger—the more notable in respect to the Nazi genocide—in attributing a corporate essence to an historical subject, e.g., as in categories like "French history" or "German history".) Individual agents who contribute to group decisions or acts introduce the element of contingency and with this the unfolding of corporate decisions as *like* the history of a self. Like the latter, the former are at once contingent—not determined externally—and deliberate: affecting change in their own character without denying its identity. It is in these terms also that we speak of the history of artistic movements like realism or romanticism, or of the history of ideologies such as Marxism or liberalism.

And so, too, I should argue, for the history of evil. Consider again the comparison cited earlier. The difference between the representation of the Nazi genocide in Himmler's statement, and Suetonius' account of murder and torture under the Caesars is— the common horror notwithstanding—a world apart; it is much sharper, in any event, than the quantitative disparity that is also evident. More fundamentally, the difference involves a reconceptualization of the subject itself—recognizable in the familiar distinction between extrinsic and intrinsic "goods" or purposes. For in Himmler's statement, and in the act of genocide it refers to, the goal intended is not designated as the means to another end, still less as a matter of personal interest or desire—both of which dominated the acts of Nero or Caligula. In it, what is undertaken becomes a matter of principle—chosen deliberately, not just to accomplish a particular end but also with an awareness of its quality *as* evil. Here evil, perversely, becomes part of the intrinsic "good"; in this sense, it resembles the ideal proclaimed by Milton's Satan, "Evil, Be thou my good!"—now expressed, however, by a human, not a mythical agent.

Admittedly, to demonstrate this distinction in terms of the Nazi genocide requires more evidence than is provided by the statement quoted from Himmler. Certainly, the opposing claim has often been made and could, in fact, draw on Himmler's speech itself: that the "Final Solution" was conceived by the Nazis instrumentally, for what they "perceived"—wrongly and criminally, but nonetheless "honestly"—as the means to another end, in the interests of the German people and, at a longer distance still, in the interests of mankind. On this account, the Nazis at least *believed* that the Jews were a threat, socially and racially; Nazi policies would then have been the means of averting this threat—a form of self-defense—which ought now to be judged with that putatively mitigating consideration in mind.

Against this defense, the argument has to be made: that the Nazis often, even in their own terms, acted *against* instrumental considerations; that neither their campaign of extermination against the Jews nor the means employed is adequately explained on instrumental grounds alone, nor can their willingness to risk losing the more general war in order to carry on that campaign; that the imagination and will for evil which characterized the means used—the rarified intentions evident in such creations as orchestras in the death camps, the edifying slogans that were part of those camps (such as *"Arbeit macht frei"* at the entrance to Auschwitz), the imaginative means of degradation that invariably accompanied the act of extermination (what Primo Levi refers to as "useless violence")—are inexplicable on utilitarian grounds alone.[4] Perhaps most important among these considerations is the emphasis on secrecy that figures in Himmler's speech and that was a constant aspect of the "Final Solution"—in the "language rules" governing public and even private references to the genocide, and in the extraordinary efforts to conceal or to destroy the evidence of its occurrence. This might be explained on prudential or utilitarian grounds—but the same evidence could be construed as involuntary, in the form of shame, an awareness of the wrong being done and an incorporation of that wrongfulness then in the act itself.

It seems to me that the evidence for the latter contention is strong—sufficiently strong, in any event, to ensure that the claim for a conception of the evil at work here as based on "principle" becomes at least as plausible as the instrumental explanation that is more commonly given. And to take the matter even that far introduces a significant marker in the "internal" history of evil— where evil has moved from extrinsic or instrumental acts to acts undertaken in the name of principle, where a decision has been made for the practice of evil with the recognition that it is evil. As with any historical shift, it is not necessary to demonstrate that this one came into existence fully formed, that there were no anticipations of it. It is enough to recognize that in the general historical context of occurrences of evil, the Nazi genocide epitomizes, if it does not disclose for the first time, a radical possibility that was, in its historical setting, so deliberate and deeply rooted that it cannot be written off or explained away as an aberration. It is better understood as evidence of another stage—conceptually as well as chronologically—in the history of evil. The evidence that evil indeed has a history thus also provides a standard by which the particular events that constitute that history can be assessed.

4

Even if everything proposed so far were granted for the sake of argument, with the Nazi genocide viewed now from the standpoint of the future, in the context of the history of evil—the question would still persist of what difference this makes to an understanding of the Nazi genocide in the present. And in one obvious sense, nothing *in* those events would have been altered: the motives, the strategies, the numbers remain the same. But two implications emerge that do bear on the representation of the Nazi genocide—past, present, and future. The first refers to the place of the genocide "in" the history of evil; here the danger that the genocide might simply be absorbed as only another item in a lengthy and harsh sequence of events is balanced by a conflicting possibility that requires the conception of an evolving history of evil. There would be both reason and desperation in the claim that with the Nazi genocide, the internal history of evil had at once been asserted and found its end—that this history was now complete, reaching a boundary by which any future instance of evil would be measured. Like the limit set by the speed of light, an outer limit would now have been defined for moral violation. Other instances of wrongdoing would henceforth be assessed in relation to this end point. Even with this conclusion, however, evil would at least have *had* a history, the Nazi genocide standing as both a literal and symbolic marker within it.

The hope that this should indeed be the case joins a sense of moral horror to a conception of history: *Could* there, among the possibilities of evil-doing, be a more extreme exemplification than that of acting on evil as a principle? And yet, the context of history in which that question now arises also compels recognition that this difficulty, too, is historical—a practical deferral that is itself subordinate to the imagination's distinctiveness as unpredictable. Insofar as evil is subject to the work of the imagination, we know enough to be wary of predictions of its end—of the claim that there is nothing more that the imagination can imagine.

The basis for this caution is more than an acknowledgment of logical possibilities. Aristotle formulated a conception of justice that a number of philosophers have plausibly transposed into contemporary terms—although he himself found no incompatibility between that conception and the practice of slavery, which its more recent versions reject. As his original conception came to be further defined in its later explication, a similar process may also apply to evil in *its* role as principle. It is more than only a truism to say here with Edgar in *King Lear* (turning his meaning slightly), "The worst is not so long as we can say this is the worst." To ask about the "future of the Holocaust," then, is also to recognize this other possibility of further "development"—a possibility that in no way diminishes the enormity evident in the Nazi genocide. One might argue, in fact, that to insist on viewing the genocide within the context of the history of evil makes its enormity more unavoidable than it is in those other accounts which, displacing it from history, tend also to obscure its moral significance.

A second aspect of the future of the Holocaust is also apparent, once the present and the future are related to each other in the framework of the history of evil. This is the alteration of moral consciousness which, as a consequence of the Nazi genocide, now marks the present and future off from the past, altering the history of evil in a way that affects the social history of mankind more generally. As Cain's murder of Abel symbolized a new and literal fact of social existence, one that would thereafter be a constant element in the construal of all human relations and institutions, so the events of the Holocaust and the act of genocide at their center articulate a fact that can now never be absent from considerations of social or moral existence, however unaware or indifferent people may be individually to those events. Genocide informs the future with a new and now constant imminence; to think seriously of the future is also to recognize this one among its grounds in the present.

In this sense, the history of the Holocaust is fixed, beyond the reach even of the extreme efforts of historical revision. For there, too, the phenomenon of genocide has become real. The revisionists deny that the Nazi genocide occurred—not the enormity it would have been if it *had* (sic) occurred. A premise of the revisionists, too, in other words, is the evil in genocide; also for them, willing or not, the possibility of what they deny is undeniable. Through the memories incorporated in social institutions, moreover—for example, in the United Nations Convention on the Crime and Prevention of Genocide—the prospect of the future is held up to constant view. The role of the mark of Cain that was intended to symbolize the evil that one person could do to another by murder is usurped now by genocide—as the victims of evil become not individuals but groups, and groups that are defined not by an act of their members (individually or collectively), but externally, by the same force that would then destroy them. No less importantly, the premeditation that is only a possible feature of individual murder appears as a necessary condition for genocide: here knowledge and the will meet. The mark of Cain was meant at once to identify the murderer and to preserve his life in order to attest to that identity. There is yet no equivalent mark of genocide: the division between the two Germanies that had served as an analogous symbol has been erased (although the uneasiness stirred by this change attests to its role as symbol). For the present, then, memory must serve as its own mark—but this itself can be assured only if evil does indeed have a history and only if the Holocaust itself has a future.

Michael R. Marrus

The Use and Misuse of the Holocaust

ABOUT A DECADE AGO, JEWISH SCHOLARS AND WRITERS BEGAN TO worry in print about the burgeoning interest in the Holocaust, and posed troubling questions about how the Jewish tragedy was becoming part of North American popular culture. These critics brooded upon the new interest in the Holocaust in literature and film that emerged, remarkably, during the 1970s. That decade saw the first in a series of new Holocaust-related institutions, among them a commission set up by the president of the United States, the publication of several important and controversial fictional accounts of the subject, as well as the showing, in the spring of 1978, of Gerald Green's dramatization *Holocaust* on four consecutive evenings of prime-time television. Concerns were raised at the time, not only about the impact on the public at large, but also about the effects on North American Jews. Were these fears justified, and have events borne out the concerns raised in the early 1980s? And a related question: To what extent have public presentations of the Holocaust taken account of the evolution in our historical understanding of the destruction of European Jewry in the work of scholars and researchers over the past twenty years or so?

A word, to begin, about context. The controversy raised over the possible implications of the popularization or the "academicization" of the Holocaust is a largely North American phenomenon, distinct from other debates, such as the *Historikerstreit* in the Federal Republic of Germany or recent confrontations in France and Poland about how the Nazi era and the massacre of European Jews should be understood. Although, as we shall see, the views of outsiders have certainly had an impact in North America, controversy here derives from a set of circumstances not generally found elsewhere—the widespread exposure of Holocaust themes in the mass media, the proliferation of university courses on the subject, the energetic involvement of Jewish community institutions, and the emergence of numerous projects for commemorative memorials and museums.

For the Holocaust to have entered the world of popular culture was particularly problematic for those with direct experience of these events. Some felt this burst of activity as a painful invasion of a private sphere, involving an unacceptable trivialization. Others were apprehensive about a presumed unhealthy fascination with the Nazi era, a continuation, it was suggested, of the original hold that Hitler had upon his followers in times past.[1] Elie Wiesel, chairman of the president's Holocaust Commission, but a lonely writer on the subject in the late 1950s, was himself ambivalent. Previously, he told one interviewer, nobody wanted to talk about the Holocaust. "Now everybody does, so I don't want to speak." Wiesel now decried the "desacralizing" of unspeakable suffering. Once the gas chambers were portrayed by NBC before 220 million Americans, he asked, why should others not try their hand—including well-meaning school teachers, eager to recreate the "experience" of the Holocaust for their students? Where would it stop, he wondered?[2] Some commentators deplored the distortions of fact evident in much of the public presentation of the Holocaust, deformations intended to serve sometimes questionable literary or political purposes. Alvin Rosenfeld identified some particularly egregious instances of this process, implying that, quite apart from matters of taste, the general understanding of the Holocaust was still much too fragile to permit "a transposition of erotic and aesthetic motives onto a landscape of slaughter."[3] In a much more polemical vein, Edward Alexander denounced the "stealing of the Holocaust"—the appropriation, often by the use of metaphor, of Holocaust terminology and images for a sometimes nefarious anti-Jewish objective.[4] Holocaust, he implied, should remain the property of the Jews.

Reflecting on this trend in a widely read article in *Commentary*, Robert Alter suggested that "serious distortions of the Holo-

caust itself and, what is worse, of Jewish life occur when the Holocaust is commercialized, theologized, or academicized—all of
which processes seem to be occurring today in varying degree and
manner."[5] Alter deplored the way in which the experience of victimization was in danger of supplanting other aspects of Jewish
identity, forming the core of a "civil religion" of American Jewry.
Jacob Neusner, one of the first to sound the alarm, referred deri-
sively to "Holocaustomania," the clear result of which was the
impoverishment of Jewish spiritual life. He deplored the way in
which Jewish public discourse, heavily imprinted with Holocaust
themes, had become "corrupted by sentimentality, emotionalism
and bathos."[6] Neusner's principal concern was the dilution of Jewish faith and commitment. But like others he also feared the abandonment by many Jews of a sense of proportion in approaching
the outside world. Rabbi Harold Schulweis deplored the "Manichean metaphysics" associated with the politicization of the Holocaust, the division of the world into "'them' and 'us,' 'goyim' and
'Jews,' . . . they, the predictable persecutors; we, the inevitable victims." "I fear the fallout from the catastrophic thinking," he went
on. "For if we teach our children that the whole world seeks our
destruction, if we teach them that the whole world always has, still
does and always will hate us, we visit the iniquity of a paralyzing
cynicism upon the third and fourth generations."[7]

Where are we now, a decade later? There can be no doubt that
"Holocaust" has entered the bloodstream of North American popular culture, in striking contrast to its absence in previous decades.
"It is not far-fetched to assume," writes one researcher in 1988,
"that a majority of the [American] population has obtained much
of its knowledge of the Holocaust from television"—the popular
medium par excellence.[8] The output of books and films has, by
some accounts, reached a saturation point. University courses continue to proliferate, served by textbooks, periodicals, specially produced instructional films, documentary anthologies, and collec-
tions of articles. The 1988 *Directory of Holocaust Institutions*
published by the United States Holocaust Memorial Council con-
tains 98 listings, and plans are under way for three major Holocaust
museums—in New York, Washington, and Los Angeles. Commemorative events and days of remembrance have become part of
the national ceremonial landscape. A 144-page guide to such ob-

servances has now appeared with the imprimatur of the Pentagon, destined for the five million members of the U.S. armed forces, around the world.[9]

In a statement introducing the second edition of this volume, President George Bush makes an optimistic claim that contrasts strikingly with the warnings we have heard: "We Americans... know all too well the horrors of the Holocaust. On the Mall in Washington, a museum is taking shape to help share that knowledge with those who visit our nation's capital. And in scores of communities across the country, our citizens are sharing in similar projects of education and commemoration. . . . Memory is our duty to the past, and it is our duty to the future. Let us strive to communicate the critical message to all: 'Never Again.'"[10] But unfortunately, soundings of American public opinion do not entirely confirm the president's assessment.

When President Ronald Reagan's visit to the German military cemetery in Bitburg in the spring of 1985 generated extensive public debate in the United States, opinion polls suggested a deeply split American public, hardly one united around themes of commemoration and "Never Again." The signals sent out by the affair were certainly confusing. A *New York Times/CBS* survey suggested that Americans were evenly divided over the visit, with 41 percent in favor and the same number opposed. Similar results emerged from a *Washington Post/ABC* poll, tilting slightly, however, toward disapproval.[11] Apparently, Bitburg generated a minor anti-Jewish reaction. Responding to a question posed by the *New York Times/CBS* pollsters as to whether "Jewish leaders in the United States protested too much over [Reagan's] visit," a substantial 38 percent agreed, including 60 percent of those who supported the visit and 18 percent of those who opposed it.

Other surveys in 1985 and 1986 tested American opinion about Nazi war criminals, sometimes asking questions directly related to the Holocaust. A Harris Poll revealed that 42 percent agreed that "Jews should stop complaining about what happened to them in Nazi Germany," and in a Roper survey 40 percent declared that "Jews should stop focusing on the Holocaust." On war criminals, 49 percent felt that the matter should be "put . . . behind us," while 41 percent thought that the search should continue.[12]

At least one-third of Americans seem to resent the periodic references to the Holocaust in public life, and tend to attribute these to unwarranted Jewish pressure or influence. More evidence came in 1986 with the controversy over Austrian presidential candidate Kurt Waldheim, and the barring of Waldheim, once elected, from entering the United States. According to a Louis Harris survey, 51 percent of Americans supported the ban on Waldheim, and 34 percent opposed it. A substantial number of those with an opinion (49 percent) believed the charges against the Austrian leader. But when asked whether they thought the charges against Waldheim were genuinely new, or were raised to keep him from getting elected, only 31 percent thought they were new, and 38 percent believed "that they were an election tactic by Jewish groups, such as the World Jewish Congress." Harris himself concluded that "there is some evidence of fairly widespread resentment against those who brought the charges."[13] Another Harris poll, of two Middle Western states, commissioned by the Anti-Defamation League (ADL), revealed that 42 percent resisted being told about what happened to the Jews in Nazi-occupied Europe. Reflecting soberly on the results of such surveys, Dennis Klein, director of the ADL International Center for Holocaust Studies, suggested that "we now live with a surfeit of awareness of the Nazi past. This suggests that memories can just as easily inundate as illuminate."[14]

However interpreted, these polls show a widespread American disinclination to join the dignitaries in remembrance and awe-inspired contemplation of the destruction of European Jewry. More indication of this trend comes from the persistent and partially successful campaign against the U.S. Justice Department's Office of Special Investigations, waged by certain American pressure groups. Created in 1977 in order to identify and deport U.S. residents or citizens guilty of Nazi war crimes, this office has managed a relatively small number of deportations, despite energetic and highly professional activity, and has seen its operations significantly trimmed without substantial public outcry. All in all, it is by no means clear that the general community has been significantly sensitized by the dissemination of Holocaust themes. To the contrary, there is some suggestion, as yet unproven, of backlash.

More pertinent, in view of the explicit warnings of ten years ago, is the impact upon the Jewish world of the substantial attention given the Holocaust since the end of the 1970s. On the surface, there is reason for satisfaction. Holocaust centers and museums continue to proliferate. Publications, media presentations, symposia, and conferences have provided an ever more sophisticated and learned encounter with the Nazi era. A remarkable surge of consciousness among Holocaust survivors and their descendants has prompted renewed efforts to commemorate, to bear witness, and to understand. As one might expect, there are problems associated with the management of such enterprises—assuring high standards of accuracy, taste, and balance in the public presentation of Holocaust themes. Politics also intrudes, shaping the interpretation of the Holocaust to suit particular interests and constituencies. Commenting on the American situation recently, the director of Yad Vashem Museums noted "the dangers of faddism, trivialization, oversimplification, or the use of the Holocaust as a metaphor for all of society's ills."[15] Notably, he pointed to what has been called the "Americanization" of the Holocaust—seeing it, in the local idiom, "as an extreme example and outcome of prejudice, discrimination, and the denial of civil rights."

In another sense, Holocaust must be portrayed in a certain way because it has become a fundamental source of American Jews' identity—how they define themselves vis-à-vis other Americans—validated by nothing less than a presidential commission.[16] Since such commissions have not been founded for other groups, such as native people, blacks, or the victims of other massacres or genocide, supporters of the commission have developed a vested interest in establishing the Holocaust as "unique"—a point to which we shall presently return. Worse, political exigencies lend weight to certain historical explanations over others, and even provide standing, occasionally, to easily detectable errors of fact. Yehuda Bauer has recently identified one such case—the frequent reference by Jews to a death toll of four million at Auschwitz, of whom 2.5 million were Jews—somehow seen as "more" catastrophic than the figure of 1,350,000 Jewish deaths (with a much smaller number of Poles than in the former computation) most widely accepted among specialists.[17] Clearly "relevance," in such cases, a clarion call of the 1960s to which legislators and public-spirited citizens still are eager to respond, can seriously warp the presentation of the historical past.

Doubtless some of these problems can be addressed with sufficient funding and expertise, as well as the necessary diplomacy to deal with public authorities. Deeper reservations persist, however, and may be less easily resolved. Like any community project, Holocaust memorials and museums become the vehicles of group needs and interests, some of which have nothing to do with the Holocaust.[18] Local rivalries play their part, as does the quest for standing among individuals, institutions, denominations, municipalities, and states. The end result may be a debasing of the coinage of memory as memorial structures proliferate and as the controls of good taste and historical accuracy become too thinly stretched. An Israeli visitor who had seen one memorial flame too many is reported to have muttered irreverently, during one visit, about *"Sho'ah flambé."*

A perennial difficulty is the manner in which Jewish presentations of the Holocaust may be distorted by what Jacob Neusner has called "the salvific myth," the idea that the Holocaust must be understood as a period of torment and disaster prior to redemption—realized in the achievement of the State of Israel.[19] For Israeli Jews this way of looking at the past reflects authentically upon their national experience, but for American Jews it does not. American Jews, after all, and many survivors among them, do not participate in the redemption that the myth prescribes. Holocaust museums, therefore, like the one soon to arise in Battery Park in New York, often purport to teach "the lessons of renewal and redemption" upon which American Jews have chosen not to act.[20] In what way, therefore, can the "lessons" so prescribed really be lessons at all?

Perhaps sensitive to such contradictions, some Jewish leaders continue to lament what British Chief Rabbi Lord Immanuel Jacobovits has called "the sanctification of the Holocaust as a cardinal doctrine in contemporary Jewish thought and teaching." In a concern that certainly echoed across the Atlantic, Jacobovits recently told a conference that Jews "must beware against nurturing and breeding a Holocaust mentality of morose despondency among our people, especially our youth."[21] To some degree this view echoes a much earlier apprehension, common immediately after the war, that dwelling upon the Holocaust would only further injure Jewish self-esteem and self-confidence. In a sensitive discussion of the Jews' inescapable "malformed consciousness" Irving Howe continues to meditate on this problem.[22] Yet others have made the point that Jews have no choice. Jews cannot help but come to terms with their catastrophic past and must, in the end, conquer the shame that is frequently associated with victimization through an understanding of what happened in those years. Put otherwise, Jewish memory is a way of keeping faith with the dead and those who have survived, making sure that their terrible suffering is not forgotten. Memory of the Holocaust, says Alvin Rosenfeld, "places primary historical and moral demands upon us, to which we must not fail to respond."[23]

Has the work of the past ten years served these ends? An evaluation may well turn upon the answer to the question: Holocaust consciousness, for what? The decade has seen mixed results within the Jewish world and, from my point of view, both disturbing and encouraging tendencies. It is perhaps too early to make an evaluation, for many of the initiatives referred to at the beginning of this chapter have still to run their course. Still, some trends seem inescapable.

One of these must surely be the growing inclination to "invoke" the Holocaust in order to serve political objectives—largely, though not exclusively, associated with particular Israeli policies.[24] Of course, what Philip Lopate has aptly called the *reductio ab Hitler* argument has always been with us.[25] "Nazism," writes Saul Friedländer, "has become one of the supreme metaphors, that of Evil."[26] But it seems to me that the more specific reference to the massacre of European Jews is relatively recent. The temptation to have recourse to it seems irresistible and not necessarily informed by anti-Jewish objectives—two particularly egregious instances that I have noted recently being a *New York Times* op-ed piece on the "Ecological Kristallnacht" and a call for the wearing of yellow Stars of David in support of Salman Rushdie.

In one view, the invocation of the Holocaust in attacks upon certain Jewish positions betrays a thinly disguised antisemitism—a crowning insult to Jews that could only be motivated by a profound, deep-seated hatred of the Jewish people. Some claim that the Holocaust analogy is one of the principal means by which antisemitism enters popular discourse. This approach highlights media campaigns against Israel and Israeli policies that have made free use of Nazi metaphors. There is no doubt that such tendencies have moved into the mainstream of Western press commentary, particularly since the 1982 Israeli invasion of Lebanon. Certain revisionist currents in Holocaust history also seem interested in portraying an association of Jews and the Third Reich. Thus writers like Rosemary Radforth Ruether and Herman Ruether, once sympathetic toward Jews, now reinterpret Zionism as a handmaiden of Nazism in a transparent effort to delegitimize the Jewish state.[27]

But Jews too invoke, and misuse, the Holocaust—now more than ever, I believe. Until recently, I would venture, such references were sparing within the Jewish world and certainly rare among Jewish leaders of international standing. Israeli prime minister Menachem Begin, for reasons possibly related as much to his personal biography as an escapee from Nazism as to his Revisionist Zionist ideology, set a new standard. In his denunciation of the Middle East policies of European countries in 1980 and in his extravagant attack on West German chancellor Helmut Schmidt the following year, Begin broke the earlier taboo, accompanying his partisan attacks with gratuitous declarations of wartime complicity.[28] During the Lebanese War there came his notorious likening of Arafat, under siege in Beirut, to Hitler in his bunker in Berlin. Prime Minister Yitzhak Shamir has followed suit. In a recent interview with Arnaud de Borchgrave, editor of the *Washington Times,* Shamir likened Arafat to Hitler, because "they belong to the same family of demagogues and totalitarians, enemies of the Jewish people, men who think nothing of killing millions to achieve their objectives."[29]

These and subsequent declarations, it seems likely, have helped remove substantial Jewish inhibitions outside Israel upon invoking the Holocaust for political purposes. The intention behind such usage is transparent—to energize political argument, at the seemingly small cost of stretching a point. For example, in a full-page advertisement in the *New York Times* supporting the Israeli government's "Solidarity Conference" in Jerusalem in April 1989, the Simon Wiesenthal Center likened calls for compromise with Palestinians to Munich and the abandonment of Czechoslovakia in 1938. "Instead of peace," the center's statement pointedly went on, "the West found war and eventually the horrors that led to Auschwitz." Underscoring, the text then went on to identify a presumably exemplary member of the PLO, one Fuzi Salim Ali Madi, "whose code name is Abu Hitler and who named his two sons Eichmann and Hitler."[30] At the "Solidarity Conference" it-self, at which American Jews predominated, the "lessons of the Holocaust" were frequently intoned. To be sure, such invocations usually contain only the most general exhortations as to policy—such as press baron Robert Maxwell's vacuous insight that "we cannot betray those who died by risking the lives of those who survived and descended from them."[31] But at least as important as the content of such hortatory messages was, and is, the image they project—of an embattled, weak, lonely, terrorized Holocaust vic-tim—that is intended to characterize the current Israeli reality. However distorted, this image registers with frightening clarity upon the contemporary Jewish consciousness.

I want to add that the misuse of the Holocaust is not a monop-oly of the Jewish right and that it is found elsewhere, if to a lesser degree. On the left, other causes prompt other distortions and other exaggerations—other variations, I believe, on the themes of Jewish vulnerability or the likely prospects of catastrophe. Thus the title of Yair Cotler's recent book, *Heil Kahane,* thus the polemical denunciation of Israeli occupation policies as leading to a *"Herren-volk* democracy," and thus recurrent calls among Diaspora Jews not to "keep silent" in the face of Israeli misdeeds with explicit refer-ence to the policies of bystanders during the Holocaust.

Behind these nightmarish associations I detect a powerful and widespread, if irrational, fear for the future of the Jewish people.[32] As is evident, most of this apprehension rivets upon Israel and what is seen as her hopelessly deteriorating standing in the world of nation-states, however interpreted. Without speculating too far in this vein, I would suggest that such fears, and the erosion of Jewish self-confidence upon which they rest, are stronger today than ever before since the end of the Second World War. Certainly the Palestinian uprising has fueled such apprehensions, presenting Israelis and Jews elsewhere with a problem that increasingly seems to them insoluble.[33]

As North American Jewry has become ever more divided on religious grounds and on matters related to Israel, there may be a

growing temptation to have recourse to the Holocaust as a sort of
ultimate weapon in argument—why not to assimilate, why to require unity (or a particular version of unity), why to donate funds
to this or that cause, or why to favor this or that Middle East policy.
At work in this manipulation of politics and catastrophe is what
some have called "the triumphalism of pain," the self-absorption
that so often accompanies suffering and victimization. For those
who are self-absorbed in this way, outside reality becomes blurred,
and sometimes ceases to exist; one's own rectitude is assured, and
the claims of others diminish or disappear. Self-righteousness is
the invariable result. Perhaps because they have confronted such
dispositions in their national culture, Israeli writers have been the
most acute in identifying and censuring this disposition. Here is
the novelist A. B. Yehoshua, for example: "We must bear in mind
that our having been victims does not accord us any special moral
standing. The victim does not become virtuous for having been a
victim. Although the Holocaust inflicted a great injustice upon us,
it does not grant us a certificate of everlasting righteousness. The
murderers were amoral; the victims were not made moral. To be
moral you must behave ethically. The test of that is daily and
constant."[34]

Seeking a remedy, the Israeli philosopher Adi Ophir calls for a
demythologizing of the Holocaust and a greater application to the
simple task of historical understanding. The problem, in his view,
is a Holocaust that has been "sanctified" and removed from all
other kinds of human tragedy and anguish. Absorbed into the
Jewish consciousness, and fashioned into a contemporary Jewish
identity, the present "Holocaust myth" not only does violence to
the past, it is dangerous for the present. It is dangerous, says
Ophir, "because it blurs the humanness of the Holocaust . . . because it makes it difficult to understand the Holocaust as the product of a human, material and ideological system; because it directs
us almost exclusively to the past, to the immortalization of that
which is beyond change, instead of pointing primarily to the future, to the prevention of a holocaust—like the one which was, or
another, more horrible—which is more possible today than ever
before but is still in the realm of that which is crooked and can still
be made straight."[35]

To be sure, it is practically impossible to counter the powerful images that move people in the present, particularly when they are fear-driven. In the long run, however, the passage of time seems likely to cool some of the passions associated with the Holocaust. Jewish community professionals in the United States have observed recently that the traditional playing upon Holocaust themes and the related sense of guilt toward contemporary Israel no longer work their magic among third- and fourth-generation American Jews. "The Holocaust experience is more removed for the new generation," one of them observed recently. "It doesn't have the same effect now. I will not put our people through the Yad Vashem wringer any more—taking them to the Holocaust museum just before we hold the caucus [for declaring donations]. You shouldn't treat people's emotions like this."[36] Media watchers have suggested that in the non-Jewish population, too, fascination with the Holocaust may have fallen off somewhat, and a more prudent, discriminating judgment of quality may govern what is to be shown in the future.[37]

More positively, I hope it will not sound self-serving for a historian to suggest that Holocaust history may help counter some of the abuses discussed here. Philip Lopate worries that a "'sensitivity' quotient operating around the Holocaust has begun to preclude any public discourse [about it] that goes beyond expressions of mourning and remorse."[38] But historians seek precisely to reduce or eliminate this "sensitivity" quotient in order to examine their subject. And few would deny that they have conducted that examination in recent years with considerable industry and success.[39] It seems to me that the increasing volume of Holocaust writing, its attendant professionalization as a field of study, and the growing integration of the Holocaust into the general stream of historical understanding contribute substantially to the demystification that Adi Ophir urges upon us. Little by little, such ways of thinking penetrate the public consciousness—just as the scholarly writing on the French Revolution has helped shape popular perceptions of the bicentennary of 1789. If true, this would be an ironic commentary on the fears of Robert Alter, ten years ago, about "naturalizing the horror by making it part of the curriculum." For whatever else it has done, the growing interest in the Holocaust within the academy has helped to generate substantial research and create a community of professional scholars able to speak knowledgeably about the matter. They, in turn, have entered the discourse within the Jewish world on the place of the Holocaust in the contemporary consciousness.

Let me offer one example, which I hope does not reflect over-optimistically on the process as a whole. A year ago saw the fiftieth anniversary of *Kristallnacht*. Since the event commemorated was not as widely known as, for example, the uprising of the Warsaw ghetto, media representatives and Jewish leaders consulted extensively with Holocaust historians about the public presentations that occurred. The results, I think, were salutary. To be sure, there were some gaffes—such as the presentation of the events being commemorated as "the beginning of the Holocaust." But more generally, from what I could see, the historians' assessments of the significance of the 1938 episode meshed constructively with the commemorative and ceremonial aspects of the occasion. An article in the *New York Times* judiciously summarized the findings of several researchers, and presented alternative historical explanations of the significance of the nationwide pogrom against the Jews of Germany and Austria.[40] PBS broadcast a sensitive documentary, "More than Broken Glass: Memories of Kristallnacht," that included even-handed commentary by Raul Hilberg and contemporary witnesses. In a sober reflection on the anniversary, Anti-Defamation League national director Abraham Foxman raised important questions of universal import while keeping a balanced historical perspective and avoiding unwarranted connections between the riotous work of the Brownshirts and the "Final Solution" that began three years later.[41]

I draw additional comfort from what I perceive to be a gradual fading of confrontations over the "uniqueness" of the Holocaust— what more than one historian has identified as a sterile debate in which the stakes seemed so much higher than the designation either sought or rejected. Commenting on related quarrels over numbers of victims, Harvard historian Charles Maier makes what I think are some pertinent observations: "Too often [such controversies] have led to an invidious competition. Each terror has its champions, and the result is a competition for victimhood. Non-Jewish victims of either the Germans or the Russians resent the Jewish claim to a more transcendent level of suffering. Jewish writers fear that their credentials of martyrdom will be impugned."[42] Doubtless, as I have argued elsewhere, the Holocaust is in an important sense "unique."[43] But, as Henry Huttenbach has noted recently, "admitting that the Holocaust took place within a broader context of criminality, need not rob it of its exclusive identity."[44] I believe that many historians (who, after all, tend to think that *every* event that they study is unique in some way) would agree with Eberhard Jäckel of the University of Stuttgart when he suggests that "uniqueness" may not be all that important. "Would it change anything had the National-Socialist murder not been unique? If that were the case, should the Federal Republic perhaps stop paying reparations, the West German Chancellor no longer pay his respects at Yad Vashem, or the citizen feel better?"[45] The obvious answer is no.

With that last comment, I am reminded of an observation on the Klaus Barbie trial by an elderly French café owner: "Well, Barbie has come and gone," he said, "but I don't feel any better." I think the café owner touched something important. It seems to me that the study and the popular presentation of the Holocaust run into difficulties when they have been deliberately undertaken to make us "feel better"—to confirm our political judgments, to enhance understanding of the Jewish predicament, or even to improve "human understanding." In my view, the contemplation of these ghastly events has its own imperative, which springs from an essential human itch to understand and to come to terms with the world as we find it. That such things could have happened is to me reason enough to ponder them in awe and study them with scientific curiosity. I doubt that we should "feel better" after coming to grips with such horrors, and I am sometimes uneasy when people seem to undertake the exercise with this in mind. Historians can never be sure about the uses to which their efforts to explain will be put, or if any use will be made at all. Most of us share a faith, however, that it is better to know, or to try to know, than to remain in ignorance. And about that, I think, there is ample evidence in the sorry record that it is our lot to explore.

David Vital

After the Catastrophe: Aspects of Contemporary Jewry

1

IT IS NECESSARY FOR ME TO BEGIN BY MAKING CLEAR WHAT I WILL *NOT* attempt to deal with in the remarks that follow. I do not intend to refer to the actual machinery mounted by the German state for the destruction of the Jewish people; to the policy which that machinery was intended to implement; or to the ideological, sociological, or pathological sources from which that policy sprang. Nor do I have any intention of dealing with the parallel, in important ways more intricate, question of the lessons and legacies that consideration of prewar and wartime Germany—state *and* people—might lead us to identify. Third, I do not propose to take up the question of the political and moral responsibility, public or private, collective or individual, of either the Germans or their various allies and collaborators. It is my very strong feeling that that is a question that they themselves—or more precisely, now that more than half a century has passed since the National Socialists were voted into the seats of power in Berlin—that their heirs and successors have to confront and make what they can of. And that is very much my feeling too regarding the larger issue of what the Christian churches for their part should finally make of what occurred and of its retrospective implications not merely for their conduct before, during, and after the war, but for their ethos and, dare I say, theology as well.

My concern in the present context is with my own people. But let it be plain: scholars more learned in the history of wartime

Jewry than I have dealt with aspects of those inexpressibly terrible years directly and in detail; for my part I have never sought, nor will I seek now, to examine what they have examined with such admirable skill and devotion. That is not my purpose at all. Nor could it be—not least because one who was fortunate enough not to be in wartime Europe at all, but who nevertheless belongs to the generation that largely failed to survive the slaughter, has reason enough not to attempt to emulate the historians of the Jewish catastrophe. I can only express my respect for those who have been blessed with the fortitude to embark on such hugely important work and the stamina to persevere at it. My own concern is different. It is with the condition of Jewry *in the wake* of the great destruction and amputation, that is, with modern Jewry as it has survived, rather than modern Jewry as it went under.

It may be noted that I say Jewry, not Judaism. It is the people, the communities, ultimately the nation, that I have in mind, not their ancient faith and religious practice. No doubt it is all too true that these terms, Jewry and Judaism, are anything but precise. In Hebrew, a single word, *yahadut,* does service for both. However, with present purposes in mind, I believe it would be unnecessarily tiresome to try to deal either with the question of how each may be distinguished from the other or with the equal and opposite question of how their respective referents overlap and intermingle. In any event, the issues that necessarily underlie any serious discussion of the condition of *Judaism* (in the strict religio-philosophical sense of that term) in the aftermath of the destruction of that great segment of Jewry that was most devoted to it are not ones that I propose to raise, let alone discuss. This is not to say that they do not merit the most serious and meticulous treatment. They do. But it seems to me that it is chiefly for those who are fully faithful to the Tradition to take them up. It will avail the secular-minded in Jewry nothing if they attempt to go much beyond the bare, admittedly melancholy observation that no evidence of such a process is yet in sight. In any event, the view of the matter that follows is not of that order.

2

One of the central and inescapable facts of public life in modern Jewry is that the destruction of European Jewry led to no sea change in the ethos and mores of the Jewish people. Here and there, small and scattered groups, and some isolated individuals as well, did try to take the measure of the events. Some reordered their lives. Some, although very few, sought to reconcile their previously established private beliefs with what they had now learned and thought they were now obliged to conclude. Certain issues and questions, hitherto ignored, or raised and discussed only in defined and somewhat limited sectors of Jewry, took on enhanced life and importance, as we shall see. But by and large, apart from the fight for political independence in the Middle East (which followed a logic of its own), consolidation and repair may be said to have characterized Jewish public life in the aftermath of the catastrophe. The huge defeat the Jewish people had suffered in the course of the war waged against them led to no deep reappraisal. Not one of the great public institutions resolved on radical restructure, let alone dissolution. No individual personality of real note, no leader of real prominence resolved on retirement from public life. Even beyond what might be termed the Jewish establishment no really new diagnosis of the condition of Jewry emerged, no fresh ideas were offered to the public for consideration and reflection. Certainly none were taken up. Such was the case even so far as the Zionists were concerned. It is perfectly true that they, the authentic adepts of the authentic Zionist position among them at all events, were able to argue—quite correctly, I venture to say—that their theses had been tragically, but persuasively, validated by events. But even they—largely because in the early years after the world war they themselves were faced with what may be termed the other great crisis of Jewry in this century—made no more than a simple, limited, and, so to speak, pragmatic attempt to reorder their affairs in, and their view of, the Jewish condition as a whole and in the Diaspora in particular. A notable trend in contemporary Israel itself is toward a softening of some of the old, fundamentally negative theses on the very propriety, let alone viability, of the Diaspora. As for the Diaspora itself—which is, and in the nature of these matters must be, my principal concern—it is not too much to say that little or nothing has changed and that the evidence of immobility is all around us. The contemporary Jewish Diaspora, apart from the great wasteland of Central and Eastern Europe itself, flourishes: seemingly brighter, more promising, and—to judge by the numbers and direction of the flow of migrants—more attractive than ever before. It seems that nothing of real consequence has changed. In all of this, the profoundly conservative character of the Jews is fully manifest—and not for the first time.

3

But fifty years have elapsed since the outbreak of the Second World War. It is rather longer than that since the profundity of Nazi Germany's hostility to the Jewish people and some idea of the support the Jews might expect to receive from other, ostensibly liberal and enlightened, states and societies in the hour of their darkest peril became clear—if only to those who were strong enough to look at the facts of the case. It is now only a little less than forty-five years since the outlines of what actually took place during the war passed into common knowledge. So is it not time enought to consider what the impact on Jewry in the aftermath of the horrors has been, time enough to begin to take stock and consider the condition in which the destruction of European Jewry has left the Jewish people?

In a preliminary way, two main avenues of discussion and exploration seem to me possible. One concerns the consequences for all Jewry of the all but total elimination, the final amputation from the body of Jewry, of what was unquestionably its heartland, its veritable core: the great East European mass. For it cannot be stressed too often, or too strongly, that in Poland and the Baltic countries, in Russia and Romania, in Czechoslovakia and Hungary, were to be found those communities that, taken together (as they should be), constituted the Jewish people in its essential European form. Taken together, they constituted the most homogeneous, the most coherent, the least assimilated, least self-conscious, most compact, and, of course, far and away the most numerous and lively—and in so many ways, the most remarkable—of all Jewish conglomerations in modern times. It is not too much to say that to all intents and purposes they were the Jewish nation—all other communities, no matter how distinguished or ancient or prosperous, being peripheral to them. It was out of the human resources gathered in this great reservoir not only of people, but of talent and energy of all kinds, that the two chief Jewish communities in our own times, the one in the United States, the other in Israel, have been largely (which, of course, is not to say entirely) constructed. It was within this society that the terms of virtually all the major internal issues in modern Jewry were set and had always seemed likely to be decided—the great exceptions being precisely those that entailed some form and some degree of *departure* from that society: assimilation and religious reform. It was the movement of ideas and the movement of people within—and out of— that great network of communities that largely shaped the cultural and political characteristics of all of modern Jewry. It was upon the movement of ideas and people that it had been generating for several generations that the future of the Jewish people seemed most likely to continue to depend. The injury done to the Jewish people as such by the annihilation of that great, marvelously pulsating society is therefore beyond measure and imagination. And therefore, if the war pursued against Jewry did not utterly destroy it, it did leave it, in the strict sense of the phrase, beyond recovery. The Jewish people could not be even remotely what it once had been. Worse, it could not be what many of its members had reasonably hoped it might become. It had always (and quite correctly) been understood that it would be from this reservoir of human talent and energy that the Jewish community in Palestine, and the independent Jewish state-to-be, would draw its future population. After all, the problem and the afflictions of that same Eastern European Jewry had precipitated, motivated, and nourished the Zionist movement in the first place. It was Jews from Eastern Europe who had brought the *yishuv* to the point of takeoff several years before the Second World War, as even some of the most hostile, but also the most knowledgeable, of the British officials responsible for dealing with it recognized by acknowledging that it would either have to be crushed physically by overwhelming force or allowed to emerge as an independent state.[1] The loss to contemporary Israel of that great community from which the Zionists had always drawn their strength, and for which they had always believed they were laboring, remains incalculably vast.

In brief, the European catastrophe has done more than leave a void in Jewry. It has left it with an injury that cannot be repaired. And thus there cannot fail to arise a further question, and a second avenue of discussion and exploration, one that concerns the impact of the catastrophe upon the thinking of what remains of Jewry. I propose to approach this latter question somewhat indirectly.

4

What could have saved the Jews of Europe? There is a clear sense in which that is an improper question to ask. What can be more useless—and in this case, more heartrending—than retrospective speculation? But unless we go some way toward tackling it, we do not even begin to approach an answer to an assuredly proper, if exceedingly difficult question: what might contemporary Jewry have learned from its loss? What, in other words, in the terms of this volume, might be the *lesson* of the Holocaust?

What we do know is what did not save them. The Jews of Europe were not saved by the mitigating effect of their persecutors' and murderers' cold self-interest. The old, well-worn argument offered up by one generation of Jews after another to the ruling power of the day and place and clutched at again by the desperate people of one ghetto after another in occupied Europe—that they, the Jews, would prove *useful* to state, economy, and society—that argument by and large fell on deaf ears. Even the status of slaves was largely refused them—on principle, and as a matter of high state and social policy. Nor were the Jews saved—not in appreciable numbers, at all events—by the civilized societies, polities, institutions, and churches of the day, even such as were declared enemies of Germany and at one time or another had the opportunity to act in charity on the Jews' behalf. Some turned a blind eye; some shrugged; some prevaricated; some relied on weighty political and social argument for doing this or refraining from doing that. But need one rehearse the negative, yet hardly unthinking cruelties committed by the various West European and North American democracies: from explicit requests to the Germans to imprint the passports of Jews with an identifying mark the better to keep them out, through blanket refusals to alter one jot or tittle of the relevant immigration laws in question, all the way to what can only be called an ambivalence of attitude to the essential matter of the physical elimination of Jewry from the European scene as reports of developments in the occupied territories began to appear on official desks in London, Washington, Geneva, and elsewhere? Nor

were the Jews saved or given material, let alone willing, assistance
by those who were actually fighting the common enemy in the
territories of the new German empire and had every military reason
to enlarge their ranks and increase the scope and intensity of their
otherwise admirable resistance. What could be more miserable
than the response of the Polish Home Army to the pleas of the
fighters in the Warsaw ghetto for arms—not outright refusal, to
be sure, but a pathetic handful of weapons tossed to the Jews in
barely disguised contempt and disbelief? What could be more
horrifying than the fate that awaited Jews who had managed to
evade ghettoization, or had escaped from death camps, taken to
the forests, and wished no more than to pursue the fight, when
they were unlucky enough to fall into the hands of the wrong group
of partisans?

   It is true that to every one of these generalizations there will be
found exceptions: instances of the most remarkable decency and
generosity and of the deepest commitment to what can only be
termed the basic moral dictates of humanity—to say nothing of
immense courage in circumstances of extreme peril. Many Jews
owed their lives to individuals or small groups scattered throughout
Europe, not excluding Germany itself, or Poland for that matter,
who offered them shelter and lifesaving assistance of a dozen other
forms. But they were just that: exceptions. The rule was otherwise.
And the rule was plainly a function of the fundamentals of the
Jewish condition. Not their wartime condition; rather their condition from time immemorial. Indeed, one great singularity of the
Holocaust (there are others) is that it tells us in stronger, clearer,
less deniable terms than any other event in the history of the Jews
what lies at the basis of that condition.

   In a famous essay, *Galut* (Exile), that truly eminent historian,
the late Yitzhak Baer, makes the following remark on the great
change that overcame the Jews in late antiquity.

> In the seventh century, the Jews still took an active military part
> in the struggle for control of Palestine between Rome and Persia,
> between Rome and Islam, which they interpreted in eschatolog-
> ical terms. But from then on, the nation definitely submitted to
> the admonitions of its teachers. God had made his will manifest;
> it was his will that the Jews should bear the yoke of foreign
> nations.

And Baer goes on:

> The Jews left the ranks of warring nations and put their fate altogether in the hands of God—a unique historical fact to which no historian has yet given its proper importance.[2]

These lines, originally written in German and published in Berlin, by Schocken, in 1936 (*"Das jüdische Volk schied aus der Reihe der kämpfenden Nationen aus und legte sein Geschick ganz in die Hand Gottes"*), could stand as the epitaph for European Jewry. The war against the Jews was nothing if not the supreme testimony to their powerlessness—to the direct and horrific consequences of their having "left the ranks of the warring nations and put their fate altogether in the hands of God." Except, of course, that God, or let us say Providence, is inscrutable, and that in practice, it was into the hands of their rulers that the Jews consigned their fate. Therein the tragedy and, at the same time, the paradox.

The ancient view, deeply ingrained in the Jewish psyche, was to regard what the redactors of the Mishna called "the ruling power" (*ha-rashut*) with grave suspicion. The advice the Sages offered the people was to exercise all possible care in their dealings with it, in fact to steer clear of it altogether if that were possible. *Hevu zehirin be-rashut*[3] was the basic injunction. But much of the force of the injunction came to be lost in modern times, notably in the West, but in parts of Central Europe as well, as the twin processes of formal emancipation and cultural switch altered the terms of the lives of the Jews out of all recognition. The old, proud prudence and the underlying distrust that informed it gave way to a curious and historically unprecedented combination of dependence and humility, even a measure of positive trust. It can be seen informing the singularly trustful, at the same time quite humble, not to say servile, spirit in which the most prominent figure of the day in American Jewry approached his head of state on the matter that forms the subject of this conference.

At the beginning of December 1942, when the essentials of what European Jewry was being subjected to were already quite well known not only to Stephen Wise and his senior colleagues among the leaders of American Jewry but to the State Department and President Roosevelt himself, Wise, it will be recalled, wrote to

Roosevelt, apologizing, as was not in itself unreasonable, for proposing to add to the president's wartime burdens, and restating the basic facts of what he there and then defined as "the most overwhelming disaster of Jewish history." He went on to remind the president that, "together with the heads of other Jewish organizations," he had succeeded in keeping the reports of the "unspeakable horrors" taking place in Europe out of the press. Finally, he asked the president to receive a delegation of major American Jewish organizations. To what specific purpose? I quote from Wise's letter to the president: "We hope above all that you will speak a word which may bring solace and hope to millions of Jews who mourn, and be an expression of the conscience of the American people."[4]

Solace and hope. . . . It is easy enough to be hard on Wise, especially in retrospect. That is not my present intention, which should be understood as no more than interpretative. Stephen Wise's wartime conduct, along with that of others who failed to make an ultimate, consistent attempt to muster their admittedly small and fearfully inadequate forces in the struggle on behalf of the Jews of Europe, can be understood only as a function of a profound and pervasive sense of weakness—an overwhelming, paralyzing belief in the utter vulnerability and helplessness of the Jews wherever they might be and in the extreme unwisdom of opposing or crossing or even merely irritating the "ruling power." The deeper implications of the refusal of the American government of the day to allow the war effort to be in any way compromised in the public mind—to be tainted, so to speak—by association with a Jewish cause or interest of any kind, even that of mere physical rescue of some of the Jews from death, constitute a separate topic, sufficiently well known to absolve me of a requirement to elaborate on it. Besides, many may think that, in any case, it is now water under the bridge, part of the larger total, irreversible tragedy. What is surely not water under the bridge, however, is the continuing contemporary difficulty of the Jews when dealing with problems related to power—of which weakness and vulnerability, in that they are no more than the complement of those very problems, form a great part, especially and crucially insofar as these bear on the collective affairs of Jewry itself.

5

A quick reading of the map of modern Jewry tends to yield the conclusion that the most notable divisions of opinion and classes of social and political behavior correspond to that undoubtedly sharp and fundamental contemporary division of the Jews into the class comprising the citizens of the State of Israel and the class that comprises the Jewish citizens of other states. Israel is evidently, and by design, a power-political structure. To use Baer's terminology, it is quite evidently one of the world's "warring nations." In contrast, Diaspora Jewry is much exercised by (and, as before the war, profoundly and even somewhat bitterly divided on) the question whether it is a nation at all. In no significant, operative sense is it a coherent political entity of any description. Plainly, it neither provides nor permits a structure of power in the sense that is relevant to the present issue, namely power to sustain conflict with hostile peoples and societies. But if all this is evident and important, it is only half the story. The deeper and, I think, much more telling distinction is a philosophical one.

In the contemporary West, generally speaking, respect for the rights of man and the citizen, the rule of law, certain well-tried methods of patient, peaceful resolution of conflict by negotiation—all these and more have come to be seen not only as immensely desirable in themselves and infinitely preferable to other, darker principles, techniques, and instruments of social and political action, but as actually in evidence, and if not perfectly and all the time, then not all that imperfectly and much of the time. They operate, they are available, and, all things considered, are maintained in fairly good repair. Moreover, of the application of these principles and the workings of the accompanying institutions in practice, the Jews of Western Europe, and now those of North America too, have been among the notable beneficiaries. What could be more natural, then, than their attachment to a view of society and its troubles, and of likely solutions to those troubles, which is intrinsically optimistic, altruistic, moralistic, and so, by extension, legalistic too, but above all *principled?* How, at a deeper level, could such a view, if it is to be sustained, fail to be profoundly dismissive of the opposing outlook: that which holds that, in important ways, men (and women) are often irretrievably at cross-purposes with each other and that, in this vale of tears, evil is endemic and ineradicable?

For of course there is another outlook. To the east and to the south of the fortunate lands of Northwest Europe and North America things were, and have long remained, otherwise—and not for the Jews alone, but for all. There is no need to recite even a reduced catalogue of the afflictions that have overcome virtually all the peoples of Central and Eastern Europe, of the Middle East and Central Asia, of both Northern and sub-Saharan Africa, and of Southern Asia and the Far East as well in our own times and before our eyes. The world outside the West is a hard world. The lessons it offers are hard too. In lands in which violence, cruelty, tyranny, and hatred are endemic there is every good reason to conclude that safety is unlikely to lie in reliance on the rules of law and common morality, perhaps not even on the native decency and good will of individual men and women. There, in consequence, one tends easily and naturally to a much greater measure of skepticism and distrust of the "other" than is usual—or perhaps even necessary— in the lands on the outer rim of Europe and in a land such as this. In a harder world one tends, if one can, to self-reliance. In a hard world, it is no more than prudent to learn hard lessons.

But is that the lesson that the Jews have learned from their very particular experience in the recent, and now so fully recorded, past? Or is it the case that those who have found a place for themselves in one of the fortunate lands have learned—or taught themselves—a lesson that differs from the one learned by those who are still part of the world of which the Destruction of European Jewry was so integral a part?

As time elapsed and as the initial shock wore off, different circles in Jewry, indeed different communities of Jews, could be seen—can still be seen, ever more clearly—not only to have been very differently placed during those terrible years and to have conducted themselves in different ways, but indeed to have inhabited different mental and philosophical universes. These are distinguished one from the other not so much by disagreement over points of traditional law or ritual (as was not infrequently the case in the past and over which there are divisions to this day), but by differences over the aims and methods, and even the propriety, of *collective action* by Jews, notably where collective action has needed to rely on the autonomous, political employment of instruments of influence and power. Seen in the perspective offered by the full sweep of Jewish history this is an ominous development. Nothing, surely, is so divisive of a social group as an issue that pertains at one and the same time both to interest and to propriety: to what is held to be desirable and to what is held to be right.

In final analysis, the division may be traced to the working out of the radical social and ideological processes precipitated in Jewry by the Emancipation—the onset of which two centuries ago we are now marking along with all other celebrators of the Great French Revolution. For the real profundity and irreversibility of the revolution the Emancipation helped to precipitate in Jewish life is revealed less in the differences between the material and formal-legal circumstances of the various sectors of the Jewish people, however important they may be in themselves, than in the philosophical, ideological, and psychic qualities that tend now to divide them. The heat with which contemporary arguments about both interest and propriety are conducted is so great, the tone so bitter, and the prospect of a meeting of minds so remote, that the notion that the long era of Jewish unity across many frontiers, always somewhat tenuous, but never wholly unreal, is finally about to end seems subject to continual reinforcement. The irony in all this, but also the puzzle, is that this has occurred while the events in wartime Europe are still part of living memory.

6

In a limited and shadowy way the historiographic problem the Holocaust presents contemporary Jewry is not wholly unlike the problem it presents other peoples and societies, even the people and society most closely involved in its perpetration. It is not that there is anything in Jewry analogous to the *Historikerstreit* in contemporary Germany. Nor, in the nature of things, could there be. Nor, indeed, so far as I can make out, is there any great debate in progress with more or less explicit and identifiable schools of thought arguing clear-cut theses of one kind or another. We have not come to that. It may be that we will not come to that for several generations, perhaps not at all. Nevertheless, there are questions that do manifestly gnaw at the hearts of all thinking members of the Jewish people wherever they may be.

One such question is that of universality. Was the Holocaust one of a class of more or less comparable events? Was it, on the contrary, in an important, indeed fundamental sense, unique? It is here that disagreement in Jewry—again, I would not call it a full-blown debate—is not wholly unlike such disagreements and debates as have occured elsewhere, and some limited and shadowy parallels and analogies between it and them may be detected. For, of course, the major historiographic problem for Jews all along has been how to situate the Holocaust *in their own history*. Was it specific to its time and place? Was it, on the contrary, characteristic of, indeed a function of, the exilic condition itself—as Baer implicitly and many others explicitly were later to contend? Was it then in some crucial and decisive sense not only an event in but also peculiar to Jewish history, and comprehensible ultimately only in its terms? Far from being one of a loose class of catastrophes such as have been inflicted on a variety of nations by one or another act of domestic or, more likely, foreign political will, is it amenable to being rendered intelligible only in terms that are specific to the Jews and to the long-standing and immensely bitter conflict in which they have been embroiled with their European neighbors and rulers these past fifteen hundred years and more?

One can see why such a view is certain to be unpopular in many circles. For one thing, it would mean that there is a clear respect in which Nazi Germany was less eccentric and more representative a state and society in and of Europe—all of Europe—than, on the whole, contemporary Europeans, historians among them, have generally liked to think and tended to argue. However, that is not the aspect of the question that concerns me here and now. What does concern me are what I take to be the deeper reasons for the increasingly strong tendency among Jews, at all events Jews in the Diaspora, to reject such a view. These seem to me to stem from other sources and to be somewhat less evident and explicit in the specialized literature than, for example, in literary and artistic criticism. They were well illustrated, for example, in the mixed and, in some quarters, awkward response to Claude Lanzmann's extraordinary film *Shoah*.

Reviewing the film for the BBC's *The Listener* some time ago, an eminently sensitive and perceptive critic who described herself as "a British child of Jewish origin," began by citing a second critic who, writing for *The New Yorker*, had made the following point:

> [Lanzmann] succeeds in making the past and the present seem one, and this appears to be an aesthetic victory. . . . It has another aspect though; implicitly the film says, that the past and the present are one—that this horror could happen again. See, the Polish peasants are still talking about how the Jews killed Christ and hoarded gold.

Thus far the New York critic. The London critic then went on to drive her objection home:

> [Pauline] Kael [of *The New Yorker*] has a point. Lanzmann's unwillingness to put the events of the Holocaust into historical context leaves him open to the accusation of pessimism. . . . Analysis which might have made the Holocaust understandable and specific to its era is missing.[5]

I find all this exceedingly telling. There is the terminology itself: Lanzmann being open to the "accusation" of pessimism. There is the corresponding notion that rendering the Holocaust "understandable" and showing it to be "specific to its era" would, in effect, remove an obstacle to *optimism*. (But is optimism the sole and proper position to hold?) And, of course, there is the articulation of the central issue, the one that turns on the question whether it was truly a unique and isolated event, or one whose causal roots ran so deep and were so pervasive that we may expect to find them running beneath and through contemporary society as well. Plainly, this latter view is one that neither of these two critics, nor very many other members of the contemporary Western intelligentsia are prepared to tolerate. Regardless of origins, loyalties, and political convictions, few are even prepared to examine it.

Can one blame them? The idea that in a hundred different ways the Jews are still beset by a profound, consistent, seemingly ineradicable refusal to accord them such standards or status, or to ascribe to them such significance or qualities, as are normally and unquestioningly accorded and ascribed to other peoples and denominations to this day is an exceedingly painful one. It is painful partly because it would entail a profound disappointment. Certainly, much has changed, and not solely on the surface of things. But equally so much has been invested in the belief that things changed for good. And that is not a belief that those who hold it can be expected to be happy to discard. It is painful too because—as is all too evident—the greater part of Jewry suffers today, perfectly understandably, from a kind of war weariness: an intense desire for peace, for relaxation of tension, for a condition in which all stress and conflict, to say nothing of the constraints and dictates of an exceptional status, can finally be consigned to the past. In a word, there is much less stomach for the struggle than there seems once to have been.

But if one does venture to look beneath the surface of things, what does one find and what is one to make of one's findings? What is one to make of endemic antisemitism in contemporary, *Judenrein* Poland? Or of the uses for, and the response to, the Protocols-of-the-Elders-of-Zion content of ostensibly anti-Israel, but in fact manifestly old-style, antisemitic propaganda such as has been mounted for decades now by the relevant state machinery of the Soviet bloc and the majority of the Arab states—both for domestic *and* for foreign consumption? Or of the particular edge that has been lent in recent years to the tension between American blacks and American Jews, not least here in Chicago? Or of the never-ending series of often unintended, but for that reason all the more revealing, expressions of the conviction that in some profound sense all Jews are responsible for all attacks upon them whatever their origin—as when the prime minister of France particularly lamented the death of non-Jews in the attack on the synagogue in the Rue Copernic in Paris in October 1980, on the grounds that they, presumably unlike the other, which is to say the Jewish, victims, were "innocent"?[6] And when the Greek Minister of Justice determined recently that the killing of a little Jewish boy in a synagogue in Rome was an action that fell quite properly "within the domain of the struggle to regain the independence of the [killer's] homeland."[7]

Needless to say, there is much much else to be said on this subject—the more so as it is difficult to form a clear and firm picture of the total situation. But let this be plain, it is not part of my purpose to offer a catalogue of charges, let alone a catalogue of woes. I only suggest that while the forms have changed and, in some societies, the content has altered, and the intensity of hostility has diminished, too, the grounds for thinking that the world is at peace with the Jews in their midst, or that the Jews are entitled to feel at peace with the world around them, appear to me to be highly questionable. It seems more likely that there has been a truce of sorts since the end of the Second World War; and that if the truce still holds, more or less, signs of erosion and fatigue are now beginning to be visible; and finally that if they are not always apparent, it is because the immediate object in view has changed. It is no longer so much the intensely alien Jewish intruder into European and American society cast, of course, as an incorrigibly vulgar and hateful agent of economic, political, and cultural corruption, burrowing under the old order, opening the gates of the city to carriers of moral plague. Instead it is Israel and its people who play the role of whipping boy. To no other national state or society is so much obsessive, venomous attention paid, so little forgiven, so much evil ascribed. The image is no longer T. S. Eliot's notorious

> The rats are underneath the piles,
> The Jew is underneath the lot. . . . [8]

and is more likely to be Peter Reading's image of

> a fat juicy jeep of Israelis

in Lebanon being shot at by a little Arab boy and shooting back because,

> . . . Well,
> nobody looks for a motive from these Old Testament shitters—
> thick hate is still in the genes. [9]

How profound is the difference? Of what other foreign and geographically remote people do serious literary members of Western (should one not say Christian or at least post-Christian?) society write hostile *poetry*? [10] Surely these are question to ponder.

But to return to my own theme. The notion that the killing off of the Jews of Europe ended the ancient conflict in which the Jewish people have been repeatedly pitted against their neighbors appears to have less substance than many, especially in the immediate wake of the Second World War, seem to have thought. In contrast, what the great slaughter did do was to weaken the capacity and, I fear, the will of large segments of the Jewish people to sustain that conflict today, in the aftermath. It did so in three principal respects.

First, the amputation of European Jewry from the body of the Jewish people drastically reduced it in numbers, in talent, and in what I can only describe as the *will* to collective—in practice, national—life. Second, it accelerated the process whereby Jewry, as a consequence of the Emancipation, along with the two great migrations, the one across the Atlantic, the other back to the ancestral Land of Israel, was breaking up into ever less cohering communities, each imbued with a distinct culture and language, each subject to specific influences and needs and so, inevitably, each intent on social purposes of its own definition. Third, notably in the Diaspora, but even to some extent in Israel as well, the Holocaust itself, by a huge paradox, has come to be thought of, and—what is more serious—commonly and frequently presented to all and sundry—as that event in the history of the Jews which necessarily overshadows all others. It is not too much to say that we are now at the point where in the public mind, Jewish *and* non-Jewish, the Holocaust bids fair to being seen as the archetypical event in the history of the Jews.

7

There are thus at least two strong tendencies in contemporary Jewry, so far as our general subject is concerned. One seeks to reduce the Holocaust's otherwise almost impossibly painful impact on mind and society by finding a place for it among the other, all-too-numerous horrors that humankind has inflicted on itself. Accordingly, when all due allowances have been made and exceptions taken into account—the precise methods employed by the SS, its material dimensions, its bureaucratic aspects, and the like—it is to be regarded as one of a kind. What is more, it is to be firmly rooted in a specific time and a specific place and a particular historical-political context.

The other tendency is so to magnify and particularize it in Jewish terms, and so to associate the Jewish people with it as—in practice, of course, not in intention—to drown out virtually all other voices and to smother virtually all other developments, facets, and qualities of Jewish life, history, and culture: in a word, to fix the image of the Jews in the terms of this vast and hugely injurious calamity above all. This last is an intensely disturbing phenomenon. If it was the archetypical event in the history of the Jews, the Jews themselves become archetypical victims.

But if, in the abstract and in a limited way, these two tendencies run counter to each other, in practice they do not really cancel each other out. On the contrary, in a crucial respect they tend to be mutually reinforcing. Both sap the foundations of the collective life of the Jews—as a distinct people, that is to say, as bearers of a culture and a language, as an old and, as one would claim and hope, in spite of everything, an honored member of the family of nations, one with a long, difficult, but in many ways splendid past, but also one with a future.

The first thesis, the one that eliminates the *particularity* of the horrors visited upon the Jews in this century, has the effect of inculcating a fundamental error, indeed a lie, so far as the Jewish experience is concerned. It is simply untrue that the long war conducted both against Judaism and the Jews in Europe (and the Middle East, too) over so many centuries, of which the wartime events in Europe were only the culminating and most horrible chapter, was of a class with other crusades, massacres, decimations, and slaughters. To hold that it was is to skew, and certainly to misconstrue, exceptionally important aspects not only of Jewish civilization, but of European civilization and of the civilization of the Muslim world as well. There is nothing to be gained and much to be lost by such an immense distortion, such a gigantic exercise in the sweeping of unpleasantness into the capacious memory holes that societies quite understandably retain for such contingencies.

The second thesis concerns the Jews themselves more directly. It is one thing to retain the memory of the Holocaust as an act of piety toward the dead and as a catastrophe the causes of which deserve to be studied and examined, not only for their own sake, but in the interests of finally reordering the life of the Jews as a people and as individuals. It is quite another to establish its memory as a (if not the) reference point as much in the communal life of the Jews as in their relations with other peoples. On the one hand, to do so is to diminish all else in Judaism and Jewry and, what is more, permanently and compulsively to fix our attention on the past. On the other it is, like it or not, to make of the Jews a people of invalids, of victims, of death. Thus in the minds of others. Thus, I fear, little by little, in their own minds as well—at any rate in the minds of those who subscribe to this view and in the minds of those—especially the young people—in whom this view has been inculcated. Nothing can be so destructive of the inner life and stability of Jewry or of its capacity to sustain present and future pressures—for there can be no question but that such pressures will continue to be exerted—as to make of the matter of the Holocaust a cult. That, above all, cannot be tolerated; and the impulse to do so, however innocent and worthy the underlying motives may be, must be resisted.

II. D · E · E · D · S

Hans Mommsen

The Reaction of the German Population to the Anti-Jewish Persecution and the Holocaust

THE PERSECUTION OF THE JEWS DURING THE THIRD REICH REACHED A climax in the almost unimaginable slaughter of five million European Jews by the *Einsatzgruppen,* in the annihilation camps, and as a consequence of brutal treatment in ghettos, concentration camps, and many other places.[1] The history of Nazi anti-Jewish policy has been the object of far-reaching international research. Of the many studies in this field the pioneering work of Raul Hilberg deserves special attention. In general, the origins and the stages of the Holocaust are well researched and well known, although some issues, among them the actual timing of the preparatory steps of the systematic genocide program and the question whether Adolf Hitler issued an explicit order or promoted the mass murder more indirectly, remain controversial.[2] The progress of research, however, has done little to clear up the question of why all this could happen without significant opposition and protests on the part of the German population. It is by now well established that a whole range of administrative units was involved in the immediate preparation as well as the implementation of the Holocaust. The armed forces, the foreign service, the local police, the civil administration, the railway system, and many others participated in a policy that put into practice what before the war had been regarded by an overwhelming majority as a fanciful goal of fanatic antisemitic rhetoric.

We are still without a convincing answer to this question or an explanation of how the terrible truth could be concealed even from those who were instrumental to the crime. The attitude of the German population has been the object of an extended debate between Anglo-Saxon and Israeli historians. In West Germany it is still widely believed that the annihilation process remained essentially secret and that the mass killings became known only to a small group of reliable Nazis. According to this view, rumors about Nazi atrocities against Jews circulated, but the ordinary citizen was not necessarily aware of them. The whole issue of knowledge of the Holocaust seems to have been so little discussed in West Germany that one could presume that something like a collective repression was at work. Marlis Steinert was among the first who examined this issue systematically. Her pioneering analysis of German public opinion and Hitler's war came to the conclusion that mass executions were sometimes known, but that the systematic annihilation and the death toll of the concentration camps were hardly ever mentioned.[3] In recent years, the studies by the Israeli scholars Dov Kulka and David Bankier, by the British historian Ian Kershaw, and by the American Sarah Gordon have enlarged the documentary evidence and broadened our perspective on this issue.[4] Also, the field study on the Bavarian conditions in the Third Reich published by Martin Broszat and Elke Frölich greatly improved our knowledge of the social practices of disobedience and compliance with Nazi orders.[5] The contribution by Heinrich Wilhelm on the role of the troop commanders and army leaders at the Eastern Front needs special attention, as does Raul Hilberg's case study on the railway transports to Auschwitz.[6]

Most experts seem to believe that large parts of the German population were unaware of the systematic liquidation of Jews, despite the fact that the deportations were not concealed from the public. Generally, this may be true for those who did not fill responsible positions in the army, in the political system, or in the society. One is puzzled, however, to find even high-ranking members of the leading elite asserting their ignorance of the systematic mass killings. In many cases it was indeed extremely difficult to prove the opposite. An outstanding example for this can be seen in Albert Speer's defense arguments against Erik Goldhagen's attempt to prove that he was well acquainted with the Auschwitz complex, including the gassing.[7] Similar problems occurred continuously in the trials against Nazi criminals. Nonetheless, obviously the claim of a great many contemporary observers after 1945 that they had had no access to reliable information about the Holocaust partly reflects an apologetic mentality.

In many respects, the moral liability of the Germans for the atrocities committed against Jews, Gypsies, and other persecuted groups must be seen independently from the question whether they knew much of the killing squads of the *Einsatzgruppen* or the gas chambers in the annihilation camps. The brutal treatment of Jews and the potential destruction of their existence must have been clear to everybody who read the discriminatory anti-Jewish ordinances that appeared in the publicly accessible *Reich Gesetzblatt* before the war. This was even more so for anybody who witnessed the deportations—and many did. Individuals might have been ignorant of the Holocaust, but they could hardly have been unaware of the basically criminal intent of the anti-Jewish legislation and other measures that undermined or destroyed the preconditions for the survival of their former Jewish neighbors.

In evaluating the attitude of the average German, Dov Kulka and his co-authors spoke of "passive complicity," because by ignoring persecution and murder he or she undoubtedly bore a co-responsibility.[8] With this argument Kulka responded to Kershaw's judgment that a majority of the German population took a position of indifference toward the "Jewish question." According to Kershaw, racial hatred in certain segments of the population and an increasing indifference on the part of the majority combined to pave the road to Auschwitz. Kulka's interpretation implies that the prevailing passivity of the Germans with respect to the escalating persecution was a necessary precondition for the implementation of the "Final Solution." Furthermore, he seems to be convinced that, by and large, the German population had a more or less clear notion of the deadly fate of the Jews. He quotes the reports on public opinion (*Stimmungsberichte*) of the Security Service (SD) and comparable material in order to show that fanatic antisemitism found considerable popular support and that even concealed threats in Nazi propaganda against Jews were frequently taken at face value. However, he leaves the problem of whether or not utterances of this kind were representative of the general public unresolved, and does not systematically study the question of the extent to which antisemitic indoctrination had been effective.

Hence, Dov Kulka perceives the passive reaction of most Germans against anti-Jewish policies as a result of a profound antisemitic indoctrination. Undoubtedly, antisemitic prejudices were widespread in Germany, and they were nourished by Goebbels's propagandistic efforts to expand the inherited cliché of the eastern Jew into an all-embracing xenophobic caricature. Nevertheless, although antisemitism had grown during the Weimar period, it was by no means virulent in all social strata in Germany.[9] Antisemitic prejudices were mainly to be found within the lower middle class. Simultaneously, the functional elites were strongly infected by a sweeping cultural antisemitism that can be traced back to the Wilhelmine period and corresponded with a deep-seated anxiety about the loss of former social privileges. In any case, the impact of racial antisemitism was rather restricted, at least in comparison with Poland and other East European countries. The Nazi success at the polls between September 1930 and March 1933 was achieved despite, not because of, racial antisemitic slogans in the propaganda campaign, which were deliberately held back by the Reich election office of the NSDAP. When Goebbels tried to mobilize a broad antisemitic boycott movement in April 1933, he met silent opposition by the public and was compelled to beat a tactical retreat. In November 1938, his expectations of popular support for the pogrom-like excesses of *Kristallnacht* also proved to be unfounded.

Sarah Gordon, in her analysis of the repercussions of antisemitic policies in the Rhineland and Westphalia, discovered evidence of considerable, if unquantifiable, dissent from the official antisemitic course. In conjunction with the interpretation of Gestapo documents, she refers to the contemporary private survey of opinion by the German psychologist Michael Müller-Claudius, who had analyzed the attitude of party members to the "Jewish question" on the basis of informal inquiries done in 1938 and in 1942. According to his findings, no more than 5 percent of the interviewed persons belonged to the hard core of fanatic antisemites who supported the eventual extinction of the Jewish race and expressly welcomed Hitler's antisemitic rhetoric.[10] The majority shared certain prejudices against Jews but would not support direct action against them and did not show any interest in their persecution. Certainly, the sample chosen by Müller-Claudius was relatively small, and it did not meet ordinary statistical standards.

Its results, however, coincide with those of the famous Abel collection and its interpretation by Peter Merkl, according to which massive antisemitic motivations prevailed within only a minority of the group of Old Fighters investigated by him.[11] Insofar as antisemitism as a primary motivation did not prevail even among the Nazi rank and file, it can certainly not be expected in the population at large. This does not mean that the public climate was not infected by radical antisemitism. After all, the minority of hard-liners met almost no open protest in consequence of increasing terrorist intimidation, and they could build on a growing political apathy, especially among the former opponents of the NSDAP.

There is no doubt that antisemitic obsessions escalated among those parts of the Nazi leadership who had entered the Party during the *Kampfzeit*. The driving force behind the pressure on the government to intensify the persecution of Jews was mostly those elements of the Nazi Party whose social integration had failed in spite of varying efforts by Party and state. This was especially true for a great many of those Old Fighters who had not found an adequate job in conjunction with the *Gleichschaltung* and who did not fit into the changed requirements after the movement phase had come to its end. The relative defeat of the Party in the rivalry with the state agencies in many realms of public life pushed the "Jewish question" into the foreground as an outlet for radicalization. The higher civil service was resolved to keep the NSDAP at bay and to prevent any direct intervention in the administration. In this they were generally successful, except in the field of municipal administration. The price the bureaucratic elites had to pay for this consisted of delivering the alleged "Jewish question" into the hands of the local and regional party functionaries, who used it as a playground to compensate for their defeat in other fields of policy. Particularly those radical elements within the NSDAP whose social energies had not been absorbed by the consolidation of the "*Führerstaat*," and who were no longer required for political mobilization through national election campaigns, were receptive to the continuous radicalization of anti-Jewish slogans, and the pressure from such people even increased, since wild actions were more firmly prohibited.

This strategy by the predominantly conservative-minded leading bureaucrats also relied on the strong conservative antisemitism
that had been symptomatic of the political mentality of German
functional elites since the Wilhelmine Empire. In general, they
welcomed the Nazi antisemitic policies only so far as they coincided
with their call for racial dissimilation of those Jewish groups who
were not assimilated to German culture. They thought that the
brutal racial antisemitism practiced by the SA and proclaimed by
"Der Stürmer" was but a "childhood disease" that would disappear within a short period. The frustrated socio-revolutionary energies of the Nazi movement were thus primarily directed against
Jews who found only marginal support in vested interests within
the German society. This was a crucial factor for the continuous
cumulative radicalization exactly in the field of anti-Jewish policies.

Two additional mechanisms have to be taken into account. On
the one hand the impact that the "aryanization" of Jewish property on all social levels had on the leading elites cannot be overestimated. In fact, the corrupting repercussions of the enrichment
through the takeover of Jewish property were far-reaching and go
some way to explain the extreme weakness of dissent against total
expropriation and deprivation of Jews by the German upper class,
even if the brutal procedure by the Nazis found much criticism.[12]
On the other hand the administration was resolved not to leave the
"leadership in the Jewish question" to the NSDAP, as Wilhelm
Frick maintained at an interministerial meeting in spring 1935.[13]
As above all Christopher Browning has shown,[14] the establishment
of special *Judenreferate* by the different departments contributed
considerably to the escalating legislative discrimination against
Jews, which continued even in 1943 and 1944, when only a limited
number of Jews still lived in the Reich. In order to preserve its
leadership, the administration felt compelled to make so many
concessions to the radical anti-Jewish wing of the NSDAP that it
not only lost the initiative that it had fought so long to preserve
but also got deeply involved in the criminal dimensions of anti-
Jewish policy, after the Reich Security Main Office introduced compulsory labor, enforced emigration, and ghettoization.

The hard-liners of the NSDAP who were pressing for an acceleration of anti-Jewish measures could rely on Hitler's personal
implicit and explicit encouragement at any time. Consequently,

the government was deprived of any means of taking coercive measures or threatening juridical sanctions against the radical antisemitic wing of NSDAP, which was bent on deliberately breaking the laws and pushing the legislative process in an increasingly radical direction. The pioneering study by Lothar Gruchmann on the role played by Franz Gürtner, the Reich Minister of Justice, in this process clearly shows the fundamental weakness of the more conservative segments of the administration when it became imperative to call an end to the cumulative radicalization in this sector.[15] In a certain sense, precisely those strategies that were meant to domesticate the radical wing of the movement resulted in a speeding up of anti-Jewish policy, because they functioned as a means of psychological compensation for the radical's lack of power in other fields of policy. The Four-Year Plan crisis and the prevention of the military intervention against Czechoslovakia in the fall of 1938, for instance, were in some respects compensated for by the November pogrom.[16]

On the occasion of the fiftieth anniversary of the pogrom night, a couple of monographic studies appeared that shed some new light on the public reaction to the antisemitic excesses. Obviously the majority responded to the violent and brutal actions by the Storm Troopers with deep moral apprehension and sometimes even with gestures of protest, well aware of the risk of being targeted for Nazi defamation and retaliation. Clearly, this was due not to a fundamental solidarity with Jewish fellow-citizens, although in many cases the victims got clandestine support from their non-Jewish neighbors, but to the traditional law-and-order mentality. Even among the participating Storm Troopers and Nazi functionaries, antisemitic motives were not necessarily paramount. The pogrom night was primarily regarded as a short-lived reminiscence of the unsatisfied expectation of violent terrorism that had prevailed during the days of the seizure of power. When criticized for their illegal actions, the Storm Troopers justified their behavior with the need for obeying orders. In almost no case did they refer to arguments of racial hatred. The gang leaders, however, pressed their men to perpetrate brutal and inhuman acts of violence. But the popular protest against the undisciplined destruction of private property did not encompass the arrest of about 26,000 Jewish citizens. For all its inhumanity, this action seemed to be justified,

148 •   HANS MOMMSEN

because it was covered by official orders given by Heydrich. This example shows that the strongly authoritarian disposition of many Germans may have had a far greater influence on their passive response toward even sterner steps of anti-Jewish persecution than antisemitic indoctrination as such.[17]

The enforced social segregation of German Jewry was intensified under the impact of the November pogrom. Simultaneously, the competence of the Party to settle this issue was definitely turned over to the Gestapo, which subsequently modified the strategies of solving the "Jewish question" in favor of regular administrative methods. Pogrom-like actions never reoccurred in the *Altreich*. The complete social and economic exclusion of the Jews who did not manage to leave the country in time eventually dissolved what was left of former social ties between Jews and "Aryans," at least within small and middle-size communities, where social contacts with Jews were immediately picked up by the Nazi press and persecuted by the Gestapo. After roughly 1939, the average German was confronted with the "Jewish question" only on rare occasions. The miserable living conditions of the remaining Jews and their complete isolation finally resulted in the psychological effect that has been described as "depersonalization" of the Jew.[18] Under the conditions of the Second World War, this psychological phenomenon contributed to the apathy toward the inhuman treatment of Jews everywhere. The terrible conditions in the ghettos were even used by Nazi propaganda to intensify the subhuman image of "the Jew." For the mass of the people, antisemitic rhetoric more and more lost any direct relation to the victims and acquired a purely abstract meaning. The average German even accepted allegations, such as that of the Jewish responsibility for the war, without putting them in the context of the realities of Jewish life.

Hence, it was symptomatic for the widespread ignorance and indifference toward the fate of Jewish fellow citizens that the "Jewish question" was only of marginal relevance in German public opinion before the "yellow star" was introduced in the fall of 1941. Suddenly it was realized that Jews were still living in Germany, and the "Jewish question" got some of its human dimension back. Consequently, as we can learn from the *Stimmungsberichte*, there were clear indications that the obligatory wearing of the Star of

David (*Kennzeichnungspflicht*) met some opposition. Later on we find the fate of the Jews discussed again when the deportations started, but this time the attention was less strong than in the fall of 1941. The issue reappeared in connection with Katyn and the Allied air offensive, but apparently it was not continuously present in political consciousness. Kulka, who uses the evidence of a remarkably broad collection of *Stimmungsberichte,* interprets the fact that the treatment of Jews played but a subordinate role in the reports as the outcome of a "national conspiracy of silence."[19] He believes that the *Stimmungsberichte* provide a relatively representative picture of the public reaction to the genocide policy. In general, however, the SD reports and analogous documentation contain only information of a strongly affirmative character and reflect actual propaganda, such as public commentaries on Jewish policy by Hitler and Goebbels. Repeatedly the SD reports contain critical remarks against anti-Jewish measures that can be explained only within the context of the contemporary antisemitic prejudices and show that fellow travelers suddenly became aware of the actual implications and the immoral dimensions of Nazi ideology. Almost all utterances make sense only against the background of the official antisemitic agitation, for example, a report from the city of Lemgo in July 1942 that some citizens criticized the deportation of women, children, and old men who, as they said, could do nobody any harm.[20] It is frequently reported that the Allied air attacks against German cities were perceived as a retaliation for the unjust treatment of Jews or, conversely, that fanatics demanded even more radical measures against Jews as a means of German retaliation. Utterances like these only reflect the official propaganda, which justified ruthless measures against Jews because of their alleged responsibility for the destruction of German cities.

Dr. Kulka is right when he concludes that there existed an overall consciousness of Nazi crimes. This is borne out by the fact that the anti-Bolshevik attacks in conjunction with Katyn reminded many of comparable German massacres of Jews. The equation of Auschwitz and Katyn that the Gestapo discovered in graffiti was clearly an oppositional gesture, and it is indicative of the one-sidedness of the SD reports that they did not record resistance in this respect. The opinion of those who rejected the persecution of Jews outright is not reflected in the reports. We have to assess it on the basis of private diaries, letters, and the results of oral history. The personal experience of complete powerlessness in the face of the early deportations of Jews is impressively depicted in Ruth Andreas Friedrich's diaries, *Der Schattenmann*, relying on notes she made during the war.[21] Her reminiscences offer an explanation as to why the "Jewish question" was obviously underrepresented in the *Stimmungsberichte*, compared with other political, social, and economic issues. Silence does not necessarily mean passive acceptance of the persecution, especially of the steps leading to the Holocaust. From other sources we can derive clear indications that relevant parts of the German population were opposed to the atrocities in the occupied territories in the East, and in particular to the anti-Jewish genocide, insofar as they became aware of the systematic character of the mass killings. In 1942 the Party Chancery still believed that it was possible to convince the German population of the necessity of uncompromising measures against the Jews. Later, the Party leadership had to realize that it might be better to restrict the official information about the deportation program to the fictitious argument that the Jews were being transferred to new settlements in the East.

This amounted to a veritable propagandistic retreat, just as Himmler's order to speed up the deportation measures in spite of the difficult transportation facilities in the later war years can be seen as response to the German population's obvious apprehension concerning the treatments of the Jews and the mass killings. If we take account of this, the moral undertone of Kulka's assertion that there existed a conspiracy of silence appears somewhat misleading. Where and how could the clandestine opposition or the dissenters on this question articulate their opinion without running the risk of becoming victims of the Gestapo terror? Instead of a "conspiracy of silence" as the outcome of an antisemitic consensus, it appears to me that those who objected to the genocide policy and did not see any means to intervene short of self-sacrifice responded with apathy. Furthermore, for the bulk of those citizens who took an indifferent attitude to the "Jewish question," it was psychologically difficult to give the rumors of mass executions and the threats in the Nazi press too much weight.

Whether the individual was able to obtain enough information to gain a more than impressionistic picture of the process leading to the "Final Solution" depended on numerous quite different factors. An analogous problem existed on the international level, especially with regard to the reluctance of Washington and London to accept the news about the Holocaust.[22] The psychological factor proved to be of crucial importance, in that many contemporaries were not ready to believe atrocities of this kind and dimension were possible at all. Uncompromising opponents of the Nazi regime were less skeptical than those who originally sympathized or supported it, such as many members of the national-conservative resistance movement of July 20, 1944. Furthermore, anyone who suspected what was going on could collect manifold but also incoherent information. In this respect, the improvisation accompanying the start of the "Final Solution" made it difficult even for the agencies that were directly involved to get a clear picture of Heydrich's intentions. As Browning has pointed out correctly, the SS bureaucracy and its helpers relied heavily on improvisation and had difficulties in coordinating the different programs, not to mention the fact that the gradual realization of the "Final Solution" was itself influenced by frequently spontaneously originating mass killings performed by local antisemitic groups, usually with the sympathies of police forces or the *Einsatzgruppen*.[23] Evidently, the genocide program was put into practice without any formal coordination on the cabinet level, although representatives of the involved departments attended the Wannsee Conference on January 20, 1942. For its part, the civil administration tried to keep its involvement as minimal as possible. The informal procedures chosen by Heydrich, who circumvented the Reich Chancery, and his use of mainly oral command chains resulted in the fact that outside the Reich Main Security Office almost nobody had an overview of the whole program. This strengthened the general impression that the executions and similar events sprang from isolated initiatives. Even the inner circle of Nazi mandarins did not have any official information, and although the perpetrators talked repeatedly of various Führer orders, Hitler seemingly avoided any formal engagement, possibly because he was instinctively aware of the extreme unpopularity of the genocide.[24]

That the extension of the killing program from the *Einsatzgruppen* to the systematic deportation of Jews in German-occupied Europe occurred in an informal climate and certainly step by step, not in the form of fully developed planning, was bound to have important effects on the nature of public reaction. Certainly, information regarding executions and atrocities in the East was abundant. Reports by soldiers on furlough in the Reich, leaks in the Party apparatus, and news about intolerable conditions in the ghettos and the concentration camps were widespread. The massacres of the *Einsatzgruppen* and the early improvised mass executions became relatively well known. The gassing operations in the annihilation camps, however, remained obscure. For the contemporary observer it was almost impossible to gain an overall picture of the annihilation process. In general, the impressions predominated that criminal actions of this kind originated in direct connection with the anti-partisan warfare and had, therefore, a more or less emergency character, or that fanatic subleaders, such as Himmler and Heydrich, had acted on their own responsibility. On December 19, 1943, the Protestant Bishop of Hanover, August Mahrarens, in a letter to the Reich Minister of Interior, demanded that the leadership of the state should do everything in its power to prevent irresponsible individuals from burdening necessary political and public programs with intolerable injustice.[25] In church circles the impression prevailed that the genocide policy was pursued by arbitrary officials.

What kind of information was available about the genocide policy? The main problem for the critical observer consisted in the difficulty of assembling divergent information into a comprehensive picture. The diaries of an engineer working in a factory in Celle, Karl Dürkefälden, prove that it was possible to arrive at an almost complete picture by collecting assorted available information, even without access to governmental sources.[26] Perhaps one had to be, like Dürkefälden, opposed to the Nazi regime from the start and free from any nationalist reservations in order to be able to do so. Dürkefälden found out the truth during the summer of 1942, when the reports of the BBC played a crucial role in confirming variegated information. In comparison to Dürkefälden, the members of the conservative resistance movement were less well informed, and it took them longer to realize the facts, although the command channels of the regime were accessible to them. Helmuth James von Moltke heard of the Wannsee Conference, but he did not gather its fateful meaning. In October 1942 Moltke got first news about the annihilation process at Auschwitz, and he compiled different information into a relatively precise picture in the spring of 1943. At the same time Prussian Finance Minister Johannes Popitz informed Ulrich von Hassell about the existence of gas killing installations in Auschwitz.[27] In general, the opposition obtained reliable evidence of the genocide policy relatively late, although it had collected detailed information about the preceding events in the occupied Polish territory. Moltke, in particular, had access to internal information through his contacts with the military espionage agency, the *Abwehr*. The informality of the implementation of the "Final Solution" helps to explain why the resisters acquired full knowledge only after the majority of the German Jews already had been deported.

The broad discussion of how the knowledge of the Holocaust eventually reached the Western world has shown the difficulty that even opponents of the Nazi regime had in believing that mass murder on this scale really could have been performed and that they were not victims of propagandistic manipulation. Kurt Gerstein, who tried to inform the Confessional Church and foreign diplomats, had a similar experience. Given this, it is not surprising that the population at large fell into silence, aside from the fact that the impact of the war brought issues of personal survival into the foreground. Not so much an antisemitic bias but the combination of an authoritarian mentality and obedience to acts of state on the one hand and moral indifference with respect to the fate of Jews and other oppressed groups on the other explains the passivity of the German population. An assessment of the attitude of members of the leading elites appears to be more difficult. Undeniably among the leading functional elites, whether they belonged to the NSDAP or not, a considerable minority supported the genocide policy against the Jews unreservedly. Heinrich Wilhelm is right in claiming that significant parts of the military elite knew about the genocide and contributed actively to it.[28] Others who should have known the facts later on claimed that they had not been involved and had not been adequately informed. In some respects, it does not matter whether leading personalities, as Admiral Dönitz maintained, spoke the truth when they declared that they had not been aware of the Holocaust. It was symptomatic of the moral erosion of German society that especially the functional elites repressed the terrible secret and avoided getting personally involved. That explains why only splinters of documentary evidence have survived and why central parts of the decision-making process are only fragmentarily documented. The experience of Jochen Klepper, who lived in a mixed marriage and tried everything to prevent his daughter from being sent to a death camp, reveals the mendacity of the leading officials of the Third Reich. Wilhelm Frick argued that he could not risk any complaint by Himmler to Hitler and that he was legally prevented from intervening in order to allow Klepper's daughter to emigrate to Sweden. Klepper, who had two-fold information, the internal orders by the Gestapo to the Jewish community in Berlin and access to high governmental circles, read Hitler's speeches and Goebbels's infamous articles on the "Jewish question" in the weekly *Das Reich* verbatim. After he failed to move Adolf Eichmann to an act of mercy, he realized that he was left with no choice but to commit suicide with his family.[29]

The moral perversion of the Nazi regime is last but not least to be seen in the attitudes of its mandarins, who repressed the deviation from their alleged petit-bourgeois moral respectability by a criminal regime without parallel. There are indications enough that Hitler himself, when confronted with the consequences of his criminal policy, also denied his responsibility and concealed the truth even from his followers. At least—unlike Himmler—he never publicly admitted his responsibility for the greatest crime of which history had ever heard. Hitler's liability is beyond question, and David Irving's assumption that Hitler did not get adequate information about the "Final Solution" before 1943 is an arbitrary construct.[30] But Hitler tended to lose contact with the real world, and he needed subordinates who were ready to turn his visionary goals into political reality. It is not unlikely that the lack of solidarity of the average German with his Jewish fellow citizen and the impact of antisemitic indoctrination of the German people at large were necessary preconditions for the mass murder. But the moral indifference of the German functional elites lay at the bottom of this terrible event.

Claudia Koonz

Genocide and Eugenics: The Language of Power

"HOW DOES IT HAPPEN THAT PEOPLE BECOME THINGS?" THE QUESTION haunts both memory and scholarship about National Socialist genocide against the Jews during World War II.[1] When we focus mainly on concentration camps, deportations, *Sonderkommando,* and mechanized mass murder, the question defies an answer. Such a teleological vantage point, however, distorts our vision by foregrounding the unique aspects of genocide and obscuring its etiology in more normal times. To complement meticulous examinations of the final stages of the "Final Solution," we need to look at the genesis of genocide within the context of the racial schemes that predated orders for extermination by several years.[2] Studies of Nazi extermination routinely include a chapter or two on eugenics and "racial science" as way stations on the road to Auschwitz. Often, these background chapters imply an inevitable descent down a slippery slope from eugenics to genocide. Steven Chorover, for example, writes, "The path was direct, from an allegedly objective brand of scientific discourse about human inequality to a purportedly rational form of moral argument about 'lives devoid of value' and then to the final solution. . . ."[3] Similarly, some participants in contemporary American debates elide the gaps between sterilization or birth control and extermination,[4] and Right-to-Lifer rhetoric glides smoothly from abortion centers to concentration camps. Although eugenics programs did institute vital preconditions for later extermination programs, they did not inevitably lead to mass murder. A set of political decisions made by fanatical leaders under wartime crises converted that potential into lethal reality.

In settings as diverse as the Soviet Union and the United States, scientists created the potential for radical racial policies without producing mass extermination.[5] And not even Nazi Party leaders imagined they could exterminate Jews, Gypsies, the disabled, and other "inferiors" except under the extreme conditions of war. Yet the universality of eugenics notions—seen against the uniqueness of genocide—inspires us to pause and think about the connections. In 1926, when the Supreme Court judged forced sterilization laws constitutional, Oliver Wendell Holmes wrote the majority decision—declaring that after so many of the nation's finest had sacrificed their lives in World War I, it would not represent a great sacrifice if the least qualified gave up their potential to reproduce. "It is better for all the world, if instead of waiting to execute the degenerate offspring for crime, or to let them starve for their imbecility, society can prevent those who are manifestly unfit from continuing their kind. . . . Three generations of imbeciles are enough."[6] Between 1907 and 1932, twenty-seven states passed compulsory sterilization laws, and by 1939 about 30,000 people had been sterilized.[7] In Germany, the Reichstag passed no eugenics measures before 1933. During the next twelve years, about 350,000 German citizens and 40,000 foreigners were sterilized. Compared to Wilhelm Frick's prediction that 10 percent (or about 500,000) Germans would be judged genetically defective and one eugenicist's estimate of an 18 percent sterilization rate, these totals seem modest.[8] Compared to the results from the interwar United States, the statistics seem staggering.[9] Still, respected American medical scientists lavished praise on the German program, which they saw as a model for their own country—at least until the outbreak of World War II.

Because of the links between world scientific opinion, eugenics, and racial hygiene, we cannot complacently regard genocide against the Jews as an atavistic outcropping of irrational forces unique to Germany. As Zygmunt Bauman notes, "It was the rational world of modern civilization that made the Holocaust thinkable."[10] Only in a modern secular society does scientific discourse wield the authority to legitimize vast social engineering schemes. Only a bureaucratized state can draw both perpetrators and victims into its web. This capability and the mentality to match, Bauman persuasively argues, stem directly from an optimism generated during the Enlightenment. Eugenic scientists, he observes, shared a "proper and uncontested understanding of the role and mission of science" as well as a

> feeling of duty towards the vision of a good society, a healthy society, an orderly society. In particular, they were guided by the hardly idiosyncratic, typically modern conviction that the road to such a society leads through the ultimate taming of the inherently chaotic natural forces and by systemic, and ruthless if need be, execution of a scientifically conceived, rational plan.[11]

Building on universally acclaimed biological discoveries, eugenicists everywhere planned for genetically improved societies.

Still, only in Germany did the eugenic and ultimately racial consensus achieve hegemony. What made the Third Reich different? In other contexts, eugenics and racial paradigms encountered considerable resistance from entrenched political and professional interests. In other words, elsewhere these novel biological approaches met with the same reception as all scientific breakthroughs. From Copernicus and Galileo to Darwin and Freud, scientific innovators have typically aroused deep hostility from dominant institutions.[12] As Bruno Latour's work brilliantly shows, even Louis Pasteur's discovery of microbes aroused massive opposition among entrenched medical and administrative interests.[13] In Nazi Germany, however, radical eugenics and race doctrines (which Hitler likened to the Copernican Revolution) coincided with the goals of a powerful state. Indeed, slogans like "National Socialism is the political expression of our biological knowledge" became platitudinous.[14] Nazism to many scientists meant applied biology. State backing brought funding for research, educational programs, and public relations. This revolution in medical knowledge and practice has attracted much scholarly attention in recent years.

Several outstanding studies of Nazi eugenics reconstruct the interface between political interests and the medical community.[15] Scholarship on what one historian termed this "murderous science"[16] focuses on medicine as a profession, scientific research, and Nazi politics. But it omits from scrutiny the vast media *Blitzkrieg* launched by state-supported eugenics projects to incite public enthusiasm for eugenics and racial science. This endeavor to create what one might call a "murderous silence" among citizens involved in bio-political activities, no less than the professionals' collaboration, was central to the "racial revolution" promised by Hitler. A well-funded Office of Racial Enlightenment (after 1934, "Racial Policies") deluged Germans with a new discourse on race, science, nature, and politics. Racial programs depended, for example, on ordinary citizens' willingness to target potential victims for sterilization, report on neighbors' "asocial" behavior, base their selection of sexual partners on racial criteria, and collect information about possible hereditary illness in their own family trees. Though it is tempting to speculate about the success of these endeavors, I will in this chapter focus on the rhetorical strategies designed to reconstruct values related to life and death, private and public spheres, "worthy" and "unworthy" individuals.

When beginning my research into the records of national and local offices of racial policy, health administrations, educational institutions, and social work agencies, I had an experience shared, I suspect, by many historians of the Nazi period. When I came across passages or paragraphs or even entire books on race, I passed over them impatiently. My notes are sprinkled with expressions like "dreck," "disgusting," "stupid," or "yet another lunatic." Like those of *Mein Kampf* itself, the inchoate formulations and flamboyant language of these broadsides make for difficult reading. But these crude, barely literate ravings merit a closer look because it was via these visual and verbal texts that racial laws drafted by the experts were fit into a new racial *weltanschauung* that transformed categories of people into abstractions.

One term stands out in this popular literature. The verb *erfassen* is translated in Cassell's in two ways: "to lay hold of, grasp, seize, comprehend; to include (as in a health program)." It meant to include people either by conversion or by coercion into an administrative network or a *weltanschauung*. Racial experts used the term in both senses: in relation to a publicity campaign to *"erfassen"* or convert a mass audience to a revolutionary biologized view of society, and in relation to the bureaucratic *"erfassung"* or "targeting" of specific types of "unfit" individuals for eugenic action. To a degree that seems extraordinary for an era without computers or television, a dense media system functioned in tandem with a bureaucratized health police in distinctively modern ways to implant new social values and to invade public and private life.

After building a dedicated following of loyal party members, Nazi leaders in 1933 faced a challenge for which they were unprepared. During the years of frenzied campaign activity, dedicated Nazis had maintained constant mobilization at fever pitch. Speaking tours, rallies, leadership training camps, ceremonies, pamphlets, posters, newspapers, and demonstrations drew mass support. After victory, however, that energy had to be redirected away from the political sphere and into safer, apolitical terrain. Overnight, the Nazi Party changed from battling against the status quo to being the status quo. Nazi "Old Fighters" saw this as their opportunity to realize still more radical tasks. They regarded the "seizure of power" (*Machtergreifung*) as a mere prelude to a more sweeping revolution that would transform people's entire value systems. Some post-1933 campaigns (most notoriously Ernst Röhm's threat of a second revolution) failed, but the call for racial revolution succeeded on a grand scale. The drive to imbue all Germans with a racial *weltanschauung* constituted a veritable "seizure of opinion" (*Meinungsergreifung*). During the early months of 1933, Minister of Education Hans Schemm called for a "moral revolution."[17] At the grassroots level, ordinary people spoke of "an immense learning in rethinking that penetrates into the deepest recesses of life." The Führer's personal charisma alone could not accomplish the task. Faith in Hitler may have brought the party to power, but now a thoroughgoing transformation of values was in order.

> Not even Hitler can work magic. Regulations that are not grasped (*erfasst*), at least in their basic intent by the majority of the population and therefore respected, will remain impotent because the resistance is too great. Therefore Hitler has tirelessly converted his ideas into enlightenment (*Aufklärung*) and sent it out to the *Volk*.[18]

This emphasis on total indoctrination reflected Hitler's own propaganda strategy, as described in *Mein Kampf*. "Every philosophy of life, even if it is a thousand times correct . . . will remain without significance for the practical shaping of a people's life, as long as its principles have not become the banner of a fighting movement."[19] The immediate challenge lay in maintaining that momentum, which might easily become mired in administrative rivalries and red tape. Guided by limitless faith in the power of propaganda, Nazi leaders launched a media campaign.

The imposition of a radically new bio-political worldview, along with scientific and bureaucratic capabilities, depended upon distinctly modern capacities. From Hitler's brilliant insights into the arts of persuasion to Goebbels's sophisticated propaganda network, Nazi leaders made their appreciation of media power clear. The post-1933 propaganda blitz blared anti-modern, nostalgic messages into private homes and public squares via the most up-to-date technology. The historian Detlev Peukert comments on this nostalgic modernism: "It was often, indeed, precisely the profuse trappings of antiquated traditionalism or reactionary utopianism in Nazi ideology that served to make more acceptable in practical, social terms the modern technologies and structures they disguised."[20] National Socialism played out in lethal form what Peukert calls "a long term pathological dimension within modern society itself" by linking a secular, industrial, welfare state to "racialist doctrines and terror."

This linkage becomes possible because of mass communications. Yet, conversion of a nation to radically new views faces a dilemma. While sophisticated media hold out the potential of unprecedented social control, these same media contain built-in constraints on their power. Michel de Certeau comments on the near impossibility of generating faith among people who have become cynical about repeated claims on their credulity. Ever since the emergence of what Jean-Jacques Rousseau termed civil religion, Europeans and Americans have been bombarded by waves of new ideals. This "multiplication of convictions" ultimately depletes the reserves of belief. De Certeau notes that "Little by little, belief became polluted, like the air and the water."[21] Already in the nineteenth century, literate citizens had been exposed to dynamic popular campaigns ranging from colonial leagues to popular health remedies. In all nations, yellow journalism took its toll, but Germans' susceptibility to hate propaganda during World War I and their subsequent disillusionment at defeat accelerated their cynicism concerning media. Some of the most prescient commentary on the impact of media on the modern self came from interwar Germany, where the silent film and radio drew mass audiences.[22] Peter Gay identifies a poignant "hunger for wholeness" among Weimar intellectuals—as well as thousands of "would be thinkers hunting for an organic philosophy of life." Patrice Petro calls our attention to the unlikely trio of Martin Heidegger, Siegfried Kracauer, and Walter Benjamin, all of whom investigated the "historical nature of subjectivity" and worried about a destabilized modern identity.[23] Later, writing during the Third Reich, Arnold Gehlen described the infinite malleability of human nature and warned about the rise of subjectivity. The demise of stable institutions like the church, the military, and local communities meant that modern individuals would increasingly fall under the regulation of state control.[24] Thus, modern citizens face a standoff between their need for a stable belief system and their reluctance to invest faith in simple solutions—even when packaged by sophisticated media techniques.

De Certeau's discussion of conventional religion and modern, secular doctrines applies to the Third Reich, as well as to contemporary industrialized society. Working against deep popular skepticism, the media replace religious communication. But, de Certeau notes, whereas an awesome "great silence" lay at the core of preindustrial belief systems, in modern societies, "the real talks constantly." Through "facts, data, and events . . . an anonymous code, information innervates and saturates the body politic . . ." This code seizes the individual. "Captured by the radio . . . as soon as he awakens, the listener walks all day long through the forest of narrativities" deployed by authoritative media. "These stories have a providential and predestining function: they organize our work, our celebrations, and even our dreams."[25] The modern self is surrounded and shaped by mass-produced images. What better a description of Nazi Germany, in which, as Goebbels is said to have quipped, "The only person who has privacy is the person who sleeps."

After a wave of modernist Weimar culture that threatened to recast the self in terms of individual fulfillment and, further, to displace fixed beliefs in God, Fatherland, and Family, Nazi leaders launched a comprehensive propaganda offensive to restabilize the self within the community and nation. Celebrations of *Blut und Boden* (blood and soil) appeared to anchor identity in tradition—

but it was a tradition created by Nazi ideologues. In a campaign to situate identity in biological concepts, an "inflated, totalitarian language"[26] told "Aryans" they belonged to a closed community of blood. "Nature," as created by racial scientists and propaganda experts, supplanted religion and politics. Building on cultural criticism from the Weimar years, Nazis called for the restoration of "natural" communities, values, and traditions. Yet, they realized the very concept of "natural" (like "traditional") had to be invented and imposed, not discovered. The author of a pamphlet on racial hygiene put it well: "Our entire cultural life has become so alienated from every natural condition of life that we have almost forgotten how to see natural phenomena as really natural."[27]

Nazi Party leaders inaugurated their racial policies simultaneously with terror against their political opponents. The symbolic significance of three measures that became public on a single day suggests important connections. On July 14, 1933, diplomats concluded the *Concordat* with the Vatican, all political parties were outlawed, and the involuntary sterilization law was announced. Here we see the convergence of a desire for stability vis-à-vis foreign nations, ruthless suppression of domestic rivals, and the beginning of a racial war against people defined as "unworthy." All people suspected of being mentally retarded, schizophrenic, depressive, alcoholic, disabled, epileptic, or otherwise disabled by genetic deficiencies were to be reported to local health officials. Their cases would be judged by special genetic health courts, and the operation would be performed without the individual's consent. Such an operation required full support of an informed, convinced populace, as well as a vast administrative network.

Every organization, Joseph Goebbels ordered in 1933, was to receive indoctrination in "the eugenic way of thinking." Dr. Walter Gross, a young physician and dedicated Nazi, was appointed to head the well-funded Office of Racial Policies—a step that signaled the centrality of its programs. Before the end of the year, training courses for health care professionals, special publications, research institutions, and public education on racial policies were established. In addition, the office created a network of regional genetic health courts to adjudicate individual cases and began to compile a total genetic census that recorded data on every citizen. Nationwide radio programs acquainted even the casual listener with this new conceptual universe. Experts at the Office of Racial Policies wrote directives, commissioned research, published popular literature, produced films, and distributed educational material. Long before even the most extreme antisemites in the Nazi leadership planned genocide, an ordinary, "unsensational" racism was deployed to define certain categories of people as things.[28]

Michel Foucault coined the term "bio-political" in writing of power and knowledge in liberal, industrialized societies, in which unspoken presuppositions constrain the options of supposedly free, autonomous individuals. Showing the ways that the discourse of modern science circumscribes perceived freedom, Foucault invokes a grid-like metaphor to describe the dissemination of new ideas. As he describes the process, it often seems that novel discourses float like miasmas on the media air. Latour's study of pasteurization, however, alerts us to the need to locate generating stations in the vast cultural grid. And both of these theoretical approaches can be applied to totalitarian societies. In Nazi Germany, fantastic theories about blood and crackpot schemes to discipline every aspect of a healthy "Aryan"'s life did not merely "seep" into the ordinary ways of thinking. *Erfassung* in both senses aimed at the twin goals: surveillance and punishment, *surveiller et punir.*[29] As Nazi ideologues, no less than Foucault, noted, ideas (like weapons) would "penetrate" deep into the national consciousness. The Nazi case study offers a chance to examine the generating stations that dispatched this lethal knowledge-power among users.

A quick survey of projects sponsored by the Office of Racial Policies suggests the range of media mobilized to carry out Goebbels's 1933 command to become "eugenically educated." Although most of us think of Leni Riefenstahl's *Triumph of the Will* as a powerful propaganda film, actually the film met with little box office success in Germany. Far more powerful were documentary shorts such as *Erbkrank* or *Sacrifice of the Past* (*Opfer der Vergangenheit*), commissioned by the office. These films played before the features in virtually all cinemas. In all, the office sponsored 350 films to propagate its views in theaters and schools. Education brought the racial message to young and old alike. Between 1933 and 1939, over 4,000 party members attended eight-day courses on racial theory. All students read "The Population

Policy ABC's" and memorized the "Ten Commandments for Se-
lecting a Mate."[30] To graduate from the gymnasium, students were
tested on questions such as "describe the spiritual characteristics of
the Nordic race."[31] Teachers' colleges taught their pupils to (using
a contemporary term) "mainstream" race into the entire curriculum. A one-day crash course for teachers in Munich in 1936, for
example, suggested how to accomplish that end, with sessions on
"The Essence of Scientific Studies among Alien Races," "Speaking
and Writing as Expression of Various Racial Attitudes (*Haltung*),"
"Public Libraries and Racial Studies," "Demographic Policies and
Racial Cultivation (*Pflege*)" (slides), "Genetic Flow and Objective
Spiritual Milieu" (*Erbstrom und objektive Geisteswelt*).[32] The Office of Racial Policies produced a lavish array of publications, including the pretentious *Neues Volk* for educated readers, the popular "*Volk* and Race" (*Volk und Rasse*) (with editions ranging
between 200,000 and 300,000), the "Goal and Path" (*Ziel und
Weg*) received by all doctors, and the *Informationsdienst* (Newsletter) limited to 5,000 medical experts.[33] Doctors were expected to
distribute racial literature in their waiting rooms. Women throughout the nation solicited donations to racial projects by selling the
Calendar of Racial Policies.[34]

   This veritable *Blitzkrieg* of publicity for Nazi bio-politics summoned party members to new tasks—and recast a message from
the pre-1933 campaigns within a new field. From the outset this
educational offensive was seen as part of an effort to remake the
entire person. Racial educators, Minister of Education Bernard
Rust told teachers, were selected on the basis of character as well as
knowledge. He looked for followers who "not only command the
pure biological facts, but also are willing and able to draw the
proper conclusions that demonstrate the National Socialist
weltanschauung."[35]

   The Office for Racial Policies dispatched its radical racial ideas
into the nation wrapped in a carefully crafted language that
blended old and new. Ambient prejudices about the handicapped,
mental and moral "defectives," Jews, Gypsies, and "less worthy
races" received shiny, respectable containers. Technocratic terminology reinforced—and did not displace—an older set of concepts.
Nor did Nazi language merely disguise reality (as George Orwell

and many others have noted); it "piggy-backed" lethal innovations on traditional-sounding concepts.

The new narrative directly contradicted conventional moral views that enjoined "normal" people to feel mercy toward the disabled. To upend such conventional maxims, a radically new vision of society was needed—and the Office of Racial Policies supplied it. No term better expresses the Nazi value system than the expression "life unworthy of living" (*lebensunwertes Leben*). This phrase did not mean that the suffering of some individuals might lead them to wish for a painless death. Rather it meant that some "genetically ill" individuals placed such a burden on the "healthy" that they ought to be prevented from bearing children (and, after 1939, from living at all). The decision rested not with the patient, but with the experts acting in the name of the community.

Photographs of infants with Down's syndrome or family portraits of feeble-minded people in popular literature, educational documentaries and newspaper "human interest" stories about the mentally ill enjoined readers to feel repulsion for these unfortunates. One pamphlet featured an illustration of a "healthy" group of seventeen smiling beautiful grandchildren from two "normal" grandparents contrasted with thirty-one tormented faces produced by two "deficient" grandparents.[36] In the short documentary film *Erbkrank*, a white-coated physician (who looks like the experimenter in the film of Stanley Milgram's experiments, *Obedience*) takes the viewer on what seems to be a tour of a human zoo of handicapped and mentally ill, while photos of healthy people highlight the contrast. The beautifully landscaped grounds and imposing architecture of the institutions further remind readers of the "good life" led by these "unworthy" people.

Financial calculations reinforced the message. Math textbooks asked students to calculate the price of a year's schooling for a normal versus an abnormal child. Gerhard Wagner, chief of the SS physicians' organization, warned that family size among "inferiors" was twice that of "normals." In the last seventy years, the "inferior" population had increased by 450 percent—as compared to an overall increase of 50 percent. Robert Proctor quotes Wagner's speech of 1935, more than one billion reichsmarks is spent on the genetically disabled; contrast this with the 766 million spent on the police, or the 713 million spent on local administration, and one sees what a burden and unexcelled injustice this places on the normal, healthy members of the population.[37]

The "insanity for equality," Wagner concluded, had produced this unjust situation, in defiance of "the natural and God-given inequality of men." A traveling educational exhibit from the national museum of genetic science informed viewers that any nation that succumbed to the "grotesque impulse" to assume the burden of caring for the weak would "destroy itself on purely economic grounds."[38] In the past, among "natural peoples" (*Naturvolk*) subnormal individuals simply died out; the "era of individualism," however, ushered in so much good will (*Wohlwollen*) that the least "worthy" reproduced their "genetically subnormal" (*blutlich unterwertig*) qualities.[39]

Two terms, "German genetic stream" (*deutscher Erbstrom*) and "German genetic property" (*deutsches Erbgut*), highlight a powerful message conveyed by the subtext of the new propaganda. Dr. Achim Gerecke explained "racial thinking" (*Rassengedanke*) in a nationwide broadcast. It was more, he said, than passive scientific knowledge because it implied also a *Forderung*, a set of expectations tied to action. Invoking mixed metaphors from nature, he called "race" a "stream" (*Strom*) that "must, wants to surge through us."

> And, as its mission, the stream does not block but transfers the inheritance from our forefathers and lets it stream on . . . It's God's will that we maintain the inheritance entrusted to us pure, clean, and healthy, to guard it so we can send it along to the next generation. Whoever is healthy and does not marry or bear children is like a leak (*Spritzer*) out of the racial stream. He will get stuck on the banks and quickly wither away.[40]

Walter Gross, in dozens of articles, reminded readers to remember "the eternal voice of the blood in the stream of German history."[41] When the "unfit" or "unworthy" bore children, their genes could pollute the national stream that flowed through everyone. The stream metaphor, which was ubiquitous in racial science publications, reminded people of unseen connections binding them together—across class, region, and generation, in sickness and in health. This rhetoric generated fear of impure genes that could, undetected, sully the national gene pool.

Flanking this fluid metaphor was a solid, stable, and rooted image: "national property" (*Erbgut*). The resultant ranking, based on qualitative contributions to the national *Gut,* incrementally dehumanized those people the experts declared to be disabled, mentally ill, asocial, Jewish, gypsy, or Slav. From medieval times, a family had seen its status in terms of property (*Gut*) but the new terminology transferred security from a familial, territorial basis to racial, national genetic property. Not only did the popular literature anchor identity in Blood and Soil (*Blut und Boden*), but it evaluated each citizen's contribution to the national ground. This redrawing of the ethical map placed "biologically" defined categories of people outside the sphere of humans to whom one owed moral behavior and constructed these "deficient" categories as a danger to public health. This new identity would be, the biopoliticians insisted, inscribed as natural. Hildegard Passow, an early convert to Nazism and a leader in Bavaria, described the process: "The total educational and indoctrination drive of the *volkish* state sees as its crowning achievement the burning of racial identity and racial feeling into the instincts and (of course) into the hearts and brains of the youth that have been entrusted to it."[42] A vision of protection and threat situated every German within a racial universe.

A new narrative manipulated powerful binary categories that held out the (specious) promise of order in a society made chaotic by democracy and economic depression. The melodrama of race cast hidden, lethal genes as a threat to both the physical and financial well-being of the healthy majority. The savior, dressed in white lab coat and flanked by formidable knowledge and health administrators, ferreted out the danger. The innocent heroine, the *Volk*, gratefully allowed herself to be protected by the ruthless experts. Like proponents of the microbe theory of contagion or advocates of the sexual etiology of mental illness, racial scientists aroused their audiences' fears of the unseen and unknown, which only they were powerful enough to excise. By their confronting the sources of illness, a cure would be forthcoming. A Manichean vision of the world created anxiety around purity and pollution,[43] and it transformed binary concepts, such as "good" and "evil," or "god" and the "devil," into "chosen" and "discarded," or "worthy" and "unworthy." More concretely, as one pamphlet put it, "A people of the feebleminded and idiots threatens to overcome our people of thinkers and poets."[44]

Official rhetoric operated on two levels simultaneously. Whereas the language of fear aroused deep *Angst*, a crisp, artificial technocratic language framed a vision of order that would ameliorate the *Angst*.[45] Science held out a fresh promise for collective and individual greatness—a hope that resonated powerfully among people disillusioned by Wilhelmine militarism, Weimar democracy, and Christian piety.

Although they recognized that when rhetorical strategies floundered state intervention would compensate, the propagators of racial utopia saw conversion as ultimately the only efficient kind of power. One early Nazi, looking back on the pre-1933 days, recalled, "Our national socialist idea would never have prevailed . . . if we had not spoken in a language that the *Volk* understood, if we had not framed sentences and words that moved millions and fulfilled their longings."[46] Gerecke spoke to his radio audience about the importance of psychological change and value change in the Nazi drive to biologize all aspects of life. "In order to arrive at racial selection, we must enlighten and educate. We don't need racial centers and little branch offices, but an educational network for racial questions."[47] One of the most highly respected eugenicists in the Nazi hierarchy, Arthur Gütt, optimistically proclaimed that overt force would disappear because, "what even today still appears as coercion, will in decades and centuries appear to the German *Volk* completely obvious (*selbstverständlich*)."[48] At the grass roots level, Hildegard Passow underscored the primacy of indoctrination over force in the new state.

> Faith and understanding (*Erkenntnis*) form the core of the person and of the *Volk*. This gives to the individual the guiding principle of his acts, meaning in his life; to the *Volk* its sense of justice and therefore its laws and political forms. . . . This feeling of justice (*Recht*) is like faith, not a delimination of rights vis-à-vis the individual, but 'the moral law in myself' as the great thinker Kant put it, simply 'Justice' (*Das Rechte*).[49]

In a society saturated by force and terror, there were limits on the extent to which the state could coerce its followers. A powerful police force could arrest political and biological enemies, but persuasion alone could produce appropriate behavior among people who supported the regime. Scientists and popularizers designed appeals to attract key audiences.

The Office of Racial Policies not only targeted potential victims but also designed special appeals to recruit particular groups of people conventionally seen as repositories of tradition and ethical beacons in their communities. Physicians and clergymen stood at the forefront of the ethical and health status hierarchies, and women participated at the lowest echelons. During the Weimar Republic, physicians had experienced downward mobility due to the increase in young doctors; clergymen lamented declining numbers of parishioners, especially among the young; and mothers complained of the "new woman" who placed career and pleasure ahead of marriage and children.[50] Even before 1933, the Nazi Party had attracted considerable support from all three groups. In the Third Reich the state offered not only renewed status, but employment opportunities and material support.

Nazification (*Gleichschaltung*) for physicians proved remarkably easy, for (as Lifton, Proctor, Klee, Kater, and Weindling point out) doctors readily perceived their own self-interest—in having Jewish doctors expelled from practice and simultaneously in hearing themselves exalted as saviors of the *Volk*. By the 1940s, half of all doctors joined the party, according to Michael Kater. Accompanying the medical rush to Nazi orthodoxy were new conceptions of the place of medicine in the bio-political state. Central to this campaign was a redefinition of "patient" and "doctor." Instead of feeling emotional and ethical responsibility to the individual, the physician became a "People's Doctor" (*Volkarzt*), and now served the national body (*Volkskörper*). This renaming shifted the unit of ethical consideration from individual to collective. The Hippocratic oath too underwent revision, so that the life that physicians swore to protect was the life of the *Volk*. Frick clarified the new ethic in 1934: "Involuntary sterilization is so clearly in the best public interest that the private interests of genetic defectives (who want to keep their disease secret) do not count."[51] One Nazi lecturer justified euthanasia to doubtful health care workers by revising Hippocrates' command: their duty was to rescue the "fit" for the future by weeding out the "unfit" in the present.[52]

Ambitious young physicians achieved remarkable upward mobility in the Nazi medical system. But material self-interest would not suffice for a regime that demanded passionate loyalty. Lifton quotes Arthur Gütt's insistence that "the true physician . . . must not only be a party member on the outside, but rather must be convinced in his heart of hearts of the biological laws that form the center of his life." Lifton described such commitment as "visionary idealism"; Peukert calls it the dream of "a utopian racial community (*Volksgemeinschaft*).[53] According to Lifton, physicians saw themselves as "the core of the mystical body of the *Volk*." As soon as the campaign for forced sterilization was announced, requests poured in to local Offices of Racial Policies from hospitals and physicians eagerly seeking authorization to participate in eugenic sterilization and abortion.[54] Medical schools offered new courses in body types, Mendel's laws, criminal biology, blood group research, and racial anthropology. By 1937, two hundred educational projects in sixty-eight locations offered refresher courses—attended by about 5,000 physicians a year.[55] State funding set the priorities for research, while public relations campaigns portrayed the medical scientist as *Volkarzt*.

Because the ranking of people according to biological value would seem to contradict conventional Christian ethics, it might be expected that the racial hygiene campaign would have aroused opposition from religious leaders. In fact, as scholarship on the contest between church and state in Nazi Germany makes clear, eugenics did not arouse much opposition in the Christian community.[56] Even racial policies that excluded people with Jewish forebears from the "Aryan" community aroused little opposition—even among the dissident Protestant Confessing Church. Each religious hierarchy reacted to eugenics and racial policies in different ways.

Catholics, especially after Pius XI delivered *castii conuubi* in 1931, knew that any intervention in life or death, whether for eugenic or humanitarian motivations, counted as a sin. Yet prelates, eagerly protecting the 1933 Concordat between the Vatican and the Nazi regime, slid away from opposition. After priests read a condemnation of eugenic policies from their pulpits in January

1934, the leadership backed away from a confrontation with state officials. Theologians distinguished between the obligation to report people who might suffer from genetic damage or to assist in eugenics operations and the actual performance of operations. Negotiations produced an exemption for all Catholic physicians not paid by public health institutions who objected on moral grounds. Moreover, a few bishops, such as Conrad Gröber, declared their enthusiasm for the "aims if not the methods" of sterilization. Physicians (mostly male) could simply refuse to participate; however, health care workers (mostly female) were told by both church and state to collaborate in eugenic operations the pope had declared immoral.

In reacting to the Nazi state, Protestant leaders divided into three camps: the fanatically pro-Nazi German Christians, the mainstream official German Evangelical Church, and the dissenting Confessing Church. Whereas the German Christians converted wholeheartedly to an almost pagan Nazified faith, the other two branches adopted its principles with somewhat less zeal. Since the 1920s, progressive Protestant health and social workers had lobbied for eugenics legislation—and when they heard about the new laws they took credit for having drafted them in the first place. Across the Protestant spectrum, no objections were raised to eugenic or racial hygiene laws. Even the dissidents limited their opposition to theological issues and stayed away from "political" concerns, such as racial policy.

The Office of Racial Policies sponsored courses for clergymen and encouraged the Protestant-led Working Committee for National Racial (*Völkisch*) Health.[57] In eugenic tracts written for the clergy, the Christian faith was not subjected to head-on criticism, but its precepts were harnessed to new conclusions. One Protestant, for example, waxing eloquent, celebrated the arrival of an instinctive "Aryan weltanschauung" that only the racially fit could grasp: "[B]ecause Adolf Hitler has made this instinct conscious, indeed desired by the *Volk*, it is now elevated as a popular and simultaneously methodological weltanschauung . . . " This awkward mix of religion, instinct, and racism epitomizes Nazi antiintellectual scientism. Already in 1933, this author continues, the Nazis removed contradictions (*Gegensätze*) from the community by "laying hands on the wounded places of the *volks*body."[58] Medical experts addressed special workshops and courses to inform clergymen about the latest laws.

Perhaps most revolutionary was the mandate to intervene in the decision-making of "unfit" individuals about reproduction (against their wishes), in contradiction to Christian precepts. Where conventional ethical injunctions urged mercy toward the weak, Nazi ethics insisted on ruthlessness. Instead of "love thy neighbor," racial educators preached "evaluate your neighbor." Praising Christian concepts, Nazi educators then inserted a racial dimension. Protestant eugenicists such as Hans Harmsen fit Christian ethics into the new guidelines, saying that the "artificial preservation of dying life" contradicted God's will.[59] A new racial religion grafted itself onto Christian terms so that Protestants and Catholics would see Nazism as an ally in their battle against social disorder. Linked to the sacred, the *Volk* became elevated to a cause that mandated sacrifice. The slogan *Gemeinnutz vor Eigennutz*, "collective over the individual good," fit Christian values.

Although it might seem paradoxical that a stridently masculinist regime recruited women to its ranks, racial programs depended on women's cooperation. Special efforts to win support from clergy and physicians were made because these community leaders commanded great respect and could sway public opinion. Different considerations framed the propaganda drive to attract women. Until 1933, calls for racial purity did not leave the realm of rhetoric. Until the experts actually began to draft legislation, no one seemed to have realized that any breeding program would require women's backing. Women played crucial roles—as mothers, of course—but also as health care workers, teachers, social workers, and community members. Given the public's shocking ignorance about genetics, actual diagnostics depended often on observations made by low-level custodians who would report on their clients' and charges' daily behavior. Women typically occupied low-paid positions from which they could make judgments (as teachers, health care and social workers, mothers, and neighborhood observers)—that is, could act as denouncers. Moreover, at the lowest rungs of the social, educational and health professions, women bore an unusually large share of responsibility for the care of the "less worthy," because government welfare agencies shunted off the hopeless cases to private, religious charitable institutions.[60]

Whereas male leaders ignored what seemed an obvious connection between breeding programs and women before 1933, women Nazis made the connection from the earliest days of the party. Hildegard Passow, in 1932, asked, "What responsibilities does Adolf Hitler assign to the woman? How does he build her into the cathedral of the German *Volkstum*?" She answered, "Hitler recognizes in the woman the protector of pure blood, of the maternal ideal to whom he has entrusted the youth and therefore the future of the *Volk*."[61] Another early Nazi convert called woman "the born transmitter of culture" because that mission required so much "intelligence, tact, organizational talent, and selflessness—repression of the dearly loved me."[62] Lydia Gotschewski, a major party organizer in the 1920s, said: "The woman does not proceed from the 'I', but rather from the 'We' and the 'You'. On our banners stands . . . one single command: Germany must live even if we must die."[63] This was "collective good" raised to the next level.

The leaders, who before 1933 had sedulously ignored women as voters, suddenly realized that the racial program that lay at the heart of Nazism required women's enthusiastic cooperation. Within weeks of Hitler's takeover, a deluge of pamphlets, textbooks, broadsides, newspaper articles, and special journals flooded the market. Even Goebbels belatedly tried to undo the damage of blatant misogyny in the Nazi movement. Unable to refute charges of prejudice against women, he dismissed accusations of Nazi misogyny as the result of a Jewish disinformation campaign. From the outset, he said, the Nazi movement was "in its nature a masculine movement . . . that does not mean any kind of degradation of the woman, no difference in status . . . because women assumed responsibility for the care of the future generation." Picking up an old theme, one ideologue declared: "The more sharply each sex limits itself to its particular sphere of responsibility, the more it will find power really to fulfill its mandates." In metaphors recalling both religious and military ideals, Goebbels concluded that the mother was the underlying guarantee (*Unterpfand*) for the eternal life of her *Volk*. "The man senses that the woman strikes a blow on her terrain just as strong as he does on his."[64] Hans Schemm told women,

I have always said that the German women in many cases have stood behind national socialism more steadfastly than the men . . . because their souls have not been burdened by too much intellectualism, because the woman fundamentally is led not by reason but by feelings.[65]

Urging women to rally against the impending racial crisis, Minister of the Interior Wilhelm Frick told his radio audience on Mothers' Day: "We find ourselves at a turning point! The salvation of Germany depends not only on the enthusiasm of our Fatherland, but depends just as much on the devotion of our women and girls to the family and motherhood."[66] These appeals recalled the urgent tones of 1914 propaganda calling on women to come to the aid of their *Vaterland* in times of crisis. But such verbiage also reinforced the gender stereotypes propagated by women Nazi leaders and anchored identity in fixed gender types. After traditional gender behavior had been displaced in Weimar culture, the Nazi message revived one aspect of tradition.[67] But women were summoned to act out conventional roles in the service of the state, not the family or even the local community. Just as propaganda praised the doctor as a *Volksarzt*, mothers heard themselves summoned as *Volksmütter*. Rather than caring for their own children (or even their own happiness), they were to devote themselves to the *Volkskörper* (racial body politic). Gentle Mother Nature became a ruthless Darwinist, willing to extinguish "unfit" life in the interests of the community. "For the German *Volk* and the national socialist revolution that serves it, fate hinges on whether the *volk* body can be numerically maintained and increased and beyond that also renewed in a valuable way."[68] Walter Gross reminded women of their vital role, but his metaphor made their lowly status clear.

You are a link in the chain of life, a little drop in the great bloodstream of your *Volk*. . . . After all, you as an individual are not at all as great and significant as you imagined you were yesterday. . . . Pause to think. We have become more humble and respectful faced with the great laws of fate. . . . We can do nothing else than humbly recognize the law of our human limitations and to recognize that as humans we have been born as what we are—not as Eskimos or Chinese, but as German people. . . . Not because we deserved it, not because we were guilty, not because

we wanted it that way. It is fate . . . and there is no choice but to
reconcile ourselves to that fate. . . . Let us . . . follow the laws of
God in deepest humility and piety.[69]

Women Nazis told the unconvinced that by honoring their racial
calling, they would win respect.

Quoting an early pamphlet entitled "Germanic Renewal Begins with the Germanic Woman,"[70] one convinced Nazi woman
picked up a familiar theme. Women, praised since the nineteenth
century as priestesses of the home, were to become the handmaids
of the racial state. A new cadre of women leaders proselytized just
after Nazi victory: "Because it is the duty of woman to complement the fighter," the new state "needs men with the will to be
100 percent man, and women with the will to embody 100 percent
their femaleness."[71] The party's director of women's education,
Auguste Reber-Gruber, declared "The woman has always served as
the best health official of the state."[72] The pages of official news-
letters for women leaders were redolent with racial messages. Margarete Unger saw women as the "tools of the state."[73]

The eugenic and racial axioms that divided humanity into
"fit" and "unfit" reinforced sharp gender divisions and generated
a vision of society putatively anchored in natural law. By inscribing
racial categories on the body and assigning roles by gender, propaganda contructed a new vision of a modern, scientific Mother Nature. As in bourgeois nineteenth-century Western society, a vigorous purity campaign was launched in the face of advancing
industrial, urban society. As in the previous century, physicians,
clergy, and women operated at the core of drives against moral and
physiological pollution. The Nazi worldview, however, held out the
promise of a comprehensive biological program that would integrate every citizen according to categories they called objective,
scientific, and natural. After religion lost its force, a new racial,
civic religion linked civic worth to putative biological traits.

CONCLUSIONS

Against the backdrop of fear, putatively biological, scientifically
authoritative binary concepts were deployed to establish a "natural" social structure. Long before even Nazi leaders planned for
genocide, these new divisions reinforced what Robert Jay Lifton

called "psychic numbing" among those who planned and administered racial programs. In this process, Lifton says, the individual disassociates himself or herself from action that he or she might otherwise find deplorable.[74] Nazi biological language facilitated that process by mobilizing science to disassociate individuals in the "chosen" categories from those cast out as "unworthy," "dangerous," and "threatening." This constituted an important step in disassociating these people from the category "human."

The invasion of daily life by state media and surveillance systems overturned bourgeois liberal notions about a "private" sphere beyond the reach of politics. Collective life overrode private rights and even thoughts. "Community," a key term in the Nazi project, underwent a transformation from regional and religious to racial marker. "Citizenship" was defined not in terms of equal access to universal rights, but in terms of bio-politics.[75] This curtailment of equality contradicted the promise of civic equality for all held out by the Enlightenment. Thus, even as racial experts' scientific optimism about their ability to perfect human society upheld one legacy of Enlightenment thought, their politics destroyed another vision inspired by Enlightenment thinkers: the ideal of equal civic rights for all citizens. We still live with the twin legacy.

As we ponder "lessons" we realize, too, that even as we deplore Nazi racial science and recoil from the simplistic, crude formulations of Nazi propaganda, some of the medical-ethical dilemmas inherent in their project have not disappeared from our society. Who ought to make health decisions? The oath of Hippocrates, for example, no longer remains in its fifth century B.C. form. Almost half of all American medical schools have modified the oath. The original read: "I will give no deadly medicine to anyone if asked, nor suggest any such counsel; furthermore, I will not give to a woman an instrument to produce an abortion." The reformed, 1964 version reads, "Most especially must I tread with care in matters of life and death. If it is given me to save a life, all thanks. But it may also be within my power to take a life: this awesome responsibility must be faced with great humbleness and awareness of my own frailty. Above all I must not play at God."[76] Daniel Callahan, in the best-seller *What Kind of Life?*, says that because financial and technical resources have become so scarce, individuals (especially those who are elderly and require expensive treatment to remain alive) can no longer make health care decisions over their own lives. Americans, he insists, must choose between investing in younger, more vigorous life and acquiescing to the personal desires of older. The possibility of life support has alerted us to the centrality of language in framing ethical dilemmas. Of course, we condemn terms like "life unworthy of living" and "fit," just as we deplore the crude eugenics experiments of the 1930s. But debates about the beginning of "life" and the "personhood" of someone in a coma remain alive. Though the Nazi dream of a total genetic census on all citizens arouses our incredulity, the three billion dollar federal Genome project promises to map our total genetic inheritance. Though no one speaks of a national "genetic property" (*Erbgut*), biologists promise that this vast data collection will enable scientists to improve the physical quality of life. Over fifty years after the Nazi propaganda blitz, powerful media establish the parameters of our vision of individual and community, person and non-person, and health and illness—shaping our idea of people as autonomous individuals or abstract things. The Nazi case study alerts us to pay attention not only to the specific victims of Nazi discourse ("Jew," "unfit," "asocial"), but to the process designed to transform any category of people from citizen to pariah.

Robert Gellately

"A Monstrous Uneasiness": Citizen Participation and Persecution of the Jews in Nazi Germany

THE NAZI DICTATORSHIP CREATED IN THE MONTHS AFTER HITLER'S AP-
pointment as chancellor on January 30, 1933, allowed German
citizens little scope for participation in the formal politics normally
associated with democracies. For the most part the political lives of
Germans consisted of membership in Nazi, or Nazified, organizations, activity at locally staged propaganda events, or voting in
occasional token elections whose results were foregone conclusions.
In view of the severe restrictions on formal political activity, it is
hard to explain why, during the latter part of the war, and especially after 1945, there grew up outside Germany a widespread
belief that Germans as a people were heavily implicated in, and
publicly and collectively accountable for, the worst crimes of the
Nazi regime. The collective guilt thesis cannot be sustained, because it is closely tied to the existence of democratic freedoms and
choices that were plainly denied to German citizens during the
period of Nazi rule. As Karl Jaspers pointed out, few if any choices
were open to ordinary Germans, so that what they did as citizens
amounted to little more than a ritualized, orchestrated, or commanded and coerced performance of duties.[1] This resolution of the
problem of collective guilt, however, seems to suggest that German
citizens were inactive and had no part in persecutions such as those
suffered by Jews in the country.

I want to suggest that the notion of citizen participation that
informs most studies of Nazi Germany is too restrictive to help us
explain how the Nazi dictatorship functioned and what role citi-

zens played. The concept of citizen participation invariably refers to formal or public political life at the level of elections and "free" organizations. I want to extend the use of citizen participation to refer to non-formal and non-organizational activities, to what might be termed the micro-politics of Nazi Germany. This conceptualization allows us to lay to rest the collective guilt charge but also to explore the limits and possibilities of citizen participation in the political life of the country. This chapter reflects the findings of a number of recent studies of "popular opinion and political dissent," and "everyday" or grassroots history, which reject the monolithic picture of the Third Reich and question the open-armed reception of all Nazi messages by the people. However, it emphasizes another aspect of popular behavior. Instead of focusing on the ways some people apparently ignored or even broke with official norms, the chapter looks at how others reinforced those norms by offering the authorities denunciations, that is, by volunteering information about suspected "criminality" that came to their attention. In this way citizens made a vital contribution to the operation of the Gestapo, and, thereby, of the Nazi terror. A surprising finding is that, with rare exceptions, this information does not seem to have been provided because of any deep commitment to Nazi ideology. In fact, some people acted out of "non-Nazi" motives recognized as so self-serving that they deeply troubled the country's leaders.

Without citizen participation, the efforts of the Gestapo to deal with political opponents and the sources of resistance would certainly have been hampered. However, when it came to isolating the Jews from the rest of the German population, tip-offs from the population were essential, not least because only with this popular surveillance would it have been possible to infiltrate the more private realms of social and sexual life. It was not necessary that everyone become antisemitic, much less violent or actively involved in officially termed "excesses," or even that most get behind official efforts. What was required was that a sufficient number of citizens come forward, for whatever reason, to supply information they alone were in a position to collect. And of course, rumors and uncertainty quickly spread, so that hardly anyone felt beyond the reach of "the Gestapo."[2]

Although the chapter shares some of the views presented in the recent literature, especially the studies dealing with "popular opinion," it differs in one important respect from the interpretation summarized by the oft-cited remark that "the road to Auschwitz was built by hate, but paved with indifference."[3] The term "popular opinion" (a genuine "public opinion" having ceased to exist in Nazi Germany) tends to emphasize *reactive* aspects of social behavior—what did people think about what was going on, what was their "mood and attitude"? Variously conceived concepts of "popular opinion" largely subordinate more active, participatory elements. Although it is certainly important to investigate the extent to which people in Germany (and the occupied territories, for that matter) reacted favorably or otherwise to antisemitic propaganda and the persecutions, it is also necessary to investigate the extent to which at least *some* citizens (and non-citizens as well) adjusted their behavior in support of the changing official stand on the Jews. In dealing with the motives for participation, it may be useful to ask whether these were affective, or instrumental, or a combination of both. My chapter suggests that at least some people were more *active* than passive or indifferent. It also challenges Otto Dov Kulka's view that the reaction of the German population to the persecution of the Jews amounted to "a kind of national conspiracy of silence."[4] My argument is that at least inside Germany proper (and to some extent also in occupied Western Europe from the spring of 1940), the transformation of Nazi theory and policy into practice required active participation at the local level of a sizable number of people in the official and semi-official endeavors to anathematize Jews and others who were out of step with the regime on the "Jewish question." The situation in Eastern Europe, especially after the beginning of the war against the Soviet Union in June 1941, was in certain important respects qualitatively and quantitatively different from the persecutions in the West. In the East, the massive killing operations behind the lines and the mechanized mass murder in death camps such as Auschwitz and Treblinka were unparalleled by experiences in Western Europe.

THE AMBIGUITIES OF THE "GOOD CITIZEN"

It would be interesting to study conceptions of the duties of the "good citizen" *(Bürger)* and their evolution over the twelve-year history of Hitler's dictatorship.[5] There was a long tradition in Germany as to how the "good citizen" should participate, and many of these civic virtues, like other social traditions, such as workers' pride in doing "good work," did not disappear overnight. In the course of consolidating power, the Nazis paid a great deal of attention to keeping up at least the appearance of legality, in part in order to maintain legitimacy in the eyes of most citizens and thus to tap their sense of civic loyalty. It was indicative that Hitler was cautious about pushing the revolution and had already begun to put the brakes on it by the summer of 1933. He later boasted publicly that the Nazi revolution was the best one of all time, for "not a single pane of glass was broken."[6] Most "good citizens" had a deep respect for the sanctity of property, and those not earmarked as opponents, such as Communists, Socialists, or Jews, more or less came to support the regime as Hitler mastered the crisis situation the country had faced since at least 1930. An alleged "Communist threat" was put down, the civil service was "restored," the Storm Troopers were reined in during the June 1934 purge, and, of course, most people welcomed the economic recovery from the depths of the depression. Even within the working class, as several oral history projects make clear, "good times" were thought to have returned.[7] For their part, Nazi leaders sought to draw on the tradition of the "good citizen," linked now to that of the "racial comrade," and to encourage Germans' "idealistic" commitment and spirit of self-sacrifice.

One way individual citizens are asked to participate in any political system pertains to assisting its enforcement agencies to uphold the existing order. The police, even one beyond the reach of the law such as the Nazi secret police, require that citizens become involved in the enforcement process by providing information about suspected crimes. In Nazi Germany, the Gestapo was intended ultimately to become a "thought police" in order to monitor new and ever-expanding areas of "criminality." Because the regime sought control and surveillance over so many novel aspects of social and political life, the scope of potential "criminality" was increasingly broadened. Several conflicting consequences ensued. On the one hand, these intentions and designs, for the most part, would have remained idle fantasies without citizen participation in the undertaking. However, in opening the door for citizens to play a role in "reproducing order," the regime also made it possible for more people than ever before to take advantage of the situation by informing the police about the "suspicious" behavior of someone they wanted out of the way. Allegations would be taken seriously no matter how apparently insignificant the "crime," at least if the charge pertained to one of the regime's designated "opponents" such as the Jews. These factors combined to produce an explosive growth of denunciations, the information volunteered from citizens who contacted the authorities to offer tip-offs.

The spread of denunciations, however, presented the regime with a genuine dilemma, and, perhaps contrary to what one might expect, leaders were of two minds about them. Although the regime required and encouraged citizen participation in order to isolate the Jews and those who refused to go along with antisemitism or other official policies, it never introduced a universal obligation to denounce all criminal deeds or even all "political criminality." One suspects that this official reserve was largely a response to the nature and extent of the denunciations that took place. By the spring and summer of 1933, and well beyond, there is evidence of chagrin in official circles about the increasing deluge of denunciations, some of which were baseless and many of which arose out of self-serving motives. Not only was this deluge a direct affront to the cherished Nazi ideal of the harmonious "community of the people" *(Volksgemeinschaft)* that was supposed to overcome the divisions and rancor of bourgeois society, but it could lead to bureaucratic tangles and disorders of various kinds. When, for example, some spouses began denouncing one another in order to obtain divorces, the regime could hardly applaud, for the result was an undermining of the mutual trust essential to marriage. An old German saying, repeated by the minister of justice, who as late as November 1944 attempted to give direction on this matter to judges across the country, notes that "the denouncer is the greatest scoundrel in the entire country."[8] This was a view shared, on numerous occasions, by some of the country's Nazi leaders.

Hitler's own early concern about the spread of denunciations reflected the official worry that runs like a red line through the course of the regime. Denunciations could obviously be used for personal, selfish purposes, purposes that not only were not intended by the regime and conflicted with some of its ideals, but worse, also disrupted the socioeconomic order. After a cabinet meeting in early May of 1933, Hitler privately confessed to Justice Minister Gürtner and another cabinet colleague that, to his dismay, "we are living in a sea of denunciations and human evil . . . so that someone denounces another and simultaneously puts himself forward as the successor." Gürtner reported Hitler as having said that the provisions of many of the Weimar Republic's business laws were such that entrepreneurs occasionally had been forced to break them in order to survive. People who gained knowledge of these commonplace illegalities, however, were retrospectively seeking to capitalize on it, thus producing a widely perceived "danger of being denounced to the attorney general or some other place at any time", which in turn was causing "a monstrous uneasiness in the economy." Hitler concluded that such denunciations should not be tolerated.[9] Easier said than done, especially given the prerequisites for the implementation of the intentions of leading Nazis.

The Gestapo, for its part, was centralized, armed with new powers of arrest and detention, and linked to a larger network of the Nazi Party and German state. In radical fashion it overcame most of the institutional problems faced by the police prior to 1933, and, with the suspension of the rule of law, it was given the upper hand in dealing with suspects. Nevertheless, the Gestapo, like Weimar's police, necessarily continued to depend on citizen participation, especially in isolating the Jews.[10] This popular involvement transformed Germany into a kind of auto-surveillance system that drastically limited the social and political spaces in which resistance, opposition, or dissent might have taken root.[11] Tracking down all forms of disobedience was a particular concern of Nazi leaders, especially after the outbreak of war in 1939. War measures called on citizens as never before to be vigilant, yet at the same time the Gestapo and justice officials warned people not to misuse the denunciation for their own purposes. But at the very moment that the Reich security officials were attempting to control the flow of information, Goebbels's "extraordinary radio measures," which outlawed listening to foreign radio broadcasts, promised that those who did not denounce known offenders were themselves to be prosecuted. As the minister of justice bitterly complained without effect, those measures actually opened the floodgates for denunciations.[12] Thus the regime often pulled in opposite directions regarding citizen participation and ultimately came up with no effective means of controlling denunciations.

CITIZEN PARTICIPATION IN GESTAPO CASE-FILES

The role of citizen participation in general and especially in the persecution of the Jews can be seen from the particular angle in Gestapo case-files, the dossiers drawn up on all suspects brought to the attention of the secret police for whatever reason. These case-files are extremely rare documents. With the exception of the 19,000 that survived in the Bavarian city of Würzburg, and the 70,000 or so in Düsseldorf, almost all others were destroyed. These dossiers are heterogeneous: some contain only a shred of paper, while others run to many pages. These materials were not tampered with at war's end to remove potentially damning information, but certain types of information were never entered in the first place. For example, no mention is made of mistreatment and torture, extortion, intimidation, or entrapment, even though these and other dirty methods were common. Anyone reading through these files will soon become aware that many begin with such cryptic remarks as "our office has been informed," or "an anonymous letter indicates," and even that a citizen appeared personally to report on "suspicious behavior."

The extent of denunciations is confirmed by the quantitative analysis of the Düsseldorf Gestapo case-files by the late Reinhard Mann. He focused on a specific subgroup of the 70,000 Gestapo dossiers, namely the 5,000 or so of those classified by the Gestapo as "local card file Düsseldorf." These cards were for internal office use by the Gestapo, and were (and still are) the reference keys to the case-files. "Local card file Düsseldorf" is divided into 52 subsections, each of which corresponds to an aspect of the Gestapo's routine preoccupations. The largest single group of case-files pertains to the Communist Party (1,050 cards), with smaller numbers of cards on virtually every other political party (including the Nazi Party), and associations of all kinds. There are also cards on the paramilitary organizations once prominent in the Weimar Republic, the police, the youth movement, pacifists, freemasons, monarchists, and the religious denominations. Other files cover topics ranging from the press, radio, art, and music to the economy and trade unionism, the resistance movement, "malicious gossip," treason, and sabotage. However, Mann's analysis deals with but 41 of the 52 categories, or 3,770 of the 5,000 case-files. From the 3,770 cards, he selected 825 by random sampling techniques for close analysis. Additional files, some of which might have come from the 1,230 formally excluded, were drawn into the investigation through the procedure of a "snowball selection" designed to trace social nets to which an individual might have belonged. For example, according to this procedure, once a file was selected in the main sample, other persons mentioned in the dossier would eventually be included in the study. An unknown number of cases would have been analyzed through the adoption of this procedure. In the tables constructed by Mann, only the 825 cases from the main sample are cited. His quantitative analysis is important because it removes much of the mystery and guesswork about what the Gestapo did on a routine basis.

Criticism of Mann's work must be tempered, of course, by the fact that it remained incomplete at his death in 1981. However, historians need to be aware of a limitation of his analysis, a consequence of his decision to eliminate those eleven categories (and 1,230 cards) mentioned above. The following were left out: "Germans returning from abroad, foreigners, Jews, emigrants, foreign workers, prisoners of war, military espionage, economic sabotage, separatism, foreign legionnaires, and racially foreign minorities." Mann explained the exclusion of these groups by observing that these cards pertained primarily to foreigners, who like "Jewish fellow-citizens were subject to different legal norms," and that inclusion of such persons "would have complicated the investigation further."[13] These comments seem evasive; they are hardly convincing grounds to exclude these groups from a study devoted to everyday life in Nazi Germany.

In spite of its limitations, however, Mann's study conveys a sense of how denunciations fitted into the routine operation of the Gestapo. Of the 825 randomly sampled files, the largest single number (213 or 26 percent) consisted of files initiated when private citizens voluntarily informed the police. Another 24 cases (or 3 percent) were opened when businesses of one kind or another reported to the authorities: these cases could be added to the tip-

offs "from the population." Additional cases that could not easily
be identified as originating with information "from the population" probably did. Mann believed that were these taken into
account, the cases initiated by private citizens would be registered
as 33 percent of all the cases "at the least."[14] In 103 cases (13
percent) no information whatsoever is given about why a proceeding was initiated.

Great care must be taken with quantitative analysis of materials
such as Gestapo case-files, especially regarding the sources that led
to the opening of a case. We know that 26 percent of all cases
began with an *identifiable* denunciation, and this must be taken
as a minimum figure. Many of the other categories of cases—such
as those that began with information "from Nazi organizations"
or from "communal and state authorities" (which together initiated 13 percent of all cases)—also apparently depended to a large
degree upon tips from citizens. With all due caution, it seems
justified to suggest that denunciations from the population constituted the single most important cause for the initiation of Gestapo
proceedings of all kinds.

These figures indicate that the regime's dreaded enforcer in all
probability would have been hampered without extensive citizen
participation. This behavior has hitherto been largely ignored or
not fully understood.[15] One important implication to draw from a
recognition of this behavior is that we ought to rethink some of
the standard interpretations of "totalitarian" terror.[16] The Nazi
terror was not an "instrument" or object that inflicted itself in
unspecified ways on the people, but part of a dynamic social process that involved ever-changing interactions between the people
and the police. There is abundant corroborating evidence in the
eyewitness accounts and in other fragmentary police reports of
various kinds from localities elsewhere in Germany.[17]

Although these statistics suggest a greater degree of citizen
participation in the routine work of the Gestapo than one might
have suspected, the secret police itself seems to have been less an
active than a reactive organization, at least in generating cases. Its
"own observations" and/or those of its "agents" initiated but 15
percent of all proceedings of the Düsseldorf Gestapo. Information
obtained through interrogations, which set in motion an additional
13 percent of the cases, indicates a more active role in these in-

stances, though originally some such undertakings may have been stimulated from a source external to the Gestapo. An important part was also played by the numerous other "control organizations" (the regular, uniformed police, the Kripo, SD, and SS), collectively responsible for initiating 17 percent of all cases, a figure, however, that raises a question about the role of the SS in the domestic police system.

It is possible that some cases were sparked off by a tip from official sources, as when a Gestapo official merely wrote in the file that "according to a confidentially disclosed report made to me today, it is alleged that the butcher Hans Schmidt remarked as follows," and so on.[18] Still, there would seem no reason for the dossier to be silent if the tip had an official or even semiofficial origin. In all likelihood the source was "from the population," but the full details of this side of the story remain hidden.[19]

CITIZEN PARTICIPATION AND THE "JEWISH QUESTION"

At the local level, the Gestapo was formally responsible for the fate of the Jews, up to and including their deportation to the death camps. Beginning in early 1933, as more and more antisemitic laws and regulations were put on the books, the Gestapo was the main official, but not the only, enforcer of the dictatorship's will. Enforcement was not hampered by the fact that there was no clear, unequivocal law outlawing all contacts between Jews and non-Jews. In fact, the absence of such a law increased the flow of denunciations; because of the vagueness of what was forbidden, denouncers could run to the authorities on the slightest whim. Anyone suspected of not accepting the letter or spirit of the measures against Jews and brought to the attention of the Gestapo was entered into one of the case-files. Some dossiers simply begin with the remark "suspicious behavior"; others state, without another word in the file, that a citizen brought to police attention for unstated reasons "continues to maintain contacts with Jews."[20] This and other "political" charges were taken extremely seriously because they might indicate that the person involved rejected the Nazi regime's doctrines on race.[21]

Social and sexual relations across the ethnic boundary were of paramount concern for a regime that saw "racial mixing" as the leading cause for the decline and fall of civilizations. The Gestapo was especially keen to stop these forbidden contacts, and the Nuremberg Laws of September 1935 provided it with a legal device to do so. Even before then, and certainly thereafter, Jews and non-Jews who kept up old friendships and social contacts were in danger of being denounced. The Gestapo dossiers reveal that some people definitely said no to Nazi antisemitism, and demonstrated what can only be called selfless heroism. However, a close examination of the dossiers of those who ran afoul of the Gestapo for failing to shun the Jews supports the view that the Gestapo was to a remarkable extent dependent upon the participation of citizens.

As the Gestapo emerged in the course of 1933 to replace the "hot" terror of the Nazi radicals, especially the Storm Troopers, with a cold, administrative, police terror, it quietly stepped up pressure on the Jews and anyone who dared sympathize with them. Although the intensification of official efforts and the presence of many enthusiastic officials in the Gestapo were important, the secret police could not on its own enforce racial policies designed to isolate the Jews. It lacked a sufficient number of officials or other operatives, and was simply not in a position to infiltrate the more intimate realm of social and sexual life.[23] The Gestapo required, and attained, more information from citizens in enforcing the racial policies designed to isolate the Jews than in other fields of operation—as shown by the general figures cited above. For example, of the 175 cases in the Würzburg files pertaining to separating Jews and non-Jews in the specific area of sexual and social relations, 57 percent began with a denunciation from a citizen. These cases involved allegations of the charge of "race defilement" or the more nebulous one of "friendship to the Jews," which might simply mean one expressed reservations about official antisemitic policies or actions. Although Mann's study indicated that information from the population initiated about one-third of all cases, this lower figure results in part from his sample, which specifically excluded the files of Jews (indeed, left out several other groups that were particularly vulnerable to denunciations, for example, the foreign workers). Some of the sympathizers with the Jews, and many who voiced doubts in public about the regime's antisemitic policies or actions, might have been covered by Mann's study if they had been accused of "malicious gossip," for example, or if their case wound up in one of the other categories covered, such as "opposition." All that can be suggested here is that had the sample been drawn from the full range of the Düsseldorf Gestapo's activities, especially if it had included Jews, then in all likelihood the overall percentage of cases that began with a denunciation would have been higher, precisely because, as the Würzburg dossiers suggest, the excluded groups were the most vulnerable to denunciations.

Besides pointing to a high degree of citizen cooperation with the Gestapo in enforcing racial-sexual policy, quantitative analysis of the Würzburg Gestapo files on allegations of "race defilement" or "friendship to the Jews" indicates that the Gestapo itself was responsible for initiating less than 1 percent of such cases. This figure constrasts sharply with the general figure of 15 percent mentioned by Mann, and underlines the importance of the Gestapo's reliance on information from external sources. That an additional 15 percent of these kinds of cases in Würzburg began with information gathered at interrogations leads one to suspect that once people were brought in for interrogation, incriminating information could be wrested from them. The main point to note here is the extent to which a study of these Würzburg files documents the participation of citizens in the enforcement process. Even paid informers or agents are conspicuous by their absence. Perhaps there was enough volunteered information to make the use of agents superfluous. In these Würzburg files, at least, it was very rare for paid agents to offer information about transgressions of racial policy. The absence of documents does not mean that agents were not more involved, but to say anything further would be overly speculative.[24]

The Gestapo acted on the information first, and worried about the reasons it was provided later. It acted on virtually all tips, at least if they pertained to important "opponents," even when the information was patently self-serving or originated from persons of dubious credibility. Indeed, the Gestapo files in Würzburg suggest that the antisemitic measures were frequently taken advantage of. It appears that on many occasions denunciations of Jews or of those who allegedly sympathized with them or disagreed with official antisemitism were offered with little or no foundation, or were

knowingly false. This impression is confirmed by both official declarations of the regime and the testimony of survivors.[25]

It is worth remembering here that denunciations cut two ways.
Not only did they make it possible to pick up the slightest signs of
dissent or disobedience in the broad area of the "Jewish question,"
for example, but also they placed structural obstacles in the way of
anyone wishing to express kindness or solidarity with the Jews.
Rumors about an "army" of Gestapo officials and informers, and
the knowledge that local enforcers—who were high-handed and
brutal at the best of times—were at their least tolerant when it
came to disagreement with official racial policies, created "invisible walls"[26] between the Jews and their neighbors, colleagues, and
former business associates. Furthermore, measures like the Nuremberg Laws of 1935 gave a new and more dangerous twist to any
form of "friendly" relations with Jews. Greeting a Jewish neighbor
or friend in the street grew inadvisable, even foolhardy, as did
continuing to socialize with Jews in the privacy of one's home—let
alone in public places such as restaurants. Any sympathy for the
plight of the Jews, or any reserve about the efficacy of antisemitic
policies or actions, was stifled, at least in part because such expressions could be used as the basis for a denunciation. It was also well
known that even the patently innocent could be charged, with
almost complete legal impunity for the accuser, especially if the
accusation was aimed at the Jews (or other important "opponents"
such as Communists) and their sympathizers. We shall never know
how much kindness might have been shown the Jews under less
foreboding circumstances. Most people in Germany decided to
avoid the race issue as far as possible and to eschew all contact with
Jewish citizens.

DENUNCIATIONS, PERSECUTION OF THE JEWS, AND THE FACES OF FASCISM

It would be interesting to compare citizen participation in the two
other "Faces of Fascism," with respect to the persecution of the
Jews. This is a large topic, and what follows is based on preliminary
investigations and offered as stimulation to further reflection and
research. One of the points that may be worth thinking about is to
move the discussion away from whether or not antisemitism was

"popular," for that implicitly places undue emphasis on affective motivation. It might be more useful to examine the extent to which citizens were prepared—for whatever reason—to offer information to the authorities that in turn made it possible to realize leaders' changing goals.

Vichy France

There were limits on the extent to which the "Gestapo system" could be exported elsewhere in Western Europe, precisely because this "system" only worked with the participation of citizens. The Gestapo's experts could piece together a police apparatus, in collaboration with native experts, but it is clear that a crucial factor in the routine functioning of these systems, just as in Germany, was the extent to which they could elicit citizens' cooperation. On occasion the same police officials who helped to create the domestic German system moved into the occupied areas, but one should not overestimate the importance of their contribution. They were dispensable in the sense that anyone could operate the levers of power; these would not move, however, without some cooperation from the population.

In Vichy France, a social environment conducive to the effective functioning of the police developed quickly. In fact, what Robert Paxton writes of France likely applied to most countries in Western Europe in the summer of 1940: "There is simply no mistaking the joy and relief which came flooding after the anguish when Marshal Pétain announced over the radio, shortly after noon on June 17, that the government he had formed the night before was seeking an armistice."[27] Paxton notes that "the most elementary promptings of normalcy in the summer of 1940, the urge to return to home and job, started many Frenchmen down a path of everyday complicity that led gradually and eventually to active assistance to German measures undreamed of in 1940."[28] Bertram Gordon adds that "the apparent totality of the German victory made even the most ardent collaborationists seem prudent in the summer of 1940. As the war progressed, opportunists of all kinds were attracted to the movements of the collaboration and each undoubtedly had its share. Denunciations and profiteering were commonplace."[29]

In a book on denunciations during the German occupation of France, André Halimi goes so far as to suggest that between three and five million letters of denunciation, signed or anonymous, were sent to various authorities in France.[30] Even if he exaggerates the number of letters, as one historian believes,[31] his many examples make clear that this kind of denunciation was far from uncommon in France, that the motives of the writers were not always "system-loyal" but frequently instrumental, and that in this way the regime reaped the benefits in terms of surveillance and control. According to fragmentary testimony from the Gestapo in France, it is clear that many Frenchmen were also willing to go to police headquarters personally in order to denounce the declared enemies of the regime. Klaus Barbie reported that in Lyons people went to kiosks set up for the purpose to give information.[32]

Fascist Italy

Raul Hilberg points out that the anti-Jewish measures of the Italians "were as thorough in appearance as any that had been drafted by German hands, but the Italian government failed to follow up its decrees and, frequently, even to enforce them."[33] Cooperation from the people was neither forthcoming nor entirely expected, even when the persecution of the Jews was stepped up and even later, when under pressure by the German occupation authorities, roundups began to seek out the Jews who had gone underground. Susan Zuccotti claims that, nevertheless, at least some assistance from civilians was attained by the police at the time of the deportations of the Jews from Italy, and that many Jews "were betrayed by Italian informers—individual citizens motivated by general antisemitism and pro-nazism, private quarrels and vendettas, their own personal involvement in illegal activities, or just plain greed. The Nazis offered rewards for information leading to the arrests of Jews, and several Italians collected. More often, the Germans received anonymous letters."[34] Meir Michaelis makes the same point and adds that "while it is true that at least four-fifths of the Jews living in Italy succeeded in eluding the grasp of the SS and that most of these were saved by Italian Aryans of all classes, it is no less true that such successes as Bosshammer [Eichmann's expert in Italy] was able to achieve were largely due to (willing and unwill-

ing) Italian collaborators."[35] Not only were local agents of the Gestapo at work, but Jews were uncovered by Fascist action squads
headed by "thugs and Jew-baiters who took advantage of the German occupation to do their worst. Not a few Jews had their hiding-
places betrayed by Italian civilians who were actuated either by
racial prejudice or by greed for gain (the Germans having offered
rewards for the denunciation of Jews). There were even a few rene-
gade Jews who made common cause with the enemies of their
people."[36] Perhaps sharing, or at least sensing, the lack of popular
support for the deportation of the Jews, Italian officials and even
the Italian police were considered incapable of the necessary "zeal"
by Germans sent to the country to conduct the deportations. An
important factor in explaining the extent of collaboration in the
persecutions was not only the oft-cited assimilation of the Jews in
Italy and the paucity of antisemitism there, but simply that many
Italians were not willing, for whatever reason, actively to support
official antisemitism.

CONCLUSION

When I began to examine the Gestapo case-files several years ago,
numerous scholarly books and articles were appearing on "everyday" or grassroots resistance and dissent. A more nuanced picture
of the dictatorship has emerged from this work. At the same time,
however, we cannot overlook the many examples in the Gestapo
case-files of the *positive* disposition of *some* citizens toward the
regime, or, more to the point here, their willing participation in
the Gestapo system. Moreover, additional forms of evidence reinforce this conclusion: the files of local Nazi Party organizations and
the memoirs, diaries, and the oral testimony of survivors. For all
kinds of reasons, some citizens cooperated, even with the regime's
dreaded secret police, and their cooperation made possible the
enforcement of racist policies such as those designed to stigmatize
and isolate the Jews. The Gestapo's activities in tracking down
other "opponents," such as the illegal Communist organizations,
or in detecting other forms of political "criminality," were also, to
a greater or lesser extent, dependent upon information supplied
by vigilant citizens and others outside the ranks of the Gestapo
itself.[37]

The question of what motivated people to inform the authorities, especially in the general area of the "Jewish question," is a complex one. Motives varied from case to case; sometimes they were mixed. Certainly, some people were moved to inform by passionately held antisemitic convictions, just as others came forward for purely personal reasons. However, motives are notoriously difficult to disentangle, and for that reason alone, it is unlikely that historians will ever be able to provide an entirely satisfactory answer.[38] For Nazi Germany, there is the further problem that many denunciations of Jews and others out of step with the regime's anti-Jewish policies cannot always be traced to affective motives such as antisemitism or even regime loyalty, but, insofar as historians can ascertain, were often linked to personal or instrumental concerns. As hard as it is to accept, it would be a delusion to think that we can explain the Holocaust, even its prelude inside Germany from 1933 to 1939, in terms of a manageable set of motives.[39]

Every question opens up some avenues for research and closes off others. The question of whether denouncers were or were not consciously motivated by antisemitism tends to draw our attention away from the intensely racist character of the actions of some German citizens. In any event, I think that our understanding of the persecution of the Jews in Nazi Germany might well be deepened if historians paid less attention to motives, and examined the linkages between racist behavior at the micro-political level and the functioning of this extremely racist system. In general we can determine that the *actions* of the denouncers were racist in that they helped the authorities identify "racial enemies," and in that they were necessary to the enforcement of racial policies. With this in mind, we can begin to grasp a certain pattern that runs through all the Gestapo cases of the kind mentioned in this essay: whatever the motives, the Nazi ideal of *Gemeinschaft* (community) divided the people of Germany into Insiders and Outsiders, "good citizens" and Jews. Those Germans who acted out the representation of this "good citizen" found it all the easier to participate in a regime whose goal was the elimination of Outsiders and to take advantage of official antisemitism. Denouncers as "good citizens" could always draw on the ideological reserves of the Nazi regime; the Jews as racial enemy number one were always Outsiders.

The Nazi regime set the tone, established the policy, offered the guidelines, and provided the powers that the police needed. The enforcement of antisemitic measures was certainly related to the zeal with which officials on the ground pursued their tasks, and there can be no doubt that the Gestapo was particularly zealous when it came to enforcing official antisemitism. Nevertheless, arguably most important to the "success" of the Gestapo in this sphere of activity was the extent to which citizens were prepared to participate—for whatever reason—by providing the kind of information required.[40] The entire apparatus would have been hampered without this cooperation. This form of citizen participation could not *simply* be commanded by the dictatorship; it had to be given voluntarily. This interpretation would seem to be supported by comparing and contrasting the German experience with what happened in Fascist Italy and Vichy France. The notion of community that splits people into Insiders and Outsiders was more intensely developed in Germany than in other European states, and this might have been an important factor in the lower rate of "successful" police operations in Italy, for example. One also thinks of the unwillingness of the Danish population to cooperate.[41] The effectiveness of the police, even obviously terroristic force such as the Gestapo, seems to have been less a result of sheer brutality than is often supposed. As a matter of fact, in the latter part of the war, the Gestapo grew ever harsher in Germany, in part as if to compensate for the erosion of its abilities to halt the growth of what it defined as "political criminality."[42] This erosion came at about the time "good citizens," who began to doubt the war's outcome, gradually ceased to provide information.[43]

Christopher R. Browning

One Day in Jozefow: Initiation to Mass Murder

IN MID-MARCH OF 1942, SOME 75 TO 80 PERCENT OF ALL VICTIMS OF THE
Holocaust were still alive, while some 20 to 25 percent had already
perished. A mere eleven months later, in mid-February 1943, the
situation was exactly the reverse. Some 75 to 80 percent of all
Holocaust victims were already dead, and a mere 20 to 25 percent
still clung to a precarious existence. At the core of the Holocaust
was an intense eleven-month wave of mass murder. The center of
gravity of this mass murder was Poland, where in March 1942,
despite two and a half years of terrible hardship, deprivation, and
persecution, every major Jewish community was still intact; eleven
months later, only remnants of Polish Jewry survived in a few rump
ghettos and labor camps. In short, the German attack on the Polish
ghettos was not a gradual or incremental program stretched over a
long period of time, but a veritable blitzkrieg, a massive offensive
requiring the mobilization of large numbers of shock troops at the
very period when the German war effort in Russia hung in the
balance.

The first question I would like to pose, therefore, is what were
the manpower sources the Germans tapped for their assault on
Polish Jewry? Since the personnel of the death camps was quite

---

This study is based entirely on the judicial records in the Staatsanwaltschaft Hamburg that
resulted from two investigations of Reserve Police Battalion 101: 141 Js 1957/62 and 141 Js 128/
65. German laws and regulations for the protection of privacy prohibit the revealing of names
from such court records. Thus, with the exception of Major Trapp, who was tried, convicted,
and executed in Poland after the war, I have chosen simply to refer to individuals generically by
rank and unit rather than by pseudonyms.

minimal, the real question quite simply is who were the ghetto-clearers? On close examination one discovers that the Nazi regime diverted almost nothing in terms of real military resources for this offensive against the ghettos. The local German authorities in Poland, above all SS and Police Leader (SSPF) Odilo Globocnik, were given the task but not the men to carry it out. They had to improvise by creating ad hoc "private armies." Coordination and guidance of the ghetto-clearing was provided by the staffs of the SSPF and commander of the security police in each district in Poland. Security police and gendarmerie in the branch offices in each district provided local expertise.[1] But the bulk of the manpower had to be recruited from two sources. The first source was the Ukrainians, Lithuanians, and Latvians recruited out of the prisoner of war camps and trained at the SS camp in Trawniki. A few hundred of these men, among them Ivan Demjanjuk, were then sent to the death camps of Operation Reinhard, where they outnumbered the German staff roughly 4 to 1. The majority, however, were organized into mobile units and became itinerant ghetto-clearers, traveling out from Trawniki to one ghetto after another and returning to their base camp between operations.[2]

The second major source of manpower for the ghetto-clearing operations was the numerous battalions of Order Police (*Ordnungspolizei*) stationed in the General Government. In 1936, when Himmler gained centralized control over all German police, the Secret State Police (Gestapo) and Criminal Police (Kripo) were consolidated under the Security Police Main Office of Reinhard Heydrich. The German equivalent of the city police (*Schutzpolizei*) and county sheriffs (*Gendarmerie*) were consolidated under the Order Police Main Office of Kurt Daluege. The Order Police were far more numerous than the more notorious Security Police and encompassed not only the regular policemen distributed among various urban and rural police stations in Germany, but also large battalion-size units, which were stationed in barracks and were given some military training. As with National Guard units in the United States, these battalions were organized regionally. As war approached in 1938–39, many young Germans volunteered for the Order Police in order to avoid being drafted into the regular army.

Beginning in September 1939, the Order Police battalions, each of approximately five hundred men, were rotated out from their home cities on tours of duty in the occupied territories. As the German empire expanded and the demand for occupation forces increased, the Order Police was vastly expanded by creating new reserve police battalions. The career police and prewar volunteers of the old battalions were distributed to become the noncommissioned officer cadres of these new reserve units, whose rank and file were now composed of civilian draftees considered too old by the Wehrmacht for frontline military service.

One such unit, Reserve Police Battalion 101 from Hamburg, was one of three police battalions stationed in the district of Lublin during the onslaught against the Polish ghettos. Because no fewer than 210 former members of this battalion were interrogated during more than a decade of judicial investigation and trials in the 1960s and early 1970s, we know a great deal about its composition. First let us examine the officer and noncommissioned officer (NCO) cadres.

The battalion was commanded by Major Wilhelm Trapp, a fifty-three-year-old career policeman who had risen through the ranks and was affectionately referred to by his men as "Papa Trapp." Though he had joined the Nazi Party in December 1932, he had never been taken into the SS or even given an SS-equivalent rank. He was clearly not considered SS material. His two captains, in contrast, were young men in their late twenties, both party members and SS officers. Even in their testimony twenty-five years later they made no attempt to conceal their contempt for their commander as both weak and unmilitary. Little is known about the first lieutenant who was Trapp's adjutant, for he died in the spring of 1943. In addition, however, the battalion had seven reserve lieutenants, that is men who were not career policemen but who, after they were drafted into the Order Police, had been selected to receive officer training because of their middle-class status, education, and success in civilian life. Their ages ranged from 33 to 48; five were party members, but none belonged to the SS. Of the 32 NCOs on whom we have information, 22 were party members but only seven were in the SS. They ranged in age from 27 to 40 years old; their average was 33½.

The vast majority of the rank and file had been born and reared in Hamburg and its environs. The Hamburg element was so dominant and the ethos of the battalion so provincial that contingents from nearby Wilhelmshaven and Schleswig-Holstein were considered outsiders. Over 60 percent were of working-class background, but few of them were skilled laborers. The majority of them held typical Hamburg working-class jobs: dock workers and truck drivers were most numerous, but there were also many warehouse and construction workers, machine operators, seamen and waiters. About 35 percent were lower-middle class, virtually all of whom were white-collar workers. Three-quarters of them were in sales of some sort; the other one-quarter performed various office jobs, both in the government and private sectors. The number of independent artisans, such as tailors and watch makers, was small; and there were only three middle-class professionals—two druggists and one teacher. The average age of the men was 39; over half were between 37 and 42, the *Jahrgänge* most intensively drafted for police duty after September 1939.

The men of Reserve Police Battalion 101 were from the lower orders of German society. They had experienced neither social nor geographic mobility. Very few were economically independent. Except for apprenticeship or vocational training, virtually none had any education after leaving the Volksschule at age 14 or 15. About 25 percent were Nazi Party members in 1942, most having joined in 1937 or later. Though not questioned about their pre-1933 political affiliation during their interrogations, presumably many had been Communists, Socialists, and labor union members before 1933. By virtue of their age, of course, all went through their formative period in the pre-Nazi era. These were men who had known political standards and moral norms other than those of the Nazis. Most came from Hamburg, one of the least Nazified cities in Germany, and the majority came from a social class that in its political culture had been anti-Nazi.

These men would not seem to have been a very promising group from which to recruit mass murderers of the Holocaust. Yet this unit was to be extraordinarily active both in clearing ghettos and in massacring Jews outright during the blitzkrieg against Polish Jewry. If these middle-aged reserve policemen became one major component of the murderers, the second question posed is how? Specifically, what happened when they were first assigned to kill Jews? What choices did they have, and how did they react?

Reserve Police Battalion 101 departed from Hamburg on June 20, 1942, and was initially stationed in the town of Bilgoraj, fifty miles south of Lublin. Around July 11 it received orders for its first major action, aimed against the approximately 1,800 Jews living in the village of Jozefow, about twenty miles slightly south and to the east of Bilgoraj. In the General Government a seventeen-day stoppage of Jewish transports due to a shortage of rolling stock had just ended, but the only such trains that had been resumed were several per week from the district of Krakau to Belzec. The railway line to Sobibor was down, and that camp had become practically inaccessible. In short the Final Solution in the Lublin district had been paralyzed, and Globocnik was obviously anxious to resume the killing. But Jozefow could not be a deportation action. Therefore the battalion was to select out the young male Jews in Jozefow and send them to a work camp in Lublin. The remaining Jews—about 1,500 women, children, and elderly—were simply to be shot on the spot.

On July 12 Major Trapp summoned his officers and explained the next day's assignment. One officer, a reserve lieutenant in 1st company and owner of a family lumber business in Hamburg, approached the major's adjutant, indicated his inability to take part in such an action in which unarmed women and children were to be shot, and asked for a different assignment. He was given the task of accompanying the work Jews to Lublin.[3] The men were not as yet informed of their imminent assignment, though the 1st company captain at least confided to some of his men that the battalion had an "extremely interesting task" (*hochinteressante Aufgabe*) the next day.[4]

Around 2 A.M. the men climbed aboard waiting trucks, and the battalion drove for about an hour and a half over an unpaved road to Jozefow. Just as daylight was breaking, the men arrived at the village and assembled in a half-circle around Major Trapp, who proceeded to give a short speech. With choking voice and tears in his eyes, he visibly fought to control himself as he informed his men that they had received orders to perform a very unpleasant task. These orders were not to his liking, either, but they came from above. It might perhaps make their task easier, he told the men, if they remembered that in Germany bombs were falling on the women and children. Two witnesses claimed that Trapp also mentioned that the Jews of this village had supported the partisans. Another witness recalled Trapp's mentioning that the Jews had instigated the boycott against Germany.[5] Trapp then explained to the men that the Jews in the village of Jozefow would have to be rounded up, whereupon the young males were to be selected out for labor and the others shot.

Trapp then made an extraordinary offer to his battalion: if any of the older men among them did not feel up to the task that lay before him, he could step out. Trapp paused, and after some moments, one man stepped forward. The captain of 3rd company, enraged that one of his men had broken ranks, began to berate the man. The major told the captain to hold his tongue. Then ten or twelve other men stepped forward as well. They turned in their rifles and were told to await a further assignment from the major.[6]

Trapp then summoned the company commanders and gave them their respective assignments. Two platoons of 3rd company were to surround the village; the men were explicitly ordered to shoot anyone trying to escape. The remaining men were to round up the Jews and take them to the market place. Those too sick or frail to walk to the market place, as well as infants and anyone offering resistance or attempting to hide, were to be shot on the spot. Thereafter, a few men of 1st company were to accompany the work Jews selected at the market place, while the rest were to proceed to the forest to form the firing squads. The Jews were to be loaded onto battalion trucks by 2nd company and shuttled from the market place to the forest.

Having given the company commanders their respective assignments, Trapp spent the rest of the day in town, mostly in a school room converted into his headquarters but also at the homes of the Polish mayor and the local priest. Witnesses who saw him at various times during the day described him as bitterly complaining about the orders he had been given and "weeping like a child." He nevertheless affirmed that "orders were orders" and had to be carried out.[7] Not a single witness recalled seeing him at the shooting site, a fact that was not lost upon the men, who felt some anger about it.[8] Trapp's driver remembers him saying later, "If this Jewish business is ever avenged on earth, then have mercy on us Germans." (Wenn sich diese Judensache einmal auf Erden rächt, dann gnade uns Deutschen.)[9]

After the company commanders had relayed orders to the men, those assigned to the village broke up into small groups and began to comb the Jewish quarter. The air was soon filled with cries, and shots rang out. The market place filled rapidly with Jews, including mothers with infants. While the men of Reserve Police Battalion 101 were apparently willing to shoot those Jews too weak or sick to move, they still shied for the most part from shooting infants, despite their orders.[10] No officer intervened, though subsequently one officer warned his men that in the future they would have to be more energetic.[11]

As the roundup neared completion, the men of 1st company were withdrawn from the search and given a quick lesson in the gruesome task that awaited them by the battalion doctor and the company's first sergeant. The doctor traced the outline of a human figure on the ground and showed the men how to use a fixed bayonet placed between and just above the shoulder blades as a guide for aiming their carbines.[12] Several men now approached the 1st company captain and asked to be given a different assignment; he curtly refused.[13] Several others who approached the first sergeant rather than the captain fared better. They were given guard duty along the route from the village to the forest.[14]

The first sergeant organized his men into two groups of about thirty-five men, which was roughly equivalent to the number of Jews who could be loaded into each truck. In turn each squad met an arriving truck at the unloading point on the edge of the forest. The individual squad members paired off *face-to-face* with the individual Jews they were to shoot, and marched their victims into the forest. The first sergeant remained in the forest to supervise the shooting. The Jews were forced to lie face down in a row. The policemen stepped up behind them, and on a signal from the first sergeant fired their carbines at point-blank range into the necks of their victims. The first sergeant then moved a few yards deeper into the forest to supervise the next execution. So-called "mercy shots" were given by a noncommissioned officer, as many of the men, some out of excitement and some intentionally, shot past their victims.[15] By mid-day alcohol had appeared from somewhere to "refresh" the shooters.[16] Also around mid-day the first sergeant relieved the older men, after several had come to him and asked to be let out.[17] The other men of 1st company, however, continued shooting throughout the day.

Meanwhile the Jews in the market place were being guarded by the men of 2nd company, who loaded the victims onto the trucks. When the first salvo was heard from the woods, a terrible cry swept the market place, as the collected Jews now knew their fate.[18] Thereafter, however, a quiet—indeed "unbelievable"— composure settled over the Jews, which the German policemen found equally unnerving. By mid-morning the officers in the market place became increasingly agitated. At the present rate, the executions would never be completed by nightfall. The 3rd company was called in from its outposts around the village to take over close guard of the market place. The men of 2nd company were informed that they too must now go to the woods to join the shooters.[19] At least one sergeant once again offered his men the opportunity to report if they did not feel up to it. No one took up his offer.[20] In another unit, one policeman confessed to his lieutenant that he was "very weak" and could not shoot. He was released.[21]

In the forest the 2nd company was divided into small groups of six to eight men rather than the larger squads of thirty-five as in 1st company. In the confusion of the small groups coming and going from the unloading point, several men managed to stay around the trucks looking busy and thus avoided shooting. One was noticed by his comrades, who swore at him for shirking, but he ignored them.[22] Among those who began shooting, some could not last long. One man shot an old woman on his first round, after which his nerves were finished and he could not continue.[23] Another discovered to his dismay that his second victim was a German Jew—a mother from Kassel with her daughter. He too then asked out.[24] This encounter with a German Jew was not exceptional. Several other men also remembered Hamburg and Bremen Jews in Jozefow.[25] It was a grotesque irony that some of the men of Reserve Police Battalion 101 had guarded the collection center in Hamburg, the confiscated freemason lodge house on the Moorweide next to the university library, from which the Hamburg Jews had been deported the previous fall. A few had even guarded the deportation transports to Lodz, Riga, and Minsk. These Hamburg policemen had now followed other Jews deported from northern Germany, in order to shoot them in southern Poland.

A third policeman was in such an agitated state that on his first shot he aimed too high. He shot off the top of the head of his victim, splattering brains into the face of his sergeant. His request to be relieved was granted.[26] One policeman made it to the fourth round, when his nerves gave way. He shot past his victim, then turned and ran deep into the forest and vomited. After several hours he returned to the trucks and rode back to the market place.[27]

As had happened with 1st company, bottles of vodka appeared at the unloading point and were passed around.[28] There was much demand, for among the 2nd company, shooting instructions had been less explicit and initially bayonets had not been fixed as an aiming guide. The result was that many of the men did not give neck shots but fired directly into the heads of their victims at point-blank range. The victims' heads exploded, and in no time the policemen's uniforms were saturated with blood and splattered with brains and splinters of bone. When several officers noted that some of their men could no longer continue or had begun intentionally to fire past their victims, they excused them from the firing squads.[29]

Though a fairly significant number of men in Reserve Police Battalion 101 either did not shoot at all or started but could not continue shooting, most persevered to the end and lost all count of how many Jews they had killed that day. The forest was so filled with bodies that it became difficult to find places to make the Jews lie down. When the action was finally over at dusk, and some 1,500 Jews lay dead, the men climbed into their trucks and returned to Bilgoraj. Extra rations of alcohol were provided, and the men talked little, ate almost nothing, but drank a great deal. That night one of them awoke from a nightmare firing his gun into the ceiling of the barracks.[30]

Following the massacre at Jozefow, Reserve Police Battalion 101 was transferred to the northern part of the Lublin district. The various platoons of the battalion were stationed in different towns but brought together for company-size actions. Each company was engaged in at least one more shooting action, but more often the Jews were driven from the ghettos onto trains bound for the extermination camp of Treblinka. Usually one police company worked in conjunction with a Trawniki unit for each action. The "dirty work"—driving the Jews out of their dwellings with whips, clubs, and guns; shooting on the spot the frail, sick, elderly, and infants who could not march to the train station; and packing the train cars to the bursting point so that only with the greatest of effort could the doors even be closed—was usually left to the so-called "Hiwis" (*Hilfswilligen* or "volunteers") from Trawniki.

Once a ghetto had been entirely cleared, it was the responsibility of the men of Reserve Police Battalion 101 to keep the surrounding region *"judenfrei."* Through a network of Polish informers and frequent search patrols—casually referred to as *Judenjagden* or "Jew hunts"—the policemen remorselessly tracked down those Jews who had evaded the roundups and fled to the forests. Any Jew found in these circumstances was simply shot on the spot. By the end of the year there was scarcely a Jew alive in the northern Lublin district, and Reserve Police Battalion 101 increasingly turned its attention from murdering Jews to combatting partisans.

In looking at the half-year after Jozefow, one sees that this massacre drew an important dividing line. Those men who stayed with the assignment and shot all day found the subsequent actions much easier to perform. Most of the men were bitter about what they had been asked to do at Jozefow, and it became taboo even to speak of it. Even thirty years later they could not hide the horror of endlessly shooting Jews at point-blank range. In contrast, however, they spoke of surrounding ghettos and watching the Hiwis brutally drive the Jews onto the death trains with considerable detachment and a near-total absence of any sense of participation or responsibility. Such actions they routinely dismissed with a standard refrain: "I was *only* in the police cordon there." The shock treatment of Jozefow had created an effective and desensitized unit of ghetto-clearers and, when the occasion required, outright murderers. After Jozefow nothing else seemed so terrible. Heavy drinking also contributed to numbing the men's sensibilities. One nondrinking policemen noted that "most of the other men drank so much solely because of the many shootings of Jews, for such a life was quite intolerable sober" (die meisten der anderen Kameraden lediglich auf Grund der vielen Judenerschiessungen soviel getrunken haben, da ein derartiges Leben nüchtern gar nicht zu ertragen war).[31]

Among those who either chose not to shoot at Jozefow or proved "too weak" to carry on and made no subsequent attempt to rectify this image of "weakness," a different trend developed. If they wished they were for the most part left alone and excluded from further killing actions, especially the frequent "Jew hunts." The consequences of their holding aloof from the mass murder were not grave. The reserve lieutenant of 1st company who had protested against being involved in the Jozefow shooting and been allowed to accompany the work Jews to Lublin subsequently went to Major Trapp and declared that in the future he would not take part in any *Aktion* unless explicitly ordered. He made no attempt to hide his aversion to what the battalion was doing, and his attitude was known to almost everyone in the company.[32] He also wrote to Hamburg and requested that he be recalled from the General Government because he did not agree with the "non-police" functions being performed by the battalion there. Major Trapp not only avoided any confrontation but protected him. Orders involving actions against the Jews were simply passed from battalion or company headquarters to his deputy. He was, in current terminology, "left out of the loop." In November 1942 he was recalled to Hamburg, made adjutant to the Police President of that city, and subsequently promoted![33]

The man who had first stepped out at Jozefow was sent on almost every partisan action but not on the "Jew hunts." He suspected that this pattern resulted from his earlier behavior in Jozefow.[34] Another man who had not joined the shooters at Jozefow was given excessive tours of guard duty and other unpleasant assignments and was not promoted. But he was not assigned to the "Jew hunts" and firing squads, because the officers wanted only "men" with them and in their eyes he was "no man." Others who felt as he did received the same treatment, he said.[35] Such men could not, however, always protect themselves against officers out to get them. One man was assigned to a firing squad by a vengeful officer precisely because he had not yet been involved in a shooting.[36]

The experience of Reserve Police Battalion 101 poses disturbing questions to those concerned with the lessons and legacies of the Holocaust. Previous explanations for the behavior of the perpetrators, especially those at the lowest level who came face-to-face with the Jews they killed, seem inadequate. Above all the perpetrators themselves have constantly cited inescapable orders to account for their behavior. In Jozefow, however, the men had the opportunity both before and during the shooting to withdraw. The battalion in general was under orders to kill the Jews of Jozefow, but each individual man was not.

Special selection, indoctrination, and ideological motivation are equally unsatisfying as explanations. The men of Reserve Police Battalion 101 were certainly not a group carefully selected for their suitability as mass murderers, nor were they given special training and indoctrination for the task that awaited them. They were mainly apolitical, and even the officers were only partly hard-core Nazi. Major Trapp in particular made no secret of his disagreement with the battalion's orders, and by Nazi standards he displayed shameful weakness in the way he carried them out. Among the men who did the killing there was much bitterness about what they had been asked to do and sufficient discomfort that no one wished to talk about it thereafter. They certainly did not take pride in achieving some historic mission.

While many murderous contributions to the Final Solution— especially those of the desk murderers—can be explained as routinized, depersonalized, segmented, and incremental, thus vitiating any sense of personal responsibility, that was clearly not the case in Jozefow, where the killers confronted the reality of their actions in the starkest way. Finally, the men of Reserve Police Battalion 101 were not from a generation that had been reared and educated solely under the Nazi regime and thus had no other political norms or standards by which to measure their behavior. They were older; many were married family men; and many came from a social and political background that would have exposed them to anti-Nazi sentiments before 1933.

What lessons, then, can one draw from the testimony given by the perpetrators of the massacre of the Jews in Jozefow? Nothing is more elusive in this testimony than the consciousness of the men that morning of July 13, 1942, and above all their attitude toward Jews at the time. Most simply denied that they had had any choice. Faced with the testimony of others, they did not contest that Trapp had made the offer but repeatedly claimed that they had not heard that part of his speech or could not remember it. A few who admitted that they had been given the choice and yet failed to opt out were quite blunt. One said that he had not wanted to be considered a coward by his comrades.[37] Another—more aware of what truly required courage—said quite simply: "I was cowardly."[38] A few others also made the attempt to confront the question of choice but failed to find the words. It was a different time and place, as if they had been on another political planet, and the political vocabulary and values of the 1960s were helpless to explain the situation in which they had found themselves in 1942. As one man admitted, it was not until years later that he began to consider that what he had done had not been right. He had not given it a thought at the time.[39]

Several men who chose not to take part were more specific about their motives. One said that he accepted the possible disadvantages of his course of action "because I was not a career policeman and also did not want to become one, but rather an independent skilled craftsman, and I had my business back home. . . . thus it was of no consequence that my police career would not prosper" (denn ich war kein aktiver Polizist und wollte auch keiner werden, sondern selbstständiger Handwerksmeister und ich hatte zu Hause meinen Betrieb. . . . deshalb macht es mir nichts aus, dass meine Karriere keinen Aufstieg haben würde).[40] The reserve lieutenant of 1st company placed a similar emphasis on the importance of economic independence when explaining why his situation was not analogous to that of the two SS captains on trial. "I was somewhat older then and moreover a reserve officer, so it was not particularly important to me to be promoted or otherwise to advance, because I had my prosperous business back home. The company chiefs . . . on the other hand were young men and career policemen, who wanted to become something. Through my business experience, especially because it extended abroad, I had gained a better overview of things." He alone then broached the most taboo subject of all: "Moreover through my earlier business activities I already knew many Jews." (Ich war damals etwas älter und ausserdem Reserveoffizier, mir kam es insbesondere nicht darauf an, befördert zu werden oder sonstwie weiterzukommen, denn ich hatte ja zuhause mein gutgehendes Geschäft. Die Kompaniechefs . . . dagegen waren junge Leute vom aktiven Dienst, die noch etwas werden wollten. Ich hatte durch meine kaufmännishce Tätigkeit, die sich insbesondere auch auf das Ausland erstreckte, einen besseren Überlick über die Dinge. Ausserdem kannte ich schon durch meine geschäftliche Tätigkeit von frühen viele Juden).[41]

Crushing conformity and blind, unthinking acceptance of the political norms of the time on the one hand, careerism on the other—these emerge as the factors that at least some of the men of Reserve Police Battalion 101 were able to discuss twenty-five years later. What remained virtually unexamined by the interrogators and unmentioned by the policemen was the role of antisemitism. Did they not speak of it because antisemitism had not been a motivating factor? Or were they unwilling and unable to confront this issue even after three decades, because it had been all too important, all too pervasive? One is tempted to wonder if the silence speaks louder than words, but in the end—as Claudia Koonz reminds us—the silence is still silence, and the question remains unanswered.

Was the incident at Jozefow typical? Certainly not. I know of no other case in which a commander so openly invited and sanctioned the nonparticipation of his men in a killing action. But in the end the most important fact is not that the experience of Reserve Police Battalion 101 was untypical, but rather that Trapp's extraordinary offer did not matter. Like any other unit, Reserve Police Battalion 101 killed the Jews they had been told to kill.

Nechama Tec

Helping Behavior and Rescue during the Holocaust

IN A DESTRUCTIVE ENVIRONMENT, EXPRESSIONS OF COMPASSION, CAR-ing, self-sacrifice, and help are rare. Nevertheless, it is also true that under conditions of extreme suffering, cooperation and mutual aid are indispensable for survival.

During World War II, for European Jews manifestations of help and care, though infrequent, were nevertheless present. In fact, without such positive reactions the Jewish death toll would have been higher.

Till recently, however, the literature on the Holocaust paid little attention to these positive acts. This prolonged silence is not surprising. The Holocaust was dominated by extreme suffering and devastation. In such an environment the compassion and help that were a part of the Jewish experience were rare and easily overshadowed by the enormity of the Nazi crimes. It is therefore understandable that students of that period focused first on the typical destruction rather than the exceptional expressions of goodness. Only after the basic outlines of the Nazi annihilation process had been examined could scholars even begin to notice the less visible, the less obvious; namely, the selflessness and compassion that were expressed in the readiness of some few to die for others. Once noticed, however, the contrast between the cruelty of the time and the ability of a few to rise above it by saving the helpless underlines the nobility of their deeds.[1]

For more than ten years I have been conducting research about compassion, self-sacrifice, and help, particularly as these touch on

Jewish rescue by Christians, and more recently about Jewish rescue by Jews. My work concentrates on Poland, the country designated by the Nazis as the center of Jewish annihilation, the place to which most European Jews were sent to die. It was also where the Nazis introduced their measures of destruction most ruthlessly and without regard to human cost. As the center of Jewish annihilation Poland provides the key to an understanding of the Holocaust in general and to the rescuing of Jews in particular. As a country in which the Holocaust drama was played out in the most gruesome ways it can teach us about similar, albeit less extreme, cases.[2]

Here I will concentrate on Jewish rescue by Poles, an activity that fits the idea of altruism. Bypassing the many definitions of the concept, I rely on one that sees altruism as behavior "carried out to benefit another without anticipation of rewards from external sources."[3] When dealing with the rescue of Jews, a distinction between two types of altruism, normative and autonomous, seems appropriate. Normative altruism refers to helping behavior that is demanded, supported, and rewarded by others. In contrast, autonomous altruism refers to selfless help that is neither expected nor rewarded by society. Indeed, autonomous altruism may be opposed by society and at times even involves grave risks to the helper. For example, society demands that a mother should donate a kidney to her child, that a child should aid an ailing parent. However, society does not ask its members to sacrifice their lives for strangers, particularly not for those whom society despises. During the Nazi occupation, saving Jews was an act above and beyond the call of duty, in that it put the actor in conflict with society's expected values. In this sense, then, those who without regard for external rewards risked their lives to protect Jews fall into the category of autonomous altruists.[4]

In those days, to rescue Jews, Poles had to overcome a number of formidable barriers. Foremost among them were the Nazi policies of Jewish annihilation. In Poland these policies were introduced early and with a high degree of ruthlessness. Among the many measures aimed at Jewish destruction was a 1941 decree that made any unauthorized move out of a ghetto a crime punishable by death. The same punishment applied to Poles who helped Jews move to the forbidden Christian world, the so-called Aryan side.[5] This law was widely publicized and strongly enforced. Executions of Christians and Jews followed,[6] and the names of the executed were widely publicized. And since the Nazis followed the principle of collective responsibility, the same punishment applied to the family members of those who defied this law. There are many cases on record where entire families of Poles were murdered, including infants, only because one of them had protected Jews.[7]

In addition to the Nazi anti-Jewish measures, the cultural climate of Poland was antagonistic toward Jews. That is, pervasive Polish antisemitism was often translated into opposition and hostility to Jewish rescue, and Poles who were eager to save Jews knew that by following their inclinations they would be inviting the censure of their fellow citizens.

Though not all forms of antisemitism were explicit, all were effective. A particularly common form, one which I refer to as diffuse cultural antisemitism, was vague and free floating. In part unconscious, this attitude was all-encompassing, as it attributed to the Jew any and all negative traits. People tended to accept this form of antisemitism without much thought or awareness, and it was expressed in such widely used utterances as "Be a good boy or the Jew will get you!"; "You are dirty like a Jew"; "Don't be a calculating Jew!"; and many, many others. In the Polish language the very term Jew (*Zyd*) is something polite people are reluctant to use. Still it is the only correct term. Others such as "a person of Mosaic faith" or "an Israelite" sound archaic, pompous, and downright phony. But one can insult a person by simply calling that person a *Zyd*. The term evokes strong negative images.

Unobtrusive and latent though it is, this diffuse cultural antisemitism acted as a foundation for all other forms. Many Poles, particularly the rescuers, found other, more explicit expressions of antisemitism objectionable, but tended to shrug off anything that reflected this subconscious type as insignificant or merely jocular.[8] Moreover, without realizing it, many of the rescuers were influenced by this diffuse kind of antisemitism. This fact in itself created an additional barrier to Jewish rescue.

Non-assimilation of the Polish Jews also interfered with their protection. For centuries Poles and Jews lived apart, in two different worlds. Each felt like a stranger in the other's world, and distinctions between them permeated all aspects of life. One of these important differences had to do with speech. In the last prewar census of 1931, only 12 percent of the Jewish population identified Polish as their native tongue, 79 percent chose Yiddish, and the rest Hebrew.[9] But more than sheer familiarity with the Polish language was involved. Even those who used the language in a grammatically correct way could still be recognized by their speech. Special phrases or expressions, even if grammatically sound, could be traced to the speaker's origins. For example, when someone bought a new garment a Jew was likely to comment by saying, "Wear it in good health"; the expression is a direct translation from the Yiddish. Special intonations or a stress on certain syllables were often identifying signs. Although most of the time Jews were unaware of their peculiar use of the language, the listening Poles were sensitive to such nuances.

Stefa Krakowska, one of the Christians I interviewed in Israel, told me about her experience with language. For over two years during the war, she hid in her house fourteen Jews, none of whom spoke Polish correctly. Constantly exposed to their way of speaking, without quite realizing what was happening, Stefa acquired some of their habits. She worked as a nurse in the hospital and at one point when talking to another nurse she asked: "Nu!? Does it mean something?" Instead of an answer she received an inquisitive look, followed by a question: "Are you Jewish?" Fortunately, her denial was accepted and the matter dropped. Such a small slip, however, could have had serious repercussions.

Language was only one of the obvious impediments to successful blending into the Polish society. Overall cultural differences were among other serious drawbacks. These differences permeated all aspects of life, including such matters as eating and drinking. For example, onion and garlic were defined as Jewish foods. For anyone who wanted to pass for a Pole, it was safest to profess a dislike for both. Also, when a man refused to drink liquor he came under suspicion. Jewish men were faced with a real dilemma. If they did not drink they would be suspect. But, unused to liquor, they feared they would easily lose control if drunk and reveal some secret. There was peril in either decision. Those who chose to drink had to make superhuman efforts to stay conscious and in control of their senses.

The survivor Jozek Braun illustrates this problem. He was about eighteen when he moved from the Warsaw ghetto to the non-Jewish world. He was protected by his good Polish papers, his flawless Polish, and his looks. He worked in a bakery where no one knew his origin. One day his co-workers, simple uneducated youths, decided to have a Christmas party. Braun, who was not used to drinking hard liquor, knew that a party meant getting drunk. Each of them had to bring a bottle of vodka. Jozek describes his dilemma:

> I, as the others, brought a bottle of vodka. But I never drank before. I knew I had to drink. I knew that if I did not they would begin to suspect me. At the same time I was scared of what would happen to me when drunk. Will I say something which would give me away? Still, I had to drink and I got drunk. I remember sitting under the table, almost paralyzed from the effects of alcohol, unable to move at all. I also remember being aware of what I was saying. I revealed nothing, just kept agreeing with their statements. And as they were getting loud and rowdy, I imitated them, still saying nothing of importance. When the conversation turned to Jews I also agreed. This way I passed the test.

When helping Jews, then, Poles had to overcome several layers of obstacles. The outer and strongest layer was the Nazi law that made helping Jews a crime punishable by death. Next were the explicit anti-Jewish ideologies and the pervasive antisemitism that made help to Jews both a highly dangerous and disapproved-of activity. In addition, some of these Poles had to overcome their own diffuse cultural antisemitism. One other serious obstacle was the inability of most Polish Jews to blend into the Christian world.[10]

Who of the Poles could overcome all these barriers? What characteristics did these rescuers have in common? As I try to answer these questions, I rely on information collected from 189 Polish rescuers and from 308 Jewish survivors who provided information about 565 Poles who helped them stay alive. When these 754 rescuers and helpers are examined in terms of social class, religion, politics, antisemitic attitudes, and friendship with Jews, the results point to a high level of diversity. Although a number of these variables show some association to the protection of Jews, none qualifies as a sufficient explanation. Only a close-range view of these helpers' life-styles and behaviors yields a cluster of shared characteristics and conditions. Before showing how these correlate with the rescue of Jews, I want to outline two case studies that illustrate these characteristics and conditions.

The peasant Jan Rybak was very short; he was the shortest man in his village. His stature was matched by an unusually slim, agile body. Though energetic and hard working, Jan was able to provide only for the basic necessities of his family. This, however, was more than most of his neighbors could claim. Busy with his own farm, he always still had time to help others with their farm chores. Whoever needed additional hands could count on Jan.

Like the rest of the villagers, he had only a few years of schooling, but unlike them he was an avid reader. He read everything that came his way—outdated magazines, newspapers, all kinds of books, even dictionaries. His hunger for ideas and the printed word gained him the nickname "philosopher." Jan was also an independent thinker and, unlike his neighbors, very tolerant. He opposed antisemitism and was courageous enough to make his position public. Unlike his neighbors, he never got drunk; nor did he, like so many of his neighbors, beat his wife. In the village Jan had a reputation as someone who liked doing favors, someone who was charitable. Passing vagrants and beggars were sure to find food and shelter in his house.

And so perhaps it was no coincidence that on a summer night in 1942 there was a gentle tap at the Rybaks' hut. There at the threshold, Jan saw a tired, disheveled man and a girl of eight or so. He recognized the man. Before the war the two of them had some business dealings. Jan learned that the father and daughter had run away during the Nazi liquidation of a ghetto. For an entire day they had been hiding and walking. The man was asking Jan for overnight shelter. Next day, he was confident, he would find more permanent lodgings. Jan knew that there was a death sentence for harboring Jews, yet he consented to the man's request. The two stayed with the Rybaks until the end of the war, for nineteen months. At the Rybaks' insistence, food was equally shared as were all kinds of outside threats. When the situation became particularly dangerous, the Jewish man was ready to leave, but the Rybaks would not hear of it unless they made proper provisions, and then the father and daughter left for only a short time. "We are in it together from the beginning till the end," Jan would say.

A few months before the end of the war Rybak returned from one of his infrequent town visits with a young Jewish woman. How did this happen? In the town, as Jan was crossing the market place, he saw excited people rushing from all directions. He soon realized that the object of their attention was a young woman dragged by two German soldiers. The crowd's movement was accompanied by the cries "Jude, Jude" (Jew, Jew). As Jan approached the scene, he recognized the prisoner as the daughter of a Jewish storekeeper who had been long since murdered by the Nazis. He moved forward, grabbed her by the arm, and said: "This is not a 'Jude,' this is my cousin." Holding on to the woman, Jan turned quickly, got into his horse-drawn wagon, and disappeared into the distance. No one made a move. When asked later what had made him act this way, Jan shrugged, saying that he did what he had to do. There was simply no other way he could have acted. The woman stayed with the Rybaks until the end of the war.

As a Pole, Jan disliked the Russians. Though open about these prejudices, he never turned away wounded or hungry Russian partisans. Asked why he had risked his life for Russians, he explained that he had to aid suffering human beings regardless of who they were. He was quick to add that his efforts on behalf of others were unrelated to the victims' nationalities. In fact, right after the war, Jan stood up for a German soldier caught by the villagers.

Seemingly very different is Felicja Zapolska, a journalist-lawyer who belonged to an old and prominent upper-class Polish family. When we met in Warsaw in 1978, she was a widow, an outspoken nationalist, much opposed to the Communist regime in Poland. I had come to interview her because during the war, as a member of the Polish underground, Zapolska was active in finding shelter for Jews who defied the Nazi policies of Jewish annihilation by living illegally among Poles. In addition, for two and a half years, Felicja and her husband had harbored a Jewish woman in their own apartment.

At first, except for her protection of Jews, there seemed to be nothing unusual about Felicja Zapolska. Then, I learned that her great-grandmother was Jewish, and that Felicja's favorite grandmother would tell stories about her Jewish mother. The grandmother wanted Felicja to know and to remember what a special human being this Jewish great-grandmother was. (Felicja hastened to assure me that this information in no way made a philosemite out of her. On the contrary, as a Polish nationalist, she did not look with favor at the Jewish presence in Poland.) Moreover, Felicja told me that her mother, though she came from a "very Polish, very patriotic family," had married a German industrialist. This, she explained, was both a social and personal tragedy. It was a poor match. A few years after Felicja's birth the couple divorced. But because of her German father, the daughter belonged to the Calvinist Church. In a predominantly Catholic country like Poland, this set Felicja apart from her contemporaries. In addition, she had spent each summer with her father, who tried to inculcate in her a love for everything German. Finally, just before the war Felicja had divorced her first husband, a member of the Polish aristocracy who was a virulent antisemite, and married another upper-class man with a more liberal, gentler disposition. In part because of this husband's prodding, she became involved in a variety of charitable activities, an involvement that continued till the present.

During the Nazi occupation the Zapolskis joined the Polish underground. Felicja's husband had access to the Warsaw ghetto and tried to persuade some Jewish friends to come to the Polish side. When these friends refused, the couple devoted themselves to helping Jewish strangers.

Among the fugitives for whom Felicja tried to find shelter was a middle-aged woman who could be easily identified by her Semitic features and her poor command of the Polish language. Adding to these inherent difficulties were the woman's uncooperative attitudes. People refused to keep her. For a while Felicja kept transferring her from place to place. When she could find no more places, she brought her to her own apartment. The neighbors were told that this newcomer was the Zapolskis' housekeeper. But the woman seemed to have learned little from her past experience. She refused to learn the Catholic prayers, a protective measure against police interrogation. And although pretending to be a housekeeper, she would talk to the neighbors about the beautiful fur coats she used to own; a definite giveaway. Listening to Felicja's many other complaints about this woman, it struck me that she had no redeeming features. Curious, I asked why she and her husband agreed to keeping such a difficult person. Taken aback, Felicja said: "What else could I have done? After all, she was a human being and I could not let her die!" As an afterthought, she added that she was protecting Jews not because she liked them but only because they were in greatest need of help.

Very different in terms of most conventional ways of classifying people, Jan Rybak and Felicja Zapolska had much in common. They shared with each other and with most of the other rescuers in my study several characteristics: (1) Individuality or separateness, which means that they did not quite fit into their social environments; (2) independence or self-reliance, that is, a willingness to act in accordance with personal convictions, regardless of how these were viewed by others; (3) an enduring commitment to stand up for the helpless and needy that expressed itself in a long history of doing good deeds; (4) a tendency to perceive aid to Jews in a matter-of-fact, unassuming way and see assistance to them as neither heroic nor extraordinary; (5) an unplanned, unpremeditated onset to the rescue, a beginning that happened gradually or suddenly, even impulsively; and (6) universalistic perceptions of Jews that defined them not as Jews but as helpless beings and as totally dependent on the protection of others. Closely connected to this last was the ability to disregard all attributes except those that expressed extreme suffering and need. Highly interdependent, these shared characteristics suggest a set of interrelated hypotheses. What follows is a selective presentation of findings to illustrate some of these hypotheses.

Most of these Polish rescuers were loosely integrated into their communities, a condition I refer to as individuality or separateness. The two examples of a peasant and an upper-class person, Rybak and Zapolska, show how each in a different way did not blend into his or her social environment. In these two cases and in others, individuality or separateness appears under different guises, but its effect upon rescue seemed to depend on other attributes and motivations.

Being on the periphery of a community means being less affected by existing social controls. With individuality, then, come fewer social constraints and a higher level of independence—in other words, an opportunity to act in accordance with personal values and moral precepts, even when these are in opposition to societal expectations. And so, to the extent that people are less controlled by their environment and are more independent, they are more likely to be guided by their own moral imperatives, regardless of whether or not these imperatives conform to societal expectations.

Rescuers in my study had no trouble talking about their self-reliance and their need to follow their personal inclinations and values. Nearly all of them saw themselves as independent (98 percent). Jewish survivors also described their rescuers as independent and as being motivated by special personal values. In addition, a quality often mentioned in the testimonies and memoirs of survivors, one that comes close to independence, is the rescuers' courage. Of the 308 Jewish survivors, the overwhelming majority (85 percent) described their helpers as courageous.

With the rescuers' view of themselves as independent came the idea that they were propelled by moral values that did not depend on the support of others but rather on their own self-approval. Again and again they repeated that they had to be at peace with themselves and with their own ideas of what was right or wrong. Consider the case of Janka Polanska, a Yad Vashem medal recipient, who saved ten Jews by hiding them in her apartment. She said:

> I have to be at peace with myself, what others think about me is not important. It is my own conscience that I must please and not the opinion of others. My father always told me that I should act in a way which should not embarrass me. . . . Public opinion is fickle, it depends on the way the wind blows. . . . At one point during the war I had to decide whether to follow my conscience or save myself. One day, Adas, the Jewish man who stayed with me, left and did not return. The Polish police came to search the house. We had a good hiding place and they did not find the others. They told me that Adas was at the police station. I was advised by all who knew about it to run away. The situation appeared hopeless. To try and save him would be suicidal. Adas looked very Jewish. Also, as a man his identity could be easily checked. [In Poland only Jewish men were circumcised.] But I could not follow the advice of others. Instead, I went to the police station. They wanted a large sum of money which I managed to get. They also demanded that I give them a grand piano and some valuable paintings. I was ready to give them everything. After I met all their demands, we were afraid that they would continue to blackmail us. They knew where we lived and they

knew at least about the existence of one Jew. I had to change apartments. I decided to tell the AK [Home Army and Polish underground] that I needed an apartment. I told them that if they could get me one I would keep arms for them. They did. All of us moved to it safely. The underground never knew that I was hiding Jews. And so, from then on, I had two illegal things, arms and Jews.

When I got Adas from the clutches of the police, I felt so light it was if I had wings. I felt so gratified; I knew I acted correctly and that I had no reason to be ashamed of myself.

Closely related to the rescuers' moral convictions and values was their long-standing commitment to the protection of the needy. This commitment was expressed in a wide range of charitable acts over a long period of time. Evidence about selfless acts also came from survivors, most of whom described their protectors as good natured and as people whose efforts on behalf of the needy were limitless and long lasting.

There seems to be a continuity between the rescuers' history of charitable actions and their protection of Jews. That is, risking lives for Jews fits into a system of values and behaviors that included helping the weak and the dependent. This linkage, however, has some limitations. Most disinterested actions on behalf of others may involve inconvenience, even extreme inconvenience. Only rarely do such acts entail that the giver may have to make the ultimate sacrifice of his or her own life. For these Poles, then, only during the war was there a convergence between historical events demanding ultimate selflessness and their already-established predispositions to help.

We tend to take our repetitive ideas and actions for granted. What we take for granted we accept. What we accept, we rarely analyze or wonder about. In fact, the more firmly established patterns of behavior are, the less likely are they to be examined and thought about. Therefore, in a real sense, the constant pressure of, or familiarity with, ideas and actions does not mean that we know or understand them; it may mean the contrary. For example, Maria Baluszko, an outspoken peasant who helped many Jews and definitely saved five, said: "I do what I think is right, not what others think is right." At first she resisted telling me that her aid to Jews was an extension of a tradition that involved helping the poor and destitute. When I touched upon her reasons for rescue she was at a loss. Then, instead of answering, she asked: "What would you do in my place if someone comes at night and asks for help? What would you have done in my place? One has to be an animal without a conscience not to help." I had no answer. Impassively, I waited for her to continue. Only at that point did she tell me: "In our area there were many large families with small farms; they were very poor. I used to help them; they called me mother. . . . I used to help. . . . When I was leaving the place people cried. I helped all the poor, all that needed help."

Closely related to this tendency is another. Namely, what we are accustomed to repeat doing, we don't see as extraordinary, no matter how exceptional it may seem to others. And so, the rescuers' past history of helping the needy might have been in part responsible for their modest appraisal of their life-threatening actions. This modest appraisal was expressed in a variety of ways. Most rescuers (66 percent) perceived their protection of Jews as a natural reaction to human suffering, and almost a third (31 percent) insisted that saving lives was nothing exceptional. In contrast, only 3 percent described the saving of Jews as extraordinary. A case in point is that of Pawel Remba, who to this day limps from an injury that occurred when he smuggled Jews out of the Warsaw ghetto during the uprising. For this and other acts on behalf of Jews, he was awarded the Yad Vashem medal. When Pawel and I met in Israel, he categorically denied that he or others like him were heroes: "I would absolutely not make heroes out of the Poles who helped. All of us looked at this help as a natural thing. None of us were heroes; at times we were afraid, but none of us could act differently."

Refusal to perceive the drama of these life-threatening and risky actions was expressed in other ways as well. Some of these Poles omitted from their accounts events that would attest to particularly noble and courageous aspects of their rescue. This tendency is apparent from a comparison of information collected from matched pairs of rescuers and rescued.

One such example is provided by the case of Ada Celka and the girl she had saved, now a woman, Danuta Brill. I interviewed Ada Celka in Poland. A governess by profession, during the war she shared a one-room apartment with her unmarried sister and invalid father. In 1942, a Jewish woman, an acquaintance, asked Ada to save her child, Danuta, a girl of eight. When Danuta came to share their small apartment, the neighbors were told that she was an orphaned relative. To my suggestion that keeping the Jewish girl must have entailed economic hardships, Ada reacted with a flat denial. She also failed to tell me a few facts that would have enhanced her image. I heard only later from Danuta, whom I interviewed in the United States, that Ada had planned and almost succeeded in smuggling Danuta's parents out of a work camp and in placing them with a Polish family in the country. This, according to the daughter, involved extraordinary efforts. Ada was not an influential person; she had few connections and no money. Her success in locating a peasant family could be ascribed to her determined willingness to try again and again. Finally, all was ready, and detailed plans for smuggling the parents out of their work camp were set in motion. On the chosen day, Ada went to the appointed place next to the camp, but she waited in vain. The day before, Danuta's parents had been deported to a death camp. Ada also never bothered to tell me that when food was scarce, which it often was, she fed her invalid father first, and then Danuta. She and her sister ate only after her father and the girl had had enough.

Whereas the Jews were glad, even eager, to praise their protectors, the rescuers were reluctant to talk about their aid. Even those who did, spoke only in timid and restrained ways. I had to prod and probe before any of them mentioned things that put them in a particularly favorable light. Instead, they consistently underplayed the risks and sacrifices inherent in their actions.

Not only did most helpers deny that their aid to Jews was heroic, they became embarrassed when this possibility was suggested to them. To underplay the heroism of their actions, half of the rescuers emphasized the fears that they had experienced during their rescuing activities. The underlying assumption in such arguments was that fears were incompatible with heroism. Felicja Zapolska was one of those who emphasized fear. She felt that "in general, those that helped were sensitive people who tried to overcome their fears. Everyone was afraid, and if anyone would tell that they were not afraid don't believe it because it has to be a lie." (In an interesting contrast, hardly any of the survivors described their protectors as fearful.) Other rescuers denied the exceptionality of their deeds by describing them as expressions of duty, or by pushing the dangers into the background, or by depicting what they had done as just another part of a dangerous environment. Some emphasized the great value of saving a life.

Given these matter-of-fact perceptions of rescue, it is not surprising that help often began in a spontaneous, unpremeditated way. Either gradually or suddenly, helping activity often started without planning or anticipation. Such an onset only underscores the rescuers' need to stand up for the poor and helpless. In fact, so strong was this need to help, so much was it a part of their makeup, that it overshadowed all other considerations.

Asked why they had saved Jews, the Poles overwhelmingly emphasized that they had responded to the persecution and the suffering of victims and not to their Jewishness. What compelled them to act was the persecution, the unjust treatment, and not the people themselves. This ability to disregard all attributes of the needy except their helplessness and dependence I refer to as universalistic perception. Evidence for its presence comes from a variety of sources. Indirect motivational data on rescue show that 95 percent of these helpers felt that they were prompted by the need of Jews for help. This is in sharp contrast to the 26 percent who claim to have helped because it was a Christian duty, or the 52 percent who saw their response as a protest against the Nazi occupation. Clearly, more than one kind of motivation was involved. Of the Jewish survivors, 81 percent said that their suffering made these Poles offer them protection. A universalistic perception is also indicated by the fact that only 9 percent of these rescuers limited their help to friends. The rest offered help to all kinds of people, including total strangers. When the sample of Jewish survivors is consulted, 51 percent of them reported that they were protected by strangers, but only 19 percent noted that they had received aid from friends.

This tendency is illustrated in the case of Dr. Estowski, who was deeply involved in helping others, Jews and non-Jews. He helped both as a member of the underground and as a private citizen. How did he describe his help to Jews?

> Whoever came to us we always managed to help. I felt that it was my duty to help people. It was not because they were Jews.

I had a simple obligation to help people. It was not for us a question of them being Jews or not, just anyone who needed help had to get it. Jews were in a specially dangerous situation; all of us who were helping were aware of this fact—that because of their difficult situation, they had to be helped the most. After all, a Pole could somehow help himself, but the Jew was in a more horrible situation and could in no way help himself.

The compelling moral force behind the rescue of Jews, the universal insistence that what mattered was the victims' position of dependence and subjection to unjust persecution, combined to make such actions universalistic. In a sense it was this moral force that motivated the rescuers, independently of personal likes and dislikes. Some of those I spoke to were aware that to help the needy in general, and the Jews in particular, one did not have to like them. Liking and helping, they knew, did not necessarily go hand in hand.[11] This becomes evident in the two cases presented earlier of Rybak and Zapolska. Also gentle Ada Celka, who expressed a deep compassion for the suffering of others, emphasized the difference between help and personal attraction when she said: "I would help anyone, anyone who needs help, but this does not mean that I like everybody."

Looking back, I hope that the discussion of the rescuers' shared characteristics throws some light upon altruistic behavior in general. Beyond that, the very presence of people willing to risk their lives for the persecuted and the helpless shows that an extremely destructive environment can lead not only to reactions of extreme evil but also to reactions of extreme goodness. It also suggests that the study of the Holocaust can instruct us both about man's inhumanity to man and about man's humanity to man. As it does, such study can have lessons and legacies beyond the particular time, place, events, and people.

III. E · N · C · O · U · N · T · E · R · S

Lawrence Langer

Redefining Heroic Behavior: The Impromptu Self and the Holocaust Experience

"THE DISASTER RUINS EVERYTHING," MAURICE BLANCHOT BEGINS HIS paradoxical commentary on *The Writing of the Disaster,* "all the while leaving everything intact." This is the contradiction we still wrestle with nearly half a century after the event. The foundations of moral behavior remain in place, as the goal if not the reality of decent societies; meanwhile, victims of the Nazi attempt to annihilate European Jewry tell tales of survival that reduce such moral systems to an irrelevant luxury. The "luxury," to be sure, remains valid for us, as we continue to strive for what is morally right; however, as these tales unfold, in written or oral narrative, the insufficiency of the idea of moral striving as a frame for hearing them, or for understanding victim behavior, becomes ever plainer. When Blanchot says that those whom accounts of the disaster threaten—presumably *us*—remain out of reach, he urges us not to abandon the confrontation but to ask why, and to seek means of narrowing the space that separates us from the event.[1]

Sometimes this seems a futile task, even for surviving victims, who in the process of remembering betray their own difficulty when they use the language of "now" to describe the experience of "then." Consider the opening paragraphs of two narratives by former victims, each in quest of a perspective to illuminate the ordeal of remembering. The first, written in 1973, is from a book called *The Victors and the Vanquished:*

> I do not want to write. I do not want to remember. My memories are not simple recollections. They are a return to the bottom of

an abyss; I have to gather up the shattered bones that have lain still for so long, climb back over the crags, and tumble in once more. Only this time I have to do it deliberately, in slow motion, noticing and examining each wound, each bruise on the way, most of all the ones of which I was least conscious in my first headlong fall. But I know I have to do it. My future stands aside, waiting until I find meaning in all that has been. I feel as if I had to overcome some almost physical obstacle, and feel drained, breathless from the effort.[2]

This victim is still consumed by her past, a sealed pain, recaptured only through struggle; her vivid imagery confirms Blanchot's conclusion that "there is no future for the disaster, just as there is no time or space [in the present] for its accomplishment."[3] Her experience seems insulated, not only from us, but from herself, the self that has survived, entered a new life, and now resists sinking back into a charnel house that even she may no longer recognize.

The second passage, written in 1986, opens a survivor narrative called *Under a Cruel Star.* The shift in tone is evident:

Three forces carved the landscape of my life. Two of them crushed half the world. The third was very small and weak and, actually, invisible. It was a shy little bird hidden in my rib cage an inch or two above my stomach. Sometimes in the most unexpected moments the bird would wake up, lift its head, and flutter its wings in rapture. Then I too would lift my head because, for that short moment, I would know for certain that love and hope are infinitely more powerful than hate and fury, and that somewhere beyond the line of my horizon there was life indestructible, always triumphant.[4]

Both the nature and the direction of the language alter, from falling to rising, from pain and anguish to rapture and hope. Authors, of course, have a right to their own mood, temperament, and vision. The problem here is that both opening paragraphs are by the *same* author, and for the *same* book, the later version, though a different translation, being virtually identical with the former one, except for the initial paragraphs. We might say that the first passage confirms Blanchot's notion that the disaster ruins everything; the second affirms its sequel, that at the same time it leaves everything intact. On the one hand, that particular disaster we call the Holocaust denies a future consistent with its violations of the self; on the other, human need requires a future where love and hope reign as motives for human conduct and aspiration despite the scope of the disaster. We as audience inhabit both worlds; and if we listen carefully to the testimonies of enough former victims, we learn that they do, too. The task before us is to understand and interpret the implications of this situation.

Memory excavates from the ruins of the past fragile shapes to augment our understanding of those ruins. What transforms "shattered bones" into "life indestructible, always triumphant"? The evolution warns us that our encounter with the narratives of former victims demands a wary intimacy with the story far beyond the passive acceptance of details. We cannot know why the author of these two introductory paragraphs decided to change the thrust of her intentions. But we do know that the first version, with its Miltonic plunge into a purely physical abyss, creates tensions for the writer and the reader that the spiritual optimism of the second version avoids. Does a self-conscious literary voice intervene here between the experience and the effect, so that language and imagery obscure even as they seek to clarify? Perhaps; perhaps not. But as we examine definitions and redefinitions of self emerging from victim narratives, we must keep in mind that each one of them represents a combat, more often than not unconscious, between fragment and form, disaster and intactness, birdsong and pandemonium. A hopeful surface story vies with a darker subtext, although—as in this instance—we scarcely recognize that the two voices are the same.

Oral testimonies of former Nazi victims slightly simplify our task, since most of these have neither time nor inclination nor gift to draw on the resources of literary artifice in their narratives. After having watched more than three hundred such testimonies, ranging in length from thirty minutes to seven hours, I've reached the conclusion that the process of recall divorced from literary effort results in a narrative form unlike the written text, equally valuable, rich in spontaneous rather than calculated effects. A member of the Norwegian underground who survived Natzweiler, Dachau, and other camps, and is writing a book about his ordeal, is asked how his oral testimony differs from his written account. "The book is different because you have more time to phrase your words," he replies. "In a book, you're also trying to be poetic—you're trying to write."[5] The equation of "writing" with "poetic," though perhaps a trifle unsophisticated, nonetheless confirms the role of style in the written memoir—that is, having time to face the conscious choice of "phrasing your words." This is a complex issue, and I mention it here only because it affects, in different ways, the sense of character that emerges from written and oral testimonies.

The "headlong fall" in the first passage quoted above unavoidably (and maybe deliberately) conjures up the image of Satan plummeting into Milton's hell, and this in turn influences our response to the experience of the victim. Such analogies rarely intrude on oral testimonies. When they do, they create a disjunctive resonance, attesting to the *in*sufficiency of familiar analogy. I am reminded, for example, of the woman who tells of being transported from Auschwitz to a labor site in Germany, looking out from the tiny window high up in her boxcar as it pauses at a small station during the journey, and exclaims: "I saw Paradise!"[6] What she saw was a group of people standing on the platform, including a mother and her child, and this normal, innocuous view, far from Edenic, nevertheless in the context of her deportation comes to represent for her a vision of Paradise. We witness a metamorphosis of meaning before our eyes, as a commonplace panorama displaces the archetypal idyllic scene, leading in turn to a spontaneous adaptation of familiar formula to an alien situation.

Devotion to orthodox versions of the self, an inability to pry oneself loose from these versions paralyzed the will of many former victims, by their own account. Rarely, however, do we find a simple opposition between paralysis and action. Oral testimonies dramatize for us, often implicitly rather than explicitly, the constantly warring impulses that bewildered the former victims. Such tensions are frequently evident in the narrative manner itself. Schifra Z., for example, born near Vilna (Vilnius), begins her testimony with perfect composure, a model of the integrated self. Slowly, as her narrative unfolds, her facial gestures and head movements, her stretching neck, the licking of her lips, her uncontrollable perspiring, and deep sighs reveal a woman increasingly possessed by rather than possessing her story. For the rest of her narrative, she alternates between control and submission, a clear illustration of the struggle to remain intact despite the disaster at the heart of her testimony.

She was between twelve and thirteen years old when German troops entered Vilna. She reports that some friendly members of the Wehrmacht asked her, "Why don't you just walk west and get out of here?" "I couldn't just walk off by myself," she tells us. "I couldn't beg, steal, I couldn't travel with false papers." It seems she is more in dialogue with herself than with us as she explains: "I couldn't see myself going off alone." Conventional moral terminology ("beg," "steal," "false,") and the sense of an inflexible persona combine to thwart the perception of a self that could respond to the urgency of the situation instead of to an inner vision of possible behavior. But when the abstract "urgency" takes on a more concrete shape, her sense of possible personae shifts dramatically.

She learns from a neighbor of the massacre of Jews in Ponary outside of Vilna, and recalls, "I decided that I wouldn't let them decide how or when I was going to die. I was going to die on my own terms, not theirs. I was not going to let them take me and put me against a wall and be shot." Out of context, statements like these resonate with the splendor of heroic determination. But as she recreates the agony of the slaughter of members of her own family, we learn along with her how provisional was *any* position under those circumstances. Her resolution to choose her own fate dissolves into one more verbal formula as the horror of the situation invades her various defenses. "We were helpless," she continues, unaware of any contradiction, "in finding our way out, and there was no way out." They had no idea, she says, why they were being killed, when they might be killed, what might happen next, or where to go. They didn't know if it was better to hide in the city, in the surrounding villages, in the forest, in a barn, with others, or alone. She admits now that they simply couldn't see their way ahead, and thus were unable to plan the best route to survival.

We encounter in this narrative memories of several versions of the self, from the reluctance to venture into unfamiliar moral terrain through the resolve to resist an imposed death sentence to total uncertainty, a kind of learned helplessness, as Jewish doom imposed by the Nazis replaced the vision of an individual, self-defined fate. Which is authentic? The question confirms the folly of searching for authenticity amidst the moral quicksand of atrocity. Schifra Z. herself unwittingly supports this conclusion when she responds to the interviewer's question at the very end about how she feels today, having gone through all this, with the surprising reply: "I believe in the goodness of man." Is this an attempt to restore the apparent order of the pre-Holocaust era, or a private concept of the self that decomposed slowly through the years of her ordeal? Perhaps as an answer to her own homiletic statement, she then adds, again with no apparent feeling of contradiction: "I believe every person has a right to be alive and to save—has a responsibility to save—his own life if he can."[7] The legacy of multiple voices is part of the heritage of survival; any attempt to resolve these voices would seem to betray or falsify that experience.

The "responsibility" of the victim to "save his [or her] own life if he can" led in unpredictable directions, hardly consistent with pre- or post-disaster ideas of the goodness of man. The "gray zone" that Primo Levi speaks of in the last of his Auschwitz memoirs represents those moments when staying alive could not be practiced as a common pursuit. Neither heroic endeavor nor selfish exploitation satisfactorily defines the options available to the victim. Narrative moments, such as the following, from one of the oral testimonies, help us to refine our appreciation of how an individual reacts when situation rather than character controls response, and what I call the impromptu self replaces the faculty of moral choice.

Having lost her proper shoes, Hanna F. is left with a dilemma: "Without shoes," she reports, "you couldn't go to work. You were dead." One evening she is standing outside her barracks when she notices a woman who is sitting on the ground and delousing her clothes. Her shoes are beside her. "I was very brave," says Hanna F., who was temporarily wearing some totally inadequate wooden clogs. She approaches the woman, surreptitiously steps out of her clogs and into the woman's regular shoes, and then, she concludes, "I walked away."[8] She looks pained while telling this story. She closes her eyes and wipes her lips, but doesn't apologize for the conduct of the impromptu self in the process of staying alive. We, however, would search in vain through familiar dictionaries of moral vocabulary for a definition of "brave" commensurate with the details of this episode.

Subversive or dismaying as it may sound, the impromptu self of the victim spontaneously detached itself from familiar value systems without apparent anguish. After liberation, that self survives in the narrative as a kind of alter ego, often unfamiliar even to the witness. "When you're hungry," admits one former victim from the Lodz ghetto, "nothing else in the world matters. . . . When you're hungry, it gets to the point where you don't mind stealing from your own sister, your own father. . . . I would get up in the middle of the night," he confesses, "and slice a piece of bread off my sister's ration. Now I—you would never picture me, and I can't even imagine myself doing that now. But it happened."[9] He is perfectly sensitive, however, to the implications of his narrative. Far from the image of the inviolable self, still our heritage from the romantic era, the impromptu self appears as a *violated* self, in part—a source of chagrin and humiliation to many witnesses—a seemingly self-violated self. One of the most distressing ironies of these oral testimonies is the ease with which, as in this instance, one is tempted to overlook the concealed persecutors, the creators rather than the inhabitants of the Lodz ghetto, and blame the victim's weakness instead.

Witnesses themselves are bewildered by the disequilibrium between the impromptu self, that followed impulse in order to stay alive, and memories of the morally distinguished life that was the goal of their prewar existence. The chronological sequence on the surface of the survivor narrative, leading through liberation to marriage, family, and/or career, cheers only the naive audience. The subtext of loss exerts its own influence on the narrative. Asked by an interviewer near the end of her testimony, "Tell me, in your life afterwards have you rebuilt some of the things that you have lost?" one former victim sabotages the illusion of continuity by exclaiming:

No, no, everything that happened destroyed part of me. I was dying slowly. Piece by piece. And I built a new family. I am not what I would have been if I didn't go through these things. . . . Life was one big hell even after the war. So you make believe that you go on. This is not something that you put behind. And people think that they can get away from it, or you don't talk about it, or you forget your fear when you lay in an attic and you know that the Gestapo is a minute away from you. And rifles always against your head. You can't be normal. As a matter of fact, I think that we are not normal because we are so normal.

Like the woman who saw Paradise in the spectacle of a mother and child standing on a railroad platform, this former victim frustrates efforts to see survival as a simple chronology of returning from an abnormal to a normal world. Without denying the reality or the significance of her present life, she insists on the discontinuity between it and her past, an unresolved and for her unresolvable stress that nurtures anxiety. After the war, she insists, they weren't allowed to fall apart because "circumstances didn't let us." Just as situation often became a form of necessity in the camps, dictating response far more than fixed principles of character, so here, according to this testimony, postwar life required an abandonment of the impromptu self with all its painful memories. "We had to educate our children," she says, "and we had to guide our children and be nice parents and make parties. But that was all make-believe [shaking her head in a strong gesture of negation]."[10] One of the surprising revelations of these testimonies is the frequency with which such a dual sense of the self emerges, with what we would have considered a solid layer of resistance, reinforced by time, turning out to be only a thin and vulnerable veneer. "Now I am talking here," another former victim concludes his testimony, "as if this were a normal thing. Inside my heart burns. My brain boils."[11]

Of course, not everyone expresses this duality. But even contrary accounts of apparently successful adaptation betray some contradiction to the careful hearer. Sigmund W., for example, insists that after coming to America in 1948, he put his camp experiences in a time capsule and decided not to think about them. "I recognized that in order to become a part of society I had a choice to make: to stay a survivor or a prisoner and be in prison for the rest of my life, or try to preserve my sanity by putting this away in my mind and integrating myself into society as if nothing had ever happened. And obviously I chose the latter." Yet, he admits, his wife tells him that for the first *ten* years of their life together, he woke up *every night* screaming. "I am fully unaware of this," he confesses, adding: "So integration into everyday life, I believe, was possible by shutting out the indescribable events that have occurred."

Just before saying this, however, he had shown a gouache portrait of himself made in Paris in 1946 by a friend and barrack-mate from the camps, and given to his brother with the observation: "This is how I remember your brother [i.e., the speaker in this testimony]." He holds his "other self" up to the camera, a prisoner in striped uniform and cap, with sallow complexion, an utterly forlorn expression on his face, a blank stare in his eyes. He chooses to present his suppressed self through the portrait, leaving to the viewer the interpretation of the human—or inhuman—condition it represents. And in fact, his strategy is shrewder and less evasive than it appears. He explains his rationale for putting his camp experiences—he was in Blechhammer, Gross Rosen, Buchenwald, Dachau, and several lesser-known labor camps—in a time capsule by arguing: "It can only be told, I think it is important to be told, but it cannot be felt, it cannot be experienced. *I* cannot even experience it." He distinguishes between making a record and letting others *know* what happened, between details and the face in the portrait, or, on the most complex level, we might say, between the concreteness of history and the suggestiveness of art.

The appeal of written narrative is based in part on the recognition of affinities, the premise that style and structure can help the imagination to penetrate strange façades, resulting in a shared intimacy with the depicted persons and events. When witnesses like the one we have just heard insist on the *unshareability* of the experience, of an estrangement even between one's present and past persona, we understand more clearly the crucial role of the impromptu self in oral testimony. That self survived in ways no longer comprehensible even to this witness, who at one point, he tells us, was so weak that he *volunteered* to die (only to be deported to another camp instead).

On the one hand, he speaks of "survival per se" as the "ultimate resistance," of the "will of survival" as the "ultimate feat." On the other, in addition to his own momentary loss of the vaunted will to survival (which led him to volunteer to die), he tells the story of a prisoner who had scooped up some gray powder that had leaked from a split bomb, thinking it was soap, being publicly *strangled* together with his Kapo and a fellow inmate for attempted insurrection.[12] He makes no effort to connect the two moments in his narrative; but an attentive audience will speculate on the implications of a memory that is never "innocent" because of the very juxtaposition that has just emerged. Oral testimony may not always engage us in the inner workings for the former victim of what I call tainted memory; but it offers some valuable insights into its genesis and consequences, and these in turn help to explain the insistence by witnesses like this one that the gulf between their experience and our sense of it is impassable.

Tainted memory, memory of that impromptu self unrecognizable even through the act of mental recovery, is a monument to ruin rather than reconstruction. This is one of the most melancholy legacies in the subtexts of these testimonies. In another example, throughout his narrative Leo G. hints at the degradation that "transpired" between victims during the worst moments of the disaster, but firmly refuses to offer details because "it can't be described." Nonetheless, after more than three hours, the interviewer asks him "What are you left with today," and to this he readily if allusively replies:

> I envy people that can get out of themself for one minute sometimes. . . . They can laugh, enjoy. You know, you see a movie. Anybody in my situation cannot laugh and enjoy, through inside, you know. Only superficially. There's always in the back of your mind everything. How can you, how can you *enjoy* yourself? It's almost a crime against the people that you lost [in his case, mother, father, and six brothers and sisters], that you can live and enjoy yourself.

He acknowledges the joy he receives from his family, his children, their marriages, their accomplishments, but he continues, "Enjoyment is cut to the end of my days. I just can't get out of myself."

"Self" here clearly operates on two levels, separated by an intervening, untranscended loss. The exasperation of this witness at his inability to explain the difference, together with his simultaneous conviction that no one would understand anyway, frames for us but does not clarify the buried dilemma of testifying. Once again, however, the careful hearer may be able to suspect what is troubling him:

> You almost need to educate them for them to understand. If they don't understand it, I don't blame them. They can't. They can't. Talking about it, all this or more, each incident needs so much explaining. It needs explaining to the other person how and why, for them to grasp it, that you could live through it.

That you could live through it without doing anything, without converting your own person to a different person than you are right now. All this you lived through, all this you saw, and you go out to work for money, drive a car or whatever. . . . How could you? . . . It should be as, you know, some people that turn away from life. It's senseless, it doesn't add up. And I and the kind of people that went through it should know that it doesn't add up. Nothing adds up. It doesn't make any sense. Nothing justifies it. To go on and on after you know what the world is like or what it was.[13]

He echoes the woman who lamented "I think we are not normal because we are so normal." If a nostalgia for the heroic spirit that enabled him and his fellow victims to endure were available, it would offer him the support he needs to restore continuity to his existence. What gnaws at his memory is the question of *how* one lived through it, and then, of how one lived through it *"without converting your own person to a different person than you are right now"* (italics added). Obviously, he cannot fall back on a heroic tradition to transcend this dilemma, because to do so would violate his sense of nothing adding up. But what else could remove the obstacles impeding his quest for an image of the integrated self?[14]

The logic of character informing his vision now is neither cause nor consequence of the humiliation he experienced through more than three years in Gross Rosen, Dora/Nordhausen, and Bergen-Belsen. "I couldn't in good conscience even tell you privately about the horrors on that train," he says about the seven-day journey in open boxcars to the latter camp.[15] But other accounts of such voyages, which include death by freezing and starvation, and even cannibalism, give us a clue to his reluctance to use the vocabulary of heroic resistance to justify—or rectify—his ordeal. His reluctance betrays not only a disinclination to speak about such things, but the absence of an idiom and a context of values to enable such a discussion.

"Nazism and its effects," writes the historian Richard J. Evans, speaking of the current *Historikerstreit* in West Germany, "cannot be made real to people who . . . were born long after the event, if they are presented in crude terms of heroes and villains." If he had added "to people who were born during the event but did not share any of its experiences," he might have been talking of the audiences of victim testimony too. "The nature of the moral choices people had to make," Evans continues, "can only be accurately judged by taking into account the full complexities of the situations in which they found themselves."[16] But it may be easier for historians, with archives of documents available for research, to reconstruct the moral complexities of Hitler's rise to power and the evolution of the Final Solution, than it is for students of the camp experience, even after a collaborative effort with the victims themselves, to assess the impact on the private (as against the public) self of such an ordeal.

One of the distinctive qualities of oral testimony is its immediacy. Even though witnesses obviously have reflected on their past before their interview, they re-encounter the duality of their experience in the process of retelling it. Oddly enough, they say little of their Nazi oppressors once the deportations have begun. They wrestle instead with the dilemma of their own identity and the impossibility of functioning as a normal self in situations so unprecedented and unpredictable. They struggle further with the incompatibility between the impromptu self that endured atrocity and the self that sought reintegration into society after "liberation." Both the nature of the "villainy" and the range of "heroic" responses during the ordeal elude traditional categories, and this unsettling quandary itself becomes the underground theme of many testimonies. For example, although a concept like "spiritual resistance" has gained increasing popularity among some commentators, including former victims, in their *written* accounts of the disaster, witnesses in the oral testimonies I have seen avoid this expression, or anything resembling it. They demur virtually unanimously when it is raised by an interviewer, as they do when the word "heroic" is introduced. Their response to such language ranges from dismay to disdain, despite the tempting offer of a verbal way out of their dilemma.

The experience apparently separating atrocity from survival, the so-called moment of liberation, provides some of the most dramatic testimony in these narratives. Through the content of their questions, interviewers *invite* witnesses to give detailed accounts of their feelings of joy when they realized that their ordeal was over. We need to understand more about how this psychology of expectation can impose itself on the reality of the situation and gradually forge a myth that would displace the truth. Asked how she felt when liberated, one witness replies: "We were weak. We were starving. We were in a state of apathy. We simply sat and stared into space."[17] Another is more graphic—and more suggestive: "And you know, when I was liberated . . . I was two days on my bed. I not was hungry, I not want dresses, I was [so] sick two days. But at this moment I realize I am alive and I have nobody and I am living." The sudden conjunction of the discontinuous (or impromptu) self that had managed to stay alive, with the continuous self (the family member who no longer had a family) receives eloquent understatement here. Terms like "spiritual resistance" and "heroic behavior" dwindle into irrelevancy.

The following brief exchange between an interviewer and this same witness illustrates the kind of well-intentioned but subtle prodding that often results when the normal world encounters the unfamiliar lineaments of atrocity:

Witness: I sometimes myself not can believe that a person can be so strong. And can lift over so many things.
Interviewer: As you did.
Witness: You know, I think I'm normal, and still be normal, and still have children, raise families, and talk and walk. [But] something *stimmt nicht.* Something is wrong here. In the chemistry something is wrong.
Interviewer: But you must be very strong and you must have had a will to have survived it.
Witness: [Shrugs, looks away.]
Interviewer: And you're here to talk about it, and to tell future generations.
Witness: I'm strong, I'm strong, *aber* [but] when I tell you I never was doing anything *really* to live. . . .
Interviewer: To help yourself. . . .
Witness: My fate push me, you know, I not help myself.

She then explains, in an apparent attempt to define what she means by "fate," that while she was in Auschwitz her parents (already murdered) came to her twice in dreams, and gave her advice that, as she now believes, saved her life. "They came to you when you needed them," the narrator encourages, hopefully. "I need them *now* too," the witness drily replies, ending the dialogue.[18]

"*Keep watch over absent meaning,*"[19] Maurice Blanchot warns in one of the gnomic fragments from *The Writing of the Disaster.* Our belief in heroic will, deeply etched on the modern sensibility by literary and scriptural traditions from ancient times to the present, intrudes on the need to understand what lies behind the troubled avowal by a former victim that despite her contented present life, something still "*stimmt nicht.*" I am reminded of the unsettling, paradoxical discovery by a former death camp inmate that one can be alive after Sobibor without having survived Sobibor. When Blanchot distinguishes between "knowledge of the disaster" (*du désastre*) and "knowledge as disaster" (*comme désastre*), he defines the frontiers separating the violated self of the witness from the inviolable self of the audience—of us. It can scarcely be accidental that he begins the passage introducing this distinction by quoting Nietzsche's question, a virtual classical formula, "Have you suffered for knowledge's sake?"[20] The disaster of the Holocaust invalidated forever whatever force that formula once retained, though Blanchot fully appreciates the possibility of "knowledge as disaster" smiting us and nonetheless leaving us untouched. This would estrange us even further from the testimonies of former victims, the burden of whose stories is the *impossibility* for them of such an eventuality.

Blanchot presses language to its limits in his efforts to prod the imagination into original vision. "Knowledge of the disaster" skirts the subversive essence of the event, while "knowledge as disaster" affirms its disruptive impact. But formulation in words is one thing, conversion to insight another matter entirely, as Blanchot himself confesses when he admits that knowledge *as* disaster (like knowledge *via* disaster) often shields us from its implications and "carries (*porte*) us off, deports (*déporte*) us [surely a scrupulously chosen term] . . . straight to ignorance, and puts us face to face with ignorance of the unknown, so that we forget, endlessly."[21] Oral testimony is a form of endless remembering, a direct challenge to us to convert our ignorance of the unknown into some appreciation of the disparate, half-articulated tensions that inhabit the former victims' narratives. We gain this appreciation not by transforming words into meaning, but by observing the process by which one meaning cancels or neutralizes another as the narratives unfold. Because so many witnesses themselves have a vivid sense of the division resulting from having survived disaster, their testimonies invite us to participate in the painful difficulties they experience reorganizing disorder. The absence of a complex verbal texture like Blanchot's in their narratives highlights the value of his commentary, which stretches language to meet the demanding requirements of atrocity; but it also reminds us of a preliminary and perhaps more urgent need—to abandon the preconceptions that our "unstretched" language offers to protect our comfortable ignorance. Blanchot follows a bold and innovative verbal path, conjuring the reader's imagination to do the same in its pursuit of this disaster's impact on the self.

Because they do *not* provide us with the kind of constant verbal stimulus that Blanchot or authors of written survivor narratives do, oral testimonies initiate us into thinking about the disaster with fewer guidelines than a reader is usually provided with. Interviewers' attempts to provoke such frames invariably fail, so we are left with unassimilated texts that demand of us what we might call interpretive remembering. Most written texts flow continuously, compelling us to follow their sinuous turns if we wish to stay mentally afloat. Oral testimonies pause in a variety of ways, one of them being moments when witnesses display visual icons, like the gouache portrait mentioned earlier, that challenge our capacity for construing silence. Many witnesses, for example, begin or end their testimonies by holding up family photographs, some of them containing a dozen persons or more. Conventional thinking responds to the dignity of the faces before us. But we are prompted to ask by the subtext of the narrative whether the point is to remind us that they once *were*, or no longer *are*, alive. Is it an effort at rescue, or an avowal of loss? Are we gazing at presence—or absence? In fact, oral testimonies offer us both, although the "un-story," as Blanchot calls it, raises the issue of how to establish a connection between consequential living, and inconsequential dying.

This is the essential dilemma for surviving victims in these testimonies. It may be the insoluble riddle of the Holocaust itself. An underlying discontinuity assaults the integrity of the self and threatens the very continuity of the oral narrative. Perceiving the imbalance is more than just a passive critical reaction to a text. As we listen to the shifting idioms of the multiple voices emerging from the same person, we are present at the birth of a self made permanently provisional as a result of fragmentary excavations that never coalesce into a single, recognizable monument to the past. A last example of multiple voices issuing from the same individual will have to illustrate this idea. They belong to Leo L., who began his encounter with Nazi oppression in a little-known labor camp called Rachotsky Mlin—the first and the worst, he calls it—followed by Auschwitz, Dachau, Sachsenhausen, Buchenwald, and Ohrdruf. Asked what effect this has had on his life, he replies almost automatically with the language of heroic enterprise: "It makes you a stronger human being to fight for the right of humanity." But other voices possess him too, since less than a minute later he adds that anyone who went through this kind of atrocity ends up "not being the way you should be." No doubt he means both; can one also *be* both? Earlier in his testimony, he had helped to define the impromptu self by deploring his inability to relate to his own tragedy. The heroic self, by definition, helps to *create* its own tragedy, and to live or die by the consequences. Leo L. crystallizes the difference by his last words, the abrupt and forlorn questions that end his two hours of testimony, and that will seem non sequiturs only to those who have not been hearing him and his fellow witnesses: "How did my mother look? When did they take her away?"[22] Unanswered and unanswerable, they remain permanent obstacles to the rebirth of the heroic self in the oral narratives of former Holocaust victims.

Alvin H. Rosenfeld

Popularization and Memory:
The Case of Anne Frank

IT HAS BEEN ESTIMATED THAT, AMONG THE ALMOST SIX MILLION JEWS who fell victim to the Nazis during World War II, at least one million and perhaps as many as 1.5 million were children. Yad Vashem in Jerusalem and other research institutions elsewhere have many of their names on record. To the world at large, however, these children all bear one name—that of Anne Frank. It is not that we lack information about the others, for more than a few of them were youthful authors and wrote diaries or other personal testimonies that have come down to us. For the most part, though, these other books remain relatively unknown, while the diary of Anne Frank is unquestionably the most widely read book of World War II. It is as if the broad public has chosen to pay tribute to the memory of the others by remembering the one child who today stands for all the child victims of the Nazi era. To the million or more who perished we have given the collective name *Anne Frank*.

What accounts for this remarkable metonymy? How has it evolved, and what might it tell us about the evolution of a more broadly encompassing popular memory of the Holocaust? These questions will form the heart of my inquiry in this chapter, which I hope may help to clarify how, on the level of popular perceptions, a sense of the past seems to be shaped less on the basis of information contained in historical documents than through the projection of single images of ubiquitous and compelling power. Through a study of the development of the image of Anne Frank, therefore, I hope to be able to reveal some of the ways in which a public memory of the Nazi era has itself been developing since the end of World War II.

About the persistence and power of the figure of Anne Frank there can be little doubt today. Simply put, she is the most famous child of the twentieth century. Her book has been translated into dozens of languages and has been read by many millions of people throughout the world. Millions more are acquainted with her story through the dramatic and film versions of her diary. Streets, schools, and youth centers bear her name, just as public statues, stamps, and commemorative coins bear her image. Youth villages, forests, and foundations have been named after her; ballets, requiems, and cantatas written for her; poems and songs composed for her. Public figures of every kind, from politicians to religious leaders, regularly invoke her name and quote lines from her book. In all of these ways her name, face, and fate are kept constantly before us.

As illustration of this phenomenon, which, far from lessening with the passage of the years, seems to be increasing in scope and intensity, consider the following. In June 1989, a series of events was held in New York City to commemorate what would have been the sixtieth anniversary of Anne Frank's birth. Mayor Koch officially proclaimed the week beginning June 12 as "Anne Frank Week." A major exhibition of photographs and texts from the Nazi era, entitled "Anne Frank in the World: 1929–1945," opened at the City Gallery on Columbus Circle and later was shown at the Cathedral of St. John the Divine and other places in New York. It drew tens of thousands of people. A gala celebrity concert honoring Anne Frank in words and music was performed under the title "Remembering Anne Frank" on the evening of June 12. Later that same night a prominent New York television channel offered the American premiere of Willy Lindwer's Emmy award–winning documentary "The Last Seven Months of Anne Frank." A second film about Jews who had been hidden by Christians during the war was also shown. Books released that day included the Doubleday critical edition of *The Diary of Anne Frank*[1] and a new school curriculum, *The End of Innocence: Anne Frank and the Holocaust*.[2] An art exhibit that opened at a prominent gallery in Manhattan featured "The Anne Frank Series." On June 13 Bill Moyers hosted on prime-time television a special program, "The Legend and the

Legacy of Anne Frank." The day after, there was an international symposium on Anne Frank; on the following day, a teacher-training workshop was convened to introduce secondary school educators to The Anne Frank Curriculum; and so it went through the week.

It should be noted that similar events took place outside of New York City: in Pennsylvania, New Jersey, Texas and elsewhere films on Anne Frank's life were screened, lectures on and readings from her book were held, musical programs were performed, and theatrical productions of *The Diary of Anne Frank* were dedicated to her memory. Senator Paul Simon of Illinois introduced a resolution to the Senate designating June 12, 1989, as "Anne Frank Day." His resolution noted that more than twenty cities nationwide would be marking the day in commemoration of Anne Frank. In Philadelphia, a new educational foundation called the Anne Frank Institute presented its annual Anne Frank Youth Award and announced plans to build the country's first Anne Frank Museum, to be constructed possibly as a replica of the Anne Frank house on the Prinsengracht in Amsterdam.

In Frankfurt, the place of her birth, a plaque marks the building where she was born, and a major exhibition on Anne Frank was mounted during 1989 at the city's historical museum. Elsewhere in West Germany large numbers of people went to see the touring exhibit "Anne Frank in the World," attended lectures and participated in symposia about her, viewed films of the period in which she lived, recalled the way she and so many others died. The exhibit, organized by the Anne Frank Foundation in Amsterdam, also toured cities throughout the United States, Great Britain, the Netherlands, Italy, and Japan. It was estimated that by the end of 1989 "Anne Frank in the World" would have been seen by 1.5 million people in over a hundred cities in Europe, Asia, and North America.[3]

The above is by no means an exhaustive list. Rather, it merely illustrates the manifold ways in which the figure of Anne Frank has won such a prominent place among us and, indeed, stands today, almost unrivaled, as a contemporary cultural icon. The question, therefore, is not one about the constancy of her presence, which by now must be taken as a given, but about its symbolic character. Why is it that, among the many millions who perished during the Nazi era, it is Anne Frank and almost she alone who stands out as such a commanding figure? What is it that she has come to represent to vast numbers of people around the world who feel so powerfully drawn to her image? Who, in short, is the Anne Frank we remember?

In seeking answers to these questions, we would do well to reflect first on the earliest signs that Anne Frank was to return from her place among the anonymous dead at Bergen-Belsen and assume a posthumous existence within popular culture of such unusual force and magnitude. The initial reception of her diary was, in fact, inauspicious. According to reports by Louis de Jong and others, several Dutch publishing houses turned down the manuscript of *Het Achterhuis* before it was finally accepted by Contact, an Amsterdam publisher.[4] The initial print run of the first edition, which appeared in June 1947, was relatively small, consisting of 1,500 copies, no doubt reflecting the sense that people were tired of the war and probably did not want to be reminded all over again of the suffering that had marked the years of occupation. The first critical notice, in fact, written by Jan Romein, Professor of Dutch History at the University of Amsterdam, sounded a strong note of pessimism about the prospects of such a story as Anne Frank's finding many readers. After praising her diary for its intelligence, vivacity, and humaneness, and also noting that the young author had perished in one of the worst of the German concentration camps shortly before liberation, Romein offered the following reflections:

> The way she died is unimportant. More important is that this young life was willfully cut off by a system of irrational cruelty. We had sworn to each other never to forget or forgive this system as long as it was still raging, but now that it is gone, we too easily forgive, or at least forget, which ultimately means the same thing.[5]

What is so remarkable about this statement is its date: April 1946. The war had ended less than a year before, and yet, as is obvious from Jan Romein's downcast words, the question of memory was already a worried one; indeed, in terms of its outcome, it may already have been a lost one. Romein's response to Anne Frank's diary (he read it in manuscript and wrote his little essay a full year before Contact brought out the first edition of the book) was conditioned by his sense that the war had swept away whatever sources of culture might effectively have opposed Nazism and that, in the postwar period, there were few signs that an active democratic counterforce could be quickly established in its stead. And so, he concluded pessimistically, "we have lost the battle against the beast in man. We have lost because we have not been able to substitute something positive for it. And that is why we will lose again."

Had this view prevailed, it is clear that Anne Frank's story would have remained a minor affair, one among the hundreds of wartime diaries kept in the archives of the Netherlands Institute for War Documentation but otherwise hardly known. As it happens, Jan Romein's reading of Anne Frank was not to be widely shared, for within a decade of his review, the diary was to capture huge audiences the world over. Later readers evidently were to fix upon aspects of Anne Frank's story that Romein either overlooked or upon which he placed only a secondary stress. Clearly, however, he was not "wrong" in his view of Anne Frank, nor was he reading her book "badly." Rather, the discoveries that he made in the diary pointed him back to the devastations from which the countries of Europe were only just emerging. The book showed him "the real hideousness of fascism, more than all the trials of Nuremberg" and summed up "the worst crime of that abominable spirit. . . : the destruction of life and talent only because of a senseless desire to destroy." Moreover, he sensed that the force of the spirit unleashed by Nazism was far from spent and that Anne Frank would hardly be its last victim. "No matter in what form inhumanity may lay traps for us, we will fall into them as long as we are unable to replace that inhumanity with a positive force." The name that Romein gave this positive force was "democracy," and he concluded his meditation on the conflict between fascism and a vital opposition to it with these melancholy words: "And with all our good intentions, we are still as far away from this kind of democracy as we were before the war."

Jan Romein's essay presented a dark view of recent history and apprehension about its legacy for Europe in the immediate postwar period. Given this sense of things, he read Anne Frank's diary in the only way he could, as an admonitory text. The book's youthful author, after all, had been murdered by the Nazis, and her death appeared to him as a warning of further devastations to come unless the spirit of nihilism unleashed by Nazism could be permanently overcome. Romein recognized Anne Frank's precocious talent, to be sure, but for all of that he found nothing in her diary that transcended his sharp sense of her horrible end and the monstrous system that destroyed her.

The essay, entitled "A Child's Voice," appeared on the front page of the Dutch newspaper *Het Parool* on April 3, 1946, and is credited with stimulating interest in Anne Frank's then still unpublished manuscript. When the book appeared the following June, it carried an introduction by Jan Romein's wife and, on the dust jacket, extracts from his essay. The early reviews, according to the Dutch scholar Gerrold van der Stroom, were uniformly favorable, speaking of the book as "a moral testament," "a human document of great clarity and honesty," and as a text that "transcends the misery" it records.[6] These terms, which were far more optimistic than those used by Romein, were to be repeated and amplified elsewhere as the diary found its way into foreign-language translations. A French edition was brought out in Paris by Calmann-Lévy in 1950; that same year, the Heidelberg publisher Lambert Schneider issued the first German-language version; in 1952 English readers were given the book when Valentine, Mitchell released the British publication, and at the same time Doubleday offered it to American readers; translations into numerous other languages were to follow within a few years. In 1955 the popular theater version, by Frances Goodrich and Albert Hackett, first played in the United States and soon was introduced to highly receptive audiences around the world.[7] Four years later, in 1959, a film version was produced and likewise proved to be an international success. The "child's voice" that had been silenced in Bergen-Belsen had now become audible to large numbers of people around the world.

What was it that they heard in this voice, and why did it appeal to them so? Unlike Jan Romein, who took away from Anne Frank's story the heavy sense "that we have lost the battle against the beast in man," most later readers found a far more buoyant message in the book. They saw Anne Frank as a young, innocent, vivacious girl, full of life and blessed with an optimistic spirit that enabled her never to lose hope in humanity, even as its worst representatives were intent on hunting her down and murdering her. They understood her story as deeply sorrowful but perhaps not as ultimately tragic, for they also found in it strains of tenderness and intimacy, courage and compassion, wit and humor, sincere religious feeling and an aspiring romantic idealism, all of which undercut the sense of historical catastrophe that Jan Romein stressed. Indeed, whereas he read it primarily as a revealing historical document, most others preferred to see the diary as a moving personal testimony, a wartime story, to be sure, but also a work of bright adolescent spirit, one that portrayed a life shadowed by daily tension and lingering threat but also inspired by nascent love and humane intelligence. In her introduction to the American edition, for instance, Eleanor Roosevelt acknowledged that Anne Frank's book made her "shockingly aware of war's greatest evil—the degradation of the human spirit," but "at the same time, Anne's diary makes poignantly clear the ultimate shining nobility of that spirit."[8] The affirmation inherent in this evaluation, its psychological harmonies reflected in the syntactic balance of the sentence, typifies much of the early response to Anne Frank's book among American readers. The reviewer for *Newsweek* wrote under the heading "Distressing Story" but highlighted Anne Frank's "courage and faith," praised her resolve to maintain her ideals in the most difficult of circumstances, and concluded by predicting that "with her vivid and appealing diary she will be remembered as a talented and sensitive adolescent whose spirit could not be imprisoned or thwarted."[9] The review in the *Saturday Review* ran under the heading "A Glory and a Doom," and, as this phrasing suggests, likewise offered a balanced reading of the book, pointing up its sorrowful aspects but ending on a note of affirmative belief that "from this one girl's diary a gleam of redemption may arise."[10]

Meyer Levin, who was to take an intense, even obsessive interest in Anne Frank, wrote a highly appreciative review for the Sunday *New York Times Book Review*, a front-page article that undoubtedly contributed to the book's early success in the United States. It also may have helped to set the terms by which the book would be understood by many of its first readers. Levin noted that "Anne Frank's voice becomes the voice of six million vanished Jewish souls," but otherwise he subordinated the historical aspect of the diary and stressed its more intimate side. He hailed it as "a warm and stirring confession," a "virtually perfect drama of puberty," which should be read "over and over for insight and enjoyment." He emphasized that although it was a story shaped by the conditions of the recent war, readers need not shy away from it, for "this is no lugubrious ghetto tale, no compilation of horrors." Rather, it was a book representative "of human character and growth anywhere," a book "that simply bubbles with amusement, love, and discovery," and that expresses "a poignant delight in the infinite human spirit." For someone who later was to carry on an impassioned campaign against those whom he accused of willfully distorting Anne Frank's diary by universalizing it, Levin did not do very much in this review to stress its particular aspects. Instead, he wrote that the diary was "so wondrously alive, so near, that one feels overwhelmingly the universalities of human nature." The types portrayed were human types, so much so that the Franks and the Van Daans were people who "might be living next door." As for the author herself, "one feels the presence of this child-becoming-woman as warmly as though she was snuggled on a near-by sofa." "Surely," Levin concluded, "this wise and wonderful young girl . . . will be widely loved."[11]

In order to give the book this emphasis—one that urged readers to cherish its youthful author rather than to mourn her—one had to read the diary in such a way as to have it appear an uplifting and not a harrowing experience. The only way to do that, though, was to dehistoricize Anne Frank's story: to see it, on the one hand, as emblematic of Jewish fate during the Nazi period, to be sure, but, on the other hand, as transcending that fate. The girl was gone, but something precious about her spirit—its ebullience, its youthful optimism, its magnanimity—would outlast her murderers. Levin, like so many others who wrote about the diary, fixed on those passages that highlighted Anne Frank's cheerfulness and serenity, and tended to play down its gloomier aspects. Neither Levin nor anyone else, obviously, could ignore the young girl's ultimate end; however, by emphasizing the tender and more ennobling aspects of youthful sentiment in the book and deemphasizing its more tragic dimension, it became possible to project an image of Anne Frank that softened somewhat the revulsion and horror that otherwise might have directed readers' responses to the diary. One wanted, in short, to be able to regard the book as an inspiring text and not a disconsolate one and to come away from it with feelings of affection for the author rather than fear for her fate or loathing for those who brought it about.

This tendency to idealize her story characterized much of the early response to Anne Frank's writing, especially among readers in America. Thus Anne Birstein and Alfred Kazin, in their introductory essay to *The Works of Anne Frank*, quoted the young girl's bedtime prayer—"I thank you God, for all that is good and dear and beautiful"—and suggested that "perhaps this was Anne's last prayer in hiding. Perhaps when she went to bed on the night of August 3, 1944 [the following day, the family was to be discovered and taken away], her last thought was of her own blessedness: her youth, her strength, her love for all the people and the growing things around her, her closeness to God, who had provided them." Perhaps. But, as Birstein and Kazin add, "there is no way of knowing." A lack of knowledge, however, did not impede the two authors from endowing Anne Frank's last night in relative freedom with an aura of prayerful hope and consolation. Indeed, Birstein and Kazin place a prominent stress on the inspirational aspects of the diary and write that it has survived "because the faithfulness with which it records an unusual experience reminds us ... of the sweetness and goodness that are possible in a world where a few souls still have good will. The *Diary* moves us because its author had the strength to see, to remember, to hope."[12]

As here, a strong desire to regard Anne Frank's story as a testament of hope characterizes much of the early reception of the diary. This wish found both a powerful fulfillment and a new impetus in *The Diary of Anne Frank*, the 1955 stage play by Frances Goodrich and Albert Hackett, which was to prove extraordinarily successful in moving mass audiences to pity and love the image of the bright young girl without, at the same time, feeling overly frightened or repelled by too stark a sense of her end. More than any other "reading" of the diary, the Goodrich and Hackett adaptation was responsible for projecting an image of Anne Frank that would be widely acceptable to large numbers of people in the postwar period. In essence, the two authors recreated Anne Frank as a triumphant figure, one characterized by such irrepressible hope and tenacious optimism as to overcome any final sense of a cruel end. As Walter Kerr, reviewing the play for the *Herald Trib-une*, put it, "Soaring through the center of the play with the careless gaiety of a bird that simply cannot be caged is Anne Frank herself. . . . Anne is not going to her death; she is going to leave a dent on life, and let death take what's left."[13] Echoing this view, the reviewer for the *New York Post* wrote that the play "brought about the reincarnation of Anne Frank—as though she'd never been dead."[14] Given the forcefulness and attractiveness of the young girl's personality, audiences would leave the theater know-ing, of course, that Anne Frank had died but nevertheless feeling that she had not been defeated.

How did Goodrich and Hackett manage to create this effect? As is well known, the playwrights took some large liberties with the text of the diary and, by playing down or simply suppressing outright the darker, more foreboding entries and highlighting more affirmative ones, they shaped an image of Anne Frank that varied more than a little from the girl's self-image in the diary. In particular, they tended to understate some of the specifically Jewish aspects of her story and instead universalized her experience as the experience of suffering humanity in general. They also gave a preponderant emphasis to her most cheerful side, ending their play with the consoling affirmation that "in spite of everything I still believe that people are really good at heart," a line that does not appear in the diary in anything like the climactic role it is made to assume in the play. As Lawrence Langer has written, this line, "floating over the audience like a benediction assuring grace after momentary gloom, is the least appropriate epitaph conceivable for the millions of victims and thousands of survivors of Nazi geno-cide."[15] Langer, of course, is right in his criticism, or at least would be right if the play had been conceived to honor the memory of the millions of victims of Nazi terror. In fact, though, the play was shaped along very different lines. As Garson Kanin, the play's first director, put it in a revealing *New York Times* interview, "This play makes use of elements having mainly to do with human cour-age, faith, hope, brotherhood, love, and self-sacrifice. We discov-ered as we went deeper and deeper that it was a play about what Shaw called 'the life force.'"[16] No brooding sense of mass death registers here. Rather, what shows through this string of lofty abstractions is nothing but an idealized sense of history, or, more accurately, no sense of it at all.

History, as Anne Frank and millions of other European Jews suffered it, was a perilous affair, but neither the playwrights nor the director had it in mind to present a grim or gloomy play. It is clear from other remarks that Kanin made to the press at the time of the play's New York opening that exposing theater audiences to anything remotely reminiscent of genocide was simply no part of his intention:

> I have never looked on it as a sad play. I certainly have no wish to inflict depression on an audience; I don't consider that a legitimate theatrical end. I never thought the original material depressing. I've never seen it as sociological, historical, or political—but as a human document. . . . Looking back, Anne Frank's death doesn't seem to me a wasteful death, because she left us a legacy that has meaning and value to us as you look at the whole story.[17]

Kanin summed up what he understood to be the "meaning and value" of Anne Frank's story in an essay he published in *Newsweek* in 1979, almost twenty-five years after the first stage production of *The Diary of Anne Frank*. Comparing her to Peter Pan and the Mona Lisa, among others, "Anne," he wrote, "remains forever adolescent. . . . [She] reminds us that the length of a life does not necessarily reflect its quality. . . . Anne lives on. She remains for us ever a shining star, a radiant presence who, during her time of terror and humiliation and imprisonment, was able to find it within herself to write in her immortal diary, 'in spite of everything I still believe that people are good at heart.'"[18] Thus sensibility, reduced here to an almost adolescent level, is made to triumph over history.

Given the liberties that the playwrights took with the text in reworking it for the popular theater and given as well this maudlin sense of it on the part of the director, it is little wonder that audiences responded as they did. The reviewer for *Variety* had this to say about the opening in New York: "Theoretically, after seeing this new play . . . one should come out depressed, hating the Nazis, hating what they did to millions of innocent people, and most particularly what they did to a little Jewish Dutch girl whose name was Anne Frank. . . . Yet 'Diary' comes off as a glowing, moving, frequently humorous play that has just about everything one could wish for. It is not grim."[19] The reviewer for the *Daily News* wrote that "as it appears on the stage of the Cort, 'The Diary of Anne Frank' is not in any important sense a Jewish play. . . . It is a story of the gallant human spirit. . . . Anne Frank is a Little Orphan Annie brought into vibrant life." About the family in hiding, this reviewer continued in his same cartoon fashion: "Without the gallantry of the human spirit, this apartment could be a hell a few stories above the earth. . . . But this place is not a hell above ground; it is a testing place in which men and women and children earn the blessed right to be alive."[20] Others responded in a similar vein, one pronouncing that Anne Frank "was destined to become a symbol of man's hope for the survival of the human spirit," another prophesying, in lofty but equally meaningless fashion, that "wherever and whenever man's inhumanity to man erupts, these characters and their conflicts will be humanly and dramatically valid," et cetera.[21] In brief, the Anne Frank who emerged through this play was fashioned to evoke the most conventional of responses about "man's inhumanity to man," the "triumph of goodness over evil," the eternal verities of "the human spirit," and other such banalities. The harshness of history was left behind, and in its place softer, more acceptable images of a young girl's gaiety and moral gallantry came to the fore.

Lawrence Langer sums up the inevitable impact on theatergoers of a play of such character: "An audience coming to this play in 1955, only a decade after the event, would find little to threaten their psychological or emotional security. . . . The authors of the dramatic version of Anne Frank's *Diary* lacked the artistic will—or courage—to leave their audiences overwhelmed by the feeling that Anne's bright spirit was extinguished, that Anne, together with millions of others, was killed simply because she was Jewish, and for no other reason."[22]

One did not encounter much criticism of this kind in the late 1950s. On the contrary, most of the reviews of *The Diary of Anne Frank* were laudatory, and the play enjoyed an instant success. It swept all of the major theater prizes—in 1956, the Pulitzer Prize, the Critics' Circle Prize, and the Antoinette Perry Award—and soon was playing before theater audiences everywhere. To this day it remains a popular play and is frequently performed in major cities and small towns throughout the world. It was followed in 1959 by a full-length motion picture, also scripted by Goodrich and Hackett, which proved to be equally popular, and, in 1967, by the first of several television adaptations. Videos, children's books, and other tie-ins have followed, as have any of a number of reissues of the original diary. As a consequence, it is no exaggeration to say that more people are probably familiar with the Nazi era through the figure of Anne Frank than through any other figure of that period with the possible exception of Adolf Hitler himself. Hers is often the first story of that time that large numbers of people come to know; for many, hers may also be the last story of its kind that they encounter and the one whose images they are most likely to retain. I would venture to surmise, indeed, that if people have read one book and only one book about the victims of Nazism, it is likely to be *The Diary of a Young Girl*. If they have seen one play and only one play, it is probably Goodrich and Hackett's *The Diary of Anne Frank*. The several film and television versions have played to millions, and millions more have been to Amsterdam to visit the house on the Prinsengracht where the diary was composed. In sum, the impact of Anne Frank on shaping the historical consciousness of vast numbers of people is almost inestimable. More than any other single work of the postwar period, her diary, in its several permutations, must be counted among the first and most abiding popular representations of the era of Nazi persecutions.

Who, though, is the Anne Frank of *The Diary of Anne Frank*? What version of the author of the original diary comes through the Goodrich and Hackett play? From some of the theater reviews that have already been cited, it is evident that the Anne of the stage resembles the Anne of the printed page in some respects but differs from her significantly in others. The major difference, as has been pointed out by more than one critic in the past, is that the Anne of the stage has been fashioned as a more universal type than the Anne of the original diary. She also appears to be imbued with a more permanently optimistic, indeed all but indestructibly affirmative, spirit. To be sure, one can find entries in the diary that illustrate Anne Frank's cheerfulness, but, if one is open to them, one can also find passages that reflect a far graver sense of the times and more than a little anxiety about events. Peering out of her hideaway windows, for instance, Anne Frank saw and recorded the brutality of the German occupation (entry of November 19, 1942):

> Evening after evening the green and gray army lorries trundle past. The Germans ring at every front door to inquire if there are any Jews living in the house. If there are, then the whole family has to go at once. If they don't find any, they go on to the next house. No one has a chance of evading them unless one goes into hiding. . . . It seems like the slave hunts of olden times. But it's certainly no joke; it's much too tragic for that. In the evenings when it's dark, I often see rows of good innocent people accompanied by crying children, walking on and on . . . bullied and knocked about until they almost drop. No one is spared— old people, babies, expectant mothers, the sick—each and all join in the march of death.[23]

The scene is vividly drawn and shows in no uncertain terms the degree to which Anne Frank was aware of what was taking place just below on the streets of Amsterdam; however, no such passage as the one just quoted appears in the stage play. Nor did Goodrich and Hackett see fit to carry over the following entry (October 9, 1942), which extends still further the young diarist's consciousness of Jewish fate during this time:

> Our many Jewish friends are being taken away by the dozen. These people are being treated by the Gestapo without a shred of decency, being loaded into cattle trucks and sent to Wester- bork, the big Jewish camp in Drente. Westerbork sounds terri- ble: only one washing cubicle for a hundred people and not nearly enough lavatories. There are no separate accommodations. Men, women, and children all sleep together. One hears of frightful immorality because of this; and a lot of the women, and even girls, who stay there any length of time are expecting babies. . . . If it is as bad as this in Holland whatever will it be like in the distant and barbarous regions [the Jews] are sent to? We assume that most of them are murdered. The English radio speaks of their being gassed.[24]

As it happens, Anne Frank and her family were themselves to be sent to Westerbork and from there to those regions in the East that are described here in such chillingly direct terms, but this is knowledge that, once again, was not incorporated into the play in any substantial way at all. By stripping the text of such passages as these, Goodrich and Hackett may have "spared" theater audiences from knowing some of the worst that Anne Frank herself knew or feared, but in the process they reduced the figure of the young girl considerably. They also detached her from her own vivid sense of herself as a Jew. Thus, in thinking about the hardships of her family's situation, the Anne of the diary was drawn to reflect upon the nature of Jewish historical experience and wrote thoughtfully about the relationship between her suffering people and its God (April 11, 1944):

> We have been pointedly reminded that we are in hiding, that we are Jews in chains, chained to one spot, without any rights, but with a thousand duties. We Jews mustn't show our feelings, must be brave and strong, must accept all inconveniences and not grumble. . . .
>
> Who has inflicted this upon us? Who has made us Jews different from all other people? Who has allowed us to suffer so terribly up till now? It is God that has made us as we are, but it will be God, too, who will raise us up again. If we bear all this suffering and if there are still Jews left, when it is over, then Jews, instead of being doomed, will be held up as an example. Who knows, it might even be our religion from which the world and all peoples learn good, and for that reason and that reason only do we have to suffer now. We can never become just Netherlanders, or just English, or representatives of any country for that matter, we will always remain Jews, but we want to, too.[25]

This passage is remarkable for the maturity of its religious insight and also for what it reveals about Anne Frank's understanding of herself as an actor within the stream of Jewish history. It was, however, deleted from the play entirely, and in its place there appears the following weak substitution: "We're not the only people that've had to suffer. There've always been people that've had to . . . sometimes one race . . . sometimes another. . . ."[26] As dramatic prose, these lines are pallid in comparison to those cited above; in addition, they are altogether without source or analogy in the diary itself and have the effect of generalizing the figure of Anne Frank to the point of deracinating her. They are, however, typical of the major thrust of the play, which has given to the world an Anne Frank who is emotionally much thinner, intellectually less thoughtful, and spiritually and psychologically far less serious than the Anne of the diary. In the play's final scene, indeed, Goodrich and Hackett sentimentalize their heroine to the point of silliness by having Otto Frank remark, "It seems strange to say this, that anyone could be happy in a concentration camp. But Anne was happy in the camp in Holland where they first took us. After two years of being shut up in these rooms, she could be out . . . out in the sunshine and the fresh air that she loved."[27] In the bathetic quality of the sentiment they express, these lines are of a piece with the Birstein and Kazin fantasy, cited earlier, about Anne Frank's bedtime prayer and may even have provoked it. Both posit an Anne Frank of the beatitudes, a saintly figure who ultimately could not be brought down by her persecutors. "No longer a child," as Goodrich and Hackett describe her at play's end, "but a woman with courage to meet whatever lies ahead." She is last seen on stage "with a soft, reassuring smile"—this, supposedly, in the presence of the armed Gestapo, which has burst in upon her family in hiding—and her final words in the play, twice repeated, are, "In spite of everything, I still believe that people are really good at heart." Adding point to this affirmation, which is intended to lift one above whatever fear or sorrow one might otherwise feel at this moment in the play, Otto Frank says just before the curtain falls, "She puts me to shame."[28] And so *The Diary of Anne Frank* ends not on a note of final doom but of moral triumph, one's faith in humankind supposedly restored by the inspiring example of the girl who, "in spite of everything," could leave us with a credo affirming belief in the goodness of man.

Following upon the initial success of the play, which was enormous, there was renewed public interest in the diary itself. Contact had not reprinted *Het Achterhuis* since 1950, but in 1955 it reissued the diary in three separate printings. There were three more printings in 1956, nine in 1957, five in 1958, and numerous other printings up to today. In fact, when it first appeared the diary had not had a notable success in Holland, but, as a result of its much greater appeal in America and the wide attention given the Goodrich and Hackett dramatic version, the book returned to the country of its origin, as Gerrold van der Stroom describes it, "via an international detour."[29] There was a similar response elsewhere. In West Germany, *Das Tagebuch der Anne Frank* also had only a modest beginning. The original Lambert Schneider edition numbered only 4,500 in 1950. In 1955, however, Fischer Bücherei took it over and reissued the book as a paperback volume, with a cover that featured the words that by now had become canonized: "Ich glaube an das Gute im Menschen." Within the first five years Fischer printed the diary no less than eighteen times and sold more than 700,000 copies to German readers.

In 1958 Fischer also brought out Ernst Schnabel's *Anne Frank: Spur Eines Kindes,* a book that traced the story of Anne Frank beyond the point of her last diary entry to her death in Bergen-Belsen. In describing the aftermath of the Frank family's experience in Amsterdam, Schnabel performed a valuable service. His book, however, is problematic on two counts: one, since it is altogether undocumented, it is impossible to verify the personal accounts of Anne Frank that the author ascribes to the various eyewitnesses he interviewed; and, two, the book tends to idealize Anne Frank and thus contributes to the mystique that was rapidly growing up around her. In his opening pages, for instance, the author asks, "What was the source in this child of the power her name exerts throughout the world? Was this power, perhaps, not something within her, but something outside of and above her?"[30] He never answers these questions in so many words, but their metaphysical thrust is apparent and would seem, once again, to point us in the direction of some special beatitude. This emphasis is heightened by the account of Anne Frank's period of incarceration in Auschwitz that Schnabel attributes to witnesses—"Anne still had her face, up to the last. Actually she seemed to me in Auschwitz even more beautiful than in Westerbork"[31]—and even more so by the account he gives of her end in Bergen-Belsen: "She died, peacefully, feeling that nothing bad was happening to her."[32] Schnabel attributes this sense of Anne Frank's death to one of the many unnamed witnesses he interviewed; however, without any way to confirm the validity of the testimony, one is simply at a loss to know the truth of the matter. Birstein and Kazin, however, take up this description of a peaceful death and quote it approvingly in their own account of Anne Frank, as do any of a number of others. It may be that Anne Frank did die in such a manner, but, given the conditions that prevailed at Bergen-Belsen during her time in the camp, it is more likely that the ravages of typhus, malnutrition, exposure, and other related horrors culminated in a far more gruesome death. The fact is, we do not know and cannot know how Anne Frank died. What is clear, however, is that the idea of her coming to a miserable end was simply incompatible with the image of Anne Frank that was developing in the period following the Goodrich and Hackett play. Most people preferred to entertain a vision of the girl that connected her to a sustaining strength rather than debilitating weakness, to an abiding goodness rather than evil triumphant. Far from being remembered as one dead child among a million or more murdered Jewish children, she was instead to be taken up and cherished as a general symbol of martyred innocence, who stood for but also transcended the lot of suffering humanity.

More recently, this image of her received a kind of spiritual-political apotheosis at the time of the Bitburg affair when President Reagan, looking to "balance" his ill-conceived visit to the German military cemetery at Bitburg, traveled to Bergen-Belsen to pay homage to the victims of the Holocaust. This is some of what the American president had to say on that occasion:

> Here they lie. Never to hope. Never to pray. Never to love. Never to kneel. Never to laugh. Never to cry.

> And too many of them knew that this was their fate. But that was not the end. Through it all was their faith and a spirit that moved their faith. Nothing illustrates this better than the story of a young girl who died here at Bergen-Belsen. For more than two years, Anne Frank and her family had hidden from the Nazis in a confined annex in Holland, where she kept a remarkably profound diary. Betrayed by an informant, Anne and her family were sent by freight car to Auschwitz and finally here to Bergen-Belsen.

> Just three weeks before her capture, young Anne wrote these words: "It's really a wonder that I haven't dropped all my ideals, because they seem so absurd and impossible to carry out. Yet I keep them, because in spite of everything I still believe that people are really good at heart. I simply can't build up my hopes on a foundation consisting of confusion, misery and death. I see the world gradually being turned into wilderness, I hear the ever approaching thunder, which will destroy us too, I can feel the sufferings of millions, and yet if I look up into the heavens, I

think it will all come right, that this cruelty, too, will end, and that peace and tranquility will return again."[33]

By the time of President Reagan's speech in May of 1985, these words had already been cited so many times as to have taken on the character of a cliché. To recite them in Bergen-Belsen, where Anne Frank and all those other anonymous dead met their end, was to make of them little more than a kitsch of hope. In themselves, to be sure, Anne Frank's words express a noble sentiment, but, given our sense of what awaited her beyond the secret annex, it is scarcely possible to quote them today and pretend that the idealism they express remains altogether intact. When the American president then added his belief that the memories evoked at Bergen-Belsen "take us where God intended his children to go—toward learning, toward healing, and, above all, toward redemption,"[34] it was clear that the Anne Frank he had hoped to conjure at gravesite had dissolved into a public rhetoric of empty piety, her image reduced to little more than vague platitudes about the power of faith to transcend human suffering. As for her historical substance, after so much had been diffused into the gathering legend of a secular saint, little was left.

With only few exceptions, this is the image of Anne Frank that prevails to this day within a large and receptive public. By and large, it is an image produced in America along conventional American lines. Given the power of American popular culture in the postwar period and the influence it has exerted in countries around the world, the American version of Anne Frank quickly took hold elsewhere. The "exceptions" alluded to above, however, are of the utmost importance to any understanding of the place of Anne Frank within the evolving memory of the Holocaust, for the fact is, her reception has not been uniformly the same at all times and in all places, any more than public perceptions of the Nazi period as a whole have been the same. For obvious reasons, the crucial agents of memory with regard to this history are the Germans and the Jews, among whom one finds complex and often subtly differentiated responses to the story under review here. Although it is not possible to offer a full-scale exposition of German and Jewish responses to Anne Frank within the remaining pages of this chapter, I shall attempt to sketch in some of the main lines of each of these and, in this manner, try to highlight some of the ways they differ from one another and from the picture drawn thus far.

As I have already mentioned, *Das Tagebuch der Anne Frank* was originally published in 1950 by Lambert Schneider Verlag. According to contemporary reports, some booksellers were reluctant at first to show the book in their shop windows out of concern it might provoke a hostile reaction; apparently no such thing occurred. The book sold moderately well; then, in the Fischer Taschenbuch edition, which first appeared in 1955, it sold extremely well and went on to become one of the most popular books of postwar German literature. The circulation numbers bear out the extent of its reception: as of August 1989, the Fischer paperback edition was in its sixty-seventh printing and had reached a total of 2,355,000 copies in circulation.[35]

The play was also to reach an unusually large audience. It opened on October 1, 1956, at major theaters in seven different cities (West Berlin, Hamburg, Düsseldorf, Aachen, Karlsruhe, Konstanz, and Dresden) and, according to the reviews, had a profoundly moving effect on audiences everywhere. Within a short time it was to play in dozens of cities across Germany and, in the late 1950s alone, to reach hundreds of thousands of people. Although it continued to be performed in the next two decades, its popularity waned somewhat. Then, in the fall of 1979, following the huge success of the NBC program "Holocaust" on German television, there was a renewal of interest in *The Diary of Anne Frank*. The play was performed numerous times in Düsseldorf, Oldenburg, Bielefeld, Wilhelmshafen, and other cities; in some of these places it was accompanied by an exhibit of photographs of Anne Frank and her family.

There are any of a number of other events that characterize the German reception of the diary and show the extent to which the figure of Anne Frank has become established as a presence within postwar German consciousness. In the 1950s, Anne Frank clubs and discussion groups formed among German youths in various cities; in 1957 some two thousand of these young people, mainly from the Hamburg area, made a pilgrimage to Bergen-Belsen to pay homage to the memory of Anne Frank; the following year more than eight thousand people participated in a similar visit to the camp; in June of 1959 an Anne Frank Village, conceived of as a haven for refugees, was inaugurated in the city of Wuppertal; that same month, special commemorative services honoring Anne Frank were held at the university and at the Paulskirche in Frankfurt and attracted large crowds; through the 1950s and 1960s, schools were named for Anne Frank in dozens of cities and towns across Germany; German school children began to take up her diary as part of their reading and crossed the border into Holland in busloads for visits to the Anne Frank house in Amsterdam; also in the 1960s, German newspapers gave wide coverage to the trial of Karl Silberbauer, the Austrian Gestapo agent who had arrested the Frank family, and to the trials of former SS major general Wilhelm Harster and two of his aides, Wilhelm Zoepf and Gertrud Slotke, who were charged with complicity in the murder of 83,000 Dutch Jews; Anne Frank's name and fate were prominently mentioned in all of these news stories; in 1979, to mark the fiftieth anniversary of her birth, the Deutsche Bundespost brought out a commemorative Anne Frank postage stamp; that same year, Lambert Schneider Verlag published a commemorative picture book chronicling the life and times of Anne Frank; in more recent years Miep Gies's memoir, translated into German, has kept the memory of Anne Frank alive for German readers, as Ernst Schnabel's book did in earlier years; television programs and the touring exhibit, "Anne Frank in der Welt," have done the same up to the present moment.

The list could be extended but, for present purposes, need not be: it is clear that from 1950, the date of the original German publication of the diary, until today Anne Frank has been projected to German audiences through virtually all of the media of popular culture. The question, therefore, is not "Do the Germans know her?," for assuredly they do. Rather, one wants to know how Germans have responded to her, what it is she means to them, how they identify themselves with her story, et cetera.

To grasp the nature of this response at anything close to its core necessitates placing the German reception of Anne Frank within the context of that struggle over historical memory that Germans call *Vergangenheitsbewältigung*. This coming-to-terms with the past, a challenge that strikes to the heart of German national identity in the postwar period, has been going on with greater or lesser degrees of willingness and success for more than four decades now. Its history is a tortuous one, for it intermingles memory with morality in ways that are extremely demanding. Left to themselves, therefore, the majority of Germans doubtless would prefer to remain disengaged from this history, even as they know, on some level, that it continues to exert powerful claims upon them.

Willing or not, there has been an on-again, off-again engagement with the traumatic history of the Third Reich since the period immediately following the end of the war. In the beginning, this encounter was an enforced one and was met with a general resistance. Most Germans, for instance, did not respond well to the Nuremberg trials, any more than they did to the documentary films of wartime atrocities that the allies encouraged them to see. These things were intended to get people to acknowledge the worst of the crimes committed by their countrymen, but in the immediate postwar period most were in no mood to wrestle with the sins of their nation, especially when they felt they were being compelled to do so by their conquerors. In contrast to this general resistance, Anne Frank's diary, in both the book and the dramatic versions, seems to have brought numbers of otherwise reluctant Germans to look back at the war and to recognize, many of them for the first time, the real nature of the Nazi persecutions. Whereas most could not allow themselves to register any shock of personal recognition in the faces of the Nazi officials brought before the Nuremberg tribunals or acknowledge any association at all with the terrifying images of the corpse mounds shown to them in the films, many were genuinely moved by the story of Anne Frank. The theater reviews of the time tell of audiences sitting in stunned silence at the play and leaving the performance unable to speak or to look one another in the eye. Many of the early book reviews also make clear that the diary of Anne Frank broke through to German readers as almost nothing previously connected to the war had been able to do. In all of these respects, the emergence of Anne Frank as a factor in postwar German consciousness signaled something new—indeed, she was among the first prods to public memory and began a debate that continues, unresolved, to this day.

In its essence, this is a debate about the nature of World War II and, in particular, about Germany's treatment of the Jews. Looking back, how do Germans understand the war and explain to themselves, even before they attempt to explain to the world, their nation's persecution and mass murder of European Jewry? These are huge and unsettling questions, and whenever they are raised they awaken complex emotional responses, ranging from indignation and rejection to shame and guilt. The story of Anne Frank could not fail to provoke this full range of responses, and indeed it did. Following productions of the play, there were often turbulent discussions within families about the Nazi period. President Heuss himself gave a well-publicized speech in Munich, in October 1957, in which he referred to these debates and said that he wanted to see them continue lest the past be forgotten. Thus, although Anne Frank's story was a painful one for Germans to confront, it was also deemed to be a necessary one. Its greatest effect was to get people to see the "other" side of the wartime experience and to enforce a realization of the sufferings their nation had caused to the innocent. No doubt it was for these reasons that many responded powerfully, almost desperately, to the message of hope that they detected in the diary and to which they gave such a heightened emphasis. The Anne Frank they would favor, indeed almost the only Anne Frank they could bring themselves to acknowledge, was the one who spoke affirmatively about life and not accusingly about her torturers. According to one contemporary commentator, the appeal of the diary to German readers was "the appeal of the forgiving faith which pervades the book and appears to make the murdered absolve the murderer."[36] According to another, the extraordinary popularity of the play should not necessarily be taken as an unqualified good, for "it lets the Germans off too lightly. It does not even begin to suggest how frightful German actions were."[37] One sees, therefore, that the response to Anne Frank had to be a highly ambivalent one among German audiences. If they were forced into too close an identification with the girl's persecutors, most would have felt assaulted by the oppressive feelings of guilt and shame evoked by a vicarious sense of complicity. As it happens, the play is contructed in such a manner as to keep these feelings from becoming overwhelming. The drama builds toward violence but never represents it as such. No one is killed, nor is a single member of the Gestapo or SS ever brought on stage. The audience observes only the people in hiding, and though it surely knows from whom they are seeking shelter, a face-to-face encounter with Germans in the role of persecutors never takes place. It is no doubt for this reason that some in the audience would be moved to identify more closely with the victims, if not specifically as Jews, then as people in a state of extreme difficulty. In the words of one of the contemporary German drama critics, "We see in Anne Frank's fate our own fate—the tragedy of human existence per se."[38]

This tendency to generalize Anne Frank's experience so that it becomes an existential and not a specifically historical one was apparently especially strong among the young. Norbert Muhlen, who attempted to gauge public reaction to the diary of Anne Frank shortly after the play first showed in West German theaters, wrote as follows:

> Many young Germans identify with Anne Frank, see in her the prototype of all youth—helpless, imprisoned, at the mercy of elders, defiant of the outside world and terrified within. And the persecution and murder of Jews seems to them to be merely a peculiar external circumstance—secondary in importance to the personal tragedy of the heroine. . . . The political basis for the tragedy shrinks in their eyes into the remote historical background.[39]

It would be impossible to suppress altogether the Jewish factor in the story of Anne Frank, just as it would be to deny the German factor, but, as indicated above and, in a curious way, as illustrated by the character of the German translation of the diary, a degree of suppression seems to be a constituent feature of the German reception of Anne Frank.

Some of the early reviews noted that the German translator, Anneliese Schütz, was not very successful in carrying over into her own language the youthful style of the teenage author of *Het Achterhuis*. What was not remarked was the more serious matter of her alterations and suppression of material from the original diary. A few examples will have to suffice. In her entry of October 29, 1942, Anne Frank mentions that she has been reading in her mother's German prayer book. The Frank family was originally from Germany, so it is not at all surprising that Mrs. Frank would pray in her native language or that Anne could read in it. In the Schütz translation, however, the reference to Anne reading the prayers "in German" is omitted. It is omitted as well in numerous other instances. In her entry of June 13, 1943, Anne refers to a birthday poem that her father has written for her and mentions that it was composed in German. German readers of the diary, however, would never know that, for once again Schütz chose to eliminate the reference to the parent's language. She did so as well in her translation of the entry of November 17, 1942, in which Anne cites a humorous "Prospectus and Guide to the 'Secret Annexe'," a parody of a hotel guide that describes various "Do's and Don't's." Among these is the following reference to language usage: "Speak softly at all times, by order! All civilized languages are permitted, therefore no German!" In the Schütz translation this becomes: "Alle Kultursprachen . . . aber leise!!!" (All civilized languages . . . but softly!!!"). The original reference to German is simply stripped from the text as if it never had appeared. There are other instances of this kind as well, all of which would seem to indicate a determined effort on the translator's part to detach the Franks from any connection to their own mother tongue. Inasmuch as language is a cultural possession that binds its speakers to one another more naturally and intimately than most other things, the severance of the Franks from German would necessarily effect a degree of severance between them and German readers of the diary. Whatever natural links would have existed between the two would have been cut by the translator's tampering with the text.

Cuts were also made elsewhere, although it is doubtful that to this day German readers of *Das Tagebuch der Anne Frank* are aware of them. For instance, in her diary entry of November 19, 1942, Anne describes the nightly search for hidden Jews, already cited above, and remarks that "the Germans ring at every front door to inquire if there are any Jews living in the house." The German translation carries over the reference to the manhünt but submerges in vaguer terms the national identity of the hunters. In her entry of May 18, 1943, Anne records the fact that "all students who wish either to get their degrees this year, or continue their studies, are compelled to sign that they are in sympathy with the Germans and approve of the New Order." The Schütz translation once again omits the specific reference to "the Germans" and in its place substitutes, more vaguely, "die besetzende Macht" ("the

occupying power"). In her entry of January 28, 1944, Anne writes
that "although others may show heroism in their war or against
the Germans, our helpers display heroism in their cheerfulness and
affection." Schütz again eliminated the reference to "the Germans" and substitutes, more abstractly, "die Unterdrückung" (the
oppression).

When one looks carefully at these changes, a pattern begins to
emerge. Whereas the effect of the previously mentioned series of
alterations was to weaken the German-Jewish identity of the Franks
by disconnecting them from German, and thereby also perhaps to
weaken any natural sympathy with the Franks that German readers
of the *Tagebuch* would have, the effect of this second series of
changes works the other way: it disconnects German readers from
any shared identity with the persecutors of the Franks by eliminating specific references to the German nationality of the criminals.
Thus, German readers are discouraged from entertaining a full
awareness of the fact that the Jews, like themselves, are also native
Germans, and they are further discouraged from the realization
that the persecutors of these Jews were their own countrymen. In a
general sense, of course, readers of the diary would be aware of the
German identity of both the Franks and those who were responsible for terrorizing them, but reading that means anything at all
does not proceed "in a general sense" but always depends upon
the apperception of minute particulars. As has been shown, however, some of the most telling features of Anne Frank's story have
never been told to German readers, who for some four decades now
have been reading a bowdlerized version of the diary.[40]

The loss in this instance is not just the familiar one that always
obtains when one reads literature in translation but something far
more troubling: through reading a distorted text, and not knowing
it, German readers of the *Tagebuch* have become familiar with a
version of Anne Frank that is incomplete and in some serious ways
inauthentic. One final illustration may suffice to bear out this
point. In her diary entry of October 9, 1942, Anne records what
she has come to learn about the camp at Westerbork to which the
Dutch Jews were being sent. She describes the physical conditions
at the camp as being woefully inadequate and then writes, "One
hears of frightful immorality because of this; and a lot of the
women, and even girls, who stay there any length of time are

expecting babies." As a girl who had apprehensions about being arrested and sent to this very same camp (apprehensions, we know, that were borne out by her later experience), Anne had cause to worry about the immorality that victimized young women at Westerbork. The German translation of the diary, however, skips this reference in its entirety and thus keeps German readers from any knowledge of the young girl's fears. Furthermore, the German translation makes no mention at all of Anne's reference, in the same diary entry, to Jews being murdered in the East. The diarist writes: "If it is as bad as this in Holland whatever will it be like in the distant and barbarous regions they are sent to? We assume that most of them are murdered." The second of these two sentences— "We assume that most of them are murdered"—was simply dropped from the German translation, as if it were a thing of no importance that the young girl lived day by day with such fearful assumptions. Once again, therefore, German readers would be deprived of gaining a full sense of the psychology of Jewish victimhood as Anne Frank experienced it. Finally, as the result of still another excision from this same entry they would be spared the shock of knowing the full extent of Anne's bitterness about the Germans. She wrote, at the conclusion of her day's notes for October 9, 1942, "Nice people, the Germans! To think that I was once one of them too! No, Hitler took away our nationality long ago. In fact, Germans and Jews are the greatest enemies in the world." The German translation handles most of this in more or less straight fashion, but then renders the final sentence as follows: "Und eine grössere Feindschaft als zwischen *diesen* Deutschen und den Juden gibt es nicht auf der Welt!" (And there is not a greater enmity in the world than the one between *these* Germans and the Jews!; italics in the original.) In its original Dutch version, Anne's pronouncement is unqualified: as she sees it, Germans and Jews are enemies, the worst enemies in the world—period. The German translation seriously qualifies her view, however, and tells German readers that Anne regarded only *"these* Germans"—the "bad" Germans—as her enemies. The others, presumably themselves included, did not fall within her judgment and therefore need not wrestle with its implications, for Anne evidently did not mean to include *them* in her harsh comment. Of course, she did, however, and in the long run it is no kindness to German readers to spare them from the full truth of her views and to encourage them instead to take comfort in her more benign sentiments about the goodness of man. She had plenty of reason to believe otherwise.

In order to achieve a comprehensive sense of the German reception of Anne Frank, obviously a good deal more needs to be said, but even from so brief a survey as the foregoing it should be possible to grasp the nature of the challenge that the diary of Anne Frank posed to people in postwar Germany. There is no doubt that for many the discovery of Anne Frank marked the beginning of a long-delayed but necessary process of self-examination, but the hard work of personal introspection and historical scrutiny has gone on fitfully and produced reactions of a highly ambivalent sort. Out of both sorrow and shame, Germans have named streets, schools, and youth centers after Anne Frank, but to this day most probably do not comprehend why, a generation ago, a significant number of their countrymen deemed it necessary to hunt down a fifteen-year-old Jewish girl and send her off to suffer and die in places like Auschwitz and Bergen-Belsen. Until that issue is joined, the German encounter with Anne Frank is destined to remain incomplete.

The Jewish reception of Anne Frank, if one can use such a unitary phrase to describe a complex, multifaceted phenomenon, comes in part as a critique of the German response just outlined above. Hannah Arendt, the distinguished German-Jewish political philosopher, was by no means alone in expressing distaste for the way Germans and others took to Anne Frank. "I think the admiration for Anne Frank, especially in Germany, was phony and that the whole business was highly unpleasant—cheap sentimentality at the expense of a great catastrophe," she wrote.[41] In expressing this view she followed Bruno Bettelheim, the Austrian-Jewish refugee and famous child psychologist, who quarreled at length with the popular reception of Anne Frank and denounced it as a means of evading the issue of the death camps. "There is good reason," he wrote, "why the enormously successful play ends with Anne stating her belief in the good in all men. . . . If all men are basically good . . . then indeed we can all go on with life as usual and forget about Auschwitz. . . . [Anne Frank's story] found wide acclaim because . . . it denies implicitly that Auschwitz ever existed. If all men are good, there was never an Auschwitz."[42]

Arendt and Bettelheim, in other respects embattled critics of the Jewish role during World War II, here represent a powerful strain of Jewish resentment toward the popular treatment of the Holocaust. They object in particular to that familiar response to Anne Frank's ordeal that reduces the enormity of Jewish suffering under German National Socialism to sentiment of the most puerile sort. Norbert Muhlen illustrates this tendency even as he seems, unwittingly, to contribute to its banal character:

> The extent to which Anne Frank has become a symbol struck me again when a young Berlin dancer—a girl raised in a strong Nazi home but without any political interests—said on mention of Anne Frank's name: "Isn't it wonderful that a girl who went through so much suffering could still say, 'I believe in the goodness of man.'"
>
> The dancer had never read the book or seen the play, yet she repeated the quotation accurately. For Anne Frank's influence has been infinitely wider than the immediate audience for the play and book. Anne Frank has become a witness and a teacher to her survivors. Thus her homecoming to the country which expelled and then killed her has become a strange but heartening kind of triumph.[43]

We have on record no reply by either Arendt or Bettelheim to this report, but it is not difficult to imagine what either one of them would have had to say to Mr. Muhlen. They would have been highly critical of his conclusions precisely because they encourage the reduction of Anne Frank to a symbol of moral and intellectual convenience. In the example Muhlen cites, Anne Frank has been seized upon by someone who has neither read her book nor seen her story on stage but nevertheless savors a sense of her as a redeeming presence. In a word, Anne Frank has become a ready-at-hand formula for easy forgiveness. Far from this development representing her triumphant homecoming to the country that first expelled and then killed her, it represents quite the reverse: the triumph of Anne Frank's former countrymen over her. In her name, they have, after all, forgiven themselves. If there is any "teaching" to be deduced from this strange turnabout, it can only be the one that Hannah Arendt pointed to—the ascendancy of cheap sentimentality over any responsible sense of history.

Others wrote out of similar concern and expressed analogous worries and resentments. Martin Dworkin, in a highly critical essay in *Jewish Frontier*, argued that both the dramatic and film adaptations of the diary "perpetrated a fundamental falsity" by presenting to the world an Anne Frank who looked like "a signally American figure of thoughtless youth." He found that the work of Goodrich and Hackett diluted the richness of Anne Frank's writing to "a familiar soft-drink flavor" and stated that the audiences seeing the film and the play "know little of the facts of the extermination of six million Jews by the Nazis and will not be led to [such] knowledge in the theater."[44] *Commentary*, which was among the first English-language journals to bring the diary to the attention of readers, likewise denounced the work of Goodrich and Hackett, its reviewer calling the play "seriously dishonest" and a "failure." "If we in America cannot present her with the respect and integrity and seriousness she deserves," the *Commentary* reviewer stated, "then I think we should not try to present her at all."[45]

When one contrasts these criticisms and others like them that appeared in the Jewish press in the late 1950s and early 1960s with the general reception accorded the dramatic and film versions of the diary, one sees that Jewish opinion was on the whole much harsher. Jews recognized, to be sure, that the figure of Anne Frank on the stage and screen would reach very large audiences who otherwise knew little of the fate of the Jews in the recent European catastrophe, but many could not sanction the serious historical compromises that accompanied the popularization of the diary. The Anne Frank projected through these media looked to them too much like an American adolescent and too little like a Jewish youth of European background. Hence, the criticism that one finds expressed time and again by Jewish writers of the period frequently turned on questions of representation. Was Anne Frank being portrayed faithfully, or was her image and that of the larger Jewish tragedy she symbolized being cheapened and distorted? These questions, which remain with us still today, marked the Jewish reception of Anne Frank right from the start.

In contrast to what one sees elsewhere, one also finds Jews placing the diary of Anne Frank within the broader context of a crime they began to call "the holocaust" and within the corpus of a body of writings that some referred to as "*hurban* literature." These terms were used as early as 1952 in places like the *National Jewish Monthly*, *Congress Weekly*, and *Jewish Social Studies*. They contrast sharply with the often more abstract terminology that one finds in the mainstream newspapers and periodicals of the time, where the discourse more readily employs phrases like "man's inhumanity to man" and "the evil of our time." Jewish opinion was shaped by the conviction that Anne Frank's death was part of the larger destruction of European Jewry and should be grasped as such. Her story, far from being unique, was, in the words of Ludwig Lewisohn, part of "the literature of the Jewish martyrdom of this age." Many others, Lewisohn wrote, "left prose and verse, left cry and chronicle, as poignant as the diary of Anne Frank."[46] To understand her properly, therefore, one should read her as a representative voice and not a singular one.

Interestingly, Meyer Levin also advocated that she be read in these terms, although he did not use such an emphasis in his *New York Times* review. However, at the same time as he wrote about Anne Frank for the *Times*, he published two independent review articles in Jewish periodicals, and in these he placed a greater stress on the specifically Jewish features of Anne Frank's story. He began his piece for *Congress Weekly* with the sentence, "At last, the voice of the six million may be heard in America," and went on to say that "this diary is without doubt the most important human document to have come out of the great catastrophe. . . . The holocaust at long last comes home, and our defenses are shattered. We weep."[47] That is not the tone Levin took in the *New York Times*. Writing as well for the *National Jewish Post*, Levin praised the diary as "the book that makes us live with all the Jews who disappeared in Europe. It is the book with which we can identify, . . . the purest record we possess of the lives of those who were exterminated." In exhorting his readers to come to know Anne Frank's story, and to get others to know it, Levin employed a mode of address that he never would have used in writing for the mainstream press: "If it means buying no other book this year, I urge every reader to get hold of this Diary. If your budget permits you ten books a year, I urge you to buy ten copies of the Diary, and to distribute them amongst your non-Jewish friends." Levin also made a plea for Jewish institutions to devote a sizable portion of their public relations budgets "to disseminate this book and its contents in every possible form." It should be "a play and a film, it should be on television and radio." Levin was clearly embarked upon a mission here. He wanted Anne Frank's story known because he detected in it "the very pulse, the frightened but courageous pulse of the six million Jews" who perished in the Holocaust.[48] To get her story out to as broad a public as possible and to preserve it in what he took to be its essential character, Levin, as is well known, wrote the first dramatic version of the diary of Anne Frank and then, when it was aborted, engaged in a furious protracted public quarrel with Otto Frank, Kermit Bloomgarden, and others connected to the Goodrich and Hackett play. The controversy went on for a long time. Levin wrote a whole book about it, which he entitled, fittingly enough, *The Obsession*, and then turned his obsessions into a novel, which he called, tellingly, *The Fanatic*. Along the way he marshaled public support for his cause from dozens of rabbis, writers, and other prominent figures and thus managed to turn a one-man crusade into an affair that seemed to speak symptomatically of a larger Jewish anxiety.

It was an anxiety that grew out of a double sense of victimhood—first, the victimization of the Jews during the war itself, and then their revictimization in the postwar period, when it sometimes seemed that others did not understand the singularity and enormity of Jewish suffering. As Ludwig Lewisohn put it, "A million Anne Franks died in horror and misery."[49] In the aftermath of that catastrophe, the least one could do was remember the dead with a proper respect.

It was against this background that Bruno Bettelheim set Jewish nerves on edge through his severe critique of the public reception of Anne Frank. In writings that he published in several different places in the early 1960s he leveled a strong attack against the wartime behavior of the Frank family and the postwar adulation of Anne Frank. As Bettelheim saw it, the girl's fate "was certainly not a necessary fate, much less a heroic one; it was a senseless fate."[50] Her family was foolish to stick together when they would have had a better chance apart. They were also foolish to try to carry on their daily existence as if the danger just outside their door could not reach them. They should have armed themselves to fight their enemies. At a minimum, they should have recognized the death threat they were under and not given in to the illusion that they could go on living their lives as they had been accustomed to in the period before the German occupation. At the very time when the death camps were being readied to receive them, Otto Frank was giving school lessons in conventional subject matter to his two daughters. Thus, Anne, in Bettelheim's view, "may well have died because her parents could not get themselves to believe in Auschwitz." Through indulging in traditional "ghetto thinking," the Franks rendered themselves defenseless and helped to bring on their terrible end.[51]

Bettelheim's charge that the Jews, in effect, had prepared the way for their own victimization was received in a hostile manner by most others, and a public debate over the wartime behavior of the Jews quickly developed. The controversy escalated a short time later when Hannah Arendt, in writing about the Eichmann trial, argued that the Jews of Eastern Europe were condemned by the Jewish Councils in the ghettos and thus perished in far greater numbers than they would have had they had no leaders at all.[52] By this time Anne Frank had already attained symbolic status as the quintessential Jewish victim, and her name and her fate were part of the argument that ensued. The polemic was so impassioned because the stakes were so high: it turned on nothing less than how Jewish historical memory was to understand and transmit the story of "the million Anne Franks who died in misery and horror."

That the question was framed in these terms makes it evident that Jewish preoccupation with the war years centered on issues that hardly arose in the discussion elsewhere. As Bettelheim put it, "The present generation of Jews cannot stop being haunted by the question: How was it possible that six million Jews died? How was it possible that we did not rush to halt the slaughter? . . . For our own protection, now and in the future, we must try to find answers."[53] The answers are still to be discovered, but the anxiety that gives rise to the questions is palpable and is, indeed, a constituent feature of Jewish consciousness in the postwar decades. There is no doubt that it has helped to influence the Jewish reception of Anne Frank and to give it a shape that one does not find elsewhere. Like others, Jewish readers of the diary know the famous passages in which the young girl speaks of her belief in the goodness of man, but most Jews do not see these passages as constituting the central teaching of the text. Haunted by an overwhelming sense of Jewish victimization, they tend to respond skeptically to idealizations of Anne Frank as a heroic figure and instead see her as one among the six million. When they speak of her legacy, therefore, they do so in very different terms than others use. The following, written as a prefatory note to a 1967 article by Otto Frank, can serve as illustration:

> Anne Frank, 15, a dark-eyed girl-child, died in the concentration camp of Bergen-Belsen in 1945. . . . She became the symbol of the Jewish past. . . . Hitler killed her and six million others. But the events recorded in her diary became part of the national memory that built the State of Israel—and the spirit behind its six-day war last June. No longer would Jews try only to survive. There would be no more martyrs. Dead heroes, if need be, but no more Anne Franks. That is her living legacy.[54]

It is doubtful that anyone other than the Jews would define Anne Frank's legacy in these terms, but among Jews this language expresses a sentiment that is by now familiar and that tends to displace the more optimistic sentiments found elsewhere. Interestingly, and revealingly, when the Goodrich and Hackett drama was first performed in Israel by the Habimah Theater group, the director, Israel Becker, changed the last line of the play. In the original version Otto Frank hears his daughter's voice repeating the celebrated words, "In spite of everything, I still believe that people are really good at heart," and he replies, "She puts me to shame." Particularly in Germany, these words registered a powerful effect. In Israel, however, where theatergoers react against the background of a very different historical experience, such a line, spoken by the dead girl's grieving father, would have made little sense. In the Habimah Theater version, therefore, Otto Frank hears his daughter's voice, shakes his head, and says, uncertainly, "I don't know, I don't know."[55] The curtain then falls leaving the audience unconsoled, sharing the father's grief and doubt. In this response, unrelieved as it is by any uplifting sense of the girl in her more buoyant moments, one may find a significant measure of the difference between a Jewish understanding of Anne Frank and her reception elsewhere.

What can we say, by way of conclusion, therefore, about the Anne Frank we remember? She is, without doubt, an omnipresent figure of postwar consciousness, but, like the war itself, she means different things to different people. Like the Germans, the Israelis have also named streets, schools, and youth centers after Anne Frank. Unlike the Germans, however, who have paid such tribute to the memory of the young girl as an act of atonement for the past and a warning for the future, the Israelis have acted out of a sense of national mourning and solidarity with the dead. Thus, in both Germany and Israel one finds a common history marked by a common symbol but shaped by very different motives and yielding diverse interpretations of the past. Elsewhere, one finds the figuration of Anne Frank similarly resting on diverse bases. Among certain Catholic writers Anne Frank is described in language of a kind usually reserved for saints. In Japan, where she is widely known, teenage girls euphemistically refer to their monthly days of menstruation by using the name of Anne Frank. Yevgeny Yevtushenko helped to immortalize Anne Frank in his famous poem on Babi Yar, but he did so through a figure of love and fantasy as well as victimization. If one were to carry out a study of the reception of the diary in the various other countries and cultures where Anne Frank is known, one would almost certainly find still other responses to the girl and the history her image reflects.

The past, as we know, is never permanently fixed but rather shifts in contour and meaning with the changing shapes of symbolization and interpretation. As we have seen, strong symbols such as Anne Frank evoke a broad range of responses and call up associations of a varied kind. A comparison of the numerous prefaces to the foreign-language editions of the diary, for instance, reveals several different versions of Anne Frank. Albrecht Goes, the author of the foreword to the Fischer edition of *Das Tagebuch der Anne Frank*, speaks abstractly about a "spirit of love" that pervades the diary. Daniel Rops, who wrote the preface to the French edition, gives us an Anne Frank touched, on the one hand, by the sensuous and, on the other, by the artist and mystic. In Storm Jameson's foreword to the British edition we confront still another Anne Frank, one who wrote brilliantly and then went to her death at Bergen-Belsen with "a profound smile . . . of happiness and faith."[56]

I cite these versions of Anne Frank in order to emphasize the plastic nature of the figure we have been examining. In looking at the crime we have come to call the Holocaust through the figure of Anne Frank, we see that "the Holocaust" is itself a variable term and is explained and understood in ways that do not readily lead to consensus. There is nothing particularly surprising about this development, although the pace at which it seems to be proceeding and the degree of divergence that it may yield are matters that warrant serious pondering by anyone interested in observing how the past is variously reconstructed and transmitted to diverse publics. We already have been given numerous versions of Anne Frank, and in the future we almost certainly will be given others. "We shall read her diary / until the Messiah comes," as a poem about her says.[57] No doubt we shall, although how we shall read her and what we shall make of her and the history that her story reflects are questions that right now remain very much open.

James E. Young

Israel's Memorial Landscape: *Sho'ah*, Heroism, and National Redemption

> *The one suitable monument to the memory of European Jewry ... is the State of Israel ... where the hope of the Jewish people is expressed ... and which serves as a free and faithful refuge to every Jew in the world who desires to live a free and independent life.*
>
> —*Davar* editorial, 1951.[1]

LIKE ANY STATE, ISRAEL REMEMBERS THE PAST ACCORDING TO ITS NAtional myths and ideals, its current political needs. Unlike that of other states, however, Israel's overarching national ideology and religion—perhaps its greatest "natural resource"—may be memory itself: memory preserved, restored, and codified. In cultivating a ritually unified remembrance of the past, the state creates a common relationship to it. The past remembered, recounted, and interpreted collectively becomes, if only vicariously, a shared experience. Having defined themselves as a people through commemorative recitations of their past, the Jews now depend on memory for their very existence as a nation.

In every community, in every corner of Israel's landscape, one is reminded of the *Sho'ah* by a plaque, a building's dedication, an inscribed tablet. Streets are named after ghetto fighters like Mordechai Anielewicz, schools after martyrs like Janusz Korczak. A granite harp in a Kiryat Gat park is entitled "Sho'ah 1933–1945" and stands beside a stone etched with a list of victims. German-Jewish refugees who arrived to build a *moshav* at Shavei-Zion near

Nahariya erected a memorial in their synagogue to 134 of their former townspeople who did not leave Germany in time. A wall-sculpture on the front of Jerusalem's Great Synagogue is dedicated both to the six million martyrs and to Israel's war dead: all of whom "died so that we might live." Denmark Square, with its skeletal boat sculpture, recalls the Danish rescue of Jews to residents of Jerusalem's Beit Hakerem neighborhood. In Haifa, the actual hull of one of these rescue boats on the former site of a refugee center reminds us that the rescue voyage begun in Denmark did not end in Sweden at all, but in Israel's Sha'ar Ha'aliya reception camp in 1948. Over time, these markers recede into consciousness, as parts of an inanimate cityscape, but they continue to function as the coordinates of daily life, even when unrecognized.

Like the Holocaust memorials of other lands, those in Israel reflect both the past experiences and current lives of their communities, as well as the state's memory of itself. At times ambivalent, at times shrill, the official approach to Holocaust memory in Israel has long been torn between the simultaneous need to remember and to forget, between the early founders' enormous state-building task and the reasons why such a state was necessary, between the survivors' memory of victims and the fighters' memory of resistance. On the one hand, early statists like Ben-Gurion regarded the *Sho'ah* as the ultimate fruit of Jewish life in exile; as such, it represented a diaspora that deserved not only to be destroyed, but also to be forgotten. On the other hand, the state also recognized its perverse debt to the Holocaust: it had, after all, seemed to prove the Zionist dictum that without a state and the power to defend themselves, Jews in exile would always be vulnerable to just this kind of destruction.[2] As a result, the early leaders found little reason to recall the Holocaust beyond its direct link to the new state.

This essential ambivalence is reflected in the ubiquitous twinning of martyrs and heroes in Israel's memorial iconography. In this mixed figure, the victims are memorable primarily for the ways they demonstrate the need for fighters; the fighters, in turn, are remembered for their part in the state's founding. When placed against the traditional paradigmatic backdrop of destruction and redemption, the memorial message in this dialectic comes into sharp relief: as destruction of the martyrs is redeemed by those who fought, the *Sho'ah* itself is redeemed by the founding of the state. In assuming the idealized forms and meanings assigned this era by the state, these memorials tend to concretize particular historical interpretations; in time, such memory grows as natural to the eye as the landscape in which it stands.

The relationship between a state and its memorials is always complex: on the one hand, official agencies are in a position to shape memory explicitly as they see fit, memory that best serves a national interest. On the other hand, once created, memorials take on lives of their own, stubbornly resistant to the state's original intentions. In some cases, memorials created in the image of a state's ideals actually turn around to recast these ideals in the memorial's image. New generations visit memorials under new circumstances and invest them with new meanings. The result is an evolution in the memorial's significance, generated in the new times and company in which it finds itself.

Rather than focusing on the officially legislated memory enacted at Yad Vashem or in Yom Hasho'ah ceremonies, however, I have chosen to limit my discussion here to the more oblique reflections of memory found in Israel's countryside and kibbutzim.[3] Although these unofficial sites often share many of the national assumptions informing the state-sponsored memory of the *Sho'ah,* they also illustrate the memorial roles played by such variables as a monument's location, the specific experiences of the makers, and the time it was built. Even though each memorial embodies a more national theme, in nuance and significance each also adds to the overall texture of national memory in Israel.

I attempt here to enlarge the text of these memorials' performance to include the times and places in which they were created, their literal conception and construction amid historical and political realities, their finished form in public spaces, their reception by surrounding communities and visitors, and their place in the constellation of national memory.[4] With these dimensions in mind, we look not only at the ways individual monuments create and reinforce particular memory of the *Sho'ah* period, but also at the ways the *Sho'ah* reenters political life here shaped by its monuments. By focusing here not on the events of the *Sho'ah,* but on its memorial legacy in Israel, I hope to emphasize the activity of memorialization over its seemingly static results. The overall performance of Holocaust memorials in Israel encompasses not just the activity that brought them into being or the constant give and take between memorials and viewers. Most important of all are the responses of viewers to their own world and lives in light of a memorialized past: the consequences of memory.

Ultimately, this is to recognize the integral part visitors play in the memorial text: how and what we remember in the company of a monument depend on who we are, why we care to remember, and how we see. When I incorporate other visitors' responses to a memorial, I acknowledge that in my sharing the memorial space with others, their responses become part of my experience, part of the total memorial text. By extension, the texts of memory here include not only the author's personal responses but this narrative as well: hence, the openly impressionistic cast to some of these descriptions. Rather than denying the quiet presence of my own observing eye, I acknowledge the shape it has conferred on these memorials, on these words. For in describing these sites in narrative here, I have unavoidably transformed plastic and graphic media into literary texts: how I critically evaluate these memorials and what conclusions I draw from them depend very much on how I have represented them—both to myself and to the reader. Thus, readers are warned against accepting my narrative reconstructions of monuments any more unquestioningly than they would the monuments' own reconstructions of events.

THE MARTYRS' FOREST AND THE SCROLL OF FIRE

In both its practical and ceremonial significance, tree planting in Israel has long played an essential part in resettling the land. On the symbolic level, early Zionist-socialists regarded "the greening of Israel" as a metaphor for the people's return from exile. Uprooted and dispersed two thousand years before, the Jews had remained rootless, hence powerless, ever since. In cultivating the land of their origin and thereby rerooting their lives in its soil, the Jews would, according to Zionist thought, derive new strength and security. The very language of this figure reinforced the seeming naturalness of the people's return, of the people's relationship to the land. Even the physical act of planting was suggestive in its mix of natural and symbolic imagery: digging one's hands into the soil, scooping out rocks and dirt and planting a seed, seemed to be a spiritual mating of a people and its land, a becoming one with it again. To work the land was to become part of it and the natural cycle it represented.

On a more practical level, early afforestation projects by the Jewish National Fund paralleled the kibbutz movement's own reason for being: to make this rocky, inhospitable land habitable. Trees provided shade for the workers, secured the soil against erosion, and protected crops from searing desert winds. The forest encouraged life itself amidst its branches and glens, gave refuge to birds and animals. Sowing and reaping demanded the kind of labor, in Zionist-socialist eyes, needed to make the new Jews strong, better prepared to withstand a hostile world. Finally, as planting a tree might signify the founding of a kibbutz, the kibbutz in turn pointed toward the birth of a state.

This link between the state's founding and tree planting is further reinforced in Israeli Independence Day, when new buildings and monuments are dedicated—and when ceremonial tree plantings are held around the country. Even the new year for trees, Tu B'shvat (the fifteenth of Shvat), is transvalued by the state. Where traditional celebration of the sap rising in the trees of the Holy Land had included partaking of the fruits of the land—for example, apples, almonds, figs, pomegranates—and sitting up late reciting Biblical passages on trees, it is now customary on this day to go out into the fields of Israel and plant saplings. Indeed, since the state's founding, it has become common to plant a tree in Israel to honor any and all of life's milestones: the birth of a child, bar or bat mitzvah, marriage, death. As a memorial gesture, tree planting remains freighted with statist meaning, now a national form of remembrance.

In cooperation with the Jewish National Fund in 1954, B'nai B'rith thus dedicated the Martyrs' Forest near Kesalon in the Judean Hills outside Jerusalem. Its first half-million trees were planted around a sanctuary hewn of rock, in B'nai B'rith's words, "as a living memorial to the six million Jews who perished in the Holocaust."[5] Since then, nearly two million trees have been planted in the forest, with another four million planned—one for each victim. This forest takes on double-edged significance: it remembers both the martyrs and the return to the land. Memory of the victims is cultivated in the founding of the State of Israel: in taking root in the land, memory of the martyrs would bind re-memberers to the state itself.

When combined with the Israeli's traditional reverence for *yedi'ath ha'aretz* (knowledge of the land), this notion of memorials as part of the natural landscape assumes still greater significance. For in Israel, nature is defined by the Society for Protection of Nature in Israel "not only [as] plant and animal life, but also the landscapes and relics of the country's past."[6] Teacher-guides still lead tours around the country, teaching a people its relationship to the land, a bond that is both sustained and created in the teaching process. If, as part of the landscape, monuments become extensions of the land, then the teacher-guides in Israel teach not only the relationship between a people and its land, but also the relationship between a people and its monuments. As a result, ancient biblical sites and Holocaust memorials alike become the landmarks by which Israelis continue to know their relationship to the land and, by extension, to their history.[7]

Several years after the Martyrs' Forest was founded, the essential bookishness of Israel's landscape found further expression in Nathan Rapoport's *Megilath-esh*—Scroll of Fire—a twenty-six-foot-tall monument planted atop the Forest's highest hill in 1971. Surrounded now by trees and brush at the end of an isolated road near Kesalon, the two great trunks of these scrolls seem almost to have sprung indigenously from the soil. On any given day, we are as likely to find busloads of schoolchildren studying the bas-relief pictographs as we are to find solitude at the monument's base.

Ironically, however, this most natural of Israeli memorials is a transplant. It was one of two monuments proposed in 1964 by Rapoport for a site in New York City's Riverside Park, between 83rd and 84th Streets—land set aside for a Holocaust memorial that was never built. In addition to the Scroll of Fire, then conceived as a monument to the Warsaw ghetto uprising, Rapoport had submitted a sculpture that depicts Artur Zygelboim, engulfed by flames, about to pitch forward—a reference to his 1943 suicide in London to protest the world's indifference to the plight of the Jews in Poland. The former monument was sponsored by the Warsaw Ghetto Resistance Organization, the latter by the Artur Zygelboim Memorial Committee. In light of the city art commission's reasons for rejecting both proposals, the Scroll of Fire's eventual removal to Israel becomes all the more significant.

After rejecting the Zygelboim sculpture as too tragic for recreational park land and too distressing for children, sculptor and member of the city arts commission Eleanor Platt turned to the Scroll of Fire. "This proposed work seems to be excessively and unnecessarily large," she wrote. "Even if it were to be smaller and in better taste, artistically, I believe that by approving it or the Zygelboim sculpture, we would set a highly regrettable precedent."[8] In the eyes of Rapoport and his sponsors, however, the crux of Platt's response came in her concluding remarks, which infuriated the Jewish community. "How would we answer other special groups who want to be similarly represented on public land?" she asked. Stunned by her reference to "special groups," the sponsors were further bewildered by Parks Commissioner Newbold Morris's opinion that "monuments in the parks should be limited to events of American history."

These American survivors of the Warsaw ghetto might have wondered what the difference was between "events of American history" and those of "Americans' history." Like many Americans, their historical memory included both old and new worlds. Enforcing a distinction between American history and their own seemed not only to disenfranchise these immigrants but also to exclude their history from American history. At the same time, it may have seemed to encourage a certain forgetfulness, whereby American memory begins at the borders and immigrants' memories are left behind. If their history was not a part of the public memory, could they still regard themselves as part of the public?

Meanwhile, back in "the land," the B'nai B'rith Israel Commission was inviting the celebrated sculptor Jacques Lipschitz to design a monumental shrine for their Martyrs' Forest. Lipschitz declined, citing an impossible backlog of unfinished projects, and recommended Nathan Rapoport for the job. When B'nai B'rith representatives visited Rapoport's New York studio in 1965, he led them immediately to a model for the Scroll of Fire. The guardians of America's public memory may not have been ready for the particularity of her immigrants' experiences in Europe, but Israel's national memory had always been defined by that of Jews everywhere, a continuum of generational memory transcending borders. By the time B'nai B'rith delivered a contract to Rapoport in June 1967, Israel had fought the Six-Day War. Rapoport asked, therefore, whether he could now devote one scroll to the heroism and martyrdom of the *Sho'ah* and one to Israel's national rebirth, leading to the reunification of Jerusalem. In stitching together the experiences of Jews in and out of Israel, he said, the Scroll of Fire would cast Jewish memory in a classically Jewish storytelling form. B'nai B'rith happily agreed, recognizing that in an unbroken narrative continuum, these two scrolls would link Jewish martyrdom and resistance, the end of exile and redemption in Eretz Israel.

When first erected in 1971, the Scroll of Fire stood alone and was visible from all directions. Now, it is surrounded by a forest of pine trees, in a clearing created by its forty by forty foot concrete base. From a distance, the monument seems as ancient as the land, two great Doric columns covered in hieroglyphs. On closer examination, we find that these are scrolls of bronze, not columns of stone. The bas-relief images are not strange, but recall familiar scenes from the sculptor's other memorials: the heroes and martyrs of Warsaw, a herald angel from Philadelphia, Korczak and his children from New York. The two leaning scrolls form an archway, open inside and at the top, allowing visitors to enter their space and listen to the wind whistling through.

The iconic narrative in the first scroll—devoted to the Holocaust era—begins with a familiar exilic motif: a family clings together, looking out in all directions while being herded off by the Nazis, whose helmets and bayonets are just visible over the heads of the Jews. In this gesture to "the last march" bas-relief on his Warsaw Ghetto Monument, itself an echo of both Titus's march and Hirszenberg's "Golus" painting, the sculptor recalls every exile in the figure of original Jewish exile from the land of Israel. This procession moves left to right, however, in a reversal of the classical exile motif, as if returning from Rome to scenes of barbed wire—and then to packed and jumbled bodies, folded over and into each other like rolls of clay. Directly above these deportations on the same scroll, fighters arise amid flame and ruin, their fists raised and weapons brandished—again, echoes of Rapoport's figures on the Warsaw Ghetto Monument.

On this kind of scroll, one can begin anywhere and eventually be taken back to the beginning; that is, the present moment in such a circle always leads to remembrance of the past. In narrative sequence here, martyrdom is followed by uprising, which leads then to liberation from the camps—followed by yet another march. The first marchers hold arms to their brows, as if to shield themselves from memory. Above them, another family with bags now marches more hopefully, eyes fixed forward in resolve. This *megillah* (scroll) of the *Sho'ah* ends with these survivors coming ashore by boat, reaching out and falling into the arms of Israelis, who are distinguished by strong limbs, kibbutz work clothing, and temple hats—all recognizable to school children here, many of whom are dressed in exactly the same way.

The second, adjoining scroll begins with the battle at Kibbutz Negba during the War of Independence: kibbutzniks rising to fight, some falling, all still in procession. The rabbi carrying a Torah scroll from Rapoport's Ghetto Monument reappears here: only now his direction is reversed. Instead of going into exile, he is returning from it. Above him, another sage looks up, his hand upraised; but instead of beseeching God, he helps to hold aloft a great menorah, carried by Israeli soldiers and workers, not Romans. The procession on the Arch of Titus is reversed here, the menorah returned from exile. The end of the narrative on this scroll comes with soldiers praying at the Western Wall, in a reunified Jerusalem.

This memorial is unabashedly literary, even bookish, in both theme and performance. As a scroll, it is meant to be read, its pictographs unfurling into a didactic historical narrative. Students and their teachers approach it as a text to read and interpret, turning this memorial space into an open-air classroom. Students listen attentively while their teacher-guides, often with a pointer—a *yad*—lead classes from image to image, explaining and commenting on each. Occasionally, teachers correct the text itself. "Will someone please tell me what's wrong with this picture," asks the teacher, pointing to a scene of a soldier, wrapped in tefillin, praying at the Western Wall. A hand shoots up immediately. "Yes?" A young boy volunteers: "The tefillin is on the wrong arm—it should be the left arm, not the right." "Very good," nods the teacher. "But why did he do that," asks the puzzled student.

"Because he was just an artist," replies the teacher, "and didn't think about details like that."

The meanings in images, even those arranged into narrative sequence, remain somewhat indirect and depend on both the teachers' commentaries and, as it turns out, the many poetic inscriptions on markers installed around the site's perimeter. In this way, the images illustrate not just the teachers' words but the monument's dedication, the sculptor's seeming epitaph, and the poet's verses: all become part of the memorial text. To the dedication, which reads "In memory of the martyred six million and in reverent celebration of Israel's rebirth," Nathan Rapoport has added what appears to be his own epitaph: "My words have been made of stone. They are silent, heavy and everlasting."

The literary message of these scrolls is echoed more explicitly still inside their portal space, where we read in Hebrew and English from Ezekiel 37:

> Behold, O my People, I will open your graves
> And cause you to come up out of your graves
> And bring you into the land of Israel
> And shall put my soul in you
> And ye shall live and I shall place you
> In your own land.

On another marker near the perimeter of the monument's platform, Nelly Sachs has contributed her own "Epitaph for the Martyrs," as if in warning to the school children swarming near its base:

> Mutely the stone speaks
> Of the martyrdom of the six million
> Whose body drifted as smoke through the air
> Silence—Silence—Silence
> You who were born afterwards
> Remember the men, women, and children in a time of violence
> Lower your heads in humility.

To these lines, one of which was pulled directly from "O the Chimneys," the Israeli poet Chaim Gouri added his voice at the cornerstone laying on October 30, 1967. His words merely affirmed the redemptory link between the martyrs and the rebirth of Israel already expressed in Ezekiel and in Sachs's poetry:

From the fires of the ruins of the Ghettos
We picked a stone all charred and broken
That stone was made here into the cornerstone
and the foundation stone.

Their words about silence notwithstanding, these pillars are never completely mute, even in their solitary setting. Between the teachers' questions, students' answers, and the poets' verses, the landscape resounds with the words of visitors making memory articulate. By themselves, these monuments in the landscape remain insensate stone and concrete, lost to meaning. But as part of a nation's memorial rituals, they are invested with national soul and significance. As such, they function as elements in a nation's symbolic infrastructure, by which ideals are legitimated and reified. Together, these markers in the wilderness comprise a cartographical matrix by which Israelis navigate their new lives in the land. Memorials such as the Scroll of Fire serve as landmarks in and around which histories are woven and a people's past is explained to itself.

MEMORIALS AND MUSEUMS ON KIBBUTZIM

Under the cover of a moonless night in 1939, a group of recently arrived immigrant-refugees from Germany set up their tents on a lonely hillock in Israel's Jezreel Valley. Within days, they had sunk a well, dug a latrine, and begun to clear the area of rocks and prickly pear. At first, they called their kibbutz Even Yitzhak (Yitzhak Rock). Later they renamed it Gal Ed (after Laban's witness pile of stones); by this gesture, the kibbutz likened itself to a monument. Like the founders of other kibbutzim at this time who had come to escape the Germans, the members of Gal Ed regarded their kibbutz as a direct response to the gathering storm in Europe. Whether established by the youth wing of He'halutz before the war or by refugees barely escaped during the war or by survivors and ghetto fighters afterwards, such kibbutzim frequently figured themselves as living memorials: to the end of life in exile, to survival in Israel. Eventually, a handful of these kibbutzim built Holocaust museums and memorials on the land itself. On the one hand, given the pioneers' socialist ideals and emphasis on the renewal of life, there might have been little time for commemorating the destruction of the *Sho'ah* at all. But in fact, some of the reasons for Holocaust memorials on the kibbutzim are tied inextricably to these same ideals.

After the *Sho'ah,* the contrast between living independently in the land of Israel and dying so horribly in Europe could not have been more stark. As life crumbled in exile, it blossomed in the Yishuv. Every daily act on the kibbutz seemed to affirm the continuation of life after Europe, the rejection of death in exile. Having borne out all of the Zionists' darkest prophecies, Europe now epitomized the *Golah,* or Exile from the land. By contrast, in the tilling of soil and cultivation of crops, the kibbutz in Israel seemed to represent the very creation of life. To some extent, this contrast is evident in every memorial exhibit to the Holocaust in Israel, but especially so in the memorials and museums on kibbutzim, which, like other memorials, reflect the image of their makers, their experiences, and their understanding of this time.

In the eyes of these pioneers, the *Sho'ah* was not the end of Jewish life as such, but only the end of Jewish life in exile. On the kibbutz, where life continued, remembrance would be gathered around the ideals and preoccupations of life in the Yishuv. For many already in Israel, in fact, this era was not merely a time of destruction, but a time of vibrant renewal and rebuilding. As a result, kibbutz museums and memorials at Lohamei Hageta'ot, Yad Mordechai, Tel Yitzhak, Givat Haim, Ma'ale Hahamisha, and Mishmar Ha'emek tend to recall primarily the resistance of kibbutz movement comrades in Europe, the musky death stench of life in exile, and the newfound ability to create and defend Jewish life in Israel. As the kibbutz exudes life and strength, it tends also to refract memory through images of life and strength, resistance and renewal.

Kibbutz Mishmar Ha'emek

One of the earliest memorials in Israel to commemorate the *Sho'ah* was dedicated in 1947, a year before the state's independence, at Kibbutz Mishmar Ha'emek—"guardian of the valley"—near Megiddo. In its theme—L'Yeldei Hagolah (to the children of the exile)—and gently cubist form, this work by Israeli portrait sculptor Ze'ev Ben-Zvi blends the artist's vision of *Sho'ah* and his own aesthetic mission. Regarded by some as Israel's "first-born sculptor," Ben-Zvi struggled most of his life to carve an "Eretz Israel art" out of Jerusalem stone. On the one hand, he did not want to become, in his words, "a mere broker between European and Oriental traditions."[9] On the other hand, he fully recognized that Eretz Israel artists could not create without a sustaining tradition of some sort. The dilemma for Ben-Zvi was that, as an artist, he necessarily remained rooted in the Golah, even as he created in the land of Israel.

Instead of seeking to resolve this conundrum, Ben-Zvi chose to humanize the cubist edges in his work and to design what he called "Temples of the Idea." These "temples" would be isolated, even hidden, public spaces where people of the land could commune with pieces of art. In this way, European forms would derive new meaning from their new contexts. As sanctuaries of art, they would encourage a contemplative turning inward: meaning in Eretz Israel art would not derive from European or Oriental traditions, but from its place in the land, the sanctification of aesthetic space, and the private response of Jews newly redeemed in the Jewish state.

Tucked away in a corner not far from the kibbutz kindergarten at Mishmar Ha'emek, Ben-Zvi's memorial "To the Children of the Golah," is the only "temple" that he actually built. It is composed of four reliefs installed in a stone wall surrounding a small, open square, three meters by fifteen meters. Originally a grassy enclosure, it has been paved over in pebbles and concrete. When we enter it, our eyes are drawn first to a large, softly cubist figure of a mother and child, and then to three progressive reliefs on the left leading to this figure. I watch as a woman in kibbutz work clothes and her child enter the space, hand in hand. The mother begins to remark on the redness of a blossom fallen to the ground when the little girl hushes her. "Don't talk here, *ema*," she says, "this is a place for quiet." Other children enter, and one by one each goes silently to a tiny figure at the far left. Nearly hidden behind a small shrub, it is a miniature relief of a child curled into fetal position. The children crouch before this little form and study it intently, before stepping to the right to the next relief.

Here four bending forms seem to rise in an arc from the ground, as if straightening from fetal to upright position. To their right, seven other figures march in a row, bunched together in profile, their hands stiffly at their sides—a stylized exilic procession. Our eyes follow them back to the figures of mother and child. The mother's long arm holds the child close; the child reaches up, its mouth opened around the word "mama" or "ema"; the mother half turns her head away. Her eyes are closed, her mouth is open slightly but buried in her shoulder as if to stifle a cry. In sequence, the figures of these children seem to emerge from earth and stone, growing, like the small plants nearby, into a disciplined little row. Stretching its limbs to mother, the child reaches up like a flower to the sun.

"Let artistic signs and symbols be set up in every private and public place," Ben-Zvi once wrote, "to express this sense of pain in our souls." This corner at Mishmar Ha'emek is both a private and public place: once a year the kibbutz holds its Yom Hasho'ah ceremonies here, at what members now call *"pin'at hagolah"*— diaspora corner. *Sho'ah* and *Golah* are twinned here in their rhyme as near-equivalents in the mind of the kibbutz, with one reciprocally known by—even substituted for—the other. In this space, one's thoughts are gathered inward, contained by the forms surrounding memory here. It is a place of quiet contemplation: birds chirp, pine and eucalyptus trees rustle overhead, young voices emanate from the school just above—all in haunting counterpart to the stone-muteness of the "Children of the Golah."

Kibbutz Ma'ale Hahamisha

Another rarely noticed memorial statue, just outside Jerusalem on the road to Ma'ale Hahamisha, molds memory of the *Sho'ah* in the figure of the kibbutz itself. This kibbutz was established as a memorial to five young members of the Polish Zionist movement Gordonia who were ambushed and killed by Arabs while working on an afforestation project near Kiryat Anavim for the Jewish National Fund in 1938. A year later, other young pioneers from Gordonia chose the site of the ambush to found a kibbutz in memory of their murdered comrades. It was named Ma'ale Hahamisha— Ascent of the Five—in a dual reference to their deaths and to their immigration to Eretz Israel. The kibbutz later served as a base for Haganah forces during Israel's War of Independence and still hosts public ceremonies on Yom Hasho'ah.

In 1961, this memorial kibbutz erected another kind of monument in its midst—a memorial within a memorial—to commemorate another of Gordonia's members, who fought and died in the Warsaw ghetto uprising. Constructed of Jerusalem stone, this statue by Andre Revesz stands at a fork in the road leading to the kibbutz and gleams white against the forest green of pine trees. Its muscular, life-size figures emerge from a rectangular, broken-topped pillar—a reference to the ghetto's destruction. A Hebrew inscription reads: "Monument to the Fighters of the Warsaw Ghetto—Eliezer Geled and His Comrades." "His comrades" in the statue include one man poised to throw a grenade, a woman cradling a child, and a muscular figure without a shirt straining to support his fallen friend, who still clutches the barrel of an automatic weapon. The kibbutz archivist insists that there is no connection between the ascent of the original five and those who "rose up" in the ghetto. But we cannot help noticing that this stone statuary also consists of five figures.

By dint of its location at a central crossroad at Kibbutz Ma'ale Hahamisha, in fact, this memorial recalls the ascent of the original five tree planters in the figure of the later five fighters who rose up in Warsaw. To some extent, the figures even displace the pioneers. Does the name of the kibbutz—Ma'ale Hahamisha—now refer to the five pioneers who fell establishing the state, or to the five ghetto fighters in the monument, or simultaneously to both sets of heroes, each now known in the figure of the other? Precisely by creating this ambiguity, the monument commemorates both sets of heroes. Thus, by recalling the memory of the young pioneers in the figure of the ghetto fighters, this memorial binds them into one image of national heroism: all are remembered now as having fallen for the state.

Kibbutz Yad Mordechai

A similar, but much more striking, instance of this exchange between memorial images of the *Sho'ah* and the state's founding can be found at Kibbutz Yad Mordechai, three miles from the Gaza Strip in the Negev. Originally located in the north near Netanya and called Mitzpe Ha'yam (Sea Lookout), this kibbutz was composed largely of Polish immigrants from the Hashomer Hatsai'r movement. In 1943, the kibbutz moved to a site near Ashkelon in the Negev, where word of the Warsaw ghetto uprising and the fate of Mordechai Anielewicz reached his comrades in May. Inspired by the uprising led by one of their own, the kibbutz adopted Anielewicz's name to memorialize the courage of its leader; and thus it became "Yad Mordechai"—literally, monument to Mordechai— arguably the first Holocaust memorial in Israel. In this case, however, it was not only a matter of the kibbutz shaping memory in its image. In light of subsequent events, it seems that the kibbutz redefined itself in Mordechai's heroic image, as well.

Five years later, one month after the dedication of the Warsaw Ghetto Monument, Kibbutz Yad Mordechai fell under Egyptian siege during Israel's War of Independence. To what extent the kibbutz wittingly enacted its heroic self-figuration may never be clear, but its desperate stand against several Egyptian battalions in May 1948 seemed to affirm a direct link between the courage of the Warsaw ghetto and that of the kibbutz in the national mind of Israel. This memorial may have led to a particular kind of self-understanding: Israelis had acquitted themselves in the memory of their fallen comrade. The consequences of memorialization, never really benign, were palpable here. As the ghetto fighters had withstood the Germans for several weeks, so a smaller number of kibbutzniks had held off the Egyptians just long enough to allow Israeli forces to regroup behind the battlelines: each resistance is now recalled in light of the other, the latter both an extension and a possible consequence of the former.

Today, Yad Mordechai is home to three major memorial spaces: a recreated battlefield on the site of Yad Mordechai's heroic stand; a large statue of Mordechai Anielewicz; and a museum whose narrative matrix links the *Sho'ah* and national independence. Kibbutz walking tours begin with the battlefield: from a strategic lookout point, we survey both the trenches of the kibbutz defenders and the cutout figures of Egyptian soldiers charging across the field below. Loudspeakers spaced over the trenches and machine-gun nests broadcast a recorded story of the battle of Yad Mordechai.[10]

In Hebrew, one arrives in Israel by "going up" (*aliya*) and exits the land by "going down" (*yerida*). At Yad Mordechai's museum, we literally descend into the exilic past, down through a dark, narrow passageway into a vault where the Jewish past is dead and buried. In this economy of images, nearly two thousand years of Jewish life in exile is represented by the shtetl and the tired remnants of a vanished shtetl life: a few weathered books, two tarnished candlesticks, faded photographs, a stack of crumbling Yiddish newspapers. Buried in this mausoleum, these artifacts are arranged as if to say that this life was hardly worth preserving anyway. The way of life in the shtetl is captured in a handful of photographs: a belt maker, umbrella maker, and metal worker, all locked in a cramped and dingy past. Accompanying captions suggest that it is a struggle for life built on trade, faith, education, community, and redemption.

As narrated in the exhibition panels, it is also a hopeless struggle, which leads to the rise of the Nazis, the ghetto, deportations, and death. The dank shtetl is turned into a suffocating ghetto, crowding relieved only by deportations to the death camps. Having reascended to the second floor, we squint as the bright light of the kibbutz pours into the exhibit hall. Set in the wall side by side, dingy black-and-white images of Jews being led away are backlighted by great picture windows filled with trees and sun-dappled lawns. On one side, light and life, teeming greenery, agriculture and construction; on the other side, darkness and death, starvation and destruction. On one side, freedom and the laws of a Jewish state; on the other side, Nuremberg laws and yellow stars, Nazis and a synagogue going up in flames. Life is here, in the orchards, in hard work, in freedom to be Jews. Death is there, in the musty shtetlach, ghettos, and concentration camps.

Then we move to a great "Wall of the Uprising," emblazoned floor to ceiling with the names of Jewish fighting groups from the ghettos, forests, camps, and allied armies. Where the martyrs are noted in their absence—abandoned and empty shtetlach, bags strewn in the streets, the very artifacts that greet visitors in the vault downstairs—the fighters are remembered in face, name, and deed. From here we move abruptly to the escape from Europe and the rescue in the promised land. The exhibition then jumps to another era: a photographic record of water pipes laid to connect the early settlements of the Negev. A caption reminds us that this water was the life-blood of the desert—and that the pipes themselves were reddened by the blood of those guarding them. By extension, the pioneers became an infusion of life's blood into the desert, the kibbutz a remnant seed from Europe now replanted in the homeland. Next come the siege between 1947 and 1948, the destruction of many of these settlements, the story of Yad Morde-chai, and the birth of the State of Israel. Three stories are told in this museum: that of a life in exile (as exemplified by the *Sho'ah*), that of resistance (as exemplified by both ghetto uprisings and the heroism of the kibbutz itself during the War of Independence), and that of redemption in the promised land.

With only three years separating the liberation of the camps and the birth of the State of Israel, the link between the Holocaust and national independence was self-evident for most Israelis in 1948. In choosing a kibbutznik living in Paris as the model for his Ghetto Monument's Anielewicz, Nathan Rapoport may have only affirmed the link he already felt between heroes of the ghetto and those of the Yishuv. Not long after the dedication of the Warsaw monument (nearly coincident with the founding of the Jewish state), Rapoport immigrated to Israel, where he was commissioned to build yet another memorial to Anielewicz at Yad Mordechai. He relates that when he arrived at the kibbutz to survey sites for the monument, he was shocked to find the kibbutz itself nearly de-stroyed. "After rebuilding your houses, then maybe you should think about statues," he advised the kibbutz.[11] But they wanted to begin with a monument and refound the kibbutz, itself a memo-rial, literally around a monument of its namesake. This was, after all, the locus of Yad Mordechai's identity. We might now ask, when the leaders of the kibbutz commissioned this monument, whom and what did they intend to commemorate? The courage of Mor-dechai Anielewicz, or the courage of the kibbutz itself, as now represented by Anielewicz?

The result is a patently Davidic figure, twelve feet high, armed with a single hand grenade instead of a sling—the third memorial space at Yad Mordechai. Garbed as a kibbutznik, almost surly, this Anielewicz turns slowly to meet his attacker. Viewed from below, the statue stands against the backdrop of a water tower partially blown away by Egyptian shelling. The kibbutz wanted to remove the tower altogether, but Rapoport insisted that it remain, for in it, he saw a simultaneous reference to the ruins of both the ghetto and life on the kibbutz. From the area of the monument itself, we look over Anielewicz's shoulder and survey the rest of the kibbutz and neighboring fields. This Anielewicz is recast as a kibbutznik to commemorate both destructions, both acts of heroic resistance, and in so doing the figure links one to the other in national continuum.

Beit Terezin At Kibbutz Givat Haim-Ichud

Unlike other kibbutz museums and memorials, Kibbutz Givat Haim's Beit Terezin was not established in the image of state or kibbutz movement. Nor was it founded to remember to the world a general meaning or record of the *Sho'ah*. Instead, it seeks to remind Israelis both of the victims who perished in Terezin and of the unique essence of this "model ghetto," which was deception itself. In the eyes of many survivors of Terezin now living in Israel, the Germans' meticulous deception there had not only succeeded in blinding victims and the world to Terezin's awful realities at the time, but also had even begun to permeate other Israelis' and survivors' remembrance of the ghetto, as well.

The fortress-town of Terezin had been built one hundred kilometers north of Prague at the end of the eighteenth century by the Austrian Emperor Joseph II, in memory of his mother, Maria Theresa. Surrounded by walls and moats, Terezin suggested itself to its German occupiers as a convenient site for herding together the Jews of the Czech Protectorate, so it was converted from an army citadel into a city concentration camp—Theresienstadt. The first transport of Jews from Prague came in November 1941; a few months later the remaining 5,000 townspeople of Terezin were evacuated to make room for another 50,000 Jews. In "giving the Jews a city," Hitler turned the victims' culture and civilized incredulity to his own advantage. Elderly Jews were promised a convalescent spa here; artists, writers, and musicians were encouraged to continue their work within Terezin's walls—all as a means of fostering the illusion of normalcy in their incomprehensible circumstances.

By 1943, when 90 percent of the protectorate's mostly assimilated Jews were housed there, many still believed it to be an alternative to the camps in the East and so welcomed the chance to live in a wholly Jewish city. In reality, however, Terezin was little more than a transit camp—a way station—on the road to Auschwitz. Thus masked, the final solution was that much easier to accomplish: of the nearly 150,000 men, women, and children who passed through this "model ghetto," only 12,000 survived the war. Some 33,000 people died in Terezin between 1941 and 1945 of disease, starvation, beatings, and shootings. Another 90,000 were eventually murdered in Auschwitz.[12]

Many of the Terezin survivors now living in Israel are still haunted by the Nazis' deception. One survivor recalls that when asked by other Israelis whether she was a survivor of the camps, she replies, "Yes, but forgive me—I was only in Terezin." She, like many survivors, feared that the Terezin of the German propaganda films and the deluded Red Cross reports would gradually displace both the reality of the ghetto and their own memory of it. It was mostly in response to this fear that members of He'halutz proposed a museum and archives devoted to Theresienstadt at Kibbutz Givat Haim-Ichud, to teach about Terezin's special circumstances. Rather than erecting a passive, silent monument that might have acquiesced in visitors' misconceptions, even reifying certain myths, the "Theresienstadt Martyrs' Remembrance Association" opened the museum in 1975 as an educational center, a critical corrective for remembrance.

Beit Terezin consists of two sections: a study center with reading room, library, and archives; and a remembrance hall housing a small exhibition. The archives contain copies of the transport cards of 150,000 Jews transported to Terezin, recording where they came from, when they arrived, and when and where they were deported. Other materials include nearly every book and article published on Terezin, diaries and letters of inmates, photographs, and whole sets of the literary and political journals printed by the children of Terezin. Set amidst lawns and trees not far from the kibbutz dining hall, the center hosts annual ceremonies and conferences on both Yom Hasho'ah and on May 6, the date Terezin was liberated in 1945.

The twelve-cornered design of the adjacent memorial hall recalls the twelve corners of the fortress city and is constructed of red brick, a reference to the red brick of the ghetto walls. A permanent exhibition on the walls displays ghetto artifacts, transport lists, and photographs to tell Terezin's story. But on entering the remembrance hall, our eyes are drawn immediately to a colorful and intricate mosaic floor, which depicts the overhead view of the ghetto itself, surrounded by river and moats. The blocks are red, the town square and parks green. In a region where the only remnant of past civilizations is often the fragments of mosaic floor, the designer Albin Glaser sought to ensure some visual trace of both the ghetto and museum, were anything ever to happen to the building itself. "After all," the curator reminds me, "all we now know of the Byzantine period here are the mosaic floors left behind. The floor is always left." In this land of ruins and new buildings, the museum founders were ever mindful of the precariousness of both memory and the houses of memory. So, as an added precaution, they have also buried a scroll inscribed with Terezin's story beneath the mosaic floor, literally embedding further meaning in this memorial edifice.

Visitors are not the only human element of memory here. The archivist at Beit Terezin, Alisa Schiller, was born in Tel Aviv to Czech immigrants who came to Israel in the 1930s. Her parents' families so longed to return, however, that they were finally persuaded to go back to beautiful Prague—just before Hitler annexed the Sudetenland. Now trapped, Alisa and her family were sent to Terezin in 1941. Only Alisa lived to see the liberation of the camp. Within months of her release, she returned to Israel, her birthplace fourteen years earlier.

Her story is part of the memory being conveyed here, but not because she tells it to every visitor (in fact, she guards her story to prevent it from dominating other parts of the museum). However, as a survivor of Terezin now keeping memory's record in order, she represents a palpable link between the memorial house here and its source in Czechoslovakia. Unlike the memorials located at the sites of destruction in Europe, memorials in Israel cannot invoke the ruins for their authority. At Beit Terezin and other museums at a geographical remove from their sources, survivors often represent this lost link to events. As part of the experiences being commemorated, they simultaneously guard the communal memory and animate the memorial text with their presence.

Kibbutz Lohamei Hageta'ot

Nowhere in Israel does the survivors' spirit animate a museum more than at Kibbutz Lohamei Hageta'ot—literally, Fighters of the Ghettos Kibbutz. Not only do the fighters who live here embody the link between memorial sites and an actual past, but their experiences have left an unmistakable imprint here on the very forms that remembrance takes. As the survivors of camps have organized remembrance of this time around their experiences as victims, the ghetto fighters and partisans recall this era in the images of their own resistance and fighting. In both cases, the survivors' and fighters' experiences have come to serve as paradigmatic figures for public remembrance.

Where other kibbutzim have recollected the period of *Sho'ah* around and in contrast to the ideals of the kibbutz movement, Lohamei Hageta'ot has defined itself explicitly in the memory of two fighting founders: Yitzhak "Antek" Zuckerman and Zivia Lubetkin. As young guards of the Zionist left wing, both fought in the Jewish Fighting Organization as deputies to Mordechai Anielewicz during the Warsaw ghetto uprising. On Anielewicz's death, "Antek" assumed command of the organization and fought until the ghetto was reduced to smoldering ruins, when he and a handful of other fighters escaped through the sewers to the "Aryan" side of Warsaw. Once outside, they joined Polish partisan units in the woods, and in August 1944, Zuckerman and Lubetkin led a Jewish brigade in the Polish Warsaw Uprising. After surviving these battles and the obliteration of the rest of Warsaw, they returned to the forests to continue fighting as partisans until the end of the war.[13]

In 1946, Lubetkin arrived in Palestine to testify to the fighters' ordeal in the ghetto and woods. The next year, when Zuckerman finally reached the land of Israel, he and Lubetkin, together with another seventy former fighters, partisans, and survivors, founded this kibbutz in their name: Lohamei Hageta'ot. Finally, these pioneers of Shomer Hatsa'ir (Young Guard) would fulfill the movement's raison d'être: settling a collective farm in Eretz Israel. Until that moment, however, despite their youthful agricultural training before the war, the Zionism of these young guards had been realized only in organizing resistance and fighting. For these Zionists, the continuity between their past lives in Europe and their new lives in Israel was forged precisely in their capacity to fight. For some, in fact, the "war" never really ended at all. After rising up in the ghetto in 1943, joining the Poles in their 1944 uprising, and fighting as partisans until 1945, they arrived in Israel in 1947 just in time for the War of Independence. In their minds, there was a direct link between fighting in Warsaw—a struggle in their words for national and economic liberation—and the founding of the state: the war for Jewish nationhood begun in Warsaw ended in Israel. Little wonder that memory's mission would be so clear after Israel's independence, that they would regard their kibbutz—the flower of Zionism—as monument to the Ghetto Fighters.

In founding the museum here in 1949, Zuckerman and his comrades literalized the more figurative memorial of the kibbutz itself. Their intent was clear from the beginning: in the words of the curator, "We wanted to build a Yishuv as a monument to what we had seen in the ghettos and camps." Instead of standing for memory, the kibbutz would actively cultivate it. Over the years, the museum here—Beit Lohamei Hageta'ot—has grown from a small archives and library housed in a hut the size of a tool shed to a grand, classically designed stone and concrete building. This and a Roman-style amphitheater were constructed within sight of an actual Caesarian aqueduct: together the aqueduct, the amphitheater, and the museum dominate the architectonic space of the kibbutz, lending it a timeless, ancient dimension.

With so few Jews left in Europe to recall Jewish life there before the war, little sign of it now exists in European memorials and museums. As a whole they tend to focus largely on the deaths of Jews during the Holocaust and on their postwar absence. In Israel, by contrast, the survivors' recollections necessarily include their lives before the war, their suffering and struggle during the war, and their return to life in Israel afterwards. In the eyes of survivors who build these museums, their experiences link Jewish life in Europe and Israel. As part of this still-unfolding historical continuum, their lives may be indelibly marked by the *Sho'ah,* but insofar as Jews continue to live and work in Israel, life itself continues. The *Sho'ah* is absorbed into a much larger historical whole— twelve years out of two millennia. This longer view of Jewish history is explicitly reflected in the configuration of the museum at

Lohamei Hageta'ot. Out of twelve exhibition halls at Lohamei Hageta'ot, only two are devoted to the killing process; the rest relate what had come before and what now comes after in Israel. Built as it was by the hands of a kibbutz plowman, Antek, who five years before sowing these fields had been commanding the Jewish rebellion in Warsaw, it could hardly have been otherwise.

The first three exhibition halls, therefore, depict what was lost in Europe: Jewish Vilna, the Shtetl Olkienicki, and the Zionist youth groups of Hehalutz. Even here, however, there is a striking contrast between the images of a withered past in Vilna and Olkienicki and the youthful vitality of the Zionist youth groups. Where Vilna and Olkienicki reek of stale old books and tired life, the images of young, kerchiefed pioneers exude vitality, optimism, and athletic strength. In contrast to the past-obsessed *yeshiva bocher* of Vilna, these teenagers look forward to new lives in Eretz Israel, where they seem already to be living. The seeds of both European destruction and Israeli rebirth have already been sown: of the Halutzim who stayed behind, most fought and died; those who came to Israel survived. Unlike the continued sentimentalization of shtetl life in Diaspora literature and art, the models and photos of shtetlach in the museum are tinged with death and decay, constructed with their end in mind.

In the next two rooms on the ground floor, killers and victims are recalled, each in succinctly suggestive images. In order to reach the killers, we descend half a flight of stairs: a descent to hell, descent to the gas chamber, descent to graves, descent to the Diaspora. The killers are represented by their effects: intricate models of the Treblinka death camp and of the Vapniarka work camp, and an SS uniform. We exit this hall to enter that of the victims, here exemplified by the story of Janusz Korczak and his orphaned children. Together, Korczak and his children represent two sides of a victim ideal: the hero who courageously refuses to abandon his charges, and orphaned children, innocent and defenseless. On this floor, we can also view a proposal for a memorial to all the children of the Holocaust—Yad Layeled. This "monument to the child" would represent not only the children of the Holocaust but, in its generic title, all children, both then and now.

On the next floor, photographs and text narrate the rise of Nazi Germany, its war conquests, its initially invincible military machine. As conquerors of powerful nations, they could not be stopped in their destruction of European Jewry. The ghettos and deportations are described in the room following, equal in space to the section on the Nazis' war: a victim's-eye view from the end of the rifle barrel. Our walking narrative continues past a model of the Anne Frank house in Amsterdam and the actual glass booth in which Adolph Eichmann sat during his Jerusalem trial. The bulletproof glass that had once preserved Eichmann is now empty and preserves only the memory of his absence, of Israeli justice served.

Then come two long halls of Auschwitz sculptures, a map of Jewish resistance in Eastern Europe, paintings and drawings from Terezin—and the Warsaw ghetto uprising. Without an explicit theme linking these sections, we fall back on the general theme of the museum: resistance. With resistance as its organizing theme, the museum highlights aspects of resistance in all events, turns all responses into acts of heroism. The map of Jewish resistance on the second floor transforms all within its perimeter into variations on the theme of resistance: the practical resistance of Eichmann's capture, partisan activity and the ghetto uprising; the spiritual resistance of Anne Frank, Auschwitz sculptures, and art from Terezin. Even Janusz Korczak exemplifies the resistance implied in facing one's death with dignity. In this sequence, the Warsaw ghetto uprising becomes the most stirring example, but it is now only one of several instances of heroism and resistance.

In the last room, on the top floor, we find more art: drawings by Marcel Janko and others, and a section on Yitzhak Katzenelson, the elegist of the Holocaust to whom this museum is dedicated. This is not transcendent art, however, but poetry and painting anchored in events themselves. The exhibition that began with a reconstructed past—models, photographs, documents—ends here in aesthetic responses to events and thereby encourages viewers' responses, as well.

To a great extent, the main operating principle of all museums is metonymic: we come to know the whole of an age, an event, or a people through the fragment presented to us. In the case of Holocaust museums in Israel, this era is delivered to us primarily through images of resistance and heroism, references to martyred children and the survivors' new lives in Eretz Israel. In each case, the representative part creates a large meaning for the whole. By remembering all the victims of the *Sho'ah* in the figure of children, for example, an exhibition suggests the innocence and defenselessness of all the victims, the irredeemable barbarity of their killers. At the same time, such a presentation also casts doubt in viewers' minds on the traditional rationalizations for such tragedy, divine justice and punishment.

Conversely, when remembrance of the Holocaust is organized around the figure of heroic uprisings, some of this same helplessness is denied: this period becomes significant not for its unprecedented destruction, but for the unprecedented spectacle of armed revolt by the Jews—who rose up against both their enemies and their own traditional responses to persecution. Armed resistance was not only possible but, in the eyes of early museum makers here, obligatory. In the end, Zionist pioneers had also overturned the traditional image of Jew as victim. One of the tragic ironies, however, may be that if fighters remember in the shape of their resistance, and survivors remember in the shape of their experiences, who can remember the death of martyrs? In addition, we might note that of the survivors in Israel after the war (nearly half the population in 1948), only the fighters had a receptive state audience. The survivors, who had simply endured, or had survived the camps by more luck than strength, remembered well their murdered families. But with rare exception, their remembrances were given little public voice until the 1960 Eichmann trial in Jerusalem.[14]

Given the five-year span in which one's people was murdered, oneself saved, and one's country founded, it might have been difficult to conceive of events any differently. We remind ourselves here that in choosing resistance as their theme, the makers of kibbutz memorials have not deliberately tried to obfuscate or diminish the far greater number of martyrs; the icons of heroism here are not the mere whitewashing of slaughter or the calculated exaggeration of Jewish resistance in Europe. Rather, in remembering the *Sho'ah,* these groups inevitably remembered themselves, their part in events, their comrades and movements who stayed in Europe. Since it was often these movements' members who made up the leadership of resistance organizations in Europe, when the kibbutz plowman remembers these years, it will be in the image of himself, recalled in the figure of fighting comrades left behind.

Franklin H. Littell

Early Warning: Detecting Potentially Genocidal Movements

AFTER "FORTY YEARS IN THE WILDERNESS," THINKING PEOPLE ARE BE-ginning to talk about the lessons of the Holocaust. At first there was silence. Then the story began to be told—in the differing idioms: the heart-stopping incident of theater, the emotion-shaping evocation of poetry and music, the hunt and capture of brute facts by the historians. Now, the scriptural time span—forty years—later, we are still seeking a consensus as to what shall be communicated—by whom, to whom, and to what end?

TELLING THE STORY OF THE HOLOCAUST

Yad Vashem and the U.S. Holocaust Memorial Museum in Washington, D.C., for example, serve different constituencies. One teaches each generation of school children, each generation in national service, in establishing the legacy in the heart of the Jewish state. The other, raised up in the capital of a pluralistic society, amidst other shrines of liberty and heritage museums, must speak to the condition of all citizens of conscience.

Survivors, rescuers, liberators, and bystanders—all are finding their voices. Those of my generation, who have grandchildren reaching maturity, are compelled to go beyond telling the story. We reach for lessons, for ways of somehow transmuting the massive destruction and trauma into lessons that will help them to find their way to better years than we in our generation have lived through in this century of genocide.

Already, in the very turn of a phrase—"century of genocide"—the frail consensus that brought us here from across the world is threatened. Do we begin the discussion with the Armenian genocide, which ushered in the twentieth century? What happens then to the moral and religious uniqueness of the Holocaust, the characteristic that Jewish philosophers and Christian theologians repeatedly affirm when they address the event in its concreteness, its specificity?

Yet the event as story—and the event as a set of lessons, too—demands a hearing. Silence, even silent respect, will no longer suffice. And a hearing is connected only through analogies and metaphors that relate to other experiences. The one who seeks to understand the Holocaust must risk entering the ground of comparison and analysis, with the risk only slightly reduced by literary paradox and philosophical dialectic.

Once we have put the question of meaning(s) and lesson(s), once we have moved beyond simply telling the story, we enter the domain of comparison, of calculation, of analysis—in short, the domain of science. This venturing forth, imperative as it is, carries with it fundamental moral and intellectual risks.

Of these risks, none is more dangerous than the possibility that the theme "Holocaust" might one day be treated with the psychological remove that Himmler in his noted Poznan address praised in the perpetrators of the crime. Already some theologians, practitioners of a discipline classically called "the Queen of the Sciences," subsume the Holocaust under the familiar rubric "theodicy." (The Jewish parallel is the drive to subsume the *Sho'ah* under the ninth of Av.) Political scientists write of a case study in military dictatorship, even of military necessity. Sociologists take refuge in the familiar categories of "antisemitism" and "race prejudice." Psychologists render the Holocaust innocuous by subsuming the topic under "aggression," "the authoritarian personality," and so on. And university administrators render it harmless by listing it with "Jewish Studies."

TEACHING THE LESSONS:
THE INTERDISCIPLINARY REQUIREMENT

To avoid being trapped in one of these blind alleys of conventional recourse, study of the Holocaust and discussion of our findings must be kept *interdisciplinary*. For twenty years, especially in connection with the Annual Scholars' Conferences, we have stressed this fundamental position. The music of poetry and the antiphonies of liturgies must converge with the keen, critical analyses of historians and the focused microscopes of other academic disciplines in a total muster of our spiritual and intellectual forces.

Above all we must prevent a premature closure. Let the story work among all those with ears to hear, eyes to see, and consciences to respond. Let the analyses be carried forward in all the academic vernaculars—not least those of theology, law, business administration, and medicine. Recent studies by Robert Ericksen, Joseph Borkin, Robert Lifton, Benno Mueller-Hill, and others have reminded us again that the quest for scientific knowledge without the compass of morality and the rudder of ethics may be a deadly passion.

The natural human tendency to diabolize the perpetrators, romanticize the victims, and apotheosize the rescuers may blind us to the fact that the Holocaust is also to be remembered as a rational program planned, supervised, and justified by professors and Ph.D.'s. The Holocaust is not something outside history. It is not something of past history: it works in us and upon us still.

There were a few monstrous figures of unprecedented evil—and hundreds of thousands who had been schooled to "obey the powers that be," hundreds of thousands who simply did what was expected of them without question or protest. There were a few who defied the idol that was the *Führerstaat*—and great mobs that went whoring after the strange gods of Nazism. There were a few rescuers of record, and Yad Vashem records them in the Avenue of the Righteous—and several hundred thousands who by small, incisive acts at the critical moment were links in chains of rescue. In honoring the dead and "remembering for the future," let us keep the human measure!

Those of us who live by our heads need especially to be reminded from time to time that before we were teachers and scientists we were human beings—and would do well to retain our humanness afterward as well.

TEACHING THE LESSONS: THE INTERFAITH REQUIREMENT

A second fundamental position: the study of the material and the teaching of the lessons must be an *interfaith* affair. More than a decade ago a fine historian of the Holocaust declared in an address to the annual meeting of the Modern Language Association: "The Holocaust is an event which only Jews can understand and only Jews can teach."[1]

Wrong! It is *wrong* to relegate Holocaust teaching to Jewish Studies. It is *wrong* to plan Holocaust conferences and seminars without reference to the history of the monochromatic, monolithic Christendom that for centuries justified laws against "Jews and heretics" and provided a low threshhold of opposition to their dehumanization, exploitation, and mass murder. It is *wrong* to allow Jewish children and Jewish students to grow up in a Manichean universe, with but few candles flickering in the Stygian darkness, without knowledge that there are non-Jews who passionately share their devotion to Jewish survival.

Let me tell you a remarkable story. Some of you will have seen the announcements of a Distinguished Professorship in Holocaust Studies to be inaugurated at Stockton State College in New Jersey. The endowed professorship carries the name of Ida E. King. Ida E. King is a black American woman who has made money and given generously. She tells a moving tale of how the Holocaust affected her consciousness and conscience, how it helped her both to empathize with the Jewish people and to be more deeply sympathetic to the sufferings of other peoples.

The Holocaust is not a sectarian Jewish preserve. To tell it and teach it calls for the best efforts of people of conscience from all religious, ethnic, and cultural sectors.

WORKING TOGETHER ON THE LESSONS OF THE HOLOCAUST

Although the telling of the story may divide us, since each account is necessarily individual, the pursuit of the lessons can bring us together.

If the modern university produced thousands of Mengeles and Freislers and Kittels, and it did (and still does produce potential ones!), Jews *and* Christians *and* other gentiles must work together to reconstruct it.

If populist movements still undermine representative government and basic human liberties by asserting the falsehood "vox populi vox Dei," then Jews and Christians have common cause to remember and to stand together against what Alexis de Tocqueville called "democracies that are not free" and Jacob Talmon called "totalitarian democracy." The NSDAP was a populist movement par excellence: in the last open election—open, but not free— before Hitler became chancellor, the average age of the Nazi voters was ten years younger than the average age of voters in the lists of the SPD, *Zentrum*, Hugenberg Nationalists, and Heuss Liberals!

Let us remember that it was low-grade politics, as well as low-grade religion, that opened the door for Hitler's reckless military adventures and murderous "Final Solution." If a small country is destroyed by the cynical deals of selfish major powers, her society shattered, her ethnic differences exacerbated by foreign interests and native fifth-columnists, and her freedom lost, should not Jews and Christians stand together against such debased and debasing *Realpolitik?*

We could talk about Lebanon, for the dictator who is moving to take over that unhappy land works with maps on which "Lebanon" and "Palestine" are both provinces of "Greater Syria." In any case, let us not forget those broken-hearted Czech statesmen who returned to Prague in November of 1938. They had not been allowed even to enter the room to present the case for their people in Munich, as Hitler and Mussolini and Daladier and Chamberlain destroyed their country and guaranteed the coming of World War II. Can you hear in your imagination the voice of Beneš as he reported to the last free Czech parliament—the last free Czech parliament for fifty years!—"We have been basely betrayed."

Among the lessons, early warning on potentially genocidal movements can be one of the most important. Of early warning signs there is a sufficiency, if we know how to read them.

A DESIGN FOR EARLY DETECTION OF POTENTIALLY GENOCIDAL MOVEMENTS

It is against the backdrop of *interdisciplinary, interfaith*, and also *international* study and discussion of the Holocaust that I am offering my fifteen-point grid as a design for screening movements and predicting consequences.

Axiom: The NSDAP was a terrorist movement for years before it ever became a criminal government with the power to commit genocide.

The essential factor in a science is *predictability*. We do not have a science if a careful reporter records an epidemic or a plague. We have a science when a sufficient number of careful students have reached a consensus and can say that if certain conditions prevail, unchecked and unchanged, there will be an epidemic.

My argument is that there are certain objective factors—in my graduate seminar, over a period of thirty years, we have arrived at fifteen of them—which, all present and in configuration, define what the ancients called a *kairos*. A modern term might be "critical mass." The presence of three or four factors may perhaps not define a crisis, but with ten or eleven or twelve, it is time for the alarm bells to ring and the danger signals to start flashing.

Potentially genocidal movements, terrorist movements, give early evidence of what they will be like if they ever come to power. According to a conservative police report prepared in 1923 in Hannover, by the time they assassinated the great cabinet minister Walther Rathenau in July of 1922, the Nazis and their immediate allies had already killed 344 political opponents. That is not a legitimate political party, operating within the covenant of good faith: it is a terrorist movement. The time to deal with it conclusively was not 1933—too late (!)—or 1938—much too late (!!). The moment of decision was 1923, at the time of the attempted *Putsch*, a treasonous action led by Hitler and Ludendorff in Munich.

If the Weimar authorities had acted decisively in the Munich of 1923, the Munich of 1938 would never have occurred. The jurists who handled the treason of Hitler and Ludendorff mildly were not sympathizers: they were good old-fashioned, well-educated, nineteenth-century liberals. To act *in time* is the essence of the matter. In explaining his movie about the rise of the Nazi Party, "The Serpent's Egg," Ingmar Bergman put it this way: "The membrane is so thin that through it you can already discern the perfectly formed body of the reptile." By 1923, the NSDAP was a perfectly formed political reptile.

Once the terrorists come to power they cannot be removed without outside intervention. In August of 1932, as the Weimar Republic was being strangled to death by parliamentary tricksters and fifth-columnists, Goebbels wrote in his diary: "Once we have the power we will never give it up. They will have to carry our dead bodies out of the ministries." Precisely! Such is the technological concentration of power in advanced societies that once a movement of that type has invested the centers of power, it cannot be dislodged except by outside help—bluntly, by war. The use of an early warning system, therefore, is to prevent the final calamities of war and the genocides from coming to pass.

A FRESH VIEW OF THE POLITICAL COVENANT

Those who by both theory and practice indicate that they are not in good faith in the political covenant, that they are *Verfassungs-widrig* (to use the language of the Bonn government's Law for the Protection of the Constitution), should be dealt with as enemies. They jeopardize the liberties and the standing of loyal oppositions, and if they attain their goal they will destroy both public liberty and the structures of representative government.

The argument presented calls into question the continuing viability of certain received truths. Take, for example, the popular slogan "the self-determination of peoples." Enshrined in Wilson's Fourteen Points, it presupposed the availability of popular rebellion. As Jefferson defined it in the Declaration of Independence, the people had the right to overthrow rulers who no longer served their interests and to replace them by others who would. In a euphoric moment, the tree of liberty might be watered every twenty years by the blood of tyrants. A people had the rulers it deserved, for all they needed was the civic courage to get rid of the despots.

The argument no longer prevails, with the end of the possibility of popular revolutions in developed countries. It no longer applies, against modern dictatorships controlling the flow of information, which command the "gatekeeper's post." It no longer applies, in reference to a regime backed by a military that is willing to use the violence against its own people that was once reserved for the natives in colonies. It no longer applies, in reference to a regime supported by ideological "true believers" who are organized into a cellular network within one loyal party that runs all civilian branches of government.

The corollary to "self-determination," the unchallenged autonomy of each and every national sovereignty, has also become untenable. We might think back to the abuse of the principle in the so-called "nonintervention" by which the guilty bystanders assisted Hitler and Mussolini to destroy the Spanish republic. But take a present case. We may reference Brazil, where special interests have whipped up nationalist indignation against foreigners who interfere with their right to destroy the rain forests for a quick profit. But that rain forest provides 40 percent of the oxygen that keeps non-Brazilians as well as Brazilians alive! Or we may refer to Bangladesh, the most densely populated nation in the world, which is disappearing before our eyes. The reckless destruction of the forests in China and northern India has guaranteed that each year tens of thousands of the people of Bangladesh will be drowned and within a generation two-thirds of what is now Bangladesh will be under water. Even so normally perspicacious an observer as Jeane Kirkpatrick recently questioned U.S. policy in a sensitive area— Panama—in the name of the principle of national sovereignty. But the self-determination, national autonomy, and unchallenged sovereignty of each nation have become ecological as well as political impossibilities.

An effective early warning system can help secure the political covenant of a free and self-governing people, in an age when the old popular safeguards are no longer effective in advanced nations.

A NEW DEFINITION OF POLITICAL LEGITIMACY

Another sector requiring a radical reorientation is the definition of legitimate government. The traditional interpretation, going back to the first articulation of international law by Hugo Grotius and Samuel Pufendorf, fitted the circumstances when kings—sometimes queens—ruled by divine right. Under these terms a regime is still said to be legitimate if it (1) maintains security and order over a given territory and (2) has been recognized by a satisfactory number of other rulers.

In an age of terrorist movements, fired by messianic dreams and apocalyptic interpretations of history, the traditional interpretation of legitimacy no longer works. Nor does its recent codex, the appeal to popular consent: every twentieth-century dictator has claimed to incorporate in his person "the will of the people." Every terrorist movement has made the same spurious claim to legitimacy.

A new definition of legitimacy is required. Looking back over years of Holocaust study, I would submit two principles: (1) a legitimate government—whether simple democracy, republic, or constitutional monarchy—is one that affords effective channels and appropriate checks and balances in reference to the will of the people; (2) a legitimate government is one that protects the full liberties of individual citizens and groups that are at a given time functioning as "loyal opposition." Kurt Leibholz, Dietrich Bonhoeffer's brother-in-law, who survived in exile and later served on the Supreme Court in Karlsruhe, perceived already in 1934 that the Nazi Third Reich could not be accredited as a legitimate government.

I would suggest that we apply such standards to the regimes— so many of them old-fashioned despotisms or modern-style dictatorships—that have over more than a decade worked systematically to delegitimize Israel. The truth is that there is not a single legitimate government in the Arab League, and there are all too few in the rest of the membership in the United Nations.

A clearer understanding of the difference between terrorists and freedom fighters is also imperative. The first question is whether the government targeted is legitimate or illegitimate. In the latter case, other rules apply. Terrorist movements commonly act to destabilize, to undermine legitimate government, and to terrorize civilian populations. Typical incidents include killing school children, shoppers, unarmed diplomats, medical convoys, and innocent passengers on airplanes, ships, or buses. Freedom fighters are irregulars—soldiers, though often out of uniform— and their targets are the police and the military.

To imply that legitimate and illegitimate governments are to be judged on the same basis and by the same standards is as unsound as to fail to distinguish between terrorists and freedom fighters.

THE SIGNS OF ILLEGITIMACY

Another way of stating the argument is this: the grid that I am proposing makes it possible to identify illegitimate political movements that will, given the chance, form criminal governments. Such regimes, once in power, cannot be overthrown by popular revolutions. It is quite possible that populist movements carried them to power. And, once in power, they can no longer assert their legitimacy and immunity from outside interference if they do not demonstrate commitment to the new standards of legitimacy.

We may now turn to the points in the grid, the "stars" that provide an early warning system for potentially genocidal movements. The identifying marks are not matters of opinion, but objectively discernible and definable actions. Five or four alone do not necessarily configure a crisis. Although not all of the points are of the same measure of importance, when nine or ten or a dozen "stars" have swung into their place in the constellation, the time has come for decisive action to defend the society and the life and liberty of its loyal citizens. To use another figure of speech, a critical mass has been reached, and, unless it is quickly and decisively contained, appalling destruction may ensue.

Let me mention the points rapidly, to center our discussion.

1. The group or movement prints, distributes, and uses antisemitic material for recruitment.

2. The group or movement makes antisemitic appeals through the media or in evangelistic meetings.

3 and 4. The same actions as 1 and 2, but directed against any other ethnic, religious, or cultural community, using the targeting in the quest for political power.

5. Members cultivate violence toward opponents—publishing slanderous charges, bombing meeting places and homes and media, beating, assassinating.

6. The movement pursues the politics of polarization, scorning the middle ground of conciliation or compromise, rejecting the politics of moderation and orderly change. If it becomes large enough, instead of functioning as a "loyal opposition," it establishes the structures of a "state within a state."

7. The group or movement deliberately drives a wedge between the generations, alienating young people from their heritage.

8. The movement maintains camps for paramilitary training, including practice in the use of antipersonnel weapons.

9. The movement maintains private armies, demonstrating in public in uniform, parading and marching to intimidate loyal citizens.

10. Leaders of the movement elaborate a quasi-religious structure of authority and sanctions, with political hymns, shrines, martyrs, liturgies.

11. Archaic tribal, clannish, or religious symbols are worn by members as public "in-group" insignia; secret passwords, handshakes, and other recognition signals are used to signal to fellow believers.

12. Induction and termination of membership are observed as pseudoreligious rites. Straying members are treated as "heretics"—subjected to exorcism, with intensive group confession applied in case of a "rescue."

13. The movement's basic unit is the closed cell, with three to seven members the standard number. This is the classic unit of a revolutionary party or intelligence operation, but it is inappropriate to exercise pressure upon a legitimate government.

14. The movement practices deception and attempts confusion of public opinion by launching one-issue "fronts," without clear identification of sponsorship, financing, and control. A great deal of money is raised this way, ostensibly for a good public purpose but actually to serve the movement's internal interests. This is the "large net," within which "innocents" are caught.

15. The movement's tactics include infiltration and subversion of public institutions and voluntary associations, luring their direction from service to the common good to augmentation of the group's drive for power. Positions controlling the schools, the police, and public safety forces are special targets.

In conclusion, let me refer to a proposal that Dr. Gideon Hausner, the prosecutor of Eichmann and longtime head of Yad Vashem, made at the International Convention of Trial Lawyers in Honolulu in 1981. After discussing the problems posed by international terrorism, Dr. Hausner recommended that the governments of the free world enter by treaty a covenant for joint action against international terrorism. Dr. Hausner's proposal needs to be brought forward again and again until it is acted upon. In the meantime, we can act as responsible citizens within our different countries to get laws enacted that will place potentially genocidal movements under the ban—along with infanticide, dueling, chattel slavery, clan feuds, widow-burning, and other practices that were once thought permissible but are now outlawed in civilized societies.

Lenore Blum, Ph.D.
Gitta Fajerstein, L.S.W.
Ira O. Glick, Ph.D.
Elizabeth Jacob, M.A.
Sondra Fineberg Kraff, L.S.W.
Louis Rosenblum, M.D.
Lya Dym Rosenblum, Ph.D.
Chaya H. Roth, Ph.D.
Elsa Roth, L.S.W.
Raya Schapiro, M.D.
Allen Siegel, M.D.
Zev Weiss, M.A.

Tellers and Listeners: The Impact of Holocaust Narratives

IN THE EARLY PART OF 1983, A PROJECT WAS STARTED IN CHICAGO whose aim was to establish a repository of audiovisual testimonials of Holocaust survivors. The founder of the project, Zev Weiss, an educator and himself a survivor (deported from Hungary to Auschwitz in 1944), believed that the time had come to make a concerted effort to transmit what we know about the Holocaust by means of systematic and well-prepared instructional materials and academic curricula. He felt that a critical factor in the transmission of this knowledge was the availability of authentic, first-hand testimonials of the Holocaust experience by those who encountered and survived it. Fueled by a vision of the broad dissemination of Holocaust information to both contemporary and future generations, he gathered a small group of interested supporters who became the backbone of the project's financial and program planning; enlisted several mental health and human service professionals to serve as interviewers for the taping sessions; and consulted, collaborated, and affiliated with the Video Archive for Holocaust Testimonies at Yale University. Thus the Holocaust Educational Foundation (HEF) was begun.

During these past six years and the completion of 128 interviews, which are now permanently stored in the Yale University Video Archive, the project has raised many challenging questions and issues about the Holocaust, about the survivors, and, perhaps most interestingly, about the nature of the project itself. In particular, we have been impressed by the special character of personal oral history and moved, both intellectually and emotionally, by our collective experience of the survivors' powerful and deeply personal stories—unrehearsed, unedited, and often never before told.

THE PROJECT

Goals

The aims of the video archive project were hammered out through group discussions. In a relatively short period of time, we identified three goals and a common frame of reference for what we were doing:

1. To establish an oral record of the Holocaust based on first-hand experiences of those who survived it. We wanted to make history come and remain alive in a central repository of Holocaust documentation so that future generations might learn, know, and remember.

2. To give voice and representation to the thousands of survivors who wished to tell the stories of their survival—what they had seen and experienced and of which they could have spoken at an earlier time if only there had been listeners. Moreover, by establishing an oral record, we believed we were helping to give voice to the thousands who were killed and were unable to speak, yet who in the midst of disaster mandated that they be remembered and that their stories be transmitted.

3. To establish and reinforce a link between those who were there and those of us who, but for an accident of history, were spared that fate. And in our role as listeners, to commit ourselves not only to the task of transmitting the past but also to that of addressing inequities of the moment and alerting and sensitizing others to the potential for future injustices.

As the project progressed, we were able to clarify these goals and elaborate upon them even as new issues and questions emerged, and we came to see our activities in different, unexpected ways. Thus, we became increasingly aware that our contribution to the gathering of oral testimony of the Holocaust was an important supplement to the growing body of written history. We realized that oral history lends a special kind of validity to events; as Thompson has observed, "It thrusts life into history itself and it widens its scope. . . . It encourages teachers and students to become fellow-workers. It brings history into, and out of, the community . . . it makes contact—and thence (brings) understanding . . . between generations."[1]

We also felt that videocassettes, in an increasingly video-oriented world, would become even more useful to future generations of educators and students in the teaching and learning of Holocaust history. It was a perception that added a new dimension of significance to what we were doing.

It became apparent to us as we went on that both tellers and listeners were actively engaged in separate yet simultaneous dual tasks. For the survivors, the duality consisted of relating their own stories while also bearing the tales of those who had died. For the listeners, the dual task was to listen for the sake of creating a historical record and, at the same time, to make a modicum of restitution for all who had been unwilling or unable to listen during the years of the atrocities and following liberation.

General Description

Since its inception in 1983, the Holocaust videotape project has been carried out at the religious school of Beth Hillel, a large Conservative synagogue located in Wilmette, Illinois, a northern suburb of Chicago. The videotapings take place on Sundays in the school library. Various classrooms are used before and after the taping sessions as hospitality rooms for the tellers and members of their families or friends who accompany them. All the rooms display a prominent array of Jewish artwork, books, children's Hebrew School assignments, and holiday celebration objects, which together help create a relaxed and unmistakably Judaic environment. Taping sessions are held once every four to six weeks, each for a maximum of ninety minutes, with three or four interviews scheduled for a single day.

Over the past six years, the project staff has consisted of Zev Weiss, HEF director, and a total of twenty interviewers—ten social workers, five psychiatrists, and five Ph.D. mental health or human service professionals. At any given time, twelve to fifteen people have been active in the project. Personal experiences with the Holocaust vary considerably among the group members: some had themselves lived through years of persecution, flight, or hiding; several were refugees who had escaped from Europe in the early Hitler years, and in some instances at the last possible moment; others had no personal contact with the Holocaust but were sensitive to it for various individual reasons.

In each session two interviewers participate to ensure that empathic contact with the teller is maintained throughout and that important information will not be missed. Different teams of interviewers are used with each of the survivors, not so much to minimize demands on interviewers' time as to enable them to cope with the stress created by the taping sessions. In addition to those who are conducting interviews, several group members provide hospitality services and support to those waiting to be interviewed and to any family members and friends who accompany them. One staff member serves as project coordinator, responsible for scheduling appointments and assigning group members to a specific function for the taping day.

Those taped include survivors who contacted the Holocaust Educational Foundation on their own initiative after learning about it from friends or through the local media, as well as individuals contacted by members of the group after being identified as survivors. The only criteria for inclusion in the project are that the individual must have had direct experience with the Holocaust during the war years and must be willing to tell his or her story before a video camera. Since the beginning of the project, no one who has requested an interview has been denied participation.

Procedures

At the beginning of the project, guidelines were established for recruiting interviewees, conducting the interviews, and carrying out follow-up contact in accordance with the project's aims and philosophy. Considerable help was obtained from the Yale University Group, headed by Professor Geoffrey Hartman. This included a workshop devoted to standards and procedures conducted by Dr. Dori Laub, director of the Video Archive for Holocaust Testimonies at Yale, in March 1983 in Wilmette. A summary description of procedures is as follows:

> During an initial telephone contact between a prospective interviewee and a project staff member, the purpose and importance of the project are explained, the credentials of the interviewers and the general procedures and format are described, and basic information about the survivor is gathered. The voluntary nature of participation is also emphasized. If the individual agrees to participate, the coordinator schedules a taping date and assigns him or her to an interview team and a support worker. One of the interviewers then makes a second phone call to the interviewee in order to gain some preliminary information about the individual, which is written down for reference during the interview, and in order to help the interviewee begin the process of recalling and telling the story. Interviewees are also encouraged at this time to bring relevant photographs and/or documents of authenticity on the day of the taping, which usually takes place within ten days of this call.
>
> At the time of the interview, the support worker and interviewers greet the interviewee and accompanying family members, serve refreshments, spend several minutes in informal conversation with those present, explain and witness the signing of the form in which the interviewee consents to the educational uses of the videotape, and briefly review the taping format. The interviewee is then escorted to the room where the taping will be done, and the two interviewers, who sit facing the interviewee out of camera range, guide the person through a sequence of major topics that he or she is asked to discuss. Using notes of the

earlier telephone conversation as guidelines, the interviewers encourage the interviewee to describe events, feelings, attitudes and long-lasting consequences. An effort is made to promote the "personal" aspects of the recounting rather than the telling of historical facts. In no instance is the veracity of information questioned, although clarification may be requested.

Immediately following the interview the support worker provides a brief period of informal conversation before leave-taking, during which time the interviewee will often comment on the taping experience or remember material omitted during the taping. Several days later one of the interviewers telephones the interviewee to inquire about any aftereffects of the experience and to offer support and help when necessary. A copy of the videotape is made available to all interviewees.

Besides being committed to the actual taping days throughout the year, HEF members meet monthly to discuss issues and problems, view tapes, assess and attempt to improve interviewing skills, and plan future work. Given the emotional effects the interviewing has had on all of the interviewers, these meetings have provided an opportunity to communicate with and find support from one another. As such, they have been of considerable value to most group members.

Demographics

Most of the 128 survivors who have been interviewed to date were residents of the greater Chicago area; a small number were visitors from other locations.

The large majority are natives of Hungary and Poland, with only a scattering from England, France, Germany, and Holland. At the outbreak of the war, essentially all were living in their countries of origin. Their age at the time ranged between infancy and mid-thirties, with the average being eighteen. Approximately 60 percent were interned in concentration camps at some point between 1941 and 1945; the remaining 40 percent spent the war years hiding in forests, rural farm houses and barns, in the homes of local gentile families or safehouses, usually not far from their places of residence. Slightly more than half of the camp survivors (55 percent) were interned at Auschwitz. About two-thirds of the camp survivors experienced more than one camp, and over a third report having been in three or more camps, a consideration that in itself is suggestive of the difficulties they encountered and the kinds of materials forthcoming in their narrations.

THE NARRATIVES

"Stories" and "Facts"

The tellers were encouraged to tell their stories in an unstructured but roughly chronological way: to give a picture of life before the war, a description of the way the Holocaust first began for them, their experiences during the war years, the events surrounding the liberation, and finally a sketch of their present life and family situation. The stories were not sifted or checked for historical accuracy. Our aim was not to add to the empirical facts of the Holocaust, but to convey the idea that each teller's unique experiences, subjective impressions, and memories were important.

The deemphasis of factual documentation in favor of subjective accounts stimulated vigorous discussions among us regarding the question, what is "fact" in oral history? We decided to give credence to any memory of past experience told with conviction and/ or feeling. We believed that receptive listening would serve as a sufficient trigger for memories to become vivid, to the extent possible in the individual instance. Each narrative was considered valid regardless of discrepancies or time distortions with respect to established Holocaust history.

There was great variation in style and emotionality among the tellers. Some told their story in a matter-of-fact, chronological mode. Some included historical background as explanation. Some spoke quickly, as if to avoid lingering and risking the resurgence of a painful emotion connected with the narrated event—as if they were able to provide the headline for their story, but no more. For others, the intensity of the emotions overshadowed the memories. Feelings from the past—pain, helplessness, rage, remorse—became evident in the telling. And for still others, the retelling of past mastery and survival skills seemed rejuvenating and even exhilarating.

Despite the uniqueness of each story, common themes emerged. Most narrators talked of the gradual change in daily life that accompanied the beginnings of Jewish persecution: the loss of basic rights and privileges such as the right to go to school, to earn a living, to shop, to go to the coffeehouse, theater, or park, as well as peculiar restrictions such as prohibitions on owning a pet, riding a bicycle, buying ice cream from a street vendor, or walking near the river. They alluded to efforts to maintain "life as ordinary"—resourceful attempts to compensate and normalize their newly distorted lives—only to realize sooner or later the futility of such attempts. Most stressed the growing isolation from friends and neighbors during this period, accompanied by disbelief that what was happening was real and that there would be no recourse to law or justice.

With the intensification of persecution, crowding seemed to become the central issue. For the most part, families were still together but were crammed on top of one another in smaller and smaller quarters. The difficulties of living with strangers, sharing kitchens and bathrooms, and loss of privacy were stressed in the recounting of this period. "They tormented us with each other," as one person put it.

Survivors who in their adolescent and young adult years had been members of youth movements were inclined to emphasize the great strength derived from these affiliations: working in a soup kitchen in the Lodz ghetto and feeling that with each ladle of soup they were saving a person's life; speaking with pride about helping children in Theresienstadt and Westerbork; referring to the resourcefulness of teaching without books or paper. Those who had become bar mitzvah in the forests of rural France spoke of achievement. Those who had sung and made love under the stars spoke of hope. And all, throughout, made reference to their youth during the war years, a youth they had all but lost.

At the height of barbarism, themes were different among those who went into hiding and those who were deported to ghettos and camps. Those in hiding were more likely to recount acts of bravery and kindness on the part of helpful gentiles upon whom their ultimate survival depended, and they were more prone to enjoy the recall of mastery and survival skills. They were also more openly emotional when expressing their guilt about leaving trapped relatives behind; one woman, who as a teenager had managed to save herself by jumping from a death train, wept and berated herself for "abandoning" her aged parents in the cattle car bound for Auschwitz.

Those who lived through deportation and concentration camps exhibited a surprising ability to remember precise dates, even during long imprisonment. They focused on the hunger they experienced, and many remembered exactly the daily rations received during each period and place of their imprisonment. Cold, fear, exhaustion, lice, and disease—especially dysentery and typhus—were prominent themes as well. And so too was the sense of shame—the shame of suffering indignities and humiliations, the shame of being singled out for suffering.

Prominent in all the narratives were recollections of losses: sudden separations from loved ones; unanticipated harm befalling a relative, friend, or person one stood next to in line; a child taken away; a younger brother shot; a mother and father led away from others. For some the dread of loss persisted for months and years on end.

There were also themes of hope and strength in the narratives. Tellers spoke about the strength derived from family and friendship ties, or from the hope that a parent or spouse or child had somehow survived. Those who survived together with a loved person spoke of a sense of triumph at having thus "beaten the odds." Some recall how self-respect and meaning were restored by a kind word, a timely warning, a lesson of the *gemarra* remembered and retold, a ritual secretly conducted on one of the Jewish holidays.

Narrators gave varying testimonies of the part played by non-Jews in their survival struggles. Some cited names of compassionate gentiles who had helped at great risk to themselves without thought of repayment. Others mentioned the bribes that were necessary to obtain false papers, safe conduct, hiding places, food, and transport. Still others spoke of betrayal by false rescuers and plunder by former neighbors or employees.

Many of the stories included feats of great daring: escapes despite the watchful eyes and threats of guards; acts of physical strength in spite of starvation and disease; and resourceful ways of hiding under the very noses of the enemy. Almost all narratives emphasized the importance of sheer luck in survival.

The chaos that was part of the liberation period in Europe is also reflected in the stories of the tellers. Many who had maintained a detailed chronology up to this point became vague and confused about the sequence of events. Almost all described disorganized, frustrating attempts to find surviving relatives and to procure housing and food. There were rare stories of miraculous reunions. But mostly, there were poignant accounts of bitter disappointments as long-held hopes of reunion (which in not a few cases had been major motivators for survival) were dashed. Some who had endured persecution, deprivation, and torture were undone by the shock of returning "home" to nothing and no one.

When they were asked to comment on ways in which their wartime experiences affect their lives today, sensitivity to cold, to dirt, and to wasting of food were prominently cited. Others talked more about their ongoing fears that such events could recur and their resolve that Jews must never let their guard down. And in this context not a few expressed the hope that their testimonies would help assure that nothing similar to their own experiences ever happens—anywhere, to anyone—again.

The Experience of Telling

We originally believed that telling their stories would have a positive effect on narrators for three reasons. One was the presence of empathic, skilled interviewers who would listen to their stories with respect and interest.

A second, more subtle and complicated reason for believing the interviews would have a salutary effect had to do with the opportunity afforded the narrator to tell his or her story in an uninterrupted, start-to-finish manner. It was our impression that although many of the survivors we interviewed had indeed spoken of their experiences, few had the occasion to tell the whole story *as* a whole story; it was our hope that telling it in a whole piece, so to speak, might have some integrating effect on the inner representation of the terrible Holocaust experience.

A related notion we entertained was that children of survivors who viewed their parents' videotapes might benefit from this experience. Here we were influenced by Epstein's impressive series of interviews with grown children of Holocaust survivors.[2] She describes a surprisingly prevalent common feature: a feeling among most of these children that there was a dark, family secret too awful and shameful to talk about, but evident through inferences, overheard bits of conversation, pieces of frightening stories recounted, or by idiosyncrasies of their parents. Many of these children had longed to know more, in order to deal more rationally with the reality of their parents' past. We hoped that by sharing the videotape with their children, our tellers could provide them with a coherent whole, helping bits and pieces of real or imagined information fall into place for them. In the best scenario, viewing the tape together might even serve as a springboard for open discussion of the pervasive if wordless Holocaust presence in the household.

A third reason for thinking the taping would have a positive impact on survivors was that they would contribute in a personal way to a permanent record of the Holocaust, one that would be preserved for posterity. We also hoped that the interview would be seen as a shared commitment on the part of the teller and listener—"a significant thing we're doing together"—and that this could have a beneficial effect even in the most difficult, painful interviews.

THE IMPACT OF THE TAPING

As a follow-up, we telephoned approximately 15 percent of the interviewees during the summer of 1989 and asked several open-ended questions about the impact of the taping session: Had they thought about the taping? Did it change anything in their or their families' lives? Did it change the way they talked about their experiences with their children? Had they shown the videotape to anyone and, if so, with what effects?

What we learned from this informal survey is that the survivors look back on the experience of telling their stories in a variety of ways, with most remembering it as a satisfying, positive experience. Although they did not think of it as having had a major impact on how they viewed their past experiences, several described the taping as having provided an "opening" to inner feelings and memories. Three said the taping stimulated a journey back to their home town and to the camps where their ordeal had taken place.

One woman reported going back to school soon after the taping to obtain a graduate degree in social work, and another said she began psychotherapy. A majority referred to the interview as having been worthwhile—worthwhile in a personal sense and worthwhile for the educational purposes for which it was intended.

As anticipated, survivors were particularly appreciative that the interview had given them an opportunity to tell their story from beginning to end in uninterrupted fashion, to shape their experience into a more coherent whole following the chronology of events as they had occurred. There were those who expressed satisfaction at having been able to convey to some extent to the listeners the awfulness and magnitude of what had happened. Others remembered how they insisted that certain names be mentioned and photographs seen, and they understood this to have been an attempt to give voice to those who had been killed and of wanting to be sure they were honoring those who, at great risk to themselves, had helped them and their families.

Although all stated that the listeners were sympathetic and sensitive, some objected to the lack of structure in the interview, feeling that they might have told more, or told it better, had they been prompted with questions. Several people commented on the constraints of limited time and some expressed what must have been true for all: the impossibility of really telling everything, of truly conveying the horror of the experience.

Reactions of family members who saw the videotapes were reported to have been gratifying in some cases and disappointing in an equal number. A few tellers said they had neither viewed the tape themselves nor allowed others to see it. Some felt they had always talked about their experiences, but that the taping had provided additional opportunities to clarify, to justify, and to answer questions never before broached. A few specifically credited the taping with instigating discussion with their children.

The tellers were unanimous in praising the project in terms of its educational value. They expressed satisfaction in knowing that the memory of their experiences would not disappear into a void, but was on record for future generations. All commented on how important it had been to be part of the project and how meaningful it was to have helped establish a repository of oral documentation.

The interviewers came to the project for many reasons. There was the overriding wish to help establish a record for future generations. There was the wish to enable survivors to give expression to their individual experiences under the support and guidance of professionally trained listeners. And there was a wish to achieve a closer identification with survivors and with this part of Jewish history. Some were drawn to the project as an expression of Jewish identity and commitment. Others sought relief from a nagging sense of guilt for not having been part of this Jewish historical horror. And for most, the project presented an opportunity to re-address issues regarding the Holocaust that remain as yet unre-solved: namely, the uniquely Jewish nature of the *Sho'ah*, as com-pared to the universal significance of man's inhumanity to mankind.

The experience of actually doing the work had an unantici-pated impact on all the interviewers. Wrapped in our professional identities as mental health professionals, we had come to the pro-ject expecting that our clinical skills would help in reducing the potential for trauma to the tellers while facilitating a profound interview in each case. In time, however, an awareness developed that we could neither prevent excessive pain nor guarantee pro-found interviews. As each survivor fashioned his or her narrative and became its teller, so too did each interviewer become a receiver of the testimony and, therefore, a listener.

Through participation in the project, the interviewers emerged with a greater appreciation of the need to teach the lessons of the Holocaust in schools and on campuses, and the need to learn about it through readings, courses, and scholarly conferences. Listening to the accounts of people whose lives were devastated while the world stood by has had the effect of increasing our discomfort with apathy as other people's lives are affected by violence and oppres-sion. Therefore, while continuing to collect Holocaust narratives, the group has embarked on a number of other related enterprises: helping to develop curricula for Holocaust studies on college cam-puses throughout the country, supporting original academic re-search and literary writings on the Holocaust, and extending our tapings to include rescuers during the war years.

Geoffrey H. Hartman

Closing Remarks

WHAT EVERY CONFERENCE NEEDS IS A NAIF OR INGENU: SOMEONE FOR whom everything is new, everything resonates. Now most speakers here are historians, and I must say to start with that I am still very much a learner, that every time historians explode a myth or correct a factual error my heart leaps up. And then, of course, it drops. I want to tell you why.

Concerning uplift: after the music last night Raul Hilberg confessed that there was *one* person he could be envious of . . . Mozart. Well, I am envious of you collectively, of your field. I have sat in this conference deprived of my usual critical nastiness: when Hilberg said something, I felt, that's right; and when Bauer said something in contradiction, I felt, *that's* right; and Steve Katz, he was right too. You transformed me for forty-eight hours into a naif, and for that I am grateful.

Yet, as I indicated, my heart also dropped; because I realized what a minefield Holocaust studies are, that they require more than usual accuracy, how for every generalization there are exceptions, how easily sentimental distortions creep in, and how disputable even the *words* are in which we express our thoughts on what happened. I knew I wouldn't last a day in that minefield: I've probably already blown myself up without knowing it. Somewhere above the eyes, in that strange forehead space where thought lodges, a figure measures everything we say against an uncompromising standard; and what is scrutinized includes inadequate yet necessary words. Because of that especial care for words, though I was glad to see in the title of the conference such charged phrases as *lessons, legacies, meaning*, these common expressions, too, under the pressure of the catastrophic events we have focused on, had to be questioned at various points.

Historians, of course, are not physicians of memory (what medicine could possibly diminish the pain of thinking about the Holocaust?); rather, they oppose the *war against memory* that human forgetfulness, whether malign or benign, brings about. And literary thinkers give no guarantee that they will make expression easier, that they will teach us to speak more smoothly—rather than sensitively, and aware of the tongues in our tongue. Yet one of the subjects I want to raise amid these complexities is: we all know that to talk about the Destruction is not like talking about the Age of Wordsworth or the Russian Revolution. Even if the historian's task is always to present the past as still, in some way, contemporaneous, in this case, because of the magnitude of the event—and as I say it I realize "magnitude" is not the right word—and because many of those who suffered that "amputation" (David Vital's phrase) are present to hear us, and want to hear us, and in part have made this conference possible—for those reasons I would like to say something about our audience today: the community we address, whether we do it as historians or as interpreters coming from the study of literature.

There are at least two communities here. I don't refer to historians and literary critics or different types of historians. That difference (types of historians et cetera) also raises issues about language, or the terms of discourse. Those quarrels, however, whether enriching or debilitating, can be overlooked for the time being. What should not be overlooked is the survivor community, which (as Raul Hilberg mentioned) has gradually moved into the historian's range of vision.

After the war it was the perpetrators and the factual reconstruction of every step of the Final Solution that had to be the focus. I also recall being haunted by the behavior of the bystanders: even today, when we have learned more about what the Germans knew or could have known, I remain, concerning the bystander, saddened and disconcerted. But although I barely escaped being a victim myself, the survivors as a group did not strike my attention fully until the Eichmann trial in 1961; I was in Chicago, and heard on radio the testimony of a survivor who had been in a *Sonderkom-*

mando. It was then I understood for the first time the power of witnessing, of testimony. Only, however, after the TV serial "Holocaust" in 1978 did survivors in the New Haven area come forward. They said: after so many in our families lost their life, must they also be deprived of their story? Bad art had a good result. Thirty-five years and more after the event, with grown families, and grandchildren in the offing, survivors wanted to tell stories more true and terrible, more authentic in their depiction of that era. They were ready to be recognized and to transmit their experiences as a "legacy"—the question was whether others were, at last, ready to listen.

The fact that we are here, both communities together, those from the academy and the survivors, as well as friends, teachers, and professionals of both communities, means that we did listen. It does *not* mean that the new and living archive of testimonies being established in New Haven, in Wilmette, and in many other places has been incorporated in the historical consciousness, or that it does not confront the historian with problems. Testimonies are not affidavits in the juridical sense, and although they are documents subject to critical inquiry—Peter Hayes has made that clear—they are not cold pieces of paper like Nazi orders of the Day or railroad schedules for the bureaucracy. Nor are they texts for literary narratologists to practice on. We don't yet have a good term to describe them, in their bewildering, verbally stumbling, and not always factually reliable immediacy. They are oral memoirs, recorded years after the eyewitness they bring. Their power to recreate the emotional and psychological milieu of survivor experience, what was done and suffered daily, cannot be overestimated, even if names or locations are sometimes inaccurately remembered in oral history and there may be a fusion between what was directly witnessed and what was heard from others. (A recent personal corroboration. Writing about a survivor I had met in the 1950s, I gave his name as "Schreiber." I had read and reread the pages where I mention him I don't know how many times. Only when I saw them in print did I realize that his name was not "Schreiber" [Scribe] but "Sprecher" [Speaker]. A mistake with its own logic— he had been a clerk in the camp—but a mistake nevertheless.) The testimonies do not need more interpretation than other documents; they need their own kind of interpretation.

Interviewing has its controllable and uncontrollable sides. How the witness or the interviewer feels on a certain day is, for example, uncontrollable. Ideally there should be a number of reinterviews, to lessen the impact of that variable and to compare the two runs of memory. More controllable is the field interest of the interviewer. A historian looking for specific information, or a psychologist wishing to understand behavior under stress, will put different questions; and they may also use a special methodology. They will produce testimonies of a different kind from those conducted by interviewers (even when the latter are trained in history or psychology) who decide to let the witness keep the initiative as long as possible, to intervene minimally. There is also the problem of the status of the witness, which Primo Levi has discussed with habitual lucidity.

That problem of status bears less on how many times a person has told the story (the stylization of memory, et cetera) than on the vantage point of the survivor. Although the persecutors' attempt to eliminate or silence the witnesses failed, researchers who seek a total picture must rely on the small proportion who survived and a still smaller proportion who could have glimpsed something beyond the immediate terror. The latter witnesses Primo Levi calls "privileged" inmates (e.g., those in sensitive clerical positions) whose life took place in the "gray zone," a region of more than usual moral ambiguity or compromise. Their account of events may therefore be distorted by apologetic motives. But the vast majority who came out of the camps were not in a position to know what was going on. "[I]n the human conditions to which they were subjected," Levi writes in his Preface to *The Drowned and the Saved*, "the prisoners could barely acquire an overall vision of their universe." Let me quote how he follows that statement up.

> The prisoners, above all those who did not understand German, might not even know where in Europe their Lager was situated, having arrived after a slaughterous and tortuous journey in sealed boxcars. They did not know for whom they worked, they did not understand the significance of certain sudden changes in conditions, or the mass transfers. Surrounded by death, the deportee was often in no position to evaluate the extent of the slaughter unfolding before his eyes. The companion who worked beside him today was gone by the morrow: he might be in the hut next

door, or erased from the world, there was no way to know. In short, the prisoner felt overwhelmed by a massive edifice of violence and menace but could not form for himself a representation of it because his eyes were fixed to the ground by every single minute's needs.[1]

Arguably, then, the very characteristic that makes the "normal" testimony valuable—its personal detail and the reflective labor of coming to grips with an event, paralyzing then and even now—is also what limits it. Yet we have increasingly learned to appreciate *local* knowledge: to note the role of accidents, to respect the probability of the improbable, to interpret rather than reject statements that are false. Just one example: a number of women survivors think it a fact that their rations in the Lager were drugged ("doped") or tampered with. Some attribute their lack of menstruation to the tampering, and one of them her lack of affect: "So that we would not feel what was being done to us." In the absence of confirming evidence, is it our duty to contradict them on this point, or to pose questions clarifying the mental state behind their assumption? Contradiction is surely the wrong response, but how interviewers should treat such statements, if they are uneasy about receiving them as part of the record, has not been openly discussed.

Perhaps there is no firm advice to be given. Yet how can we know if we do not face the issue? For those trained to heed the form in which thoughts are expressed, the statement has its own poignancy. It could lead to acceptable rather than aggressive questions. "How long did that feeling of being drugged last? How much came through nevertheless? Does having been drugged *then* make it harder for you to tell your story *now*? Or does it make it less painful?"

You may claim that this line of questioning goes in a psychological direction; perhaps so; yet questioning, I would suggest, insofar as it is called for here, should be done in such a way that the initiative is not taken from the witness. I might have my own theory (is the feeling of being drugged related to shock?, which would still leave unexplained why the drug image is chosen from among other expressive possibilities), but rather than impose a theory the aim should be to allow the one who has suffered all this to have her own word, even if it contradicts what I seem to know.

The task of both historian and literary interpreter is not complete unless this archive of testimonies has pervaded our consciousness and challenged some of our terms of discourse. Larry Langer has said that "our encounter with the narratives of former victims demands a wary intimacy with the story far beyond the passive acceptance of details." That *wary intimacy* cannot come without both real acceptance and analysis—an examination not so much of the factual yield (other sources offer more information and accuracy) but of the language, of the way things impinged, of the social and psychological detail that often escapes the historian's net; an examination too of the personal mode by which we have traditionally transmitted (rather than censored or questioned) experience. For there comes a point at which programmed analysis— analysis for a particular end, even the end of historical precision— turns antagonistic, especially to the story-telling form. Walter Benjamin, indeed, surmised that modern psychological refinement would eventually prevent the transmission of traditions in the form of story-telling—an analytic criterion, or the qualifying it enforces, would compel a divorce between "truth" and "transmissibility" as effectively as theology once did. We would see, or communicate, only what a certain doctrine might permit. We would have meanings, then, and lessons, but not a legacy. In the Jewish tradition, however, at least so far, doctrinal theology has not triumphed; and even if modern conditions reduce the gift of story-telling, or abbreviate it into a gift for jokes, we know that stories are still an essential bond between generations. It may even be that the transition to print culture, from oral to written modes of communication, is being modified by mixed forms like the testimonies.

Except this afternoon, we have not talked at this conference about teaching and education; yet the one thing I am dogmatic about is the power and value, in a presentational frame—a frame for which we need the intellectual wariness as well as empathy of the historian—the *educational* power and value of witness accounts of the Holocaust. Even if we cannot accommodate the two bodies of knowledge—discursive history and this archive of stories—without rough edges and doubts and moments of emotion that threaten the hygiene, the distancing, we academicians adopt, there is every reason to respect oral memoirs even in their most aggadic form. Let us not judge prematurely between the two forms of communication, or quickly harmonize the discursive and oral history. They do different things; yet they may supplement each other even when they stand apart. For example: you can't know if you weren't there, but these witness accounts bridge some of the distance, even as the voice of the survivor tells you insistently that you can't know.

So I ask the historians in this audience to look carefully at this archive, which so many at Yale and the Holocaust Educational Foundation of Illinois are in the process of building and preserving, and to think of the best educational uses for it. Listen to that little voice which comes from some corner of the room, after hearing academic sermons called lectures that try so hard not to be sermons, that is, to stay emotionally clean . . . "Professor, have we really learned anything from what happened?" Or that other voice, more dramatic, but by now also more expected. "I was there."

The term "therapeutic alliance" has passed into common use; what is being asked in this case is also an alliance, but with a supportive dimension that does not aim to cure or to console, but rather to obtain a truthful, if less distanced, history that includes the persons who suffered it. The location of that history, moreover, is not in the witness alone: the experience resonates in the listener as long as there is one. And it is an interesting if disconcerting fact that the impersonality we usually attribute to the researcher may be located as much in the witness as in the maieutic interviewer or interpreter. The witness's stance is not, of course, an objective one, but it is nevertheless an objectification in which the teller does not feel it is only *his* tale. The survivor, in fact, who tells the story often does not feel it to the extent that he thinks he should (like grieving without being able to weep), while the listener—that is, you and I, who cannot tell the story—supplies a field of resonance equivalent to the feeling that once was present and may return.

We talk too glibly in literary studies of a "community of interpreters": in the case of oral testimonies there can be no transmission without witness *and* interviewer *and* interpreter. The process involves a sort of community building, with distinct roles, but also mutual recognition. The oral testimonies are far from self-interpreting even when they fascinate: without a Larry Langer they remain inarticulate, though they have a raw power of figuration and an eloquently fractured idiom. And for theory buffs they provide a challenge too: this genre is a provocation not only to professional history-writing but also to literature, both high and popular. To popular modes because, while nothing is immune from popularization (witness the glossy talk show celebrating the witness), the testimonies do not, generally, give a heroic or even a comfortable picture of the survivors; and to high literature because the unsophistication and verbal stumble of most testimonies doom conventional notions of the *mot juste*.

I would like to say more; I must conclude; I would ask you in this, as in other modes of representation, and heeding Langer, to trust the tale, not the teller, yet to give the teller by the alliance I have mentioned the trust that allows a continued gathering and handing on of this legacy.

Notes on the Contributors

YEHUDA BAUER (Ph.D., Jerusalem) is academic chairman of the Institute of Contemporary Jewry, head of the International Center for the Study of Antisemitism, and Professor of History at the Hebrew University. Among his many publications are *The Holocaust in Historical Perspective* (1978), *American Jewry and the Holocaust* (1981), *A History of the Holocaust* (1982).

CHRISTOPHER R. BROWNING (Ph.D., Wisconsin) has taught at Pacific Lutheran University since 1974, where he is now Professor of History. He is the author of numerous important articles and monographs, including *The Final Solution and the German Foreign Office* (1978) and *Fateful Months: Essays on the Emergence of the Final Solution* (1985), and he is currently preparing *The Final Solution,* a volume in the Yad Vashem comprehensive history of the Holocaust.

SAUL FRIEDLÄNDER, Professor of History at the universities of Tel Aviv and California at Los Angeles, has published, among many significant titles, *Pius XII and the Third Reich* (1966), *Prelude to Downfall: Hitler and the United States, 1939–1941* (1967), *When Memory Comes* (1979), and *Reflections of Nazism* (1984).

ROBERT GELLATELY (Ph.D., London School of Economics and Political Science) is Professor of History at Huron College, University of Western Ontario. He is the author of *The Politics of Economic*

Despair (1974) and *The Gestapo and German Society: Enforcing Racial Policy, 1933–1945* (1990).

GEOFFREY H. HARTMAN (Ph.D., Yale) is Karl Young Professor of English and Chairman of the Comparative Literature Department at Yale, as well as Revson Project Director at Yale's Video Archive for Holocaust Testimonies. In addition to numerous works of literary criticism, he has edited *Bitburg in Moral and Political Perspective* (1986).

PETER HAYES (Ph.D., Yale) is Associate Professor of History and German at Northwestern University and the author of *Industry and Ideology: IG Farben in the Nazi Era* (1987), which received the Biennial Book Prize of the Conference Group for Central European History of the American Historical Association.

RAUL HILBERG (Ph.D., Columbia), John G. McCullough Professor of Political Science at the University of Vermont, pioneered the study of the Holocaust and is widely celebrated for his monumental *The Destruction of the European Jews* (1st ed., 1961; 2nd ed., 1985).

STEVEN T. KATZ (Ph.D., Cambridge) is Professor of Philosophy and Chair of the Department of Near Eastern Studies at Cornell University and the author or editor of numerous books, including *Post Holocaust Dialogues: Studies in Twentieth Century Jewish Thought* (1983). Harvard University Press will shortly publish his three-volume work *The Holocaust in Historical Context*.

CLAUDIA KOONZ (Ph.D., Rutgers) is Professor of History at Duke University and the author of several widely cited essays, as well as *Mothers in the Fatherland: Women, the Family, and Nazi Politics* (1987).

BEREL LANG (Ph.D., Columbia), Professor of Philosophy and Humanistic Studies at the State University of New York at Albany, is the author of, among other works, *Act and Idea: Aspects of Nazi Genocide* (1990).

LAWRENCE LANGER (Ph.D., Harvard) holds the Alumnae Chair in English at Simmons College. His publications include *The Holocaust and the Literary Imagination* (1975), *The Age of Atrocity: Death in Modern Literature* (1978), *Versions of Survival: The Holocaust and the Human Spirit* (1982), and *Holocaust Testimonies: The Ruins of Memory* (1991).

FRANKLIN H. LITTELL (Ph.D., Yale; D. Theo., Marburg) is Emeritus Professor of Religion at Temple University and the Ida E. King Distinguished Visiting Professor of Holocaust Studies at Stockton State College (N.J.). He has served on both the International Council of Yad Vashem and, since its inception, on the U.S. Holocaust Memorial Council. Among his many publications are *The German Church Struggle and the Holocaust* (with Hubert G. Locke, 1974) and *The Crucifixion of the Jews* (1975).

MICHAEL R. MARRUS (Ph.D., Berkeley) is Professor of History at the University of Toronto. He has written *The Politics of Assimilation: The French Jewish Community at the Time of the Dreyfus Affair* (1971), *Vichy France and the Jews* (with Robert Paxton, 1981), *The Unwanted: European Refugees in the Twentieth Century* (1985), and *The Holocaust in History* (1987).

HANS MOMMSEN (Ph.D., Tübingen) is Professor of Modern History at the University of the Ruhr in Bochum, Germany. Widely recognized as the most articulate representative of the "functionalist" school of German historians, his publications include *Beamtentum im Dritten Reich* (1966), *Nationale Frage und Arbeiterbewegung* (1979), and *Die verspielte Freiheit: Der Weg der Republik von Weimar in den Untergang 1918 bis 1933* (1989). He is perhaps best known to English speakers for his essay "The Realization of the Unthinkable: The 'Final Solution of the Jewish Question' in the Third Reich" (English translation, 1986).

ALVIN H. ROSENFELD (Ph.D., Brown) is Professor of English and Director of Jewish Studies at Indiana University. He has published, among other works, *Confronting the Holocaust: The Impact of Elie Wiesel* (co-edited with Irving Greenberg, 1979), *A Double Dying: Reflections on Holocaust Literature* (1980), *The Murders at the Bullenhuser Damm* (by Günther Schwarberg, co-translated with Erna Rosenfeld, 1984), and *Imagining Hitler* (1985).

NECHAMA TEC (Ph.D., Columbia) is Professor of Sociology at the University of Connecticut at Stamford and the author of *Dry Tears: The Story of a Lost Childhood* (1982), *When Light Pierced the Darkness* (1986), and *In the Lion's Den: The Life of Oswald Rufiesen* (1990), among many works.

DAVID VITAL (Ph.D., Oxford) currently serves as Nahum Goldmann Professor of Diplomacy at Tel Aviv University and Klutznick Professor of Jewish Civilization at Northwestern University. He is the author of seven books, including *The Origins of Zionism* (1975), *Zionism: The Formative Years* (1982), *Zionism: The Crucial Phase* (1987), and *The Future of the Jews: People at the Crossroads?* (1990).

JAMES E. YOUNG (Ph.D., California, Santa Cruz) is Assistant Professor of English and Judaic Studies at the University of Massachusetts at Amherst. He is the author of *Writing and Rewriting the Holocaust* (1988) and the forthcoming *The Texture of Memory: Holocaust Memorials and Meaning in Europe, Israel, and America,* and is Guest Curator of "The Art of Memory," an exhibition to be installed at the Jewish Museum in New York in 1992.

Notes

Introduction

1. Kenneth Seeskin, "What Philosophy Can and Cannot Say about Evil," in *Echoes from the Holocaust,* ed. Alan Rosenberg and Gerald Myers (Philadelphia: Temple University Press, 1988), p. 102.

2. Hans Mommsen, "Die Realisierung des Utopischen: Die 'Endlösung der Judenfrage' im 'Dritten Reich'," *Geschichte und Gesellschaft* 9 (1983): 420.

3. For both quotations, see Istvan Deak, "The Incomprehensible Holocaust," *New York Review of Books* (September 28, 1989), pp. 68, 72.

4. Arno Mayer, *Why Did the Heavens Not Darken?* (New York: Pantheon Books, 1988), pp. viii, xv, 3.

5. See Christopher Browning, "The Holocaust Distorted," *Dissent* 36 (1989): 397–400; Daniel Goldhagen, "False Witness," *The New Republic* (April 17, 1989), pp. 39–44; Lucy S. Dawidowicz, "Perversions of the Holocaust," *Commentary* 88 (October 1989): 56–60; and J. P. Stern, "Germans and the German Past," *London Review of Books* (December 12, 1989), pp. 7–8.

6. In Rosenberg and Myers, eds., *Echoes from the Holocaust,* p. 103.

The "Final Solution": On the Unease in Historical Interpretation

I wish to thank Geulie Arad, Dan Diner, Eichanan Friedländer, Carlo Ginzburg, and Wulf Kansteiner, as well as members of the Critical Theory Seminar at UCLA, for their most valuable insights. This text was originally published in *History and Memory: Studies in Representation of the Past,* vol. 1, no. 2 (Autumn 1989); and in German translation in Walter H. Pehle, *Der Historische Ort des Nationalsozialismus* (Frankfurt: Fischer, 1990).

1. Walter Benjamin, "Geschichtsphilosophische Thesen," in *Illuminationen. Ausgewaehlte Schriften* (Frankfurt: Suhrkamp, 1961), pp. 268–69. The English translation is entitled *Illumination* (New York: Harcourt, Brace and World, 1969) p. 254.

2. For the significance of Walter Benjamin's redemptive vision of history, see Stephane Moses, "The Theological-Political Model of History in the Thought of Walter Benjamin," in *History and Memory,* vol. 1, no. 2 (Autumn 1989).

3. Arno Mayer, *Why Did the Heavens Not Darken? The "Final Solution" in History* (New York: Pantheon, 1989), p. xv.

4. Charles S. Maier, *The Unmasterable Past* (Cambridge: Harvard University Press, 1988), p. 92.

5. Raul Hilberg, in *Writing and the Holocaust,* ed. Berel Lang (New York: Holmes & Meier, 1988), p. 274. See also Saul Friedländer, "From Antisemitism to Extermination: A Historiographical Study of Nazi Policies Towards the Jews and an Essay in Interpretation," *Yad Vashem Studies* 16 (1984): 49–50.

6. See Martin Broszat and Saul Friedländer, "A Controversy About the Historicization of National-Socialism," *New German Critique,* no. 44 (Spring/Summer 1988): 81–126.

7. See, especially, Walter Laqueur, *The Terrible Secret* (Boston: Little, Brown, 1980), but also Hans Mommsen, "Was haben die Deutschen vom Voelkermord an den Juden gewusst?" in *Der Judenpogrom 1938. Von der "Reichskristallnacht" zum Voelkermord,* Walter H. Pehle, ed. (Frankfurt am Main: Fischer, 1988). This seems no less true for the Jewish Yishuv in Palestine; see, for instance, Dina Porat, *The Blue and Yellow Stars of David* (Cambridge, Mass.: Harvard University Press, 1990).

8. Robert Conquest, *The Great Terror: Stalin's Purge of the Thirties* (London: Macmillan, 1969), and, particularly, *The Harvest of Sorrow: Soviet Collectivization and the Terror-Famine* (New York: Oxford University Press, 1986).

9. For an analysis of this fuzziness, see Nathan Rotenstreich, "Can Evil be Banal?," *The Philosophical Forum,* vol. 16, nos. 1–2, (1984–85).

10. Stanley Cavell, *In Quest of the Ordinary: Lines of Skepticism and Romanticism* (Chicago: University of Chicago Press, 1988), p. 155.

11. Sigmund Freud, "The 'Uncanny'," *Collected Papers* 4 (New York: Basic Books, 1959), p. 385.

12. For further analysis, we would need a new category equivalent to Kant's category of the sublime, but *specifically meant to capture inexpressible horror.* In *Reflections of Nazism* (New York: Harper & Row, 1984), I tried to describe one of the elements of the *Rausch* as the exaltation stemming from vision of utter destruction.

13. Alan Montefiore, "The Moral Philosopher's View of the Holocaust," in *European Judaism,* Marcel Marcus, ed. (London, 1977), pp. 13–22.

14. Eberhard Jaeckel, "Die elende Praxis der Untersteller," *Historikerstreit* (Munich: Piper, 1987), p. 118.

15. Some aspects of this issue were discussed at a conference held by the Center for Biomedical Ethics at the University of Minnesota in May 1989.

16. Otto Dov Kulka, "Critique of Judaism in European Thought: On the Historical Meaning of Modern Antisemitism," *The Jerusalem Quarterly* 52 (Fall 1989), p. 5.

17. Letter to the author, June 29, 1989.

18. Joern Ruesen, "The Development of Narrative Competence in Historical Learning—An Ontogenetical Hypothesis Concerning Moral Consciousness," *History and Memory,* vol. 1, no. 2.

19. If the Nazi reaction to the threat of modernity was the dream and realization of a racial utopia from which all racially different—inferior—nocive elements would be eliminated, then persecutions and extermination of the "nocive" elements within the domain belonging to the *Volksgemeinschaft* are indeed explainable in terms of this mad logic. But how should one interpret, in such a case, the fact that the various "asocial" and "inferior" elements were left untouched outside of the limits assigned to the *Volksgemeinschaft* (homosexuals and the mentally ill were not shipped to camps or killing installations from France, Greece, or Poland), whereas one specific group was hounded to the most hidden recesses of the whole continent in order to be exterminated? And if the fear of Bolshevism and its annihilation practices—the most radical "social therapy" engendered by the rise of industrial societies and modernity—were at the root of the Nazi exterminations, one wonders why the first victims of annihilation were not the Communist political prisoners in concentration camps, Communist resistance fighters caught by the Germans all over the continent, etc. In short, the "Final Solution" can only very indirectly be linked to the very real upheavals and anxieties created by modernity, and this not without the prism of antisemitism.

20. Joern Ruesen, "Development."

21. The almost unavoidable fall back into the "exemplary" creates an extraordinary problem for literary and artistic representation. I have

tried to indicate elsewhere that ultimately, the "tragic-didactic" mode of representation of the *Sho'ah* was almost unavoidable, but entirely out of touch with present-day artistic and literary sensitivity. See Saul Friedländer, "The Shoah between Memory and History," *The Jerusalem Quarterly,* no. 53 (Winter 1990): 722.

22. Isaac Deutscher, *The Non-Jewish Jew and Other Essays* (London, 1968), pp. 163–64.

Holocaust and Genocide: Some Comparisons

1. See my article "Is The Holocaust Explicable?" in *Remembering for the Future* (Oxford: Pergamon Press, 1989), vol. 2, pp. 1967–75.

2. Yitzhak Arad et al, ed., *Documents on the Holocaust* (Jerusalem: Yad Vashem, 1981), pp. 344–45.

3. Yehuda Bauer, "Jews, Gypsies and Slavs—Policies of the Third Reich," in *UNESCO Yearbook on Peace and Conflict Studies* (Westport, Ct.: Greenwood Press, 1985), pp. 73–100.

Ideology, State Power, and Mass Murder/Genocide

1. I have omitted footnotes in order to use the space available here for the fullest possible development of my thesis. Full references and pertinent supporting material will appear in my forthcoming multi-volume study, tentatively entitled *The Holocaust in Historical Context*.

The History of Evil and the Future of the Holocaust

1. For an account of the former of these revisionist efforts, see the exchange between Martin Brozsat and Saul Friedländer, "A Controversy about the Historicization of National Socialism," *New German Critique* 44 (1988):81–126. The second group of writers referred to, who in varying degrees inculpate the Jews in their own destruction, come from a notable variety of ideological and historical directions—including, for example, not only Hannah Arendt's extravagent claims in *Eichmann in Jerusalem* but Raul Hilberg's conception of "anticipatory compliance" in his classic, *The Destruction of the European Jews*.

2. For the distinction of "external" versus "internal" history, see R. G. Collingwood, *The Idea of History* (Oxford: Clarendon Press, 1946), pp. 213 ff.

3. On this and the other Poznan speeches, see Bradley F. Smith, *Heinrich Himmler* (Stanford: Hoover Institution, 1971).

4. For an elaboration of this claim, see Berel Lang, *Act and Idea in the Nazi Genocide* (Chicago: University of Chicago Press, 1990), chap. 2.

The Use and Misuse of the Holocaust

1. Saul Friedländer, *Reflections of Nazism: An Essay on Kitsch and Death*, trans. Thomas Weyr (New York: Harper & Row, 1986), p. 27. Cf. Modris Eksteins, *Rites of Spring: The Great War and the Birth of the Modern Age* (Boston: Houghton Mifflin, 1989) for some related views.

2. Paula Hyman, "New Debate on the Holocaust," *New York Times Magazine*, September 14, 1980, pp. 65–68. See especially Elie Wiesel, "Does the Holocaust Lie beyond the Reach of Art?" *New York Times*, April 17, 1983.

3. Alvin Rosenfeld, "The Holocaust According to William Styron," *Midstream*, December 1979, p. 49.

4. Edward Alexander, "Stealing the Holocaust," *Midstream*, November 1980, p. 49. Cf. Yehuda Bauer, "Whose Holocaust?" in *Genocide and Human Rights*, Jack N. Porter, ed. (Washington, D.C.: University Press of America, 1982), pp. 35–46.

5. Robert Alter, "Deformations of the Holocaust," *Commentary*, February, 1981, p. 49.

6. Jacob Neusner, *The Jewish War against the Jews: Reflections on Golah, Sho'ah and Torah* (New York: Ktav Publishers, 1984), chap. 6; idem, *Stranger at Home: "The Holocaust," Zionism, and American Judaism* (Chicago: University of Chicago Press, 1981), p. 80.

7. "Transmitting Our Faith," *Direction*, December 1982, p. 4.

8. Judith E. Doneson, "History and Television, 1978–1988: A Survey of Dramatizations of the Holocaust," *Dimensions: A Journal of Holocaust Studies*, vol. 4, no. 3 (1989):23.

9. *Days of Remembrance: A Department of Defense Guide for Annual Commemorative Observances*, DoD/FMP.18 [1989].

10. Ibid, p. 2.

11. Adam Clymer, "Public Is Split on Bitburg, Poll Finds," *New York Times*, May 8, 1985.

12. "Summary of Salient Questions Posed by the Roper and Harris Surveys of American Opinion on the Holocaust and Nazi War Criminals (1985-1986)," ADL International Center for Holocaust Studies, 1986.

13. Louis Harris, "Americans Favor Keeping Waldheim Out of U.S.," press release, July 14, 1986.

14. Dennis B. Klein, "The Will to Forget," *New York Times*, May 5, 1986.

15. Yitzhak Mais, "Institutionalizing the Holocaust," *Midstream*, December 1988, pp. 16-20.

16. Ian Buruma has recently noted how, in another context, "the search for identity politicizes activities—religion, scholarship, philosophy—which should not be subject to political aims, and it depoliticizes the very spheres of public life that should be; party politics, international relations, and so on." "From Hirohito to Heimat," *New York Review of Books*, October 26, 1989, p. 43.

17. Addressing an Israeli audience, Bauer refers to "the conscious or unconscious effort made in this country to create a Holocaust myth that is totally different from the reality it supposedly relates to. If two-and-a-half million Jews were gassed at Auschwitz, that is 'better' for propaganda than the truth, as though the truth were not horrible enough." "Auschwitz: The Dangers of Distortion," *Jerusalem Post International Edition*, September 30, 1989, p. 7. For a quite different complaint by another Israeli writer see Shlomo Avineri, "Holocaust: A Shift in Focus," ibid., August 26, 1989, p. 8.

18. See James E. Young, "The Texture of Memory: Holocaust Memorials and Meaning," *Holocaust and Genocide Studies* 4 (1989): 63-76.

19. Neusner, *Stranger at Home*, p. 90.

20. See, for example, the manner in which the aftermath of the Holocaust is to be portrayed for the public in the Battery Park Holocaust Museum being planned for New York City. *A Living Memorial to the Holocaust: Museum of Jewish Heritage* (New York, [1988]): " . . . Palestine posed the only answer for the majority of survivors. This Saved Remnant now aspired, above all else, to Eretz Yisrael, the Land of Israel. . . . Sooner or later, each Holocaust survivor realizes that he or she bears a crucial message for every man, woman and child in the modern world. That message is borne partly in the lessons of the War Criminals trials, which have continued to resonate to the present day and which the Museum will present. But it resides even more strongly in the affirmative resolution of the survivors to teach the lessons of renewal and redemption—forged by a journey through darkness into light—which ultimately only they can convey."

21. Immanuel Jacobovits, "Some Personal, Theological and Religious Responses to the Holocaust," *Holocaust and Genocide Studies* 3 (1988):371–72.

22. "What lies at the root of such feelings is not just the memory of Nazi murders. The crucial fact is that the Nazis systematically *humiliated* the Jews, that they stamped upon the Jews their marks of sadism and superiority, that they made the Jews grovel and hop, that, with at least some success, they cunningly undermined the humanity of the Jews; and surely this must have shaken Jewish self-understanding and self-regard." Irving Howe, "American Jews and Israel," *Tikkun*, May/June 1989, p. 71.

23. Alvin H. Rosenfeld, "The Holocaust in Jewish Memory and Public Memory," *Dimensions*, Fall 1986, p. 12.

24. See Deborah E. Lipstadt, "Invoking the Holocaust," *Judaism*, Summer 1981, pp. 335–43.

25. Philip Lopate, "Resistance to the Holocaust," *Tikkun*, May/June, 1989, p. 56.

26. Friedländer, *Reflections of Nazism*, p. 71.

27. See Rosemary Radforth Ruether and Herman J. Ruether, *The Wrath of Jonah* (New York: Harper & Row, 1989).

28. See Yehuda Bauer, "Begin and Schmidt," *Jerusalem Post International Edition*, March 14-20, 1982; Susan Hattis Rolef, "Use and Misuse," *Jerusalem Post International Edition*, April 29–May 6, 1984.

29. "Shamir Compares Arafat to Hitler," *Canadian Jewish News*, March 9, 1989.

30. *New York Times*, April 6, 1989.

31. Prime Minister's Conference on Jewish Solidarity with Israel, "United We Stand," insert in the *Jerusalem Post International Edition*, week ending April 1, 1989.

32. According to a recent Hanoch Smith Research Center poll, a striking 68 percent of Israelis agreed "that the Arabs would commit a holocaust against the Jews in Israel if they could." (*New York Times*, April 2, 1989.) Eighty-one percent of Likud voters felt this way, as did 48 percent of Labor voters.

33. See the comments of Dedi Zucker in "License for Violence," *Jerusalem Post International Edition*, July 29, 1989.

34. A. B. Yehoshua, *Between Right and Right*, trans. Arnold Schwartz (Garden City, N.Y., 1981), p. 17. Cf. Avishai Margalit, "The Kitsch of Israel," *New York Review of Books*, November 24, 1988, p. 23.

35. Adi Ophir, "On Sanctifying the Holocaust: An Anti-Theological Treatise," *Tikkun*, vol. 2 (1987), p. 63.

36. Charles Hoffman, "The 'Me Generation' and Israel," *Jerusalem Post Internationl Edition*, June 17, 1989.

37. Doneson, "History and Television," p. 27.

38. Lopate, "Resistance to the Holocaust," p. 59.

39. I have tried to summarize recent historiography in *The Holocaust in History* (New York: New American Library, 1989).

40. Peter Steinfels, "On the Road to Extermination: Historians Ponder Lessons of Kristallnacht," *New York Times*, November 9, 1988.

41. Abraham H. Foxman, "When the West Lost Its Bearings," *Dimensions*, vol. 4, no. 2 (1988):27–29.

42. Charles S. Maier, *The Unmasterable Past: History, Holocaust, and German National Identity* (Cambridge, Mass.: Harvard University Press, 1988), pp. 192–93, n. 28.

43. Michael R. Marrus, *The Holocaust in History* (Hanover, N.H.: University Press of New England, 1987), pp. 18–25.

44. Henry R. Huttenbach, "Locating the Holocaust on the Genocide Spectrum: Towards a Methodology of Definition and Categorization," *Holocaust and Genocide Studies* 3 (1988):291.

45. Eberhard Jäckel, "The Miserable Practice of the Insinuators: The Uniqueness of the National-Socialist Crime Cannot Be Denied," *Yad Vashem Studies* 19 (1988):111. See the related point of Hagen Schulze: "Would National-Socialist crimes be somehow deemed less reprehensible even if some comparisons were possible? And did not a denial of comparability also lead to evasive moral judgments? The absolute singular could be seen as an aberration, outside history, and thus as not morally binding any more than the crime of someone clearly insane." Quoted in Maier, *Unmasterable Past*, pp. 53–54.

After the Catastrophe: Aspects of Contemporary Jewry

1. One of the greater historiographical absurdities that one encounters in the present context is the notion that modern Israel resulted from, was, so to speak, born of, the Holocaust—perhaps as a bone thrown to the unfortunates by belatedly and guiltily benevolent powers as compensation for miseries suffered. Nothing could be further from the truth, as even a superficial examination of British and American policy in the immediate postwar period will show.

2. Jizchak [Yitzhak] Fritz Baer, *Galut* (Berlin: Schocken, 1936), p. 14. English translation by R. Warshow (New York, 1947), pp. 18–19.

3. "Be heedful of the ruling power for they bring no man nigh to them save for their own need: they seem to be friends such time as it is to their gain, but they stand not with a man in his time of stress." Avot, 2:3.

4. Wise to Roosevelt, December 2, 1942. S. S. Wise Papers, Archives of the American Jewish Historical Society.

5. Saskia Baron in *The Listener,* October 15, 1987.

6. "The near hysteria which has swept the country since the bomb explosion (at the synagogue on the Rue Copernic) shows how very near the skin are French susceptibilities to the charge of anti-semitism. The fact that the Jewish community in France, which is the fourth biggest Jewish community in the world, is well integrated in the establishment has long been manifest. At the same time M [Raymond] Barre himself, in an unguarded moment, showed that the average Frenchman still regards Jews as a race apart when he protested that the bomb had killed 'innocent French people' when it had really been meant for Jews." Thus the Paris correspondent for *The Times* [London], October 9, 1980.

7. *New York Times,* February 13, 1989.

8. "Burbank with a Baedeker: Bleistein with a Cigar," in T. S. Eliot, *Collected Poems 1909–1962* (New York: Harcourt Brace Jovanovich 1970), p. 33.

9. "Cub." *Times Literary Supplement,* March 23, 1984.

10. It must be conceded that Reading's poem is somewhat more ambiguous than Eliot's, less forthright too. When, following its publication in the *Times Literary Supplement,* there was a fuss which was immediately reflected in the columns of both the *TLS* and *The Times* itself, the editor of the *TLS* defended his contributor on the grounds, in part, that his poem was complex and had been misunderstood. But *had* it been misunderstood? One of the fiercest attacks was based precisely on it having been taken as arguing that "since clearly the duty of such vermin [the Israelis] is to be fired on and patiently accept their extinction, they had no motive to retaliate. [And] to associate the Jewish religion, first with excrement . . . and then with hatred that is genetically determined— what is this, if not antisemitism, in its pure, unreconstructed form." (Roger Scruton, "Race hatred the antis ignore," *The Times* [London], April 3, 1984.)

For the author of this chapter a poem speaking of "a fat juicy jeep of Israelis" being shot at—whereupon "one of the front seat occupants oozed red"—evoked an older image: "Und wenn das Judenblut vom Messer spritzt, dann geht's noch mal so gut" (from what was in its time one of the most popular variants on the official Nazi marching song, the "Horst Wessel Lied").

I pointed this out to the Editor of the *TLS,* but he was unwilling to publish my letter, replying, courteously enough, that like so many others I had evidently misunderstood both the poem and the poet's intention.

The Reaction of the German Population to the Anti-Jewish Persecution and the Holocaust

1. For detailed information about the pertinent literature and the sources cited in this chapter, see Hans Mommsen, "Was haben die Deutschen vom Völkermord an den Juden gewusst," in *Der Judenpogrom 1938. Von der "Reichskristallnacht" zum Völkermord,* Walter H. Pehle, ed. (Frankfurt: Fischer, 1988), pp. 176 ff.
2. Christopher Browning, *Fateful Months: Essays on the Emergence of the Final Solution* (New York: Holmes & Meier, 1985), pp. 8 ff.
3. See Marlis Steinert, *Hitler's War and the Germans* (Athens, Ohio: Ohio University Press, 1977), pp. 140–47.
4. Otto Dov Kulka, "'Public Opinion' in Nazi Germany and the Jewish Question," *The Jerusalem Quarterly* 25/26 (1982):38 ff; Ian Kershaw, "German Popular Opinion and the 'Jewish Question', 1939–1943: Some Further Reflections," in *Die Juden im nationalsozialistischen Deutschland/The Jews in Germany, 1933–1945,* Arnold Paucker, ed. (Tübingen: J. C. B. Mohr, 1986), pp. 365–408; Sarah Gordon, *Hitler, Germans, and the 'Jewish Question'* (Princeton: Princeton University Press, 1984).
5. Martin Broszat, Elke Fröhlich, and Falk Wiesemann, eds., *Bayern in der NS-Zeit. Soziale Lage und politisches Verhalten der Bevölkerung im Spiegel vertraulicher Berichte,* vol. 1 (Munich: Oldenbourg, 1977).
6. Hans-Heinrich Wilhelm, "Wie geheim war die Endlösung?," in *Miscellanea. Festschrift für Helmut Krausnick zum 75. Geburtstag,* Wolfgang Benz, ed. (Stuttgart: Deutsche Verlags-Anstalt, 1980), pp. 136 ff; Raul Hilberg, "German Railroads/Jewish Souls," *Society* 14 (December 1976):60–74.
7. See Erik Goldhagen, "Albert Speer, Himmler and the Secrecy of the Final Solution," *Midstream* 17 (October 1971):43–50; Hans Mommsen, "Spandauer Tagebücher. Bemerkungen zu den Aufzeichnungen Albert Speers im Internationalen Militärgefängnis 1946–1966," *Politische Vierteljahresschrift* 17 (1976):111 f.
8. See Otto Dov Kulka and Aron Rodrigue, "The German Population and the Jews in the Third Reich: Recent Publications and Trends

in Research on German Society and the 'Jewish Question'," *Yad Vashem Studies* 16 (1984):435; Kershaw, "German Popular Opinion," pp. 380 f.

9. See D. L. Niewyk, *The Jews in Weimar Germany* (Baton Rouge: Louisiana State University Press, 1980).

10. Michael Müller-Claudius, *Der Antisemitismus und das deutsche Verhängnis* (Frankfurt: J. Knecht, 1948), pp. 169 ff; cf. Kershaw, "German Popular Opinion," pp. 374 ff.

11. Peter Merkl, *The Making of a Stormtrooper* (Princeton: Princeton University Press, 1980), pp. 222 ff.; compare Gordon, *Hitler,* pp. 55 ff.

12. Cf. Johannes Ludwig, *Boykott, Enteignung, Mord. Die 'Entjudung' der deutschen Wirtschaft* (Hamburg: Facta Oblita, 1989); Avraham Barkai, *Vom Boykott zur 'Entjudung'. Der wirtschaftliche Existenzkampf der Juden im Dritten Reich 1933–1943* (Frankfurt: Fischer, 1988).

13. Cf. Lösener Files, Institut für Zeitgeschichte (IfZ), F71/2.

14. Christopher Browning, "The Government Experts," in *The Holocaust: Ideology, Bureaucracy, and Genocide,* Henry Friedländer and Sybil Milton, eds. (Millwood, N.Y.: Kraus International, 1980), pp. 189 ff.

15. Cf. Lothar Gruchmann, *Justiz im Dritten Reich. Anpassung und Unterwerfung in der Ära Gürtner* (Munich: Oldenbourg, 1988), pp. 487 ff.

16. See Hans Mommsen, "Die Funktion des Antisemitismus im 'Dritten Reich': Das Beispiel des Novemberpogroms," in *Antisemitismus. Von religiöser Judenfeindschaft zur Rassenideologie,* Günter Brakelmann and Martin Rosowski, eds. (Göttingen: Vandenhoeck & Ruprecht, 1989), p. 186.

17. See Dieter Obst, "'Reichskristallnacht'. Reaktionen der Bevölkerung auf den Novemberpogrom" (Ph.D. diss., Bochum, 1989).

18. Ian Kershaw, *Popular Opinion and Political Dissent in the Third Reich: Bavaria, 1933–1945* (Oxford: Clarendon Press, 1983), p. 275.

19. Cf. Kulka, "'Public Opinion' in Nazi Germay," p. 45.

20. Quoted by Gordon in *Hitler,* p. 193.

21. Ruth Andreas-Friedrich, *Der Schattenmann. Tagebuchaufzeichnungen 1938–1945,* new ed. (Frankfurt: Suhrkamp, 1983), pp. 103 ff.

22. Walter Laqueur, *The Terrible Secret: Suppression of the Truth about Hitler's "Final Solution"* (Boston: Little, Brown, 1980), pp. 202 ff.

23. See Arno J. Mayer, *Why Did the Heavens Not Darken? The "Final Solution" in History* (New York: Pantheon, 1988), pp. 236 ff; and the controversy in Eberhard Jäckel and Jürgen Rohwer, eds., *Der Mord an den Juden im Zweiten Weltkrieg* (Stuttgart: Deutsche Verlags Anstalt, 1985), especially pp. 114 ff.

24. Cf. Hans Mommsen, "The Realization of the Unthinkable: The 'Final Solution of the Jewish Question' in the Third Reich," in *The Policies of Genocide: Jews and Soviet Prisoners of War in Nazi Germany*, Gerhard Hirschfeld, ed. (London: Allen & Unwin, 1986), pp. 114, 117 ff.

25. Quoted in Eberhard Klügel, *Die lutherische Landeskirche Hannover und ihr Bischof 1933–1945. Dokumente* (Berlin: Lutherisches Verlagshaus, 1965), p. 203.

26. See Herbert and Sybille Obenaus, *"Schreiben, wie es wirklich war!" Aufzeichnungen Karl Dürkefäldens aus den Jahren 1933–1945* (Hanover, 1985), pp. 111 ff.

27. Helmuth James von Moltke, *Briefe an Freya 1939–1945* (Munich: 1988), p. 420; Ulrich von Hassell, *Die Hassell-Tagebücher 1938–1944. Aufzeichnungen vom Anderen Deutschland* (Berlin: Siedler, 1988), p. 365, also p. 330.

28. Wilhelm, "Wie geheim war die Endlösung," pp. 136 ff.

29. Jochen Klepper, *Unter dem Schatten Deiner Flügel. Aus den Tagebüchern: Die Jahre 1932–1942* (Stuttgart: Deutsche Verlags-Anstalt, 1956), pp. 1130 ff.

30. Cf. Martin Broszat, "Hitler und die Genesis der 'Endlösung'. Aus Anlass der Thesen von David Irving," *Vierteljahrshefte für Zeitgeschichte* 25 (1977): 739–75.

Genocide and Eugenics: The Language of Power

I would like to thank Peter Hayes for his editorial help and Andrew Gordon, Alex Keyssar, Joanne Passaro, and William Reddy for their thoughtful discussions of language and bio-political issues.

1. For example, in this volume Yehuda Bauer describes the "intellectual shift" that categorized people into abstractions; Nechama Tec asks why a few ordinary people resisted this lethal conceptual revolution and did not see people as things; and Steven Katz writes of an ideology driven by state power.

2. This does not mean that murderous eugenic policies had uniquely Germanic roots, as implied by such studies as Yves Ternon and Socrate Helman, *Le Massacre des aliéns. Dès Théoriciens nazis aux practiéns SS* (Paris: Casterman, 1971).

3. Stephan Chorover, *From Genesis to Genocide* (Cambridge, Mass.: MIT Press, 1979).

4. Amitai Etzioni, *Genetic Fix: The Next Technological Revolution* (New York: Harper & Row, 1973), pp. 102, 120, 130.

5. As Loren Graham notes, while Communists welcomed many eugenics ideas, they did not have access to a powerful, organized state;

"Science and Values: The Eugenics Movement in Germany and Russia in the 1920s," *American Historical Review* 82 (1977): 1133–64.

6. Jacob H. Landman, *Human Sterilization: The History of the Sexual Sterilization Movement* (New York: Macmillan, 1932), pp. 14–15.

7. Allan Chase, *Legacy of Malthus* (New York: Knopf, 1976); and Mark Haller, *Eugenics: Hereditarian Attitudes in American Thought* (New Brunswick, N.J.: Rutgers University Press, 1963).

8. Wilhelm Frick, "Bevölkerungs- und Rassenpolitik" (Langensalza, 1933), a pamphlet based on a speech given on June 28, 1933, p. 7. Here Frick guessed that as many as 500,000 Germans might be affected.

9. Equal numbers of men and women were sterilized. Because sterilized people automatically could not marry, an individual's sterilization became public knowledge. In a system that enjoined all citizens to reproduce, the victims faced not only personal loneliness but public ostracism. Jews were not subjected to eugenic scrutiny, and, except for the notorious concentration camp experiments, were not sterilized; Daniel Kevles, *In the Name of Eugenics* (New York: Knopf, 1985). One advocate of sterilization suggested that over ten million Americans might be candidates; Paul Popenoe, "Eugenic Sterilization in California: The Number of Persons Needing Sterilization," *Journal of Heredity* 19 (September 1928):405–11.

10. Zygmunt Bauman, *Modernity and the Holocaust* (Ithaca: Cornell University Press, 1989), pp. 13, 15.

11. Zygmunt Bauman, "The Scandal of Ambivalence," unpublished paper, quoted with the permission of the author.

12. Thomas Kuhn, *The Structure of Scientific Revolutions,* 2nd ed. (Chicago: University of Chicago Press, 1970), pp. 52-92. Bruno Latour discusses developments when "the forces are pulling in the same direction"; *The Pasteurization of France,* trans. Alan Sheridan and John Law (Cambridge: Harvard University Press, 1988), p. 120.

13. Latour, *Pasteurization,* pp. 146–50. On p. 148 he says, "There are not two ways of proving and convincing. There is no essential difference between the human or social sciences and the exact or natural sciences, because there is no more science than there is society."

14. Theobald Land, quoted in Robert Proctor, *Racial Hygiene: Medicine under the Nazis* (Cambridge: Harvard University Press, 1988), p. 30. This phrase reappeared throughout local discussions; see the racial education reports in Nordrhein-Westfälisches Staatsarchiv Münster (hereafter NWSM), Prov. Schulkollegium/6452.

15. Götz Aly and Karl Heinz Roth, *Die restlose Erfassung. Volkszählen, Identifizieren, Aussondern im Nationalsozialismus* (Berlin: Rotbuch, 1984); Gisela Bock, *Zwangssterilisation im Nationalsozialismus.*

Studien zur Rassenpolitik und Frauenpolitik (Opladen: Westdeutscher, 1986); Christian Ganssmüller, *Die Erbgesundheitspolitik des Dritten Reiches. Planung, Durchführung und Durchsetzung* (Cologne: Böhlau, 1987); David Gasman, *The Scientific Origins of National Socialism* (London: Macdonald, 1971); Michael Kater, *Doctors under Hitler* (Chapel Hill: University of North Carolina Press, 1989); Ernst Klee, *Was sie taten—Was sie wurden. Ärzte, Juristen und andere Beteiligte am Kranken- oder Judenmord* (Frankfurt: Fischer, 1986); Fridolf Kudlien, *Ärzte im Nationalsozialismus* (Cologne: Kiepenheuer & Witsch, 1985); Robert Jay Lifton, *Nazi Doctors: Medical Killing and the Psychology of Genocide* (New York: Basic, 1986), p. 88; Proctor, *Racial Hygiene;* Karl Heinz Roth, ed., *Erfassung zur Vernichtung* (Berlin: Gesundheit, 1984); Paul Weindling, *Health, Race and German Politics between National Unification and Nazism, 1870–1945* (Cambridge: Cambridge University Press, 1989).

16. Benno Müller-Hill, *Murderous Science, Elimination by Scientific Selection of Jews, Gypsies and Others: Germany 1933–1945,* trans. George R. Fraser (New York: Oxford University Press, 1988).

17. "Hans Schemm an die Frauen auf dem Nürnberger Parteitag," *NS Frauenkorrespondenz,* nr. 35 (September 8, 1933); Bundesarchiv Koblenz (hereafter BAK), NSD/47/37–39.

18. Margarete Pessel, "Ein Kapitel Rassenhygiene für die Frauen," *NS Frauenkorrespondenz,* nr. 17 (April 19, 1933).

19. Adolf Hilter, *Mein Kampf,* trans. Ralph Mannheim (Boston: Houghton Mifflin, 1943), p. 380.

20. Detlef J. K. Peukert, *Inside Nazi Germany: Conformity, Opposition, and Racism in Everyday Life,* trans. Richard Deveson (New Haven: Yale University Press, 1987), p. 181; David Schoenbaum, *Hitler's Social Revolution,* 2nd ed. (New York: Norton, 1980); Hans Mommsen, "Die Realisierung des Utopischen: Die 'Endlösung der Judenfrage' im 'Dritten Reich'," *Geschichte und Gesellschaft* 9 (1983):381–420.

21. Michel de Certeau, *The Practice of Everyday Life,* trans. Steven Rendall (Berkeley: University of California Press, 1988), pp. 178–79. In *Langages totalitaires. Critique de la raison, narrative l'economie* (Paris: Hermann, 1972), pp. 1–9, Jean Pierre Faye addresses some of these issues brilliantly. For an analysis of Nazi euphemism, see Heinz Pächter, *Nazi Language* (New York: Frederick Ungar, 1944).

22. Dagmar Barnouw, *Weimar Intellectuals and the Threat of Modernity* (Bloomington: Indiana University Press, 1988).

23. Peter Gay, *Weimar Culture* (New York: Harper & Row, 1968), pp. 70–101; Patrice Petro, *Joyless Streets: Women and Melodramatic*

Representation in Weimar Germany (Princeton: Princeton University Press, 1989), p. 49.

24. Jürgen Habermas, *The New Conservatism: Cultural Criticism and the Historians' Debate,* ed. and trans. Shierry Weber Nicholdon, intro. Richard Wolin (Cambridge: MIT Press, 1990), pp. 34–35. Cf. Arnold Gehlen, *Der Mensch* (Berlin: Junker & Dünnhaupt, 1940); an English translation was published in 1987.

25. Certeau, *Practice of Everyday Life,* pp. 185–86.

26. Faye, *Langages totalitaires,* p. 385.

27. "Ein Kapitel Rassenhygiene für die Frauen," *NS Frauenkorrespondenz,* 1932–34; BAK/NSD/47/37–39.

28. Peukert, *Inside Nazi Germany,* p. 223.

29. Michel Foucault, *Surveiller et punir* (Paris: Gallimard, 1975).

30. *Das bevölkerungspolitische ABC* (Munich: Lehmanns, 1934), in Staatsarchiv München (hereafter StAM), NSDAP/147. See also Karl Ludwig Rost, *Sterilisation und Euthanasie im Film des "Dritten Reiches"* (Husum: Matthiesen Verlag, 1987), esp. pp. 59–75.

31. Bericht Lormann, "Umschulung für den neuen Staat," NWSM/Prov. Schulkollegium/6452.

32. "Veranstaltungen der rassenkundlichen Julischulung 1936," StAM/993. Certeau discusses the flooding of modern life by media—in contrast to H. Arendt's notion of the ideological emptiness at the core of totalitarian systems.

33. Proctor, *Racial Hygiene,* pp. 75–79.

34. Elfriede Dürk, "Werbeaktion für den Kalender," *Neues Volk* (December 11, 1936): StAM/NSDAP/350–51.

35. Rust to WKV (PMVKV), December 15, 1933; NWSM/Prov. Schulkollegium/6452.

36. Dr. Hermann Vellguth, *Blut und Rasse. Ausstellung des Deutschen Hygiene-Museums, Dresden.* This catalogue of a traveling exhibit from 1936 is in StAM/Gesundheitsämter 498.

37. Quoted in Proctor, *Racial Hygiene,* p. 181.

38. Vellguth, *Ausstellung,* p. 18.

39. Bulletin of the Bayerischer Taubstummen-Fürsorgerverband, *Bildung und Arbeit* (October 1935), StAM/NSDAP/981.

40. Achim Gerecke, "Die Erziehung zu rassischem Denken," radio address, July 17, 1933, BAK/R39/49/B1.1–7. He compared each racially educated person to a "link" in a chain of his ancestors—very much in the way that pre-industrial culture defined family in cross-generational terms. However, medieval families saw stability in terms of "Gut" (property) not "Erbgut."

41. Walter Gross, "Ewige Stimme des Blutes im Strom deutscher Geschichte," *Neues Volk*, vol. 1, no. 2 (August 5, 1933):3.

42. Hildegard Passow, "Geschichte, Blut und Boden," *NS Frauenkorrespondenz* 9 (March 4, 1933), p. 4.

43. Mary Douglas, *Purity and Danger: An Analysis of Concepts of Pollution and Taboo* (London: Routledge & Kegan Paul, 1979). Douglas collapses the smug assumption of radical difference between "the primitives" and "civilized people" like ourselves.

44. *Volk und Rasse. Ausstellungskatalog*, StAM / Gesundheitsämter 498.

45. Viktor Klemperer, *LTI. Notizbuch eines Philogen* (Frankfurt: Röderberg, 1987), pp. 105–28. The book was first published in 1946, and its author was a refugee from Nazism. I thank Regine Othmer-Vetter for bringing this volume to my attention.

46. Plenio to Bishop Müller, Obersdorf, August 5, 1934, EZA / 1 / C3 / 393.

47. Gerecke, "Erziehung," BAK / R39 / 49 / B1.6.

48. *Nachrichtendienst der Reichsfrauenführerin*, 5:9 (September 1936).

49. Hildegard Passow, "Geschichte, Blut und Boden," *NS Frauenkorrespondenz*, nr. 9 (March 4, 1933), p. 3.

50. On the convergence of medical opinion and concern for motherhood, cf. Weindling, *Health, Race*, pp. 245–69.

51. Frick, "Anzeigepflicht der Ärzte bei Erbkranken," Berlin, August 25, 1934; NWSM / Reg. Arnsberg, Medizinalwesen IM / 13157 / B1.63.

52. Prof. Büchner, "Die Gesetzte der ärtzlichen Ethik im Eid des Hippokrates," November 18, 1941; Erab. Ordin. Archiv Freiburg, B2 / 48 / 21 / Bl.128.

53. Robert Jay Lifton, "The Genocidal Mentality," *Tikkun* (May / June 1990):30–31; Peukert, *Inside Nazi Germany*, p. 220.

54. Hauptstaatsarchiv Stuttgart (hereafter HSAS), E 151 k VI.8 / 8 "Gesundheitswesen. Kosten der Duchführung des Gesetzes zur Verhütung erbkranken Nachwuchses, 1935–1938." I am grateful to Robert Gellately for informing me about this file.

55. Proctor, *Racial Hygiene*, pp. 82–85; Weindling, *Health, Race*, pp. 551–64.

56. Kurt Nowak, *"Euthanasie" und Sterilisierung im Dritten Reich. Die Konfrontation der evangelischen und katholischen Kirchen mit dem Gesetz zur Verhütung erbkranker Nachwuchses* (Göttingen: Vandenhoeck & Ruprecht, 1978).

57. Gütt, RMdI to Central Ausschuss für die Innere Mission der DEK Berlin Dahlem, January 14, 1935, B1.275, which also informed Protestant clergy that all support for eugenics must harmonize with specifically National Socialist goals.

58. D. O. Hartwich, "Denkschrift," Bremen, July 12, 1934; Evangelisches Zentralarchiv in Berlin (hereafter EZA) / 1 / C3 / 393.

59. Church council meeting, December 18, 1934, Volksgesundheit. Harmsen, "Innere Mission und Gesetz zur Verhütung erbkranken Nachwuches," pp. 12 ff,; EZA / 1 / A2 / 170.

60. A report from Innere Mission social workers asked plaintively, "Sind die Quellen leiblichen Elends und sittlicher Nöte, die noch vor wenigen Jahren einen weiteren Ausbau unserer Anstalten für die gefährdete Jugend wünschenswert machten, verstiegt? Sind unsere Fürsorgeheime, ja alle Arbeiten der IM überflüssig geworden? Nein." 62. *Jahresbericht der Fürsorgeheime evangelische schulentlassene Mädchen* (Leonberg and Obersingen: 1933 / 34), HSAS, J 150 358a / 33, 62.

61. Hildegard Passow, "Adolf Hitler, der Baumeister des neuen Reiches," *NS Frauenkorrespondenz*, nr. 9 (March 4, 1933), pp. 1–2.

62. Pgn. Else Schaudt, "Die deutsche Frau im Dritten Reich," *NS Frauenkorrespondenz*, BAK / NSD / 47 / 37–39.

63. Lydia Gottschewski, "Eine neue Frauengeneration wächst heran," *NS Frauenkorrespondenz*, BAK / NSD / 47 / 37–39.

64. Dr. Goebbels, "Pflichten und Rechte der deutschen Frau im nationalsozialistischen Deutschland," Rede auf der Amtswalterinnentagung des Gaues Gross-Berlin, *Amtliche Frauenkorrespondenz*, nr. 8 (February 15, 1934). The man was "der Intendant" and the woman "der Regisseur des Lebens." "Ihrer Natur nach eine männliche Bewegung. . . . Das ist durchaus keine Degradierung der Frau, keine Unterscheidung im Rang" because women assumed responsibility for "die Fürsorge für das kommende Geschlecht." "Je schärfer sich jedes Geschlecht auf seine eigenen Aufgabenkreise beschränkt, umso mehr wird es Kraft finden, sie auch wirklich zu erfüllen."

65. Hans Schemm an die Frauen auf dem Nürnberger Parteitag, *NS Frauenkorrespondenz*, nr. 35 (September 8, 1933), BAK / NSD / 47 / 37–39.

66. Radio Broadcast, Mothers' Day, 1934, *Friedrich Manns Pädagogisches Magazin*, Heft 1400 (Langensalza: Beyer, 1934), pp. 7–10.

67. Petro, *Joyless Streets*, pp. 220–24. Here Petro emphasizes the continuity of melodramatic expression as well as the shift during the Third Reich toward more stable and polarized gender images.

68. Julius Schwab, Friedrich W. Meyer, Emil Jörns, "Vorschläge für die Errichtung eines Erbpflegeamtes," BAK / R39 / 102.

69. Walter Gross, *Nationalsozialistiche Rassenpolitik. Eine Rede an die deutschen Frauen* (Berlin: Rassenpolitisches Amt der NSDAP, 1934), pp. 8, 12, 22. I thank Rudolph Binion for telling me of this pamphlet.

70. "Die deutsche Erneuerung geht über die deutsche Frau." E. Bosch, *Die Katholiken und das Hakenkreuz* (Munich: NS Frauenschaft-Reichsleitung, n.d.), p. 5; BAK/NSD/47/12.

71. Nachrichtendienst, "Reichstagung der Gaufrauenschaftsleiterinnen. Grundsätzliches zur deutschen Frauenarbeit," *Amtliche Frauenkorrespondenz,* ed. Deutsches Frauenwerk, nr. 10 (March 15, 1934), article nr. 11.

72. "Nationalpolitische Erziehung der Frau," lecture to Red Cross, Berlin, April 4, 1936, *Nachrichtendienst der Reichsfrauenführerin,* 5:9 (September 1936), p. 309; BAK/NS47/16.

73. M. Unger, "Der Staat und wir Frauen," *NS Frauenkorrespondenz* 6 (January 15, 1934), BAK/NSD/47/37–39.

74. Lifton, "The Genocidal Mentality," p. 31; cf. also the chapter, "Consequences," in my *Mothers in the Fatherland: Women, the Family, and Nazi Politics* (New York: St. Martin's, 1987).

75. Michel Foucault, *The History of Sexuality,* vol. 1, trans. Robert Hurley (New York: Vintage, 1978), pp. 139–60. Here Foucault traces from the seventeenth century the increasing claims of the state over not only the accumulation of capital but over human "bio-power" that includes Nazi eugenics. Foucault mentions in passing the ways in which a new set of concepts created new hegemonies and identities.

76. Lawrence K. Altman, "Despite Many Shifts, Oath as Old as Apollo Endures in Medicine," *New York Times,* May 15, 1990, p. B6.

"A Monstrous Uneasiness": Citizen Participation and Persecution of the Jews in Nazi Germany

1. For a discussion of collective guilt see Michael R. Marrus, *The Holocaust in History* (Hanover, N.H.: University Press of New England, 1987), pp. 84 ff. See also Bradley F. Smith, *Reaching Judgment at Nuremberg* (New York: Basic Books, 1977), pp. 113 ff.

2. For a discussion of the Gestapo and some of the myths surrounding it, see Robert Gellately, *The Gestapo and German Society: Enforcing Racial Policy 1933–1945* (Oxford: Clarendon Press, 1990).

3. The remark is from Ian Kershaw, *Popular Opinion and Political Dissent in the Third Reich: Bavaria, 1933–1945* (Oxford: Clarendon Press, 1983), p. 277, cited, for example, approvingly by Richard J. Evans,

In Hitler's Shadow (New York: Pantheon, 1989), p. 71, and more critically by Mary Nolan, "The *Historikerstreit* and Social History," *New German Critique* 44 (Spring/Summer 1988):78.

4. Otto Dov Kulka, "'Public Opinion' in Nazi Germany: The Final Solution," *The Jerusalem Quarterly* 26 (1983):43. See also Otto Dov Kulka and Aron Rodrique, "The German Population and the Jews in the Third Reich," *Yad Vashem Studies* 26 (1984):434, where Germans as a whole are charged with "passive complicity." According to Joel Feinberg, "Collective Responsibility," in his *Doing and Deserving* (Princeton: Princeton University Press, 1970), pp. 244–45, common law classifies complicity under four categories: "perpetrators," "abettors," "inciters" (all of whom are "accomplices"), and "criminal protectors." What one should understand as "passive complicity" is not specified by Kulka and Rodrique. For a discussion of the theme that modern dictatorships "find it at once more necessary and more difficult than autocrats of earlier vintage to secure reliable and comprehensive information on the state of public opinion," see Aryeh L. Unger, *The Totalitarian Party* (New York: Cambridge University Press, 1974), pp. 221 ff.

5. The concept of the "good citizen," is, of course, a theoretical construct, and an idealized representation. Any representation can be drawn on by different groups and for different purposes, at any time, and this is done if and when it is of use. How the representation is used will depend on the imagination and motives of the groups and individuals involved. So one might ask how the representation of the "good citizen" was used in Nazi Germany, and what interests were served.

6. See the remark in the Reichstag on January 30, 1937, in Max Domarus, *Hitler. Reden und Proklamationen 1932–1945,* vol. 1, pt. 2 (Munich: Süddeutscher Verlag, 1965), p. 665.

7. On the return of the "good times" see Ulrich Herbert, "'Die guten und die schlechten Zeiten'. Überlegungen zur diachronen Analyse lebensgeschichtlicher Interviews," in *"Die Jahre weiss man nicht, wo man die heute hinsetzen soll,"* Lutz Niethammer, ed. (Berlin: J. H. W. Dietz Nachf., 1983), pp. 67 ff. For a recent analysis of the appeals of Nazism to the elite, see Fritz Stern, "National Socialism as Temptation," in his *Dreams and Delusions: The Drama of German History* (New York: Knopf, 1987), pp. 147 ff. For Italy see Luisa Passerini, "Oral Memory of Fascism," in *Rethinking Italian Fascism,* David Forgacs, ed. (London: Lawrence & Wishart, 1986), pp. 185 ff.

8. See Hans Boberach, ed., *Richterbriefe. Dokumente zur Beeinflussung der deutschen Rechtsprechung 1942–1944* (Boppard: Harald Boldt, 1975), p. 171.

9. See Lothar Gruchmann, *Justiz im Dritten Reich 1933–1940. Anpassung und Unterwerfung in der Ära Gürtner* (Munich: Oldenbourg, 1988), p. 835.

10. For the evolution of the police see Gellately, *The Gestapo and German Society*, chaps. 1 and 2.

11. On the relationship between the growth of auto-surveillance and the difficulties of resistance, see Robert Gellately, "Surveillance and Disobedience: Aspects of the Political Policing of Nazi Germany" in *Germans against Nazism: Nonconformity, Opposition and Resistance in the Third Reich*, Francis R. Nicosia and Lawrence D. Stokes, eds. (Oxford: Berg Publications, 1990). For the perspective from the German Democratic Republic see the recent publication of *Gestapo-Berichte über den antifaschistischen Widerstandskampf der KPD 1933 bis 1945*, thus far 2 of 3 vols. (Berlin: Dietz, 1989), passim.

12. The attitude of German politicians and police officials to denunciations is discussed at length in Gellately, *The Gestapo and German Society*, passim. For recent literature on the war and the population in Germany see Wolfgang Michalka, ed., *Der Zweite Weltkrieg. Analysen, Gründzüge, Forschungsbilanz* (Munich: Piper, 1989), passim. See also Klaus Drobisch, "'Kriegsschauplatz Innerdeutschland'. Sicherheitspolizeiliche Vorbereitungen und Einübungen seit 1935/36," in *Der Weg in den Krieg*, Dietrich Eichholtz and Kurt Pätzold, eds. (Cologne: Pahl-Rugenstein, 1989), pp. 41–66.

13. Reinhard Mann, *Protest und Kontrolle im Dritten Reich. Nationalsozialistische Herrschaft im Alltag einer rheinischen Grossstadt* (Frankfurt: Campus, 1987), p. 105, n. 27.

14. Ibid., p. 293.

15. For an introduction see Robert Gellately, "The Gestapo and German Society: Political Denunciation in the Gestapo Case Files," *Journal of Modern History* 60 (1988):654 ff; Martin Broszat, "Politische Denunziationen in der NS-Zeit. Aus Forschungserfahrungen im Staatsarchiv München," *Archivalische Zeitschrift* 73 (1977):221 ff.

16. For a critique of treatments of the terror in the literature on Nazi Germany see Robert Gellately, "Rethinking the Nazi Terror System: A Historiographical Analysis," *German Studies Review* (1991, forthcoming).

17. Cf. Jörg Kammler, "Nationalsozialistische Machtergreifung und Gestapo—am Beispiel der Staatspolizeistelle für den Regierungsbezirk Kassel," in *Hessen unterm Hakenkreuz. Studien zur Durchsetzung der NSDAP in Hessen*, Eike Hennig, ed., 2nd ed. (Frankfurt: Insel, 1984), pp. 506 ff.; Bernd Hey, "Zur Geschichte der westfälischen Staatspolizeistellen und der Gestapo," *Westfälische Forschungen* 37 (1987):58

ff. See the accounts of Peter Brückner, *Das Abseits als sicherer Ort* (Berlin: Wagenbach, 1980), p. 145; Dietrich Güstrow, *Tödlicher Alltag. Strafverteidiger im Dritten Reich* (Berlin: Severin und Siedler, 1981), pp. 148 ff; Ruth Andreas-Friedrich, *Der Schattenmann. Tagebuchaufzeichnungen 1938–1945* (Frankfurt: Suhrkamp, 1983), pp. 25 ff; Else R. Behrend-Rosenfeld, *Ich stande nicht allein. Leben einer Jüdin in Deutschland 1933–44* (Munich: Beck, 1988), pp. 226 ff; Lotte Paepcke, *Ich wurde vergessen. Bericht einer Jüdin die das Dritte Reich überlebte* (Freiburg: Herder, 1979), pp. 60 ff.

18. See, for example, Hauptstaatsarchiv Düsseldorf: Gestapo 17,922.

19. See Staatsarchiv Würzburg: Gestapo 753, for one of the rare denunciations from the SD. The denouncer was married, Protestant, and not a Party member.

20. See, for example, Staatsarchiv Würzburg: Gestapo 3705; 4953; 4202. Note the following illustrations of denunciations, as actually summarized in the Würzburg Gestapo case-files:

1. "On 5 March 1936 around 18:00 hours the Political Department of the Würzburg Police Directory [the Gestapo] was informed that a Jew and a young woman were presently in the 'Cafe Michael' at the Market Place. The said Jew was allegedly pressing his attentions on the young woman in such a way that a suspicion of race defilement is not out of the question." (Gestapo 3839)

2. "On 20 May 1937, Frau Margareta Schmidt, resident in Würzburg, Rimparerstrasse 2, appeared and declared on behalf of the servant girl of the family Berg, Würzburg, Friedenstrasse 38, that she wished to report that the married tax inspector Rohm was engaged in a love affair with the Jew Mayer. Almost every day Rohm went to the Alhambra to play chess and used the opportunity to look up the Jew. Besides that, the servant girl claims to have observed recently how the Jew Mayer sought to let Rohm into her apartment, although because someone came by, she did not succeed in this. The servant girl is prepared to give more exact details if summoned, and to cooperate in the surveillance of Rohm. Frau Schmidt wishes to bring the name of the servant girl on 21 May 1937." (Gestapo 10822)

3. Anonymous letter, Würzburg, 2 May 1941 to the Gestapo: "Fräulein Else Totzke [28 years of age] entertains a very close friendship with a 15-year-old Jewish girl Schwacher, Schillerstrasse. Fräulein Schwacher has already informed Totzke that she does not wish to be visited in the present times. Nevertheless, Fräulein Totzke continues to come, almost every day, and remains for many hours, mostly from noon to the evening, leaving just before Frau Schwacher returns home. Fräulein Totzke does

not seem to have a normal turn and she appears to be pressing this on the girl. . . . I live in the immediate neighborhood and have observed these visits for weeks. Every German can and must know the laws, only they do not appear to exist for Fräulein Totzke." (Gestapo 16015).

4. The following example of a denunciation involving a Polish worker is taken from Staatsarchiv Würzburg: Gestapo 6962; 8548. Head Doctor Ludwig Brack, St. Josef's hospital, Schweinfurt reported to the local magistrate 11 August 1941 a matter which came to his attention during office hours: "Today, the father Richard Bauer from Holzhausen brought his daughter Cäcille for an examination to see if she were pregnant. With great probability there exists a pregnancy of three months. Because of the youthful age I asked Herr Bauer as to the father of the child. Thereupon I got the answer: He is a Pole. I feel myself duty bound to make this report in order to protect the remaining youth of the village."

(With the exception of Totzke, all other names have been changed in keeping with official regulations for the use of these materials.)

For a brief comparison of the enforcement of racial policies aimed at the Jews and Poles inside Germany see Gellately, *The Gestapo and German Society*, chap. 8. I am presently working on a larger study of the Polish workers.

21. See, for example, Staatsarchiv Würzburg: Gestapo 8135. For an exploration of the Würzburg data for other purposes, see H. G. Adler, *Der verwaltete Mensch. Studien zur Deportation der Juden aus Deutschland* (Tübingen: J. C. B. Mohr, 1974), passim.

22. On resistance to Nazi antisemitism and a discussion of the literature, see Gellately, *The Gestapo and German Society*, chap. 6.

23. Issues surrounding Gestapo personnel are discussed in ibid. See also Adolf Diamant, *Gestapo Frankfurt a. M.* (Frankfurt: W. Steinmann & Boschen, 1988), pp. xii ff. For the relatively small number of Gestapo employees in the SS see Robert Lewis Koehl, *The Black Corps: The Structure and Power Struggles of the Nazi SS* (Madison: University of Wisconsin Press, 1983), pp. 159 ff.

24. The Würzburg Gestapo's 175 cases of "race defilement" and "friendship to Jews" began as follows: 99 (57 percent) with "reports from the population"; 0 (0 percent) "from businesses"; 1 (0 percent) with "observations of the Würzburg Gestapo and V-Persons"; 26 (15 percent) "from interrogations"; 8 (5 percent) with "information from other control organizations"; 0 (0 percent) from "communal or state authorities"; 15 (9 percent) with "information from NS organizations"; 6 (3 percent) from "political evaluations"; there was no information on why a case began in 20 dossiers (11 percent). These figures are published in Gellately, "Political Denunciation," p. 670.

25. Misuse of denunciations by the population at large is discussed in Gellately, *The Gestapo and German Society*, passim. For examples of survivor and eye witness testimony, see above, n. 17.

26. The phrase is from the title of Ingeborg Hecht, *Als unsichtbare Mauern wuchsen. Eine deutsche Familie unter den Nürnberger Rassengesetzen* (Hamburg: Hoffman and Campe, 1984).

27. Robert Paxton, *Vichy France: Old Guard and New Order, 1940–1944* (New York: Norton, 1975), p. 8.

28. Ibid., p. 19.

29. Bertram M. Gordon, *Collaborationism in France during the Second World War* (Ithaca: Cornell University Press, 1980), p. 339.

30. André Halimi, *La Délation sous l'occupation* (Paris: Editions A. Moreau, 1983), p. 7. By the looks of it, the French had as little success in stopping the flood of anonymous letters of denunciation (especially of Jews) as the Germans. See David Pryce-Jones, *Paris in the Third Reich* (New York: Holt, Rinehart & Winston, 1981), pp. 140–41.

31. John F. Sweets, *Choices in Vichy France: The French under Nazi Occupation* (New York: Oxford University Press, 1986), p. 246, n. 79.

32. See Tom Bower, *Klaus Barbie: Butcher of Lyons* (London: Michael Joseph, 1984), pp. 51 ff.

33. Raul Hilberg, *The Destruction of the European Jews,* rev. ed., vol. 2 (New York: Holmes & Meier, 1985), p. 660.

34. Susan Zuccotti, *The Italians and the Holocaust: Persecution, Rescue, Survival* (New York: Basic Books, 1987), pp. 136–37. See also Edward R. Tannenbaum, *The Fascist Experience: Italian Society and Culture, 1922–1945* (New York: Basic Books, 1972), p. 317.

35. Meir Michaelis, *Mussolini and the Jews: German-Italian Relations and the Jewish Question in Italy, 1922–1945* (Oxford: Clarendon Press, 1978), p. 389.

36. Ibid.

37. See, for example, Detlev Peukert, *Die KPD im Widerstand. Verfolgung and Untergrundarbeit an Rhein und Ruhr 1933 bis 1945* (Wuppertal: Hammer, 1980), pp. 89 ff. For evidence that fell into the hands of the Gestapo of how the left overestimated the number of Gestapo agents (*V-Leute*) inside the underground Socialist movement, see the files (*Warnungslisten*) discovered near Karlsbad in November 1938, now in the Bundesarchiv Koblenz, R58/517, pp. 3 ff. I am now engaged in a study of the Gestapo's confidential informers. For a brief introduction see Walter Otto Weyrauch, *Gestapo V-Leute* (Frankfurt: V. Kostermann, 1989), passim.

38. Mann (*Protest und Kontrolle*, p. 293) found that 24 percent of those who offered information on all forms of suspected "political"

crimes to the Gestapo did so for "system loyal" reasons; 37 percent aimed to "clear up personal conflicts"; he found no evidence in 39 percent of these cases. Thus, it might be said that 76 percent of all denunciations were not based on obvious Nazi motives.

39. Kulka and Rodrique ("The German Population and the Jews," p. 435) correctly point out that "the degree to which the population agreed with 'the basic principles behind the persecution' while 'criticizing the methods', will probably never be known."

40. See Hans Mommsen, "The Realization of the Unthinkable: The 'Final Solution of the Jewish Question' in the Third Reich," in *The Policies of Genocide*, Gerhard Hirschfeld, ed. (London: Allen & Unwin, 1986), p. 129: "The genesis of the Holocaust offers a deterrent example of the way in which otherwise normal individuals can be led astray when they live in a permanent state of emergency, when legal and institutional structures collapse, and when criminal deeds are publicly justified as national achievements."

41. Hannah Arendt (*Eichmann in Jerusalem*, rev. ed. [New York; Viking, 1965], p. 179) remarks: "What in Denmark was the result of an authentically political sense, an inbred comprehension of the requirements and responsibilities of citizenship and independence, was in Italy the outcome of the almost automatic general humanity of an old and civilized people." Cf. Werner Best, *Dänemark in Hitlers Hand* (Husum: Husum, 1988), pp. 19 ff.

42. An indication of how the Gestapo became judge, jury, and executioner by early 1945 in some areas inside Germany can be seen, for example, from a letter of January 26, 1945, in which the Gestapo in Düsseldorf was given the power of execution over foreign workers; Düsseldorf was told that it was no longer necessary to obtain prior consent from Berlin headquarters (the RSHA). See Hauptstaatsarchiv Düsseldorf: RW 34/29, p. 3. See the important book by Ulrich Herbert, *Fremdarbeiter, Politik und Praxis des 'Ausländer-Einsatzes' in der Kriegswirtschaft des Dritten Reiches*, 2nd ed. (Berlin: J. H. W. Dietz Nachf., 1985), passim. See also Bernd A. Rusinek, *Gesellschaft in der Katastrophe, Terror, Illegalität, Widerstand. Köln, 1944/45* (Essen: Klartext, 1989), passim.

43. There was a flurry of "reports" (*Anzeigen*) that made their way to the "People's Court" in the wake of the failed plot on Hitler's life in July 1944, but the extent to which these flowed from the population at large or from local state or Party offices remains to be investigated. See the figures in Wolfgang Schumann and Olaf Groehler et al., *Deutschland im zweiten Weltkrieg*, vol. 6 (Cologne: Pahl-Rugenstein, 1985), p. 266.

One Day in Jozefow: Initiation to Mass Murder

1. For ghetto-clearing in the various districts of the General Government, the following are the most important judicial sources. For Lublin: Staatsanwaltschaft Hamburg 147 Js 24/72 (indictment of Georg Michalson) and StA Wiesbaden 8 Js 1145/60 (indictment of Lothar Hoffmann and Hermann Worthoff); for Warsaw, StA Hamburg 147 Js 16/69 (indictment of Ludwig Hahn); for Krakau, Landgericht Kiel 2 Ks 6/63 (judgment against Martin Fellenz); for Radom, StA Hamburg 147 Js 38/65 (indictment of Hermann Weinrauch and Paul Fuchs); for Bialystok, StA Dortmund 45 Js 1/61 (indictment of Herbert Zimmermann and Wilhelm Altenloh), and *Documents Concerning the Destruction of Grodno*, ed. Serge Klarsfeld (Publications of the Beate Klarsfeld Foundation); for Galizia, LG Münster 5 Ks 4/65 (judgment against Hans Krüger), and LG Stuttgart Ks 5/65 (judgment against Rudolf Röder).

2. For the Trawniki units, see StA Hamburg 147 Js 43/69 (indictment of Karl Streibel).

3. StA Hamburg 141 Js 1957/62 gegen H. and W. u.a. (hereafter cited as HW), 820–21, 2437, 4414–15.

4. HW, 2091.

5. HW, 1952, 2039, 2655–56.

6. HW, 1953–54, 2041–42, 3298, 4576–77, 4589.

7. HW, 1852, 2182; StA Hamburg 141 Js 128/65 gegen G. u.a. (hereafter cited as G), 363, 383.

8. G, 645–52.

9. HW, 1741–43.

10. HW, 2618, 2717, 2742.

11. HW, 1947.

12. G, 504–14, 642, 647.

13. HW, 2092.

14. HW, 1648; G, 453.

15. G, 647.

16. G, 624, 659.

17. HW, 2093, 2236.

18. HW, 1686, 2659.

19. HW, 2717–18.

20. HW, 1640, 2505.

21. HW, 1336, 3542.

22. G, 168–69, 206–7.

23. G, 230.

24. HW, 2635.

25. HW, 1540, 2534, 2951, 4579.

26. G, 277.
27. HW, 2483.
28. HW, 2621, 2635, 2694.
29. HW, 1640, 2149, 2505, 2540, 2692, 2720.
30. HW, 2657.
31. HW, 2239.
32. HW, 2172, 2252, 3939; G, 582.
33. HW, 822–24, 2438–41, 4415.
34. HW, 4578.
35. G, 169–70.
36. G, 244.
37. HW, 2535.
38. HW, 4592.
39. HW, 1640, 2505, 4344.
40. G, 169–70.
41. HW, 2439–40.

Helping Behavior and Rescue During the Holocaust

1. A few recent examples of such titles are Phillip Hallie, *Lest Innocent Blood Be Shed* (New York: Harper & Row, 1979); Peter Hellman, *Avenue of the Righteous* (New York: Atheneum, 1980); Samuel P. Oliner and Pearl M. Oliner, *The Altruistic Personality, Rescuers of Jews in Nazi Europe* (New York: The Free Press, 1988); Kazimierz Iranek-Osmecki, *He Who Saves One Life* (New York: Crown Publishers, Inc., 1971); Alexander Ramati, *The Assisi Underground: The Priests Who Rescued Jews* (New York: Stein & Day Publishers, 1978); Nechama Tec, *When Light Pierced the Darkness: Christian Rescue of Jews in Nazi-Occupied Poland* (New York: Oxford University Press, 1987).

2. Tec, *When Light Pierced the Darkness*, p. 11.

3. Jacqueline R. Macaulay and Leonard Berkowitz, *Altruism and Helping Behavior* (New York: Academic Press, 1970), pp. 1–9.

4. This theoretical distinction has been suggested by David L. Rosenham, "The Natural Socialization of Altruistic Autonomy," in Macaulay and Berkowitz, eds., *Altruism and Helping Behavior*, pp. 251–68.

5. Lucy S. Dawidowicz, ed., *A Holocaust Reader* (New York: Behrman House, Inc., 1976), p. 67.

6. Wladyslaw Bartoszewski, "Egzekucje Publiczne W Warszawie W Latach, 1943–1945" (Public executions in Warsaw), *Biuletyn Glownej Komisji Badania Zbrodni Niemieckiej W Polsce*, no. 6 (1946); 211–24;

Emanuel Ringelblum, *Notes from the Warsaw Ghetto* (New York: Schocken Books, 1975), p. 236; Tatiana Berenstein et al., eds., *Exterminacja Zydow Na Ziemiach Polskich W Okresie Okupacji Hitlerowskiej* (Jewish Extermination in Poland during Hitler's Occupation) (Warsaw: Zydowski Instytut Historyczny, 1957), pp. 121–22; Dawidowicz, *A Holocaust Reader*, pp. 67–68.

7. Tec, *When Light Pierced the Darkness*, chap. 3, pp. 52–69.

8. Ibid., p. 56.

9. Antony Polonsky, *Politics in Independent Poland, 1921–1939* (Oxford: The Clarendon Press, 1972), p. 40.

10. Ibid., p. 69.

11. The description and discussion of rescuers follows closely my book, *When Light Pierced the Darkness*, pp. 188–91.

Redefining Heroic Behavior: The Impromptu Self and The Holocaust Experience

1. Maurice Blanchot, *The Writing of the Disaster* (*L'Écriture du désastre*), trans. Ann Smock (Lincoln: University of Nebraska Press, 1986), p. 1.

2. Heda Kovály and Erazim Kohák, *The Victors and the Vanquished* (New York: Horizon Press, 1973), p. 1. The citation is from Part One, "The Victors: Memoirs of Heda Margolius Kovály," trans. and ed. Erazim Kohák. Part Two comprises "The Vanquished: Perspective of Erazim Kohák."

3. Blanchot, *The Writing of the Disaster*, p. 2.

4. Heda Margolius Kovály, *Under a Cruel Star: A Life in Prague, 1941–1968*, trans. Franci Epstein and Helen Epstein with the author (Cambridge, Mass.: Plunkett Lake Press, 1986), p. 5.

5. Fortunoff Video Archive for Holocaust Testimonies at Yale, tape T-1123. Testimony of Arne L.

6. Tape T-107. Testimony of Edith P.

7. Tape T-11. Testimony of Schifra Z.

8. Tape T-18. Testimony of Hanna F.

9. Tape T-2. Testimony of Leon W.

10. Tape T-285. Testimony of Hanna H.

11. Tape T-192. Testimony of Viktor K.

12. Tape T-55. Testimony of Sigmund W.

13. Tape T-158. Testimony of Leo G.

14. Here and elsewhere, I use "integrated" as a contrasting rather than a descriptive term. The idea of an integrated self is probably mostly

mythical to begin with, though under normal circumstances—the reverse of the Holocaust universe—the armor preserving its external appearance seems more secure. The "integrated" self of the former victim adapts to society's conventions by re-embracing goals like marriage, family, career. Oral testimonies reveal the existence of multiple selves that usually function in more-or-less satisfactory versions of equilibrium. Some may see this merely as a reflection of the general human condition, though I believe that the exceptional nature of the former victims' experience is a crucial differentiating factor.

15. Tape T-158. Testimony of Leo G.

16. Richard J. Evans, *In Hitler's Shadow: West German Historians and the Attempt to Escape from the Nazi Past* (New York: Pantheon Books, 1989), p. 120.

17. Tape T-65. Testimony of Irene W.

18. Tape T-845. Testimony of Eva K.

19. Blanchot, *The Writing of the Disaster*, p. 42.

20. Ibid., p. 3. Blanchot also speaks of knowledge "via disaster" (*par désastre*), fusing consciousness even more keenly with the event. Apparently trying to convey Blanchot's unorthodox sense of verbal and mental intimacy, his translator renders *par désastre* as "knowledge disastrously," suggesting in English what is less obvious in the original French—literally, a new grammar of thought.

21. Ibid., p. 3.

22. Tape T-729. Testimony of Leo L.

Popularization and Memory: The Case of Anne Frank

1. *The Diary of Anne Frank: The Critical Edition,* ed. David Barnouw and Gerrold van der Stroom, trans. Arnold J. Pomerans and B. M. Mooyaart-Doubleday (New York: Doubleday, 1989).

2. Karen Shawn, *The End of Innocence: Anne Frank and the Holocaust* (New York: International Center for Holocaust Studies, Anti-Defamation League of B'nai B'rith, 1989).

3. *Legacy: The Newsletter of the Anne Frank Center* (June 1989): 2.

4. Louis de Jong, "The Girl Who Was Anne Frank," *The Reader's Digest* (October 1957), p. 118.

5. Jan Romein's essay is reprinted in *A Tribute to Anne Frank,* ed. Anna G. Steenmeijer (Garden City, N.Y.: Doubleday & Company, 1971), p. 21; in a slightly altered translation, it also appears in *The Diary*

of Anne Frank: The Critical Edition, pp. 67–68; the citations here are to the version in *A Tribute to Anne Frank.*

6. *The Diary of Anne Frank: The Critical Edition,* p. 71.

7. The text of the play was published as *The Diary of Anne Frank,* by Frances Goodrich and Albert Hackett (New York: Random House, 1956).

8. "Introduction" to *Anne Frank: The Diary of a Young Girl* (New York: Pocket Books, 1953), p. ix.

9. *Newsweek,* June 16, 1952.

10. *Saturday Review,* July 19, 1952, p. 20.

11. *The New York Times Book Review,* June 15, 1952, pp. 1, 22.

12. *The Works of Anne Frank,* with an Introduction by Ann Birstein and Alfred Kazin (Garden City, N.Y.: Doubleday & Company, 1959); the Birstein-Kazin essay is also printed as the Introduction to *Tales from the House Behind* (New York: Bantam Books, 1966).

13. *Herald Tribune,* October 23, 1955.

14. *The New York Post,* October 8, 1955.

15. Lawrence Langer, "The Americanization of the Holocaust on Stage and Screen," in *From Hester Street to Hollywood,* ed. Sarah Blacher Cohen (Bloomington: Indiana University Press, 1983), p. 216.

16. *The New York Times,* October 2, 1955.

17. *The Herald Tribune,* October 2, 1955.

18. *Newsweek,* June 25, 1979.

19. *Variety,* October 6, 1955.

20. *Daily News,* October 6, 1955.

21. *B'nai B'rith Messenger,* February 3, 1956; *Congress Weekly,* December 19, 1952.

22. Langer, "The Americanization of the Holocaust," pp. 214–15.

23. *Anne Frank: The Diary of a Young Girl,* p. 49.

24. Ibid., pp. 34–35.

25. Ibid., pp. 186–87.

26. Goodrich and Hackett, *The Diary of Anne Frank,* p. 168.

27. Ibid., pp. 172–73.

28. Ibid., pp. 170, 174.

29. *The Diary of Anne Frank: The Critical Edition,* p. 74.

30. Ernst Schnabel, *Anne Frank: A Portrait in Courage,* trans. Richard and Clara Winston (New York: Harcourt, Brace & World, 1958), p. 16.

31. Ibid., p. 167.

32. Ibid., p. 185.

33. President Reagan's address at Bergen-Belsen is collected in Geoffrey Hartman, ed., *Bitburg in Moral and Political Perspective* (Bloomington: Indiana University Press, 1986), pp. 253–55.

34. Ibid., p. 255.

35. The figures were given to me by an editor at Fischer Verlag, in Frankfurt, August 1989.

36. Cited in "In the Hearts of Men: The Progress of Anne Frank's 'Diary,'" *The Wiener Library* 12 (1958): 45.

37. Cited in Emanuel Litvinoff, "Berlin's High Noon," *Jewish Observer and Middle East Review* (February 8, 1957), 13.

38. *Theater der Zeit,* June 1957.

39. Norbert Muhlen, "The Return of Anne Frank," *The ADL Bulletin* (June 1957): 2.

40. Passing reference to changes in the diary was made in an article that appeared in *Der Spiegel,* April 1, 1959; a fuller account is given in *The Diary of Anne Frank: The Critical Edition,* pp. 72–73. Readers who wish to trace the changes described and analyzed in this essay would do well to consult the new German critical edition, *Die Tagebücher der Anne Frank* (Frankfurt am Main: S. Fischer Verlag, 1988).

41. Hannah Arendt, "Letter to the Editor," *Midstream* 8 (September 1962): pp. 85–87.

42. Bruno Bettelheim, "The Ignored Lesson of Anne Frank," *Harper's,* November 1960, p. 46.

43. "The Return of Anne Frank," *The ADL Bulletin* (June 1957): 8.

44. Martin Dworkin, "The Vanishing Diary of Anne Frank," *Jewish Frontier,* April 1960, pp. 9, 10.

45. Algeine Ballif, "Anne Frank on Broadway," *Commentary,* November 1955, pp. 466–67.

46. Ludwig Lewisohn, "A Glory and A Doom," *Saturday Review,* July 19, 1952, p. 20.

47. Meyer Levin, "A Classic Human Document," *Congress Weekly,* June 16, 1952.

48. "At Long Last We Have a Real Story of Jews under Nazism," *National Jewish Post,* June 20, 1952.

49. *Saturday Review,* July 19, 1952.

50. Bruno Bettelheim, "The Ignored Lesson of Anne Frank," *Harper's,* November 1960, p. 46.

51. Bruno Bettelheim, "Freedom from Ghetto Thinking," *Midstream* (Spring 1962):16–25.

52. Hannah Arendt, *Eichmann in Jerusalem: A Report on the Banality of Evil* (New York: Viking, 1963).

53. "Freedom from Ghetto Thinking," *Midstream* (Spring 1962):16.

54. "The Living Legacy of Anne Frank: The Memory behind Today's Headlines," *Ladies Home Journal*, September 1967, p. 87.

55. "The 'Diary' in Israel," *New York Times*, February 17, 1957.

56. For Albrecht Goes, see "Vorwort," *Das Tagebuch der Anne Frank* (Frankfurt am Main: Fischer Bücherei, 1955); for Daniel Rops, see "Préface," *Journal de Anne Frank* (Paris: Calmann-Levy, 1950); for Storm Jameson, see "Foreword," *Anne Frank's Diary* (London: Valentine, Mitchell, 1952).

57. G. Boogaard, "Poem on May 5," in *A Tribute to Anne Frank*, p. 53.

Israel's Memorial Landscape: Sho'ah, Heroism, and National Redemption

1. From an editorial in *Davar*, one of Israel's daily newspapers, on the occasion of Holocaust Remembrance Day, April 22, 1951, the first to be observed after the parliament's remembrance day act. Compare this to Thomas Friedman's contemporary observation that "Israel today is becoming Yad Vashem with an air force," in his *From Beirut to Jerusalem* (New York: Farrar, Strauss & Giroux, 1989), p. 281.

2. In a bulletin prepared for army commanders on Holocaust Remembrance Day in Israel, the meaning of Holocaust memory is made explicit: "The Zionist solution establishing the State of Israel was intended to provide an answer to the problem of the existence of the Jewish people, in view of the fact that all other solutions had failed. The Holocaust proved, in all its horror, that in the twentieth century, the survival of the Jews is not assured as long as they are not masters of their fate and as long as they do not have the power to defend their survival." See "Informational Guidelines to the Commander," as quoted in Charles S. Liebman and Eliezer Don-Yehiya, *Civil Religion in Israel: Traditional Judaism and Political Culture in the Jewish State* (Berkeley and Los Angeles: University of California Press, 1983), p. 184.

3. This essay is adapted from a chapter in the author's full-length study, *The Texture of Memory: Holocaust Memorials and Meaning in Europe, Israel, and America* (New Haven and London: Yale University Press, 1992), which includes discussion of all the state's remembering institutions, including Yad Vashem and Yom Hashoah Vehagvurah (Holocaust and Heroism Remembrance Day).

4. For example, see James E. Young, "The Biography of a Memorial Icon: Nathan Rapoport's Warsaw Ghetto Monument," *Representations* 26 (Spring 1989): 69–106.

5. *B'nai B'rith in Israel: A Traveler's Guide* (Washington, D.C.: B'nai B'rith International, n.d.), p. 14.

6. See Shaul Katz, "The Israeli Teacher-Guide: The Emergence and Perpetuation of a Role," *Annals of Tourism Research*, vol. 12, no. 1 (1985): 66.

7. Born in the nineteenth-century Jewish pioneers' need to familiarize themselves with the terrain, a series of Sabbath tours promoting *yedi'ath ha'aretz* eventually gained respectability as an academic course of study. This was partly a result of the early Zionist-socialists' agricultural devotion to the soil, and partly to the mytho-geography of the land. In both cases, the land had become the Jews' newest unexplored text. Place-names never referred merely to geographic location, but to entire biblical stories, each rife with historical meaning. In an ironic way, a journey through the land of the book likened itself to a journey through the book itself. These tours have since been institutionalized in the extremely popular "Society for the Protection of Nature in Israel," which has become the leading organizer for nature walks in Israel.

8. Quoted in "City Rejects Park Memorials to Slain Jews," *New York Times,* February 11, 1965, p. 1; and in "2 Jewish Monuments Barred from Park," *New York World Telegram and Sun*, February 10, 1965, p. 1.

9. From Haim Gamzu, "Ben-Zvi 1904–1952," in *Ben-Zvi: A Portrait Album* (New York, 1962), unpaginated.

10. See Margaret Larkin, *The Six Days of Yad Mordechai* (Israel: Yad Mordechai Museum, 1965).

11. See Richard Yaffe, *Nathan Rapoport: Sculptures and Monuments* (New York: Shengold, 1980), unpaginated.

12. See Yehuda Bauer, *A History of the Holocaust* (New York and London: Franklin Watts, 1982), pp. 189–91.

13. See Zivia Lubetkin, *In the Days of Destruction and Revolt* (Israel: Ghetto Fighters' House, 1981).

14. As an engrossing spectacle, this trial might even be said to have transcended its juridical function to serve as a mass commemoration of the victims. Many regard it as as much a memorial process as a legal process. See, for example, Annette Wieviorka, *Le Procès Eichmann* (Brussels: Editions Complexe, 1989).

Early Warning: Detecting Potentially Genocidal Movements

1. *Teachers College Record* (February 1979): 533.

Tellers and Listeners: The Impact of Holocaust Narratives

The authors are founding members of the Holocaust Educational Foundation, Wilmette, Illinois.

1. Paul Thompson, *The Voice of the Past: Oral History* (New York: Oxford University Press, 1988), p. 21.

2. Helen Epstein, *Children of the Holocaust: Conversations with Sons and Daughters of Survivors* (New York: G. P. Putnam's, 1979).

Closing Remarks

1. Primo Levi, *The Drowned and the Saved* (New York: Summit Books, 1988), p. 17.